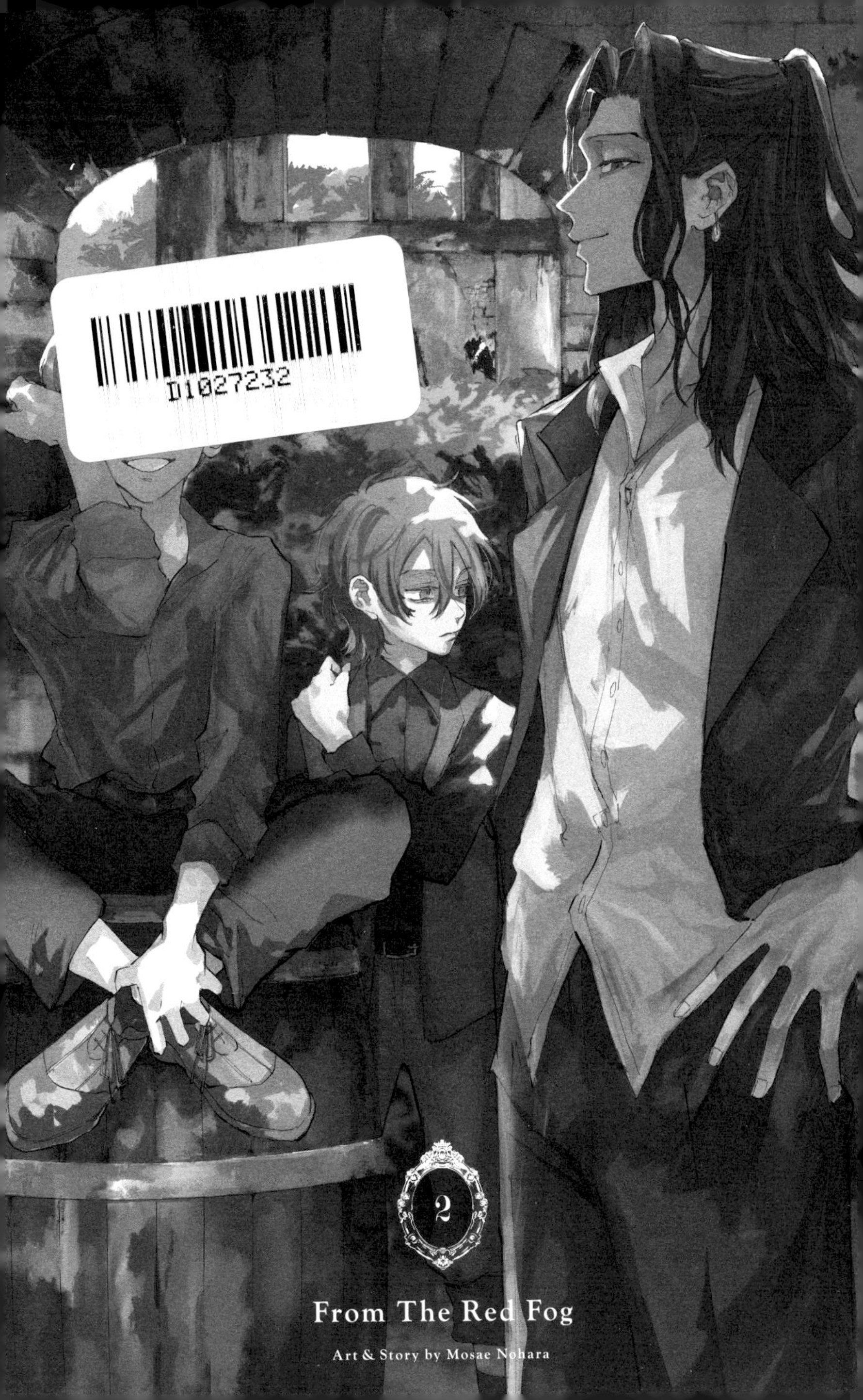
2
From The Red Fog
Art & Story by Mosae Nohara

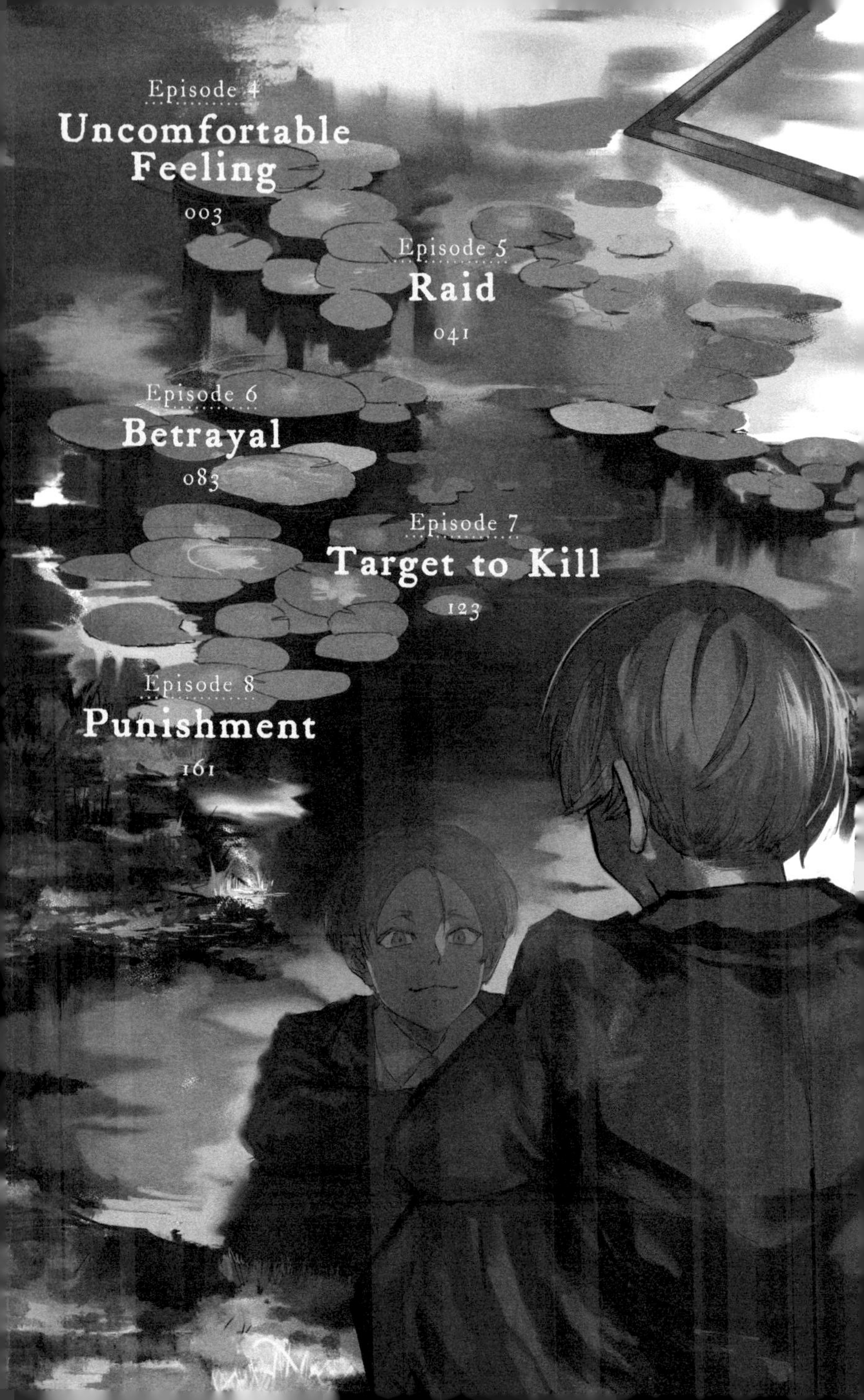

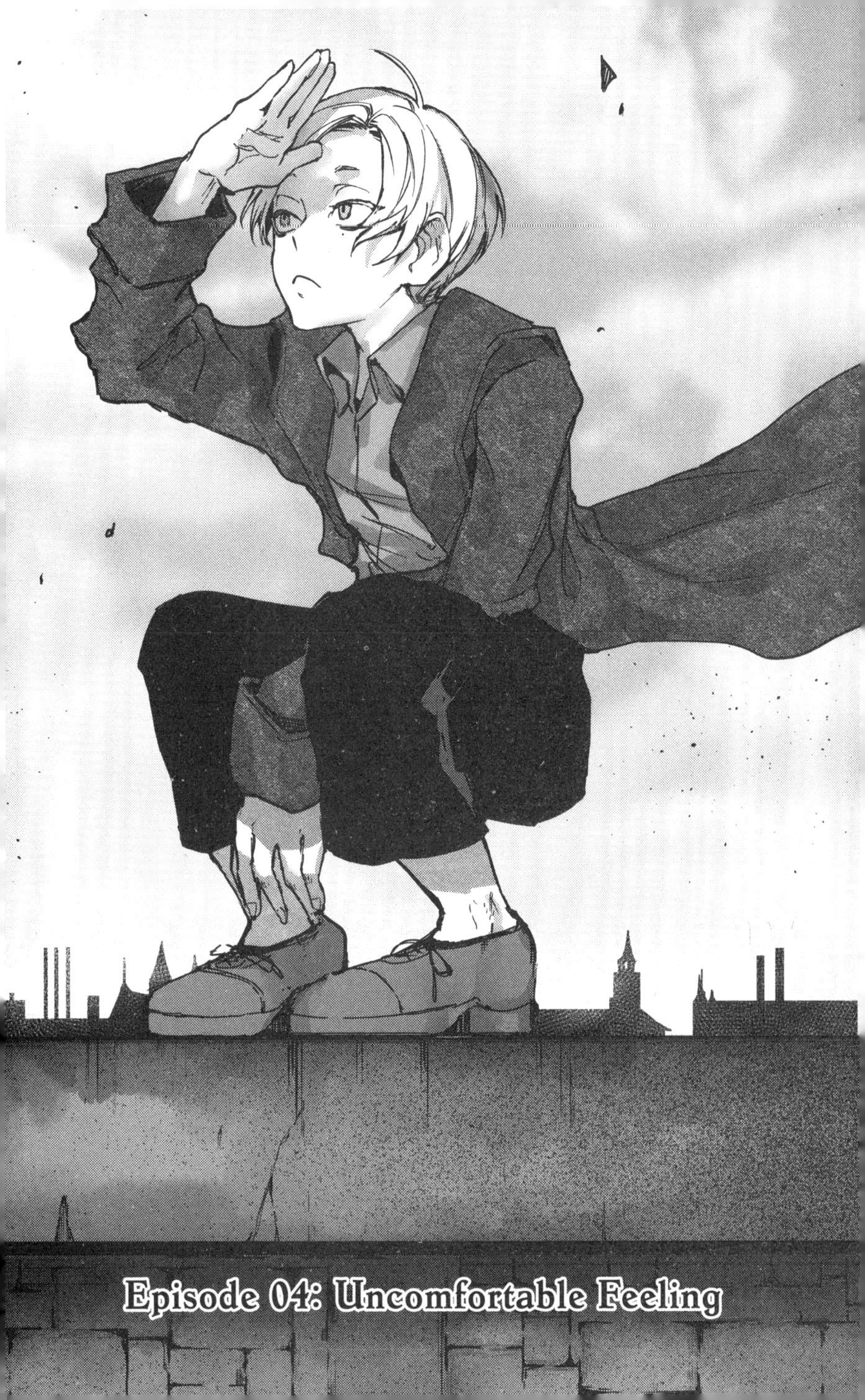

Episode 04: Uncomfortable Feeling

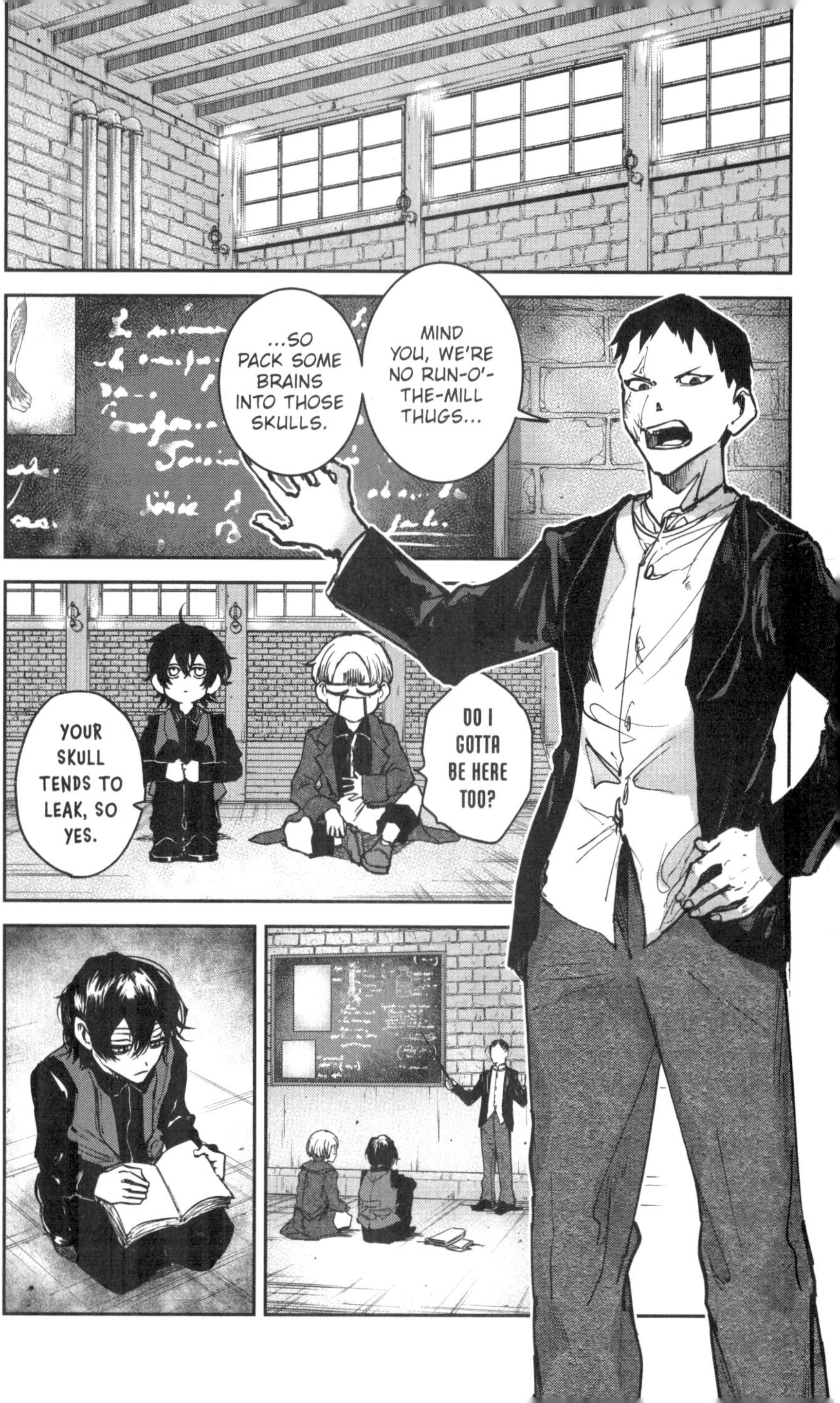
MIND YOU, WE'RE NO RUN-O'-THE-MILL THUGS...
...SO PACK SOME BRAINS INTO THOSE SKULLS.
DO I GOTTA BE HERE TOO?
YOUR SKULL TENDS TO LEAK, SO YES.

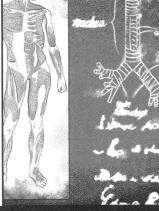

NOTHING NEW FOR ME...

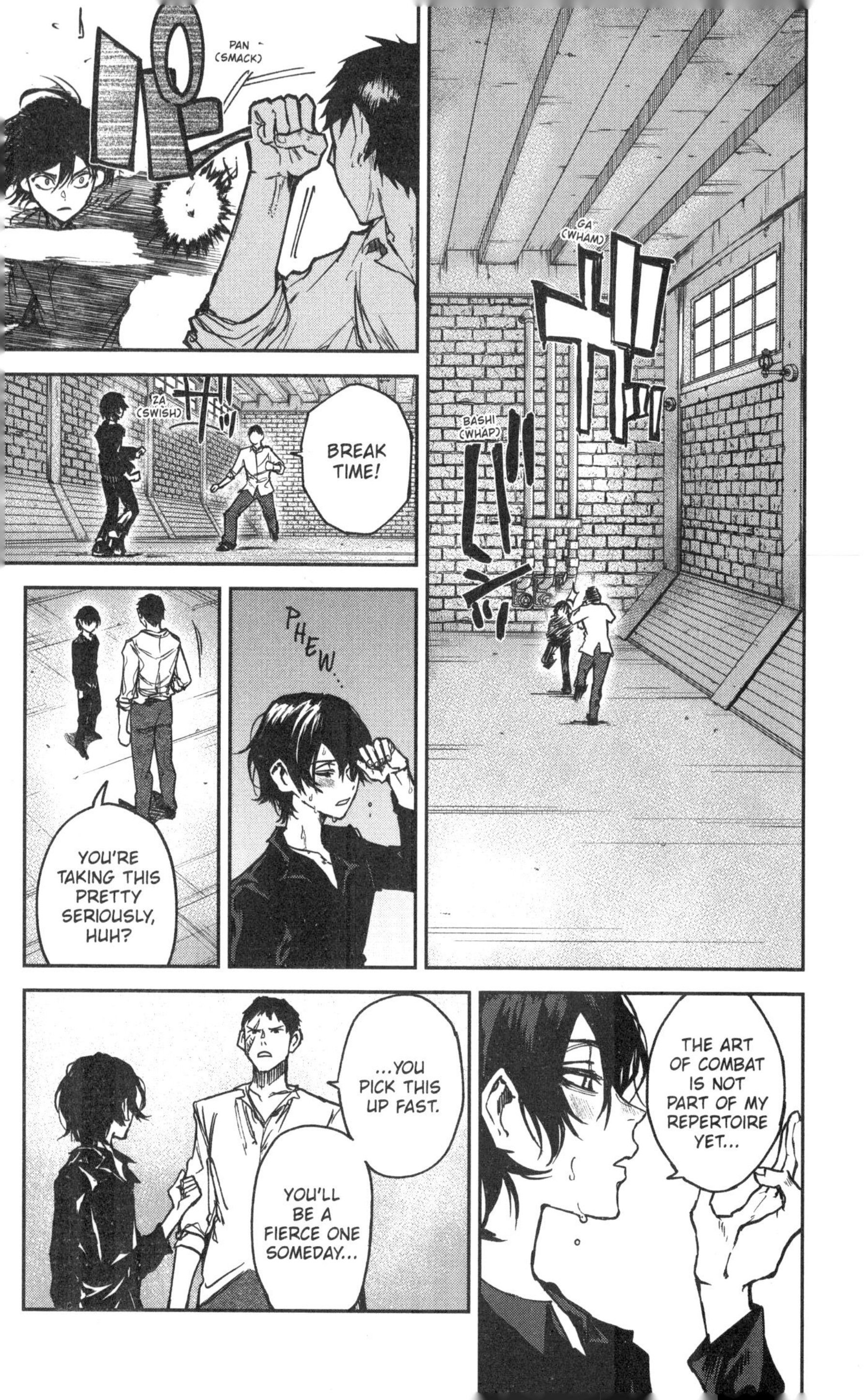
GA (WHAM)
BASHI (WHAP)
PAN (SMACK)
ZA (SWISH)
BREAK TIME!
PHEW...
YOU'RE TAKING THIS PRETTY SERIOUSLY, HUH?
THE ART OF COMBAT IS NOT PART OF MY REPERTOIRE YET...
...YOU PICK THIS UP FAST.
YOU'LL BE A FIERCE ONE SOMEDAY...

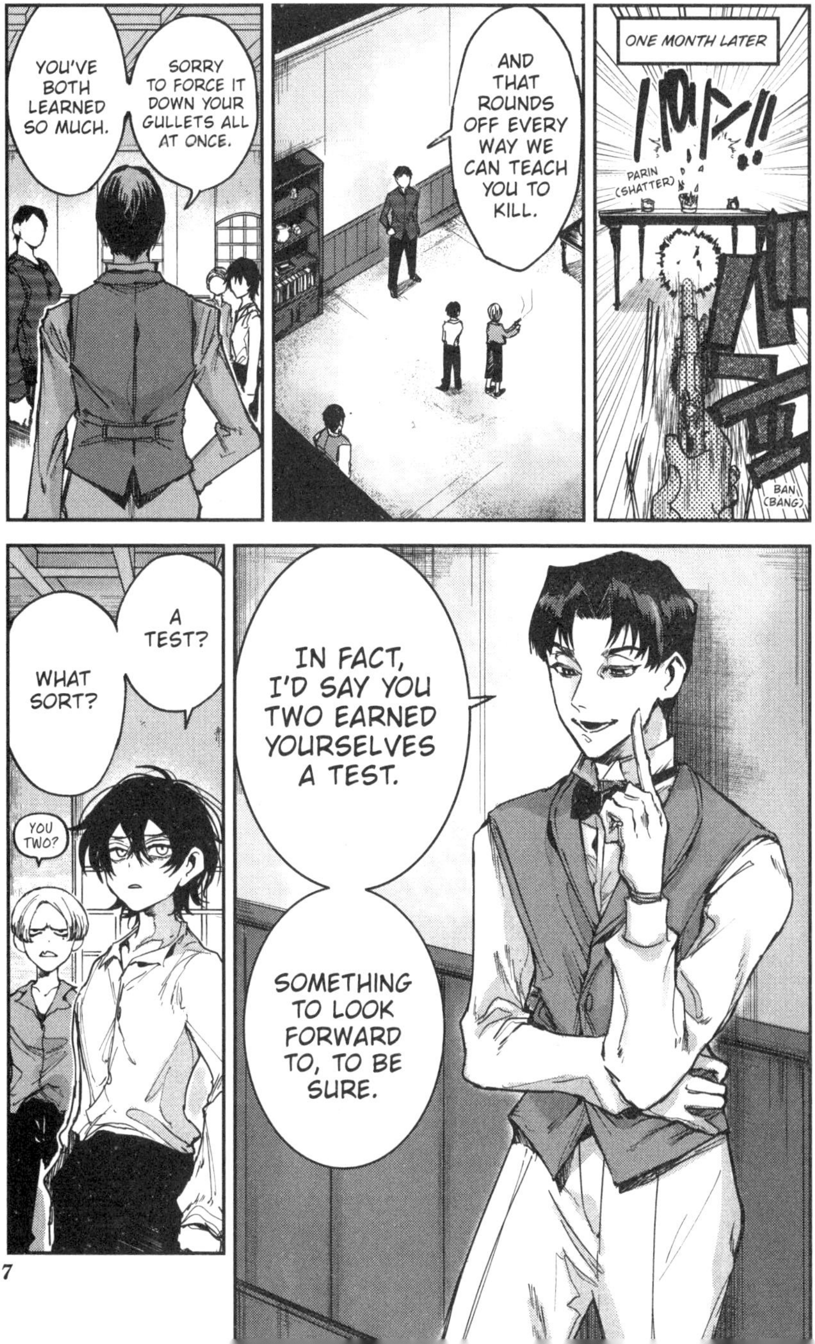
ONE MONTH LATER
PARIN (SHATTER)
BAN (BANG)
AND THAT ROUNDS OFF EVERY WAY WE CAN TEACH YOU TO KILL.
SORRY TO FORCE IT DOWN YOUR GULLETS ALL AT ONCE.
YOU'VE BOTH LEARNED SO MUCH.
IN FACT, I'D SAY YOU TWO EARNED YOURSELVES A TEST.
SOMETHING TO LOOK FORWARD TO, TO BE SURE.
A TEST?
WHAT SORT?
YOU TWO?

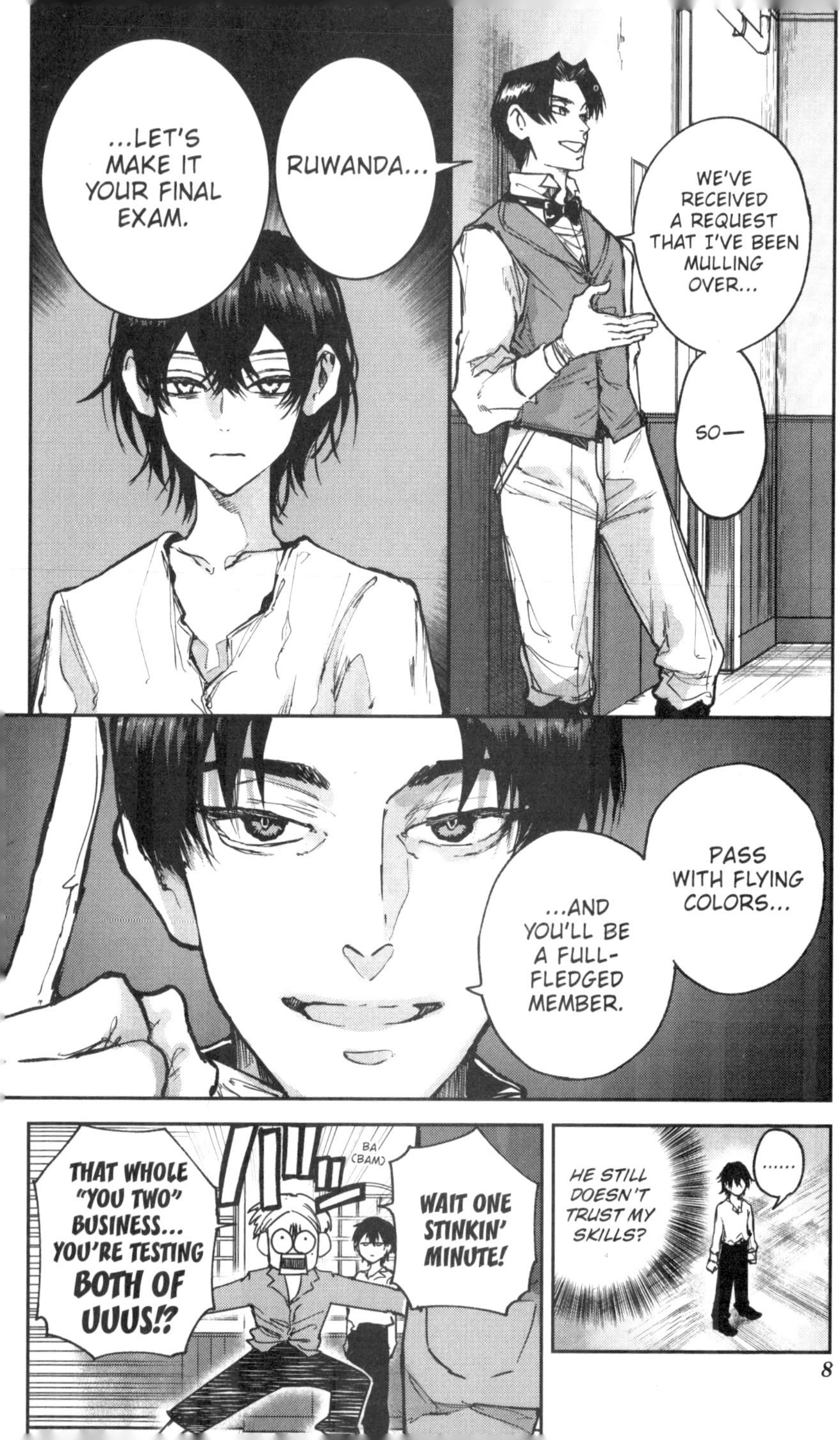
WE'VE RECEIVED A REQUEST THAT I'VE BEEN MULLING OVER...
SO—
RUWANDA...
...LET'S MAKE IT YOUR FINAL EXAM.
PASS WITH FLYING COLORS...
...AND YOU'LL BE A FULL-FLEDGED MEMBER.
......
HE STILL DOESN'T TRUST MY SKILLS?
BA (BAM)
WAIT ONE STINKIN' MINUTE!
THAT WHOLE "YOU TWO" BUSINESS... YOU'RE TESTING BOTH OF UUUS!?

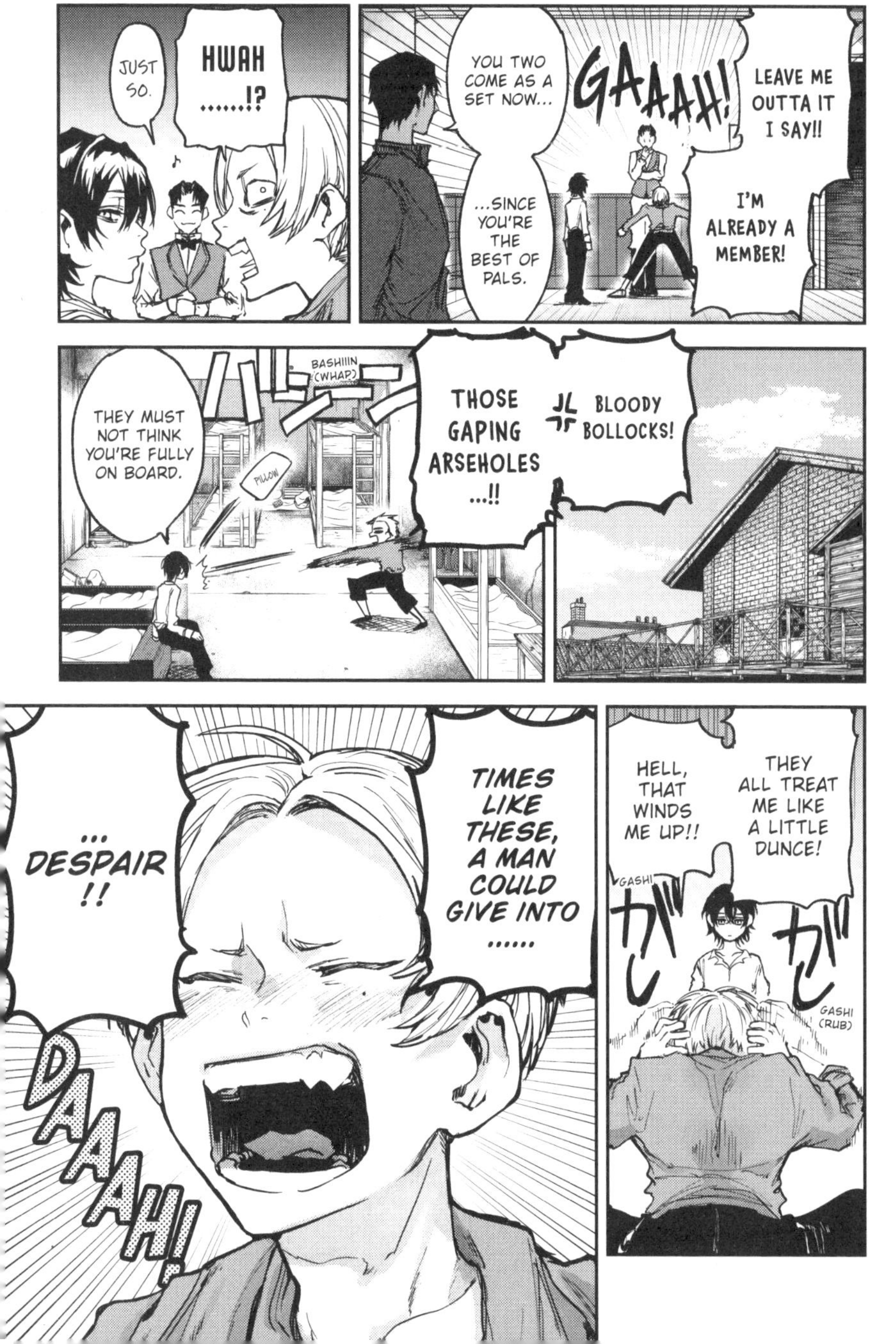
LEAVE ME OUTTA IT I SAY!!
GAAAH!
YOU TWO COME AS A SET NOW...
I'M ALREADY A MEMBER!
...SINCE YOU'RE THE BEST OF PALS.
HWAH ......!?
JUST SO.
BLOODY BOLLOCKS!
THOSE GAPING ARSEHOLES ...!!
BASHIIIN (WHAP)
PILLOW
THEY MUST NOT THINK YOU'RE FULLY ON BOARD.
THEY ALL TREAT ME LIKE A LITTLE DUNCE!
HELL, THAT WINDS ME UP!!
GASHI
GASHI (RUB)
TIMES LIKE THESE, A MAN COULD GIVE INTO ......
... DESPAIR !!
DAAAAH!

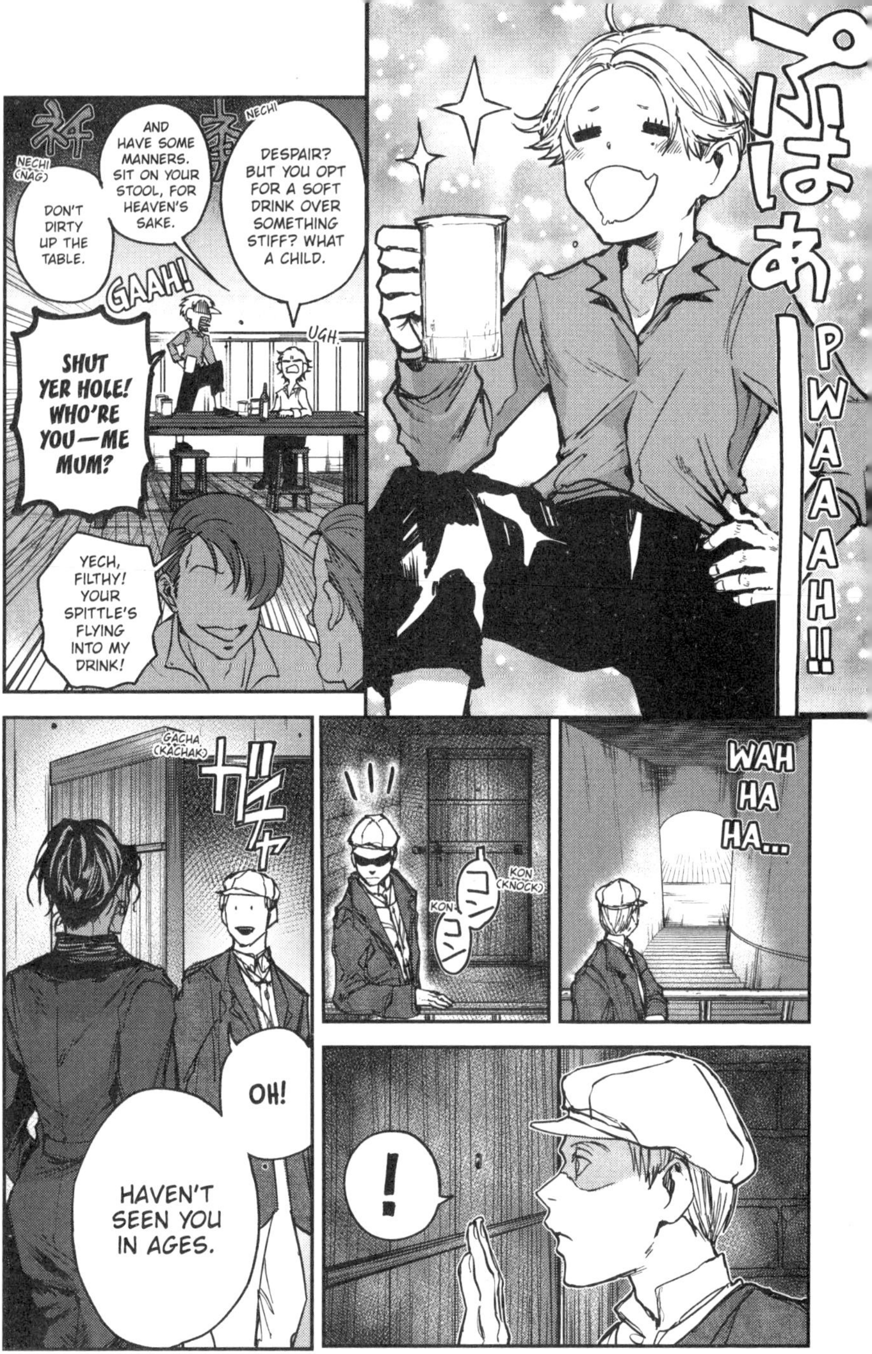
ぷはあー
PWAAAAAH!!
NECHI
DESPAIR? BUT YOU OPT FOR A SOFT DRINK OVER SOMETHING STIFF? WHAT A CHILD.
AND HAVE SOME MANNERS. SIT ON YOUR STOOL, FOR HEAVEN'S SAKE.
NECHI (NAG)
DON'T DIRTY UP THE TABLE.
GAAH!
UGH.
SHUT YER HOLE! WHO'RE YOU—ME MUM?
YECH, FILTHY! YOUR SPITTLE'S FLYING INTO MY DRINK!
WAH HA HA...
KON (KNOCK)
コン
KON
コン
!
GACHA (KACHAK)
ガチャ
OH!
HAVEN'T SEEN YOU IN AGES.

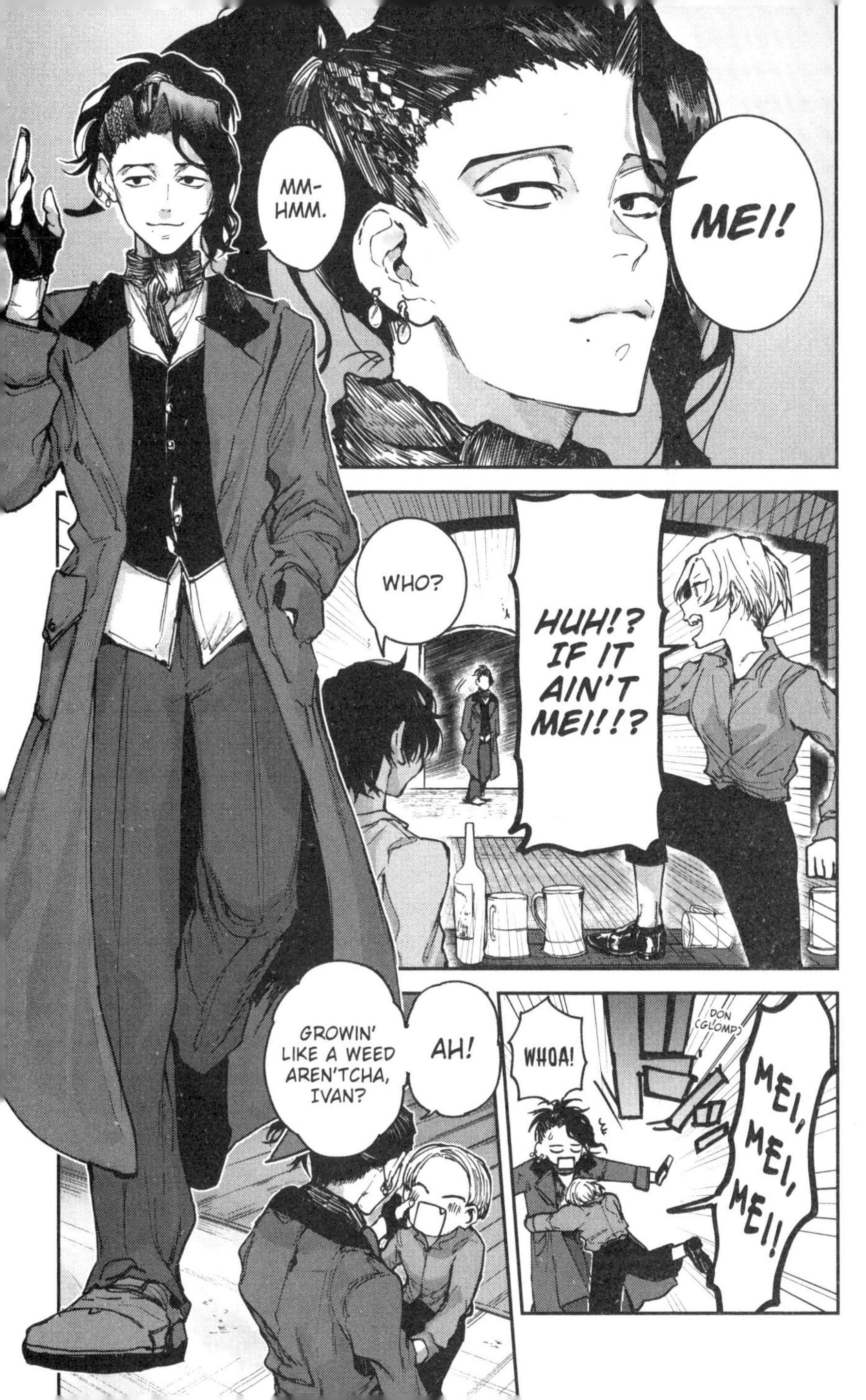

MEI!
MM-HMM.
HUH!? IF IT AIN'T MEI!!?
WHO?
DON (GLOMP)
MEI, MEI, MEI, MEI!!
WHOA!
AH!
GROWIN' LIKE A WEED AREN'TCHA, IVAN?

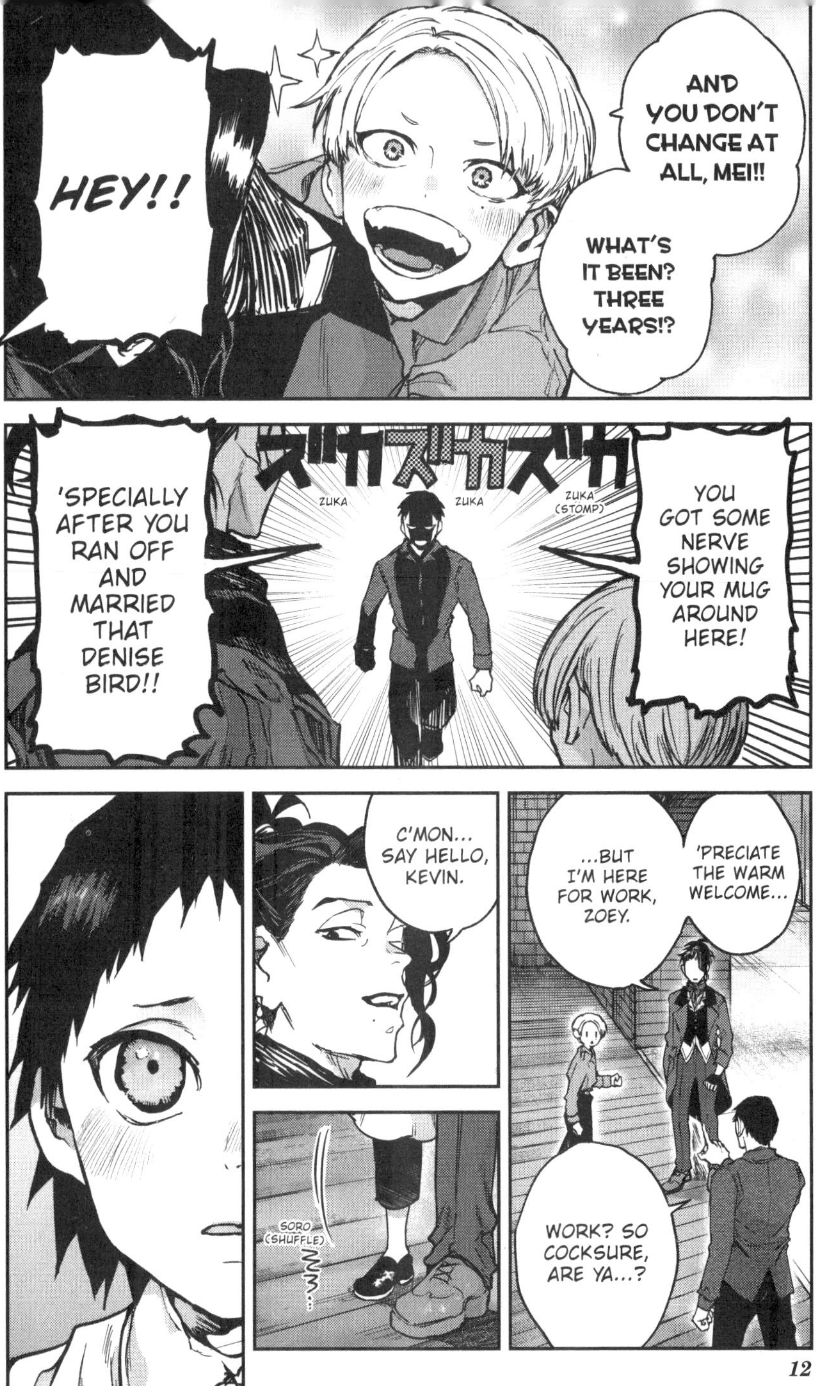
AND YOU DON'T CHANGE AT ALL, MEI!!
WHAT'S IT BEEN? THREE YEARS!?
HEY!!
ZUKA ZUKA ZUKA (STOMP)
YOU GOT SOME NERVE SHOWING YOUR MUG AROUND HERE!
'SPECIALLY AFTER YOU RAN OFF AND MARRIED THAT DENISE BIRD!!
'PRECIATE THE WARM WELCOME...
...BUT I'M HERE FOR WORK, ZOEY.
WORK? SO COCKSURE, ARE YA...?
C'MON... SAY HELLO, KEVIN.
SORO (SHUFFLE)

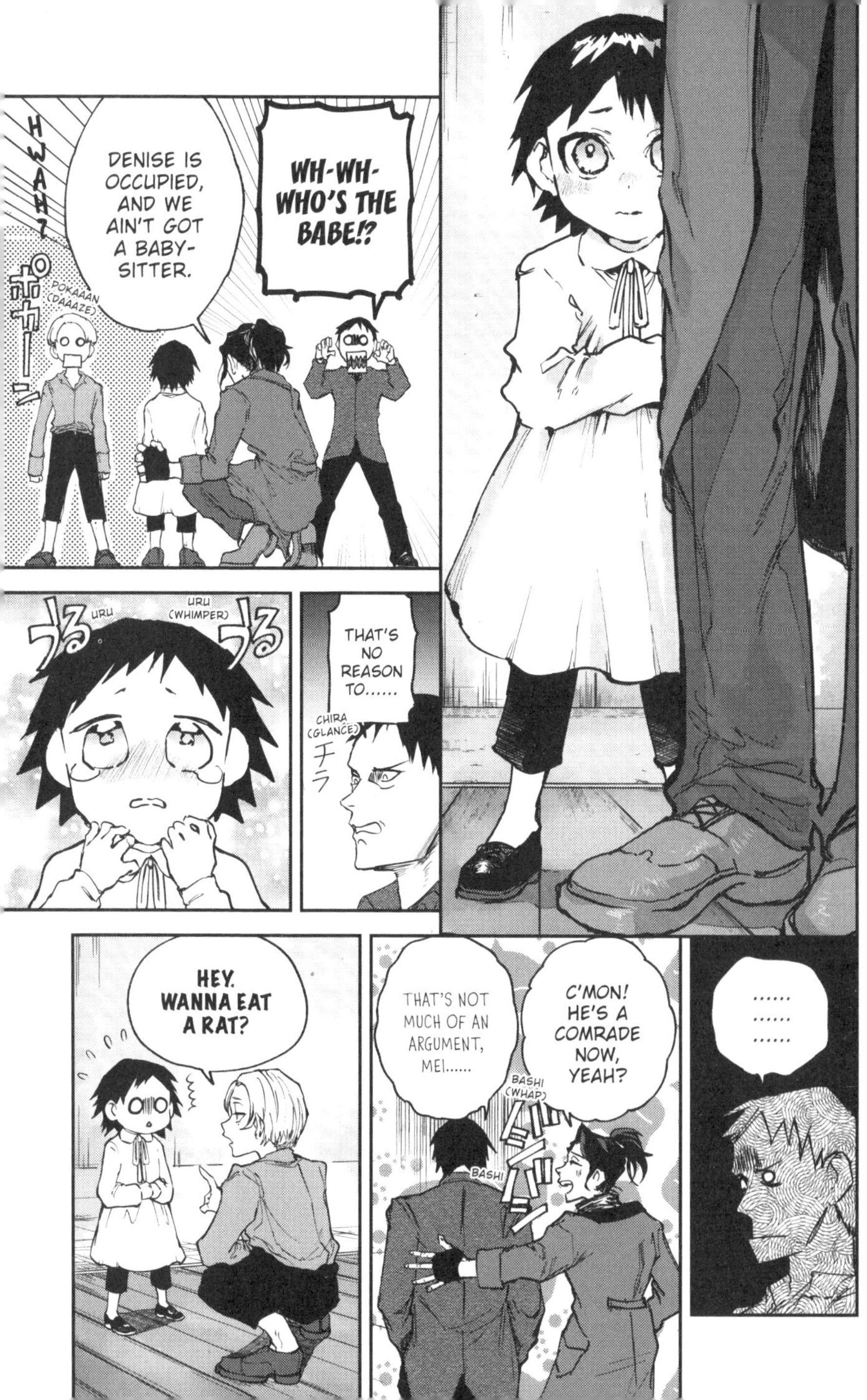
WH-WH-WHO'S THE BABE!?
DENISE IS OCCUPIED, AND WE AIN'T GOT A BABY-SITTER.
HWAH?
ポカーン
POKAAAN (DAAAZE)
THAT'S NO REASON TO......
チラ
CHIRA (GLANCE)
うる
URU (WHIMPER)
うる
URU
......
......
......
C'MON! HE'S A COMRADE NOW, YEAH?
THAT'S NOT MUCH OF AN ARGUMENT, MEI......
BASHI (WHAP)
BASHI
HEY. WANNA EAT A RAT?

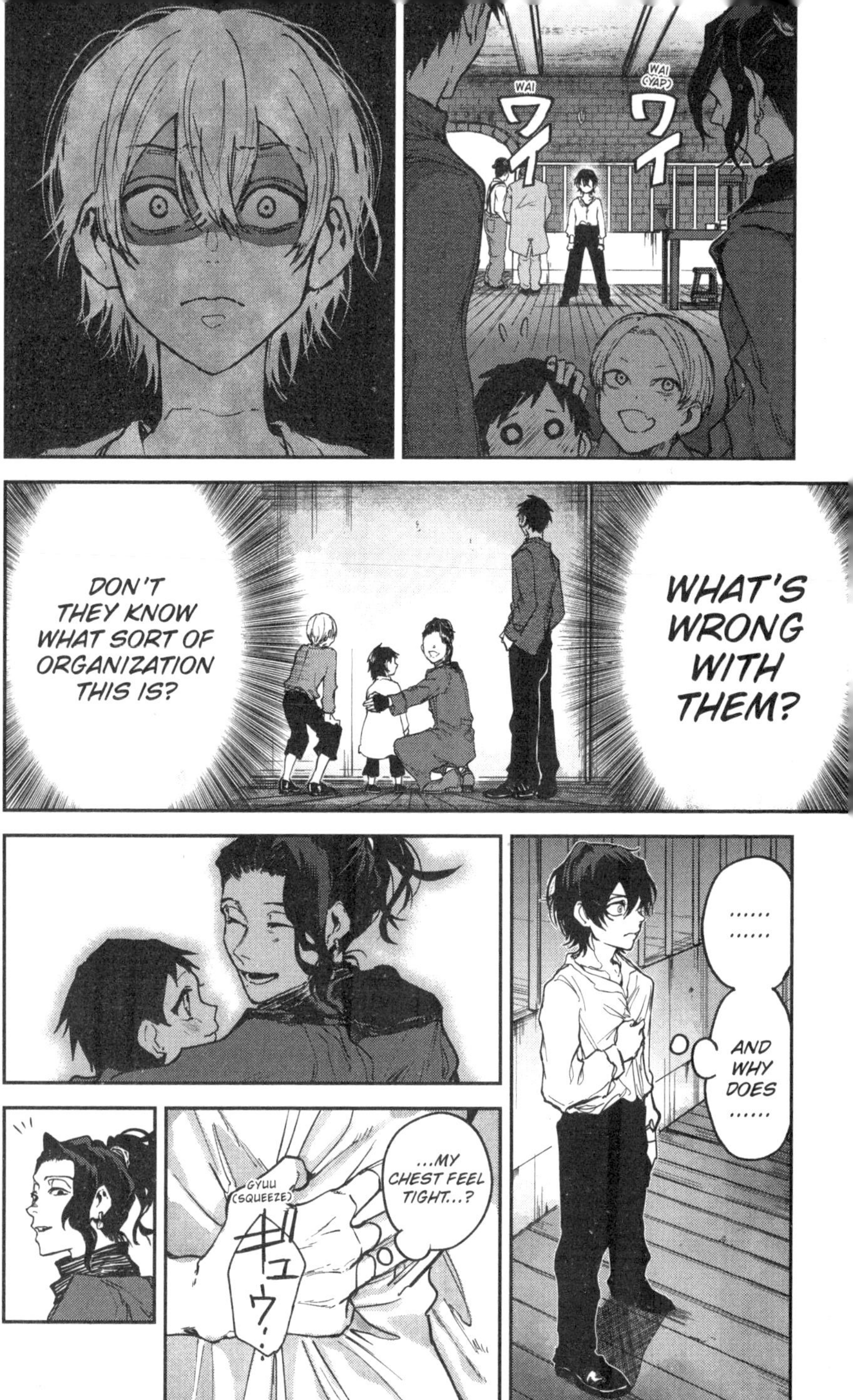
WAI (YAP)
ワイ
WAI
ワイ
WHAT'S WRONG WITH THEM?
DON'T THEY KNOW WHAT SORT OF ORGANIZATION THIS IS?
....
AND WHY DOES......
...MY CHEST FEEL TIGHT...?
GYUU (SQUEEZE)
ギュウ

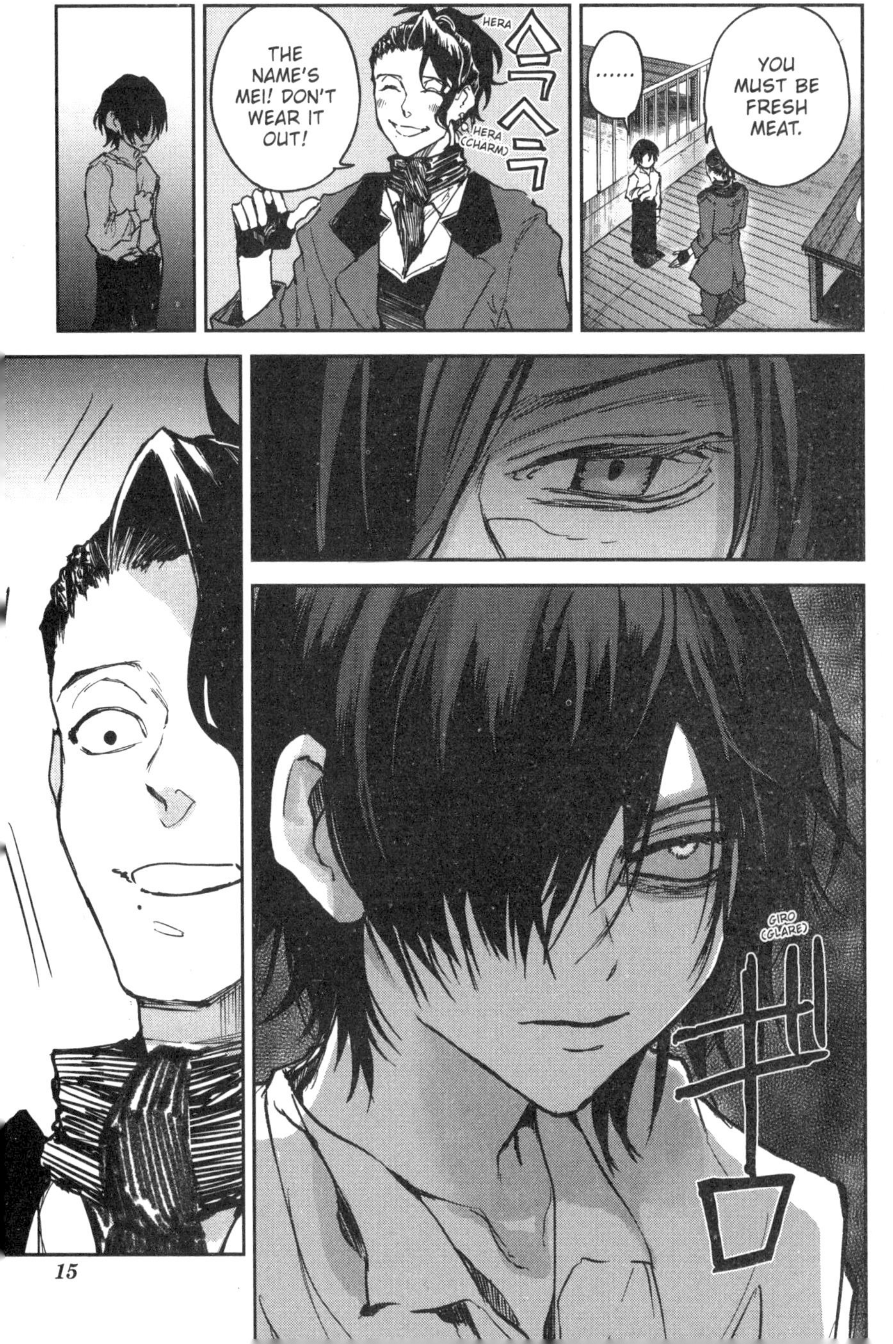
YOU MUST BE FRESH MEAT.
......
HERA
HERA (CHARM)
THE NAME'S MEI! DON'T WEAR IT OUT!
GIRO (GLARE)

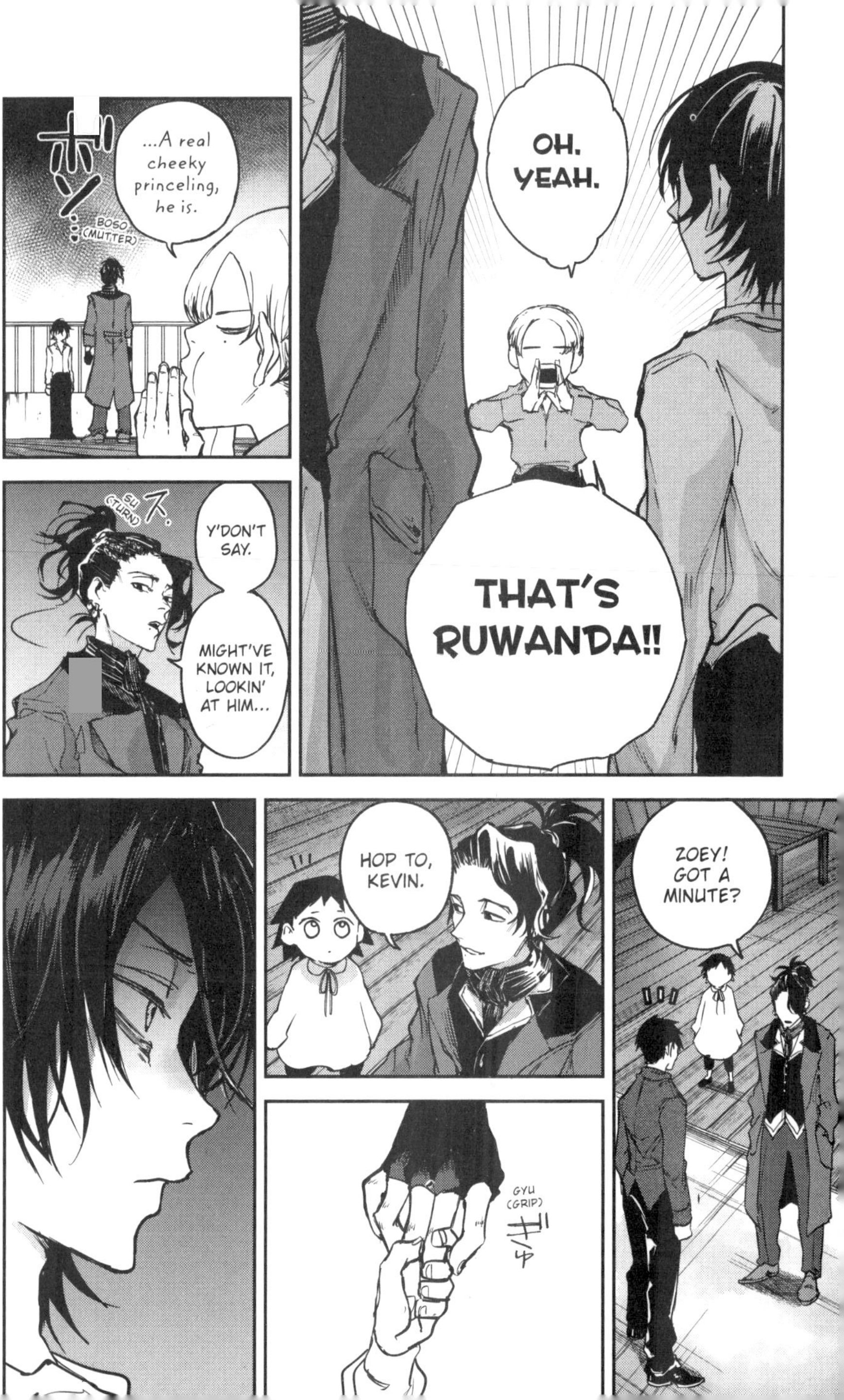
OH. YEAH.
THAT'S RUWANDA!!
...A real cheeky princeling, he is.
BOSO (MUTTER)
Y'DON'T SAY.
MIGHT'VE KNOWN IT, LOOKIN' AT HIM...
SU (TURN)
ZOEY! GOT A MINUTE?
HOP TO, KEVIN.
GYU (GRIP)

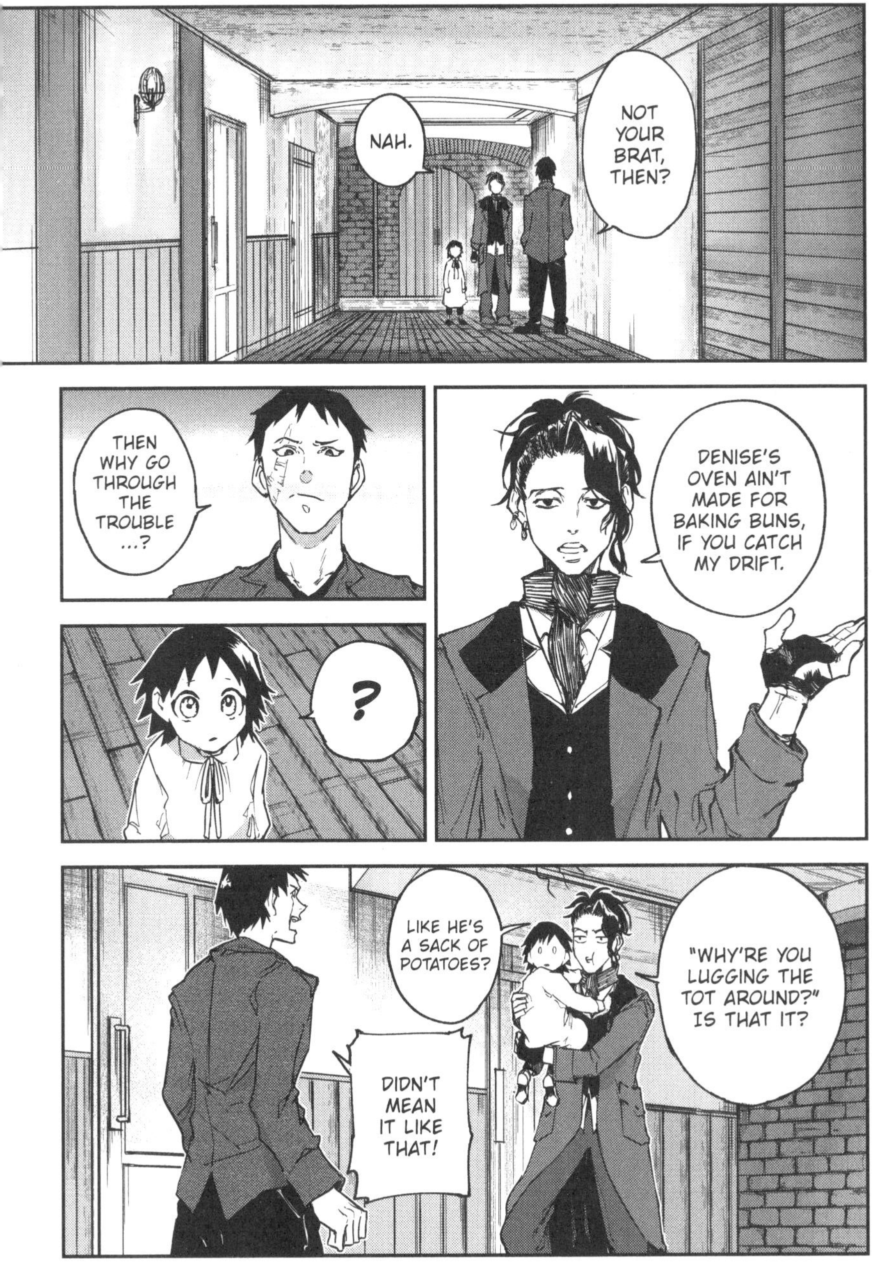
NOT YOUR BRAT, THEN?
NAH.
DENISE'S OVEN AIN'T MADE FOR BAKING BUNS, IF YOU CATCH MY DRIFT.
THEN WHY GO THROUGH THE TROUBLE ...?
?
"WHY'RE YOU LUGGING THE TOT AROUND?" IS THAT IT?
LIKE HE'S A SACK OF POTATOES?
DIDN'T MEAN IT LIKE THAT!

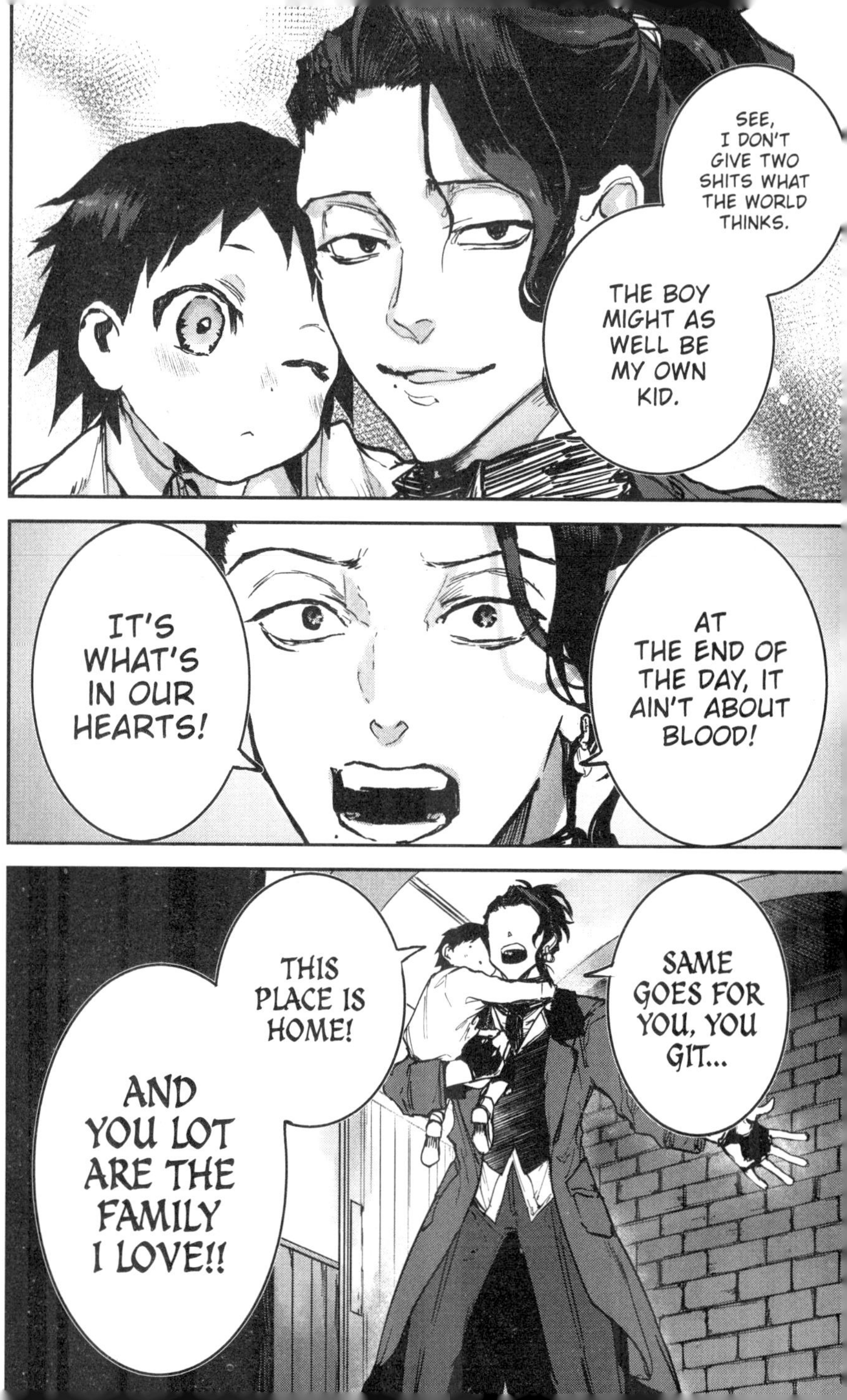
SEE, I DON'T GIVE TWO SHITS WHAT THE WORLD THINKS.
THE BOY MIGHT AS WELL BE MY OWN KID.
AT THE END OF THE DAY, IT AIN'T ABOUT BLOOD!
IT'S WHAT'S IN OUR HEARTS!
SAME GOES FOR YOU, YOU GIT...
THIS PLACE IS HOME!
AND YOU LOT ARE THE FAMILY I LOVE!!

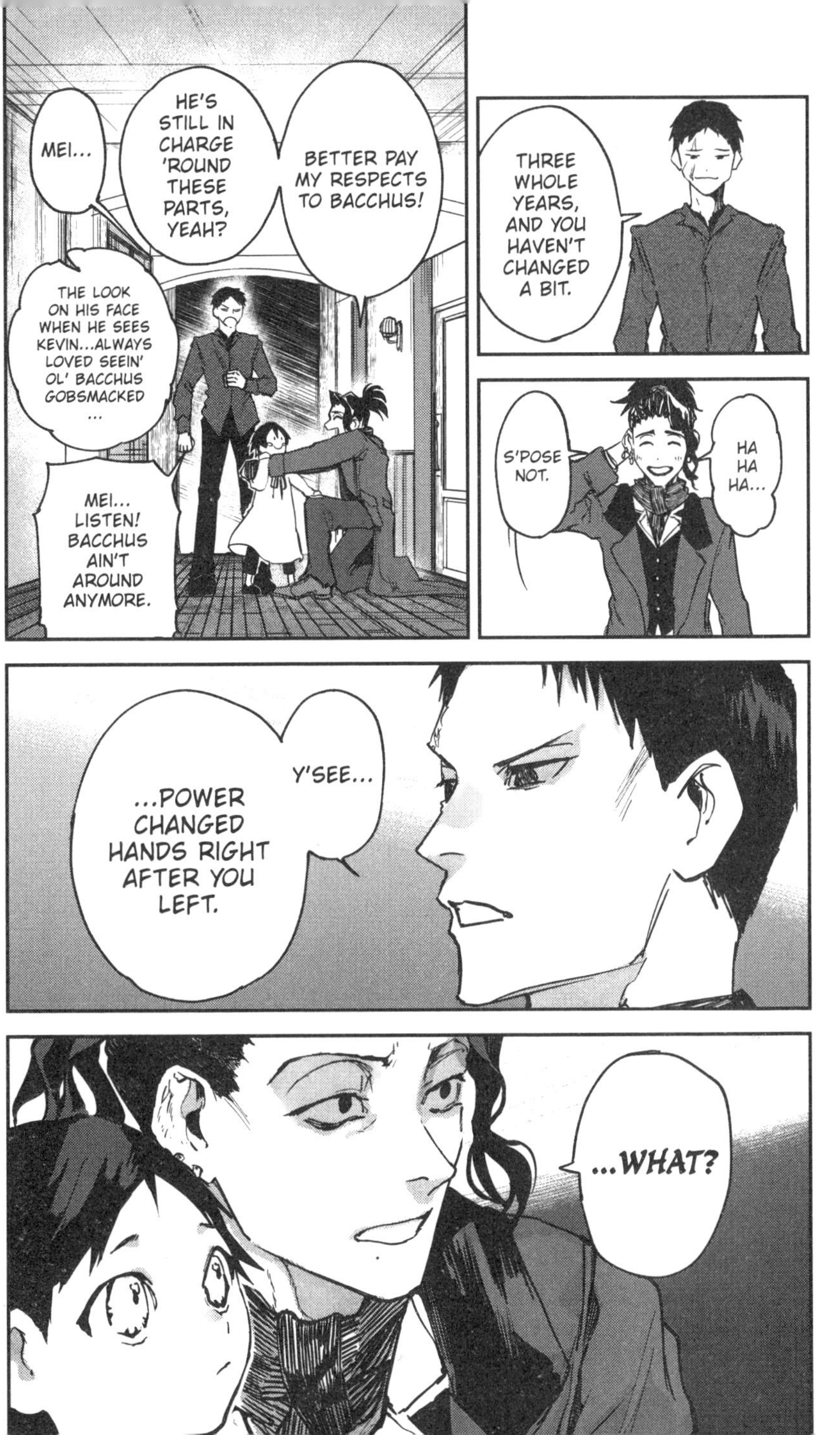
THREE WHOLE YEARS, AND YOU HAVEN'T CHANGED A BIT.
HA HA HA...
S'POSE NOT.
BETTER PAY MY RESPECTS TO BACCHUS!
HE'S STILL IN CHARGE 'ROUND THESE PARTS, YEAH?
MEI...
THE LOOK ON HIS FACE WHEN HE SEES KEVIN...ALWAYS LOVED SEEIN' OL' BACCHUS GOBSMACKED...
MEI... LISTEN! BACCHUS AIN'T AROUND ANYMORE.
Y'SEE...
...POWER CHANGED HANDS RIGHT AFTER YOU LEFT.
...WHAT?

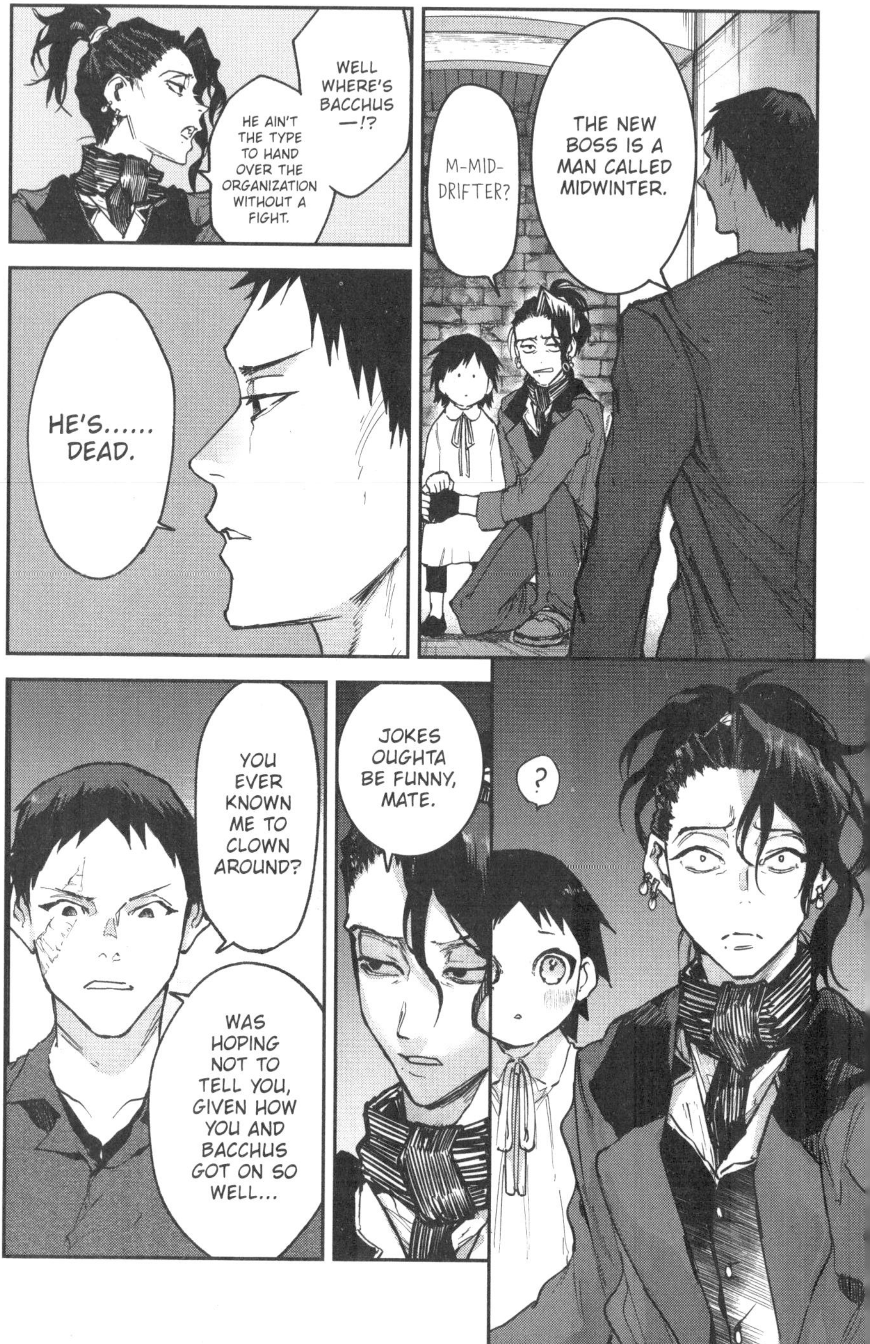
THE NEW BOSS IS A MAN CALLED MIDWINTER.
M-MID-DRIFTER?
WELL WHERE'S BACCHUS—!?
HE AIN'T THE TYPE TO HAND OVER THE ORGANIZATION WITHOUT A FIGHT.
HE'S...... DEAD.
?
JOKES OUGHTA BE FUNNY, MATE.
YOU EVER KNOWN ME TO CLOWN AROUND?
WAS HOPING NOT TO TELL YOU, GIVEN HOW YOU AND BACCHUS GOT ON SO WELL...

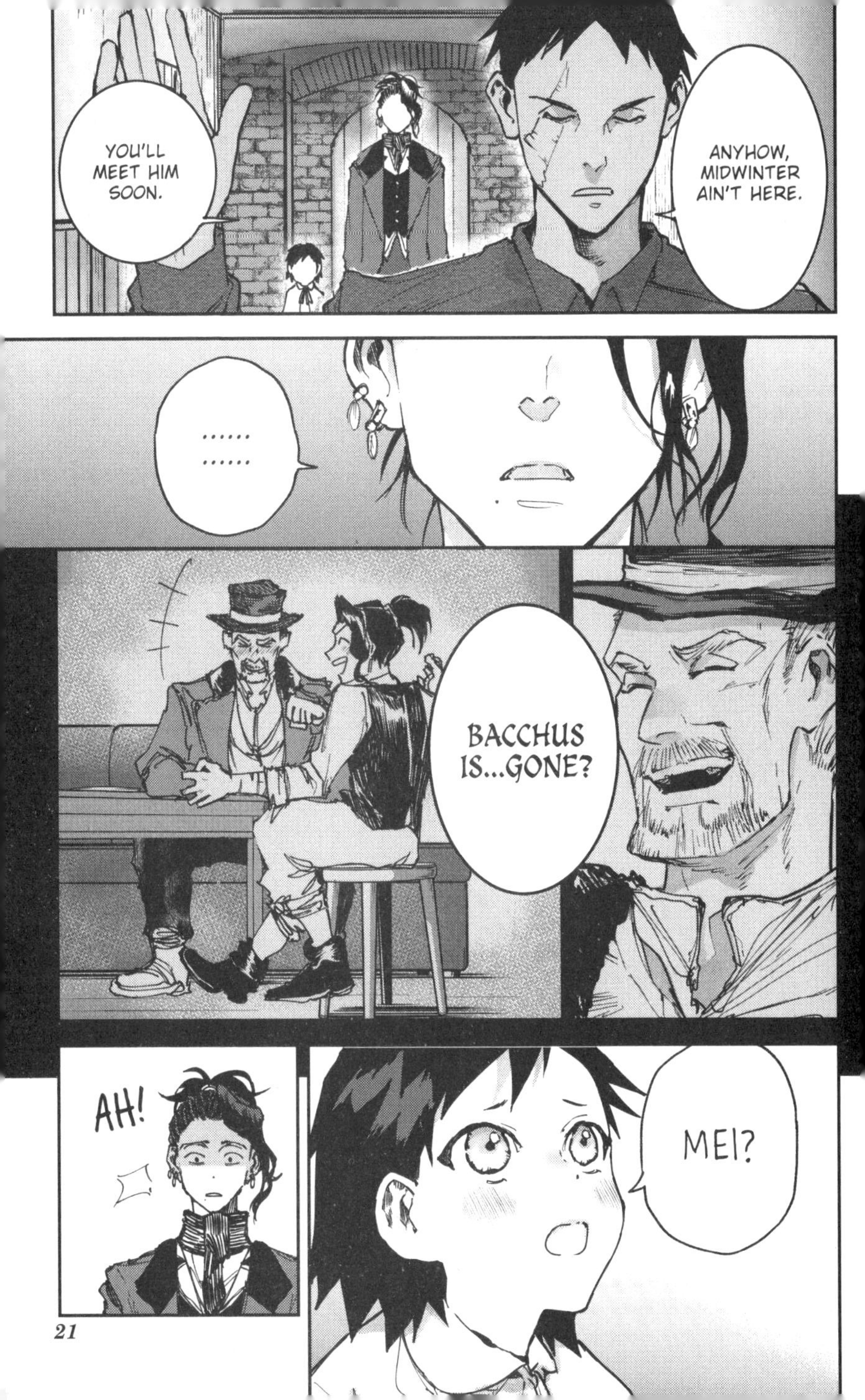
ANYHOW, MIDWINTER AIN'T HERE.
YOU'LL MEET HIM SOON.
......
......
BACCHUS IS...GONE?
MEI?
AH!

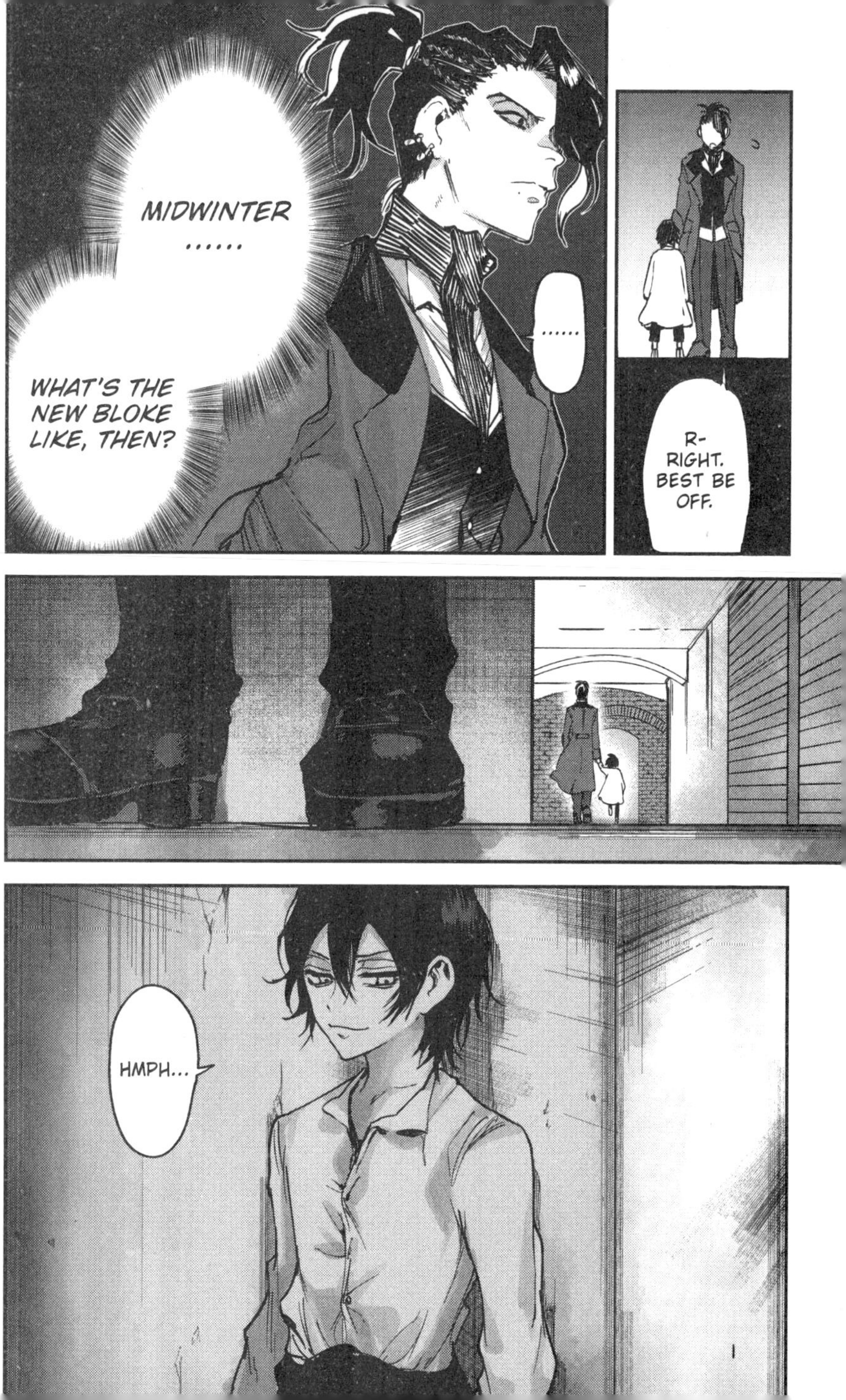
R-RIGHT. BEST BE OFF.
MIDWINTER ......
......
WHAT'S THE NEW BLOKE LIKE, THEN?
HMPH...

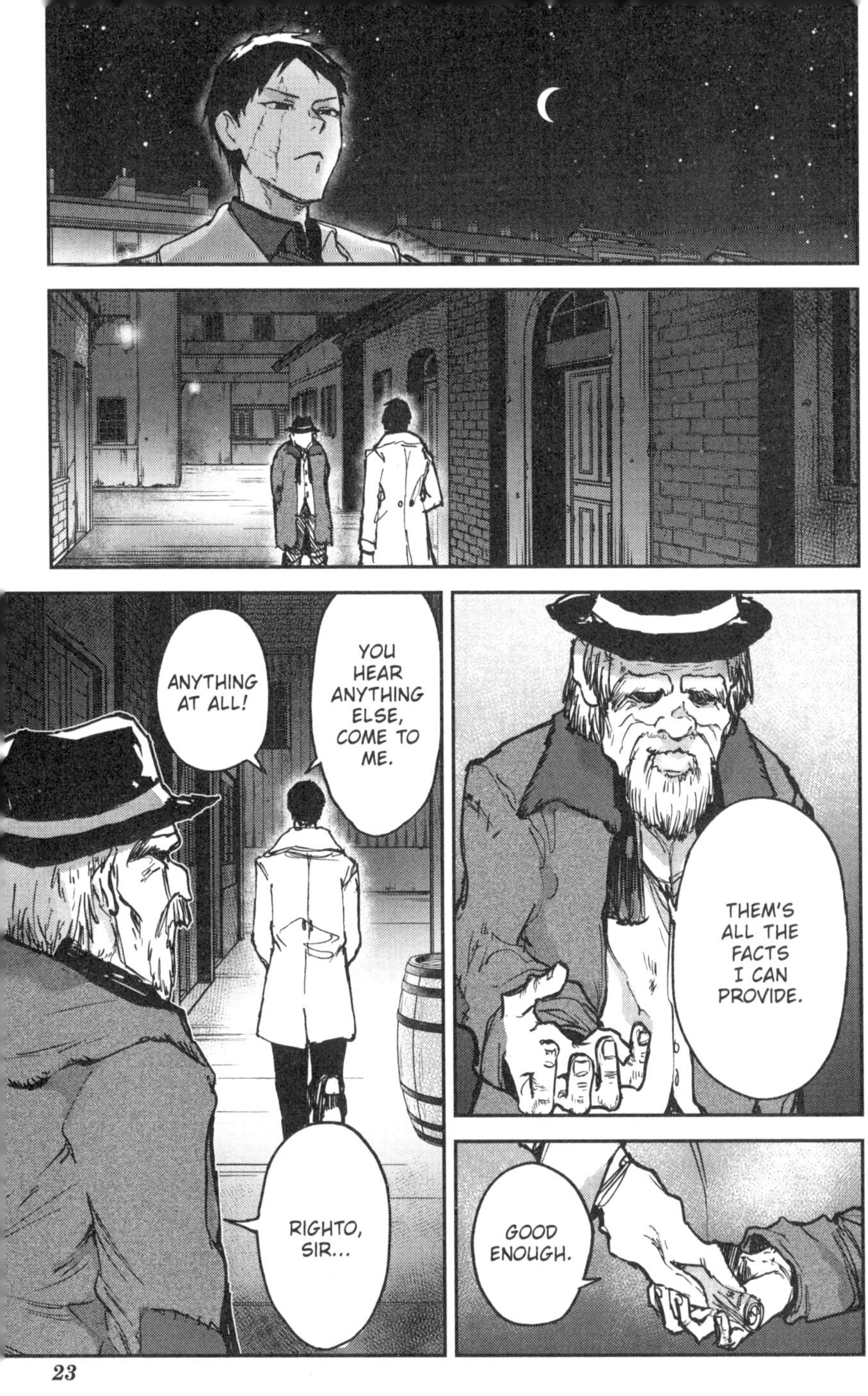
THEM'S ALL THE FACTS I CAN PROVIDE.
GOOD ENOUGH.
YOU HEAR ANYTHING ELSE, COME TO ME.
ANYTHING AT ALL!
RIGHTO, SIR...

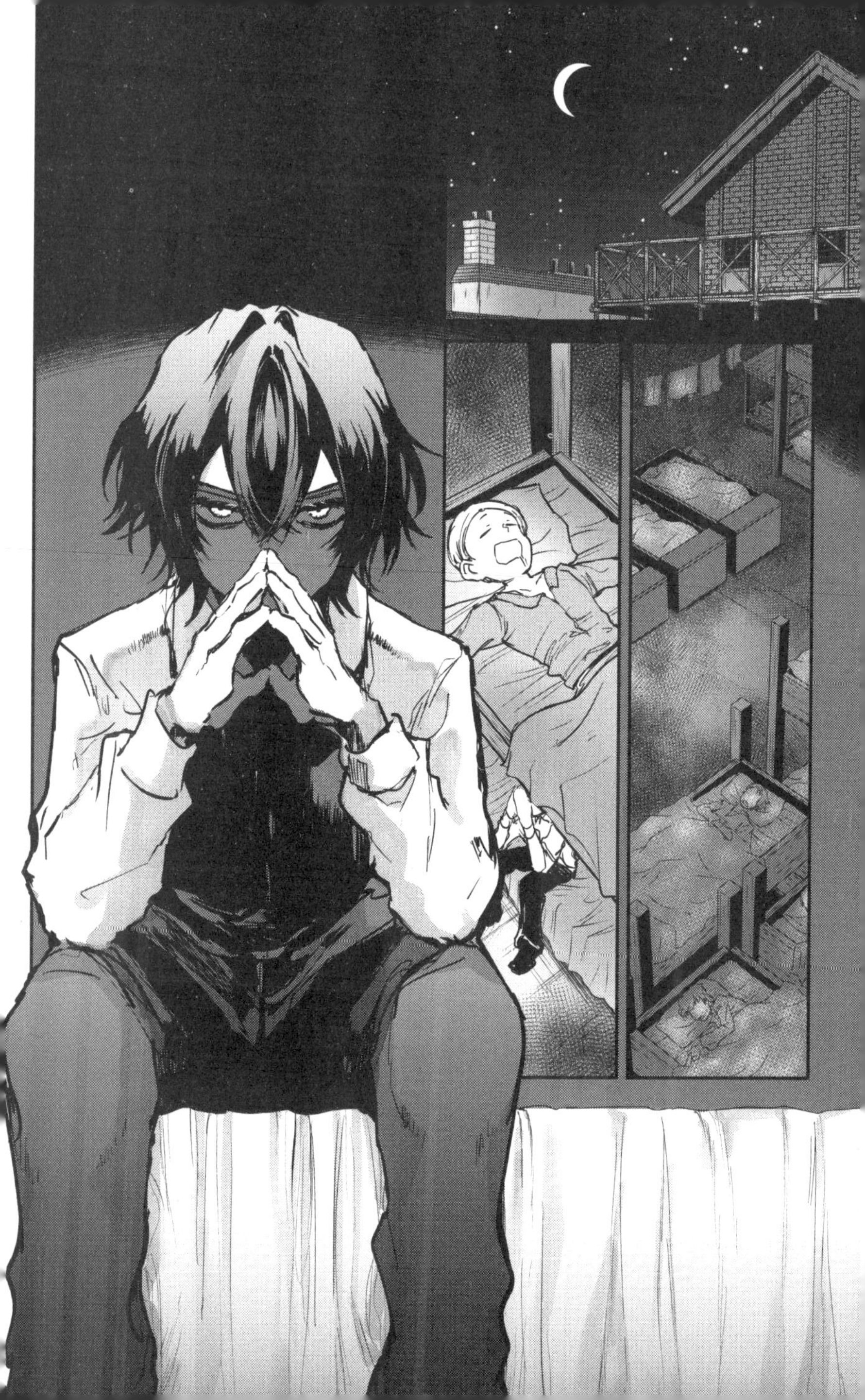

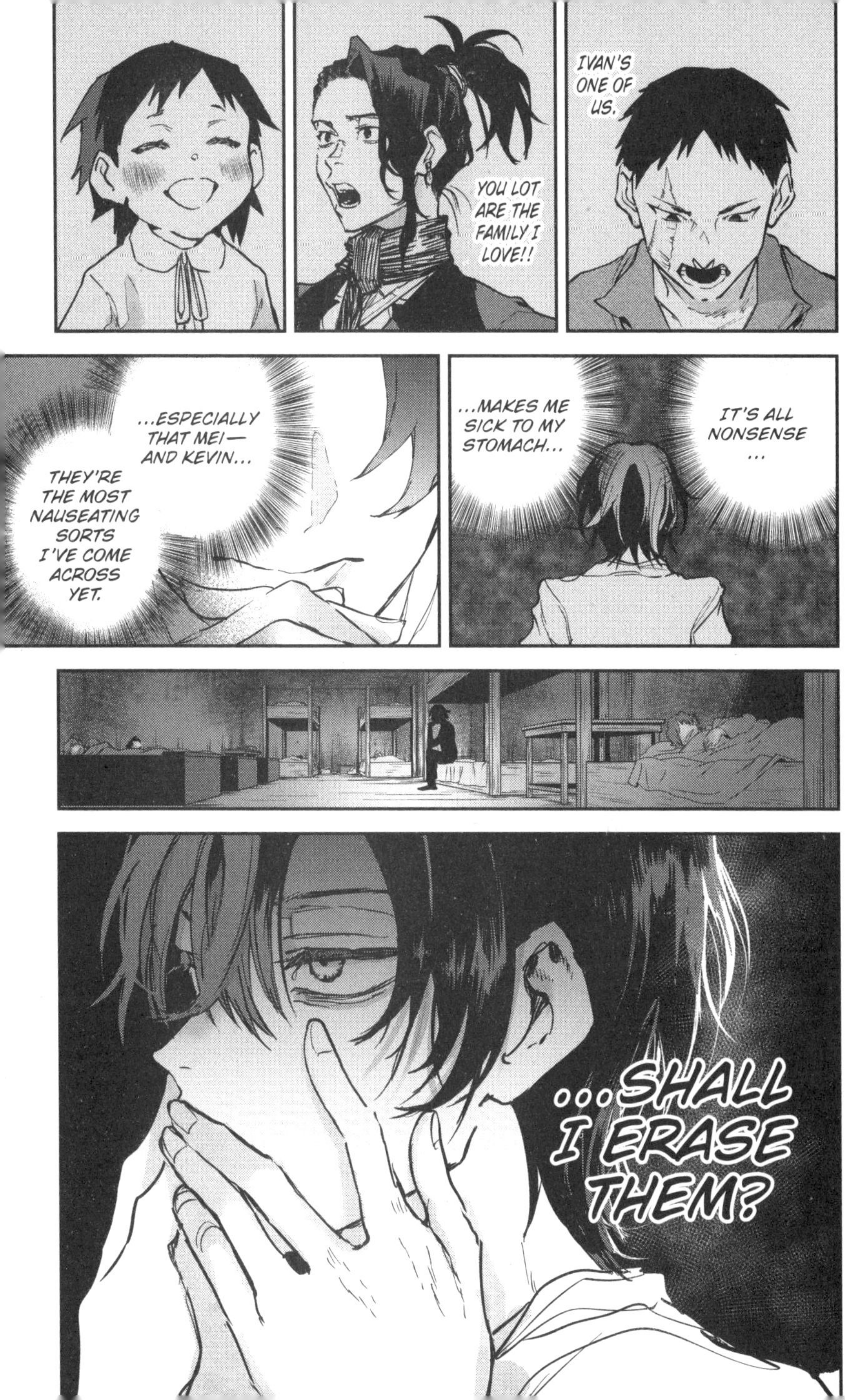
IVAN'S ONE OF US.
YOU LOT ARE THE FAMILY I LOVE!!
IT'S ALL NONSENSE ...
...MAKES ME SICK TO MY STOMACH...
...ESPECIALLY THAT MEI— AND KEVIN...
THEY'RE THE MOST NAUSEATING SORTS I'VE COME ACROSS YET.
...SHALL I ERASE THEM?

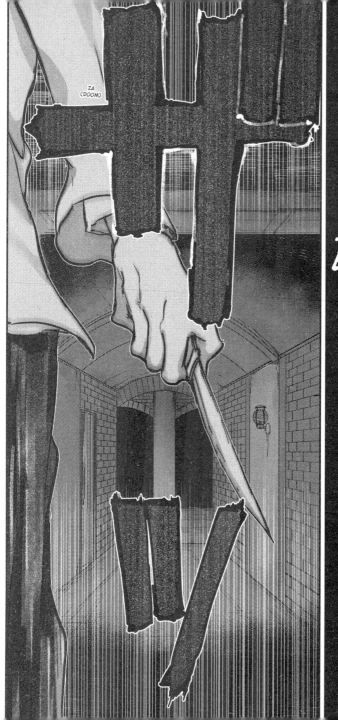

ZA
(DOOM)

I WILL ERASE ALL WHO ARE IN MY WAY.

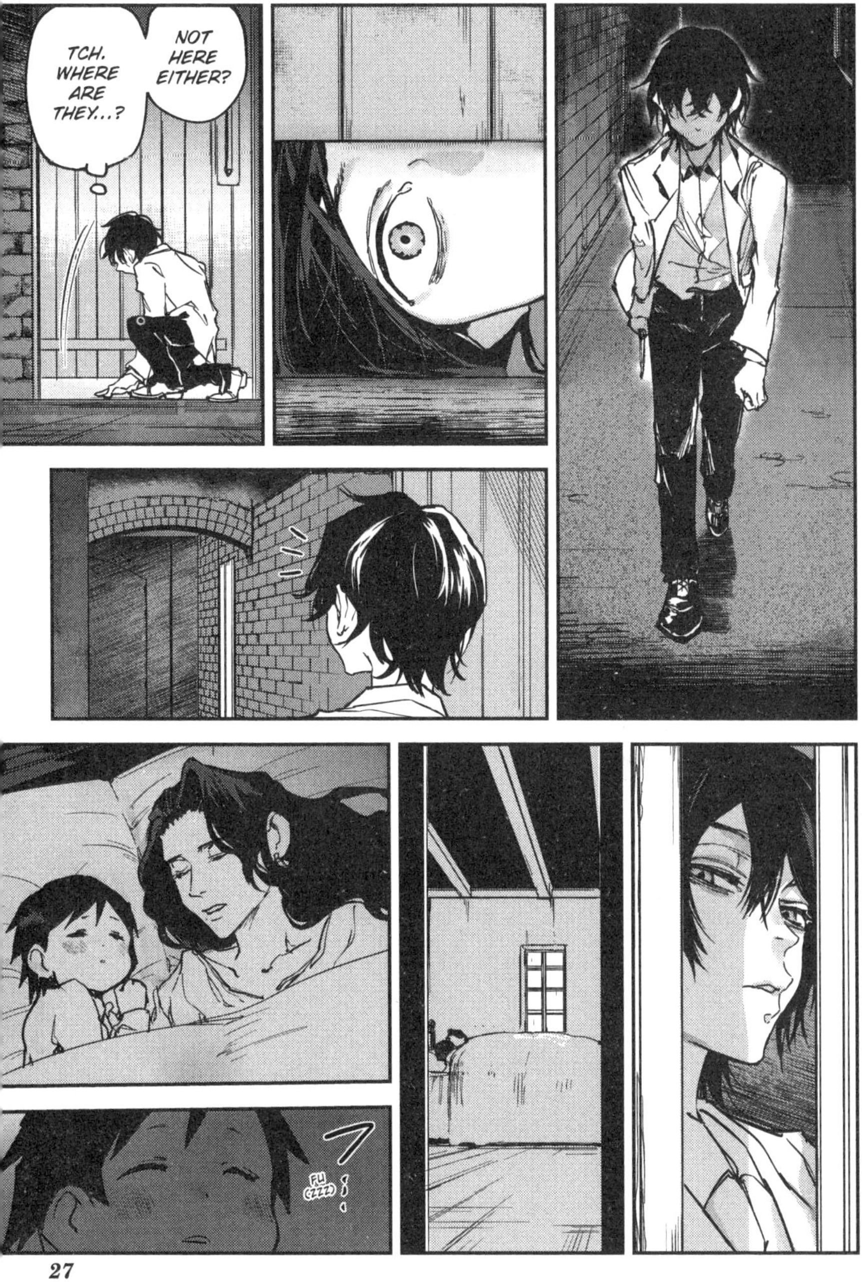
NOT HERE EITHER?
TCH. WHERE ARE THEY...?
FU (ZZZ)

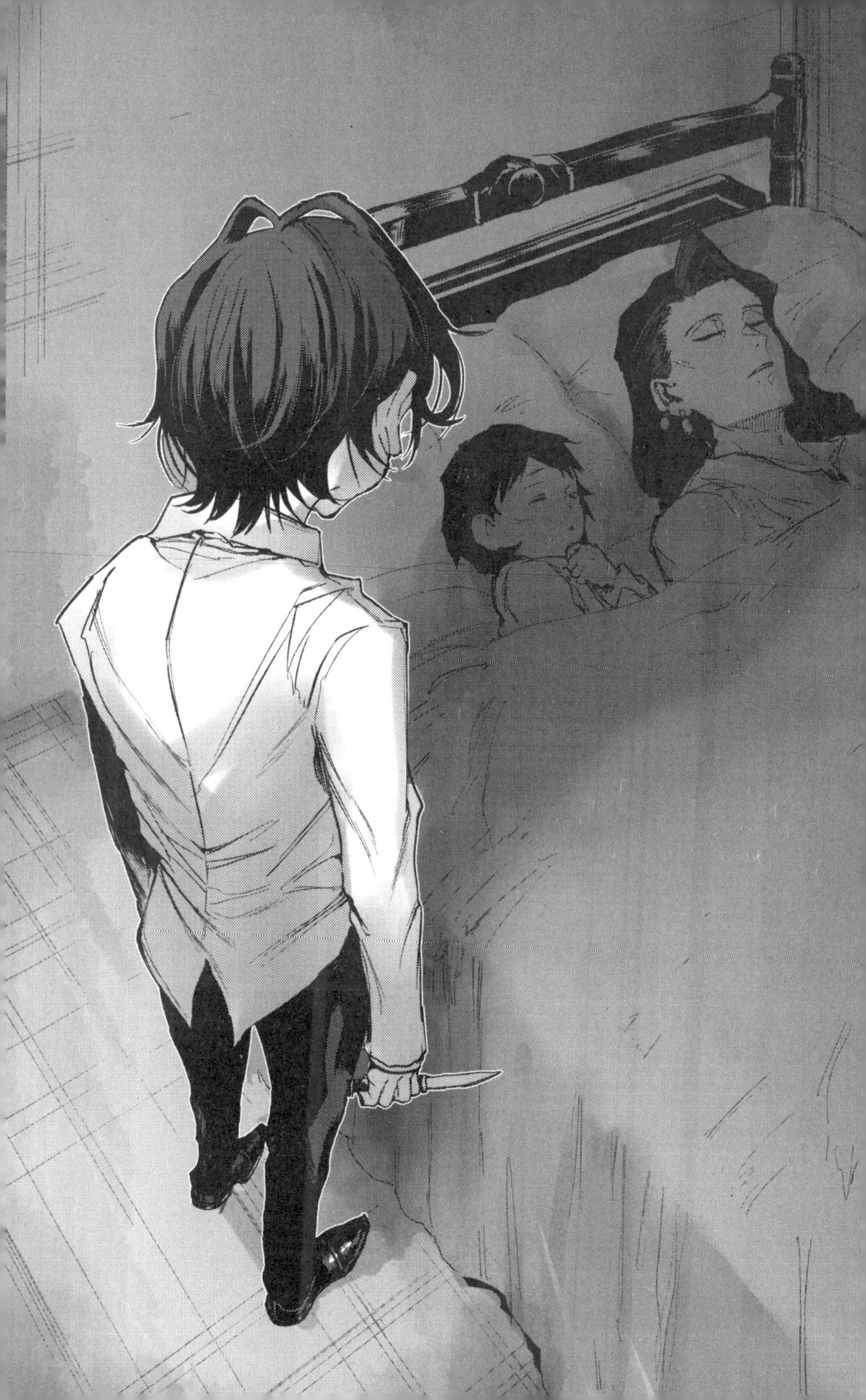

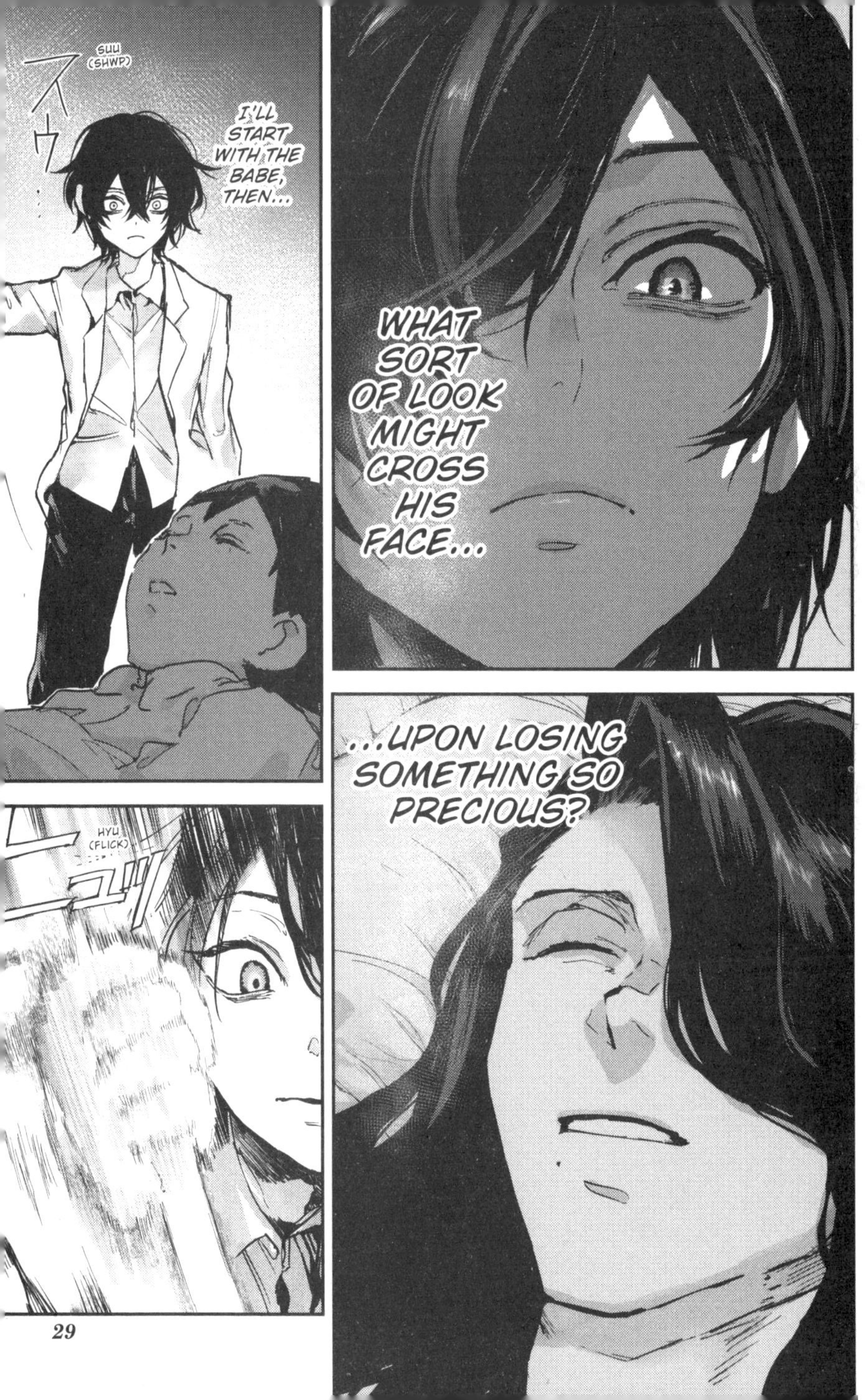
WHAT SORT OF LOOK MIGHT CROSS HIS FACE...
SUU (SHWP)
I'LL START WITH THE BABE, THEN...
...UPON LOSING SOMETHING SO PRECIOUS?
HYU (FLICK)

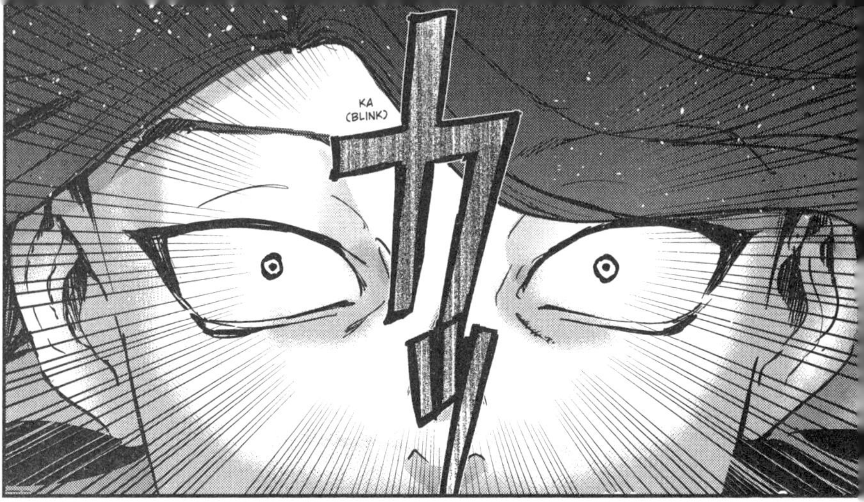
KA
(BLINK)
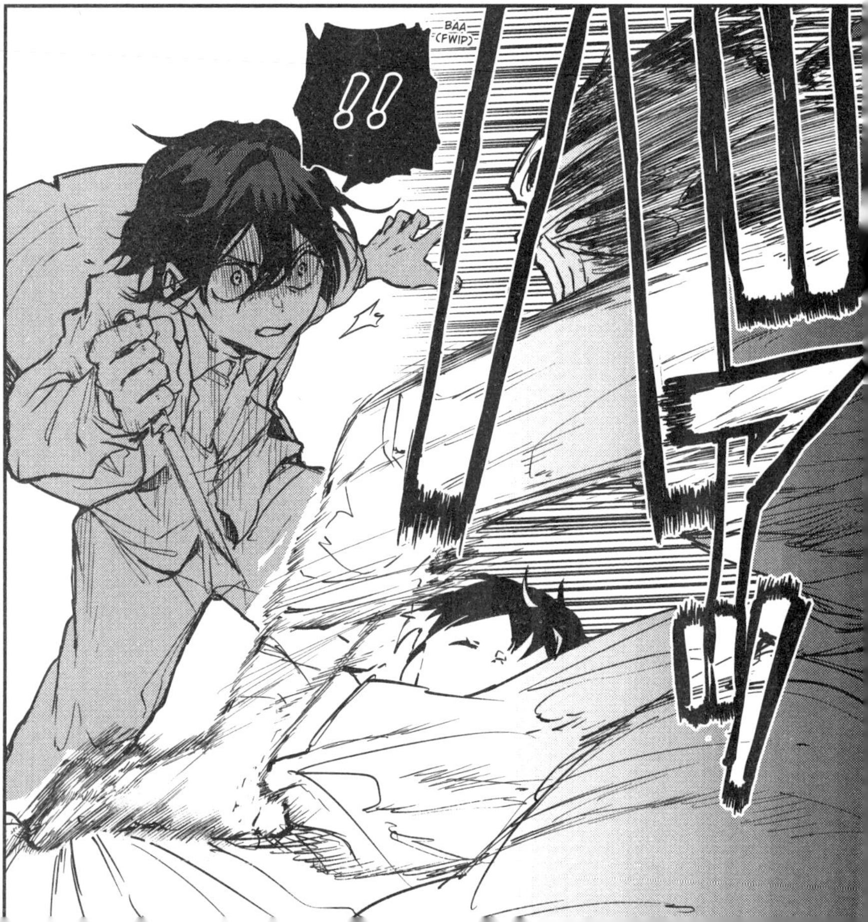
BAA
(FWIP)
!!

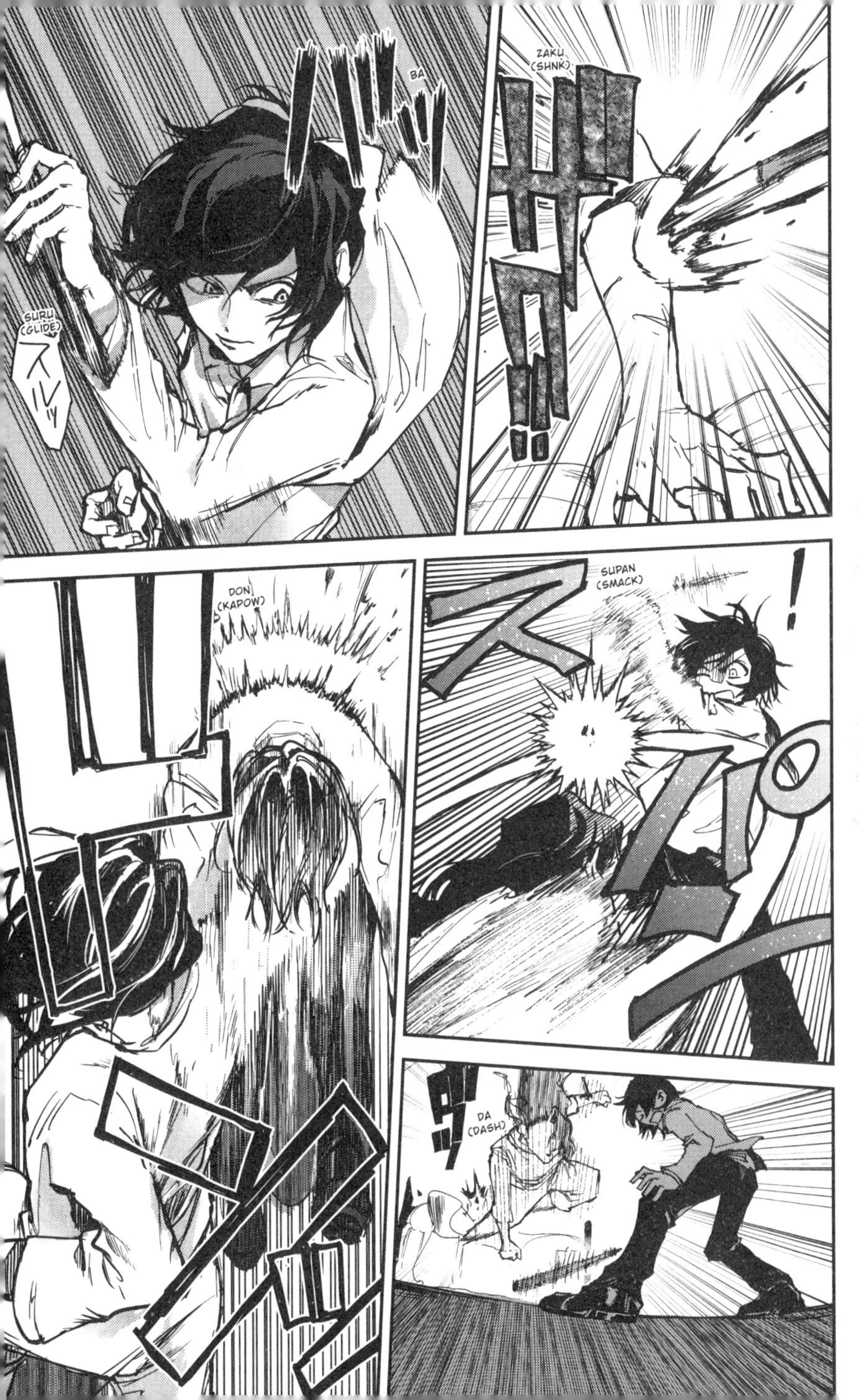
ZAKU
(SHNK)
BA
SURU
(GLIDE)
SUPAN
(SMACK)
DA
(DASH)
DON
(KAPOW)

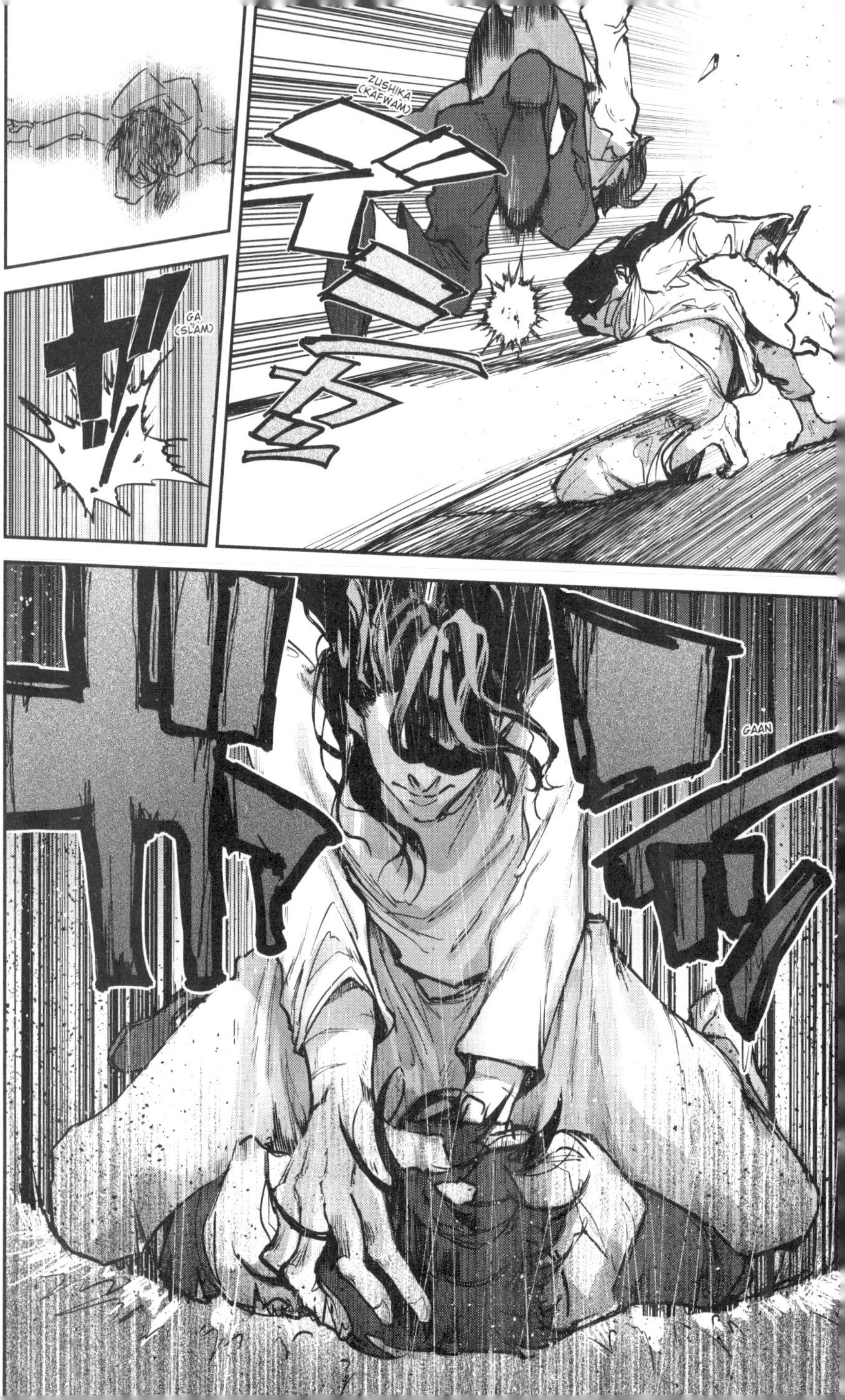
ZUSHIKA
(KAFWAM)
GA
(SLAM)
GAAN

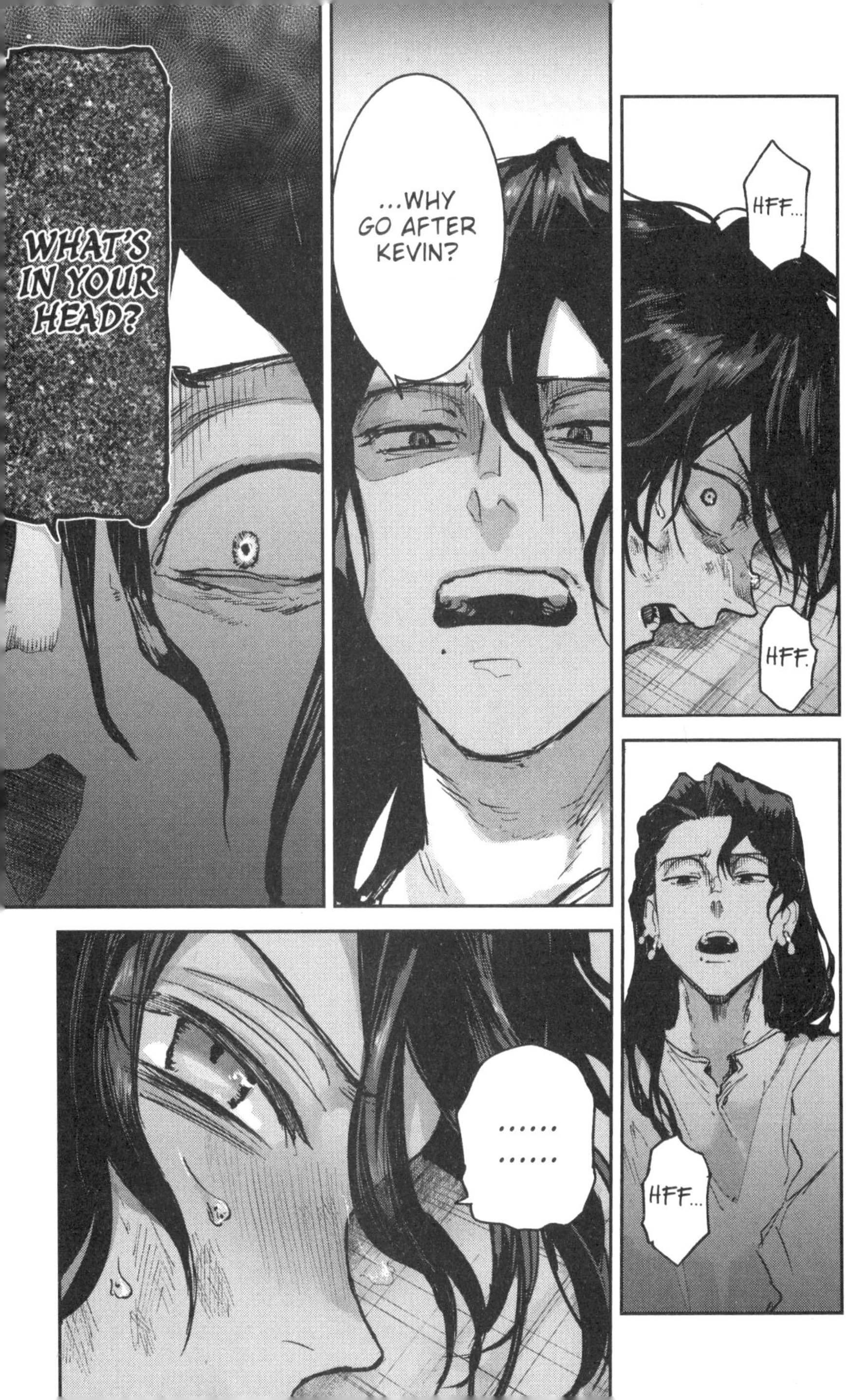
HFF...
HFF.
HFF...
...WHY GO AFTER KEVIN?
WHAT'S IN YOUR HEAD?
......
......

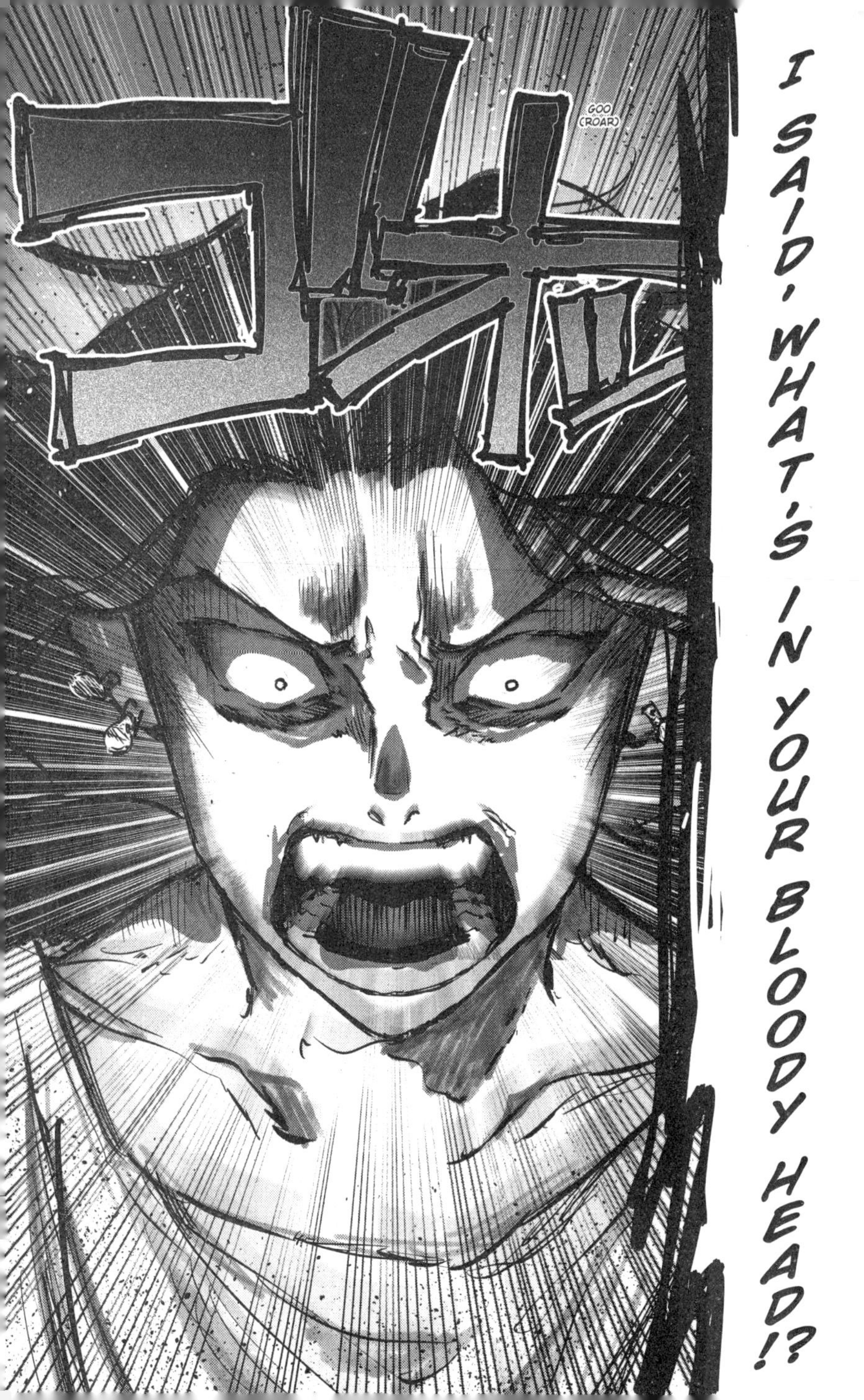
I SAID, WHAT'S IN YOUR BLOOODY HEAD!?
GOO (ROAR)

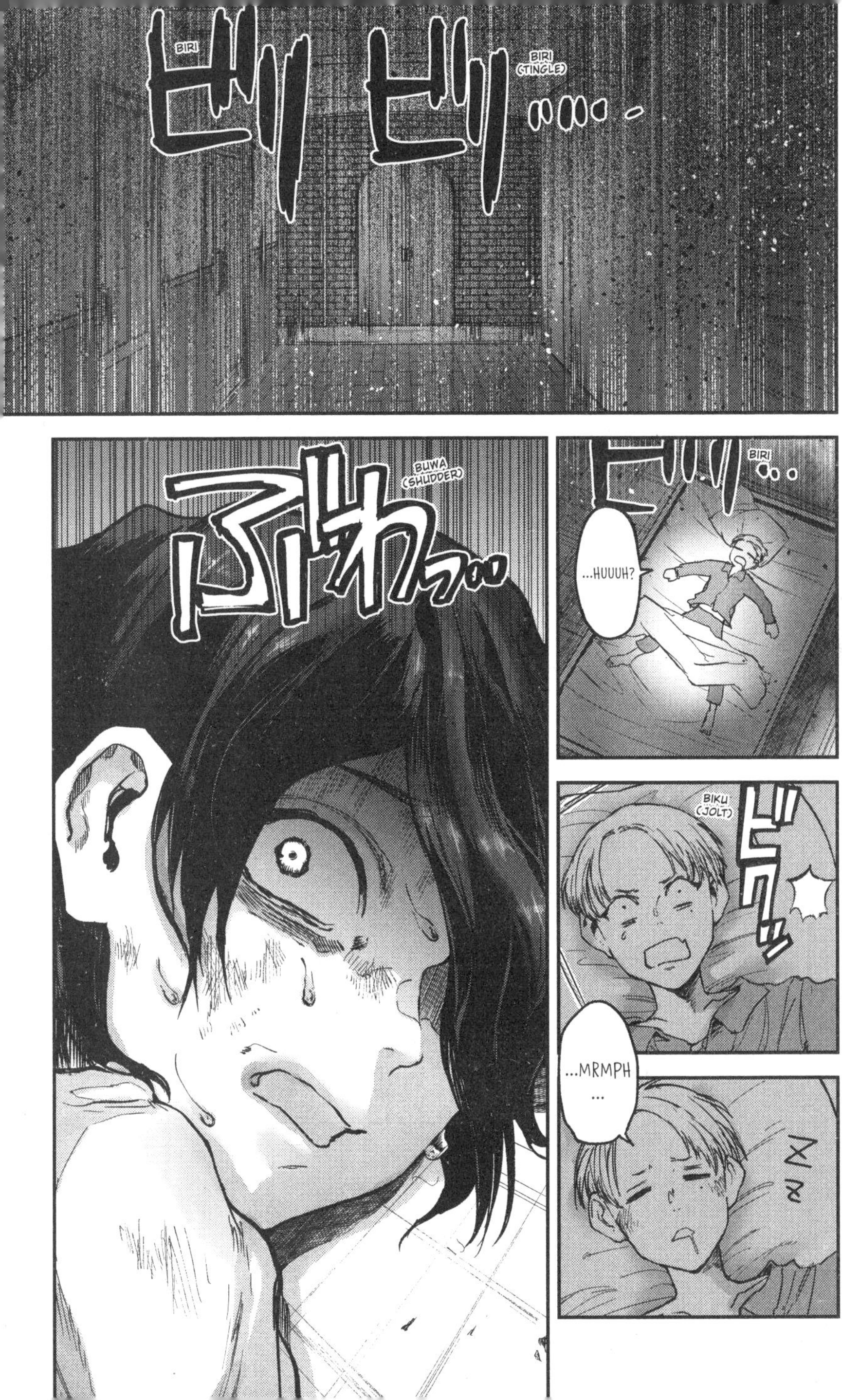
BIRI
BIRI (TINGLE)
BIRI
...HUUUH?
BIKU (JOLT)
...MRMPH ...
BUWA (SHUDDER)

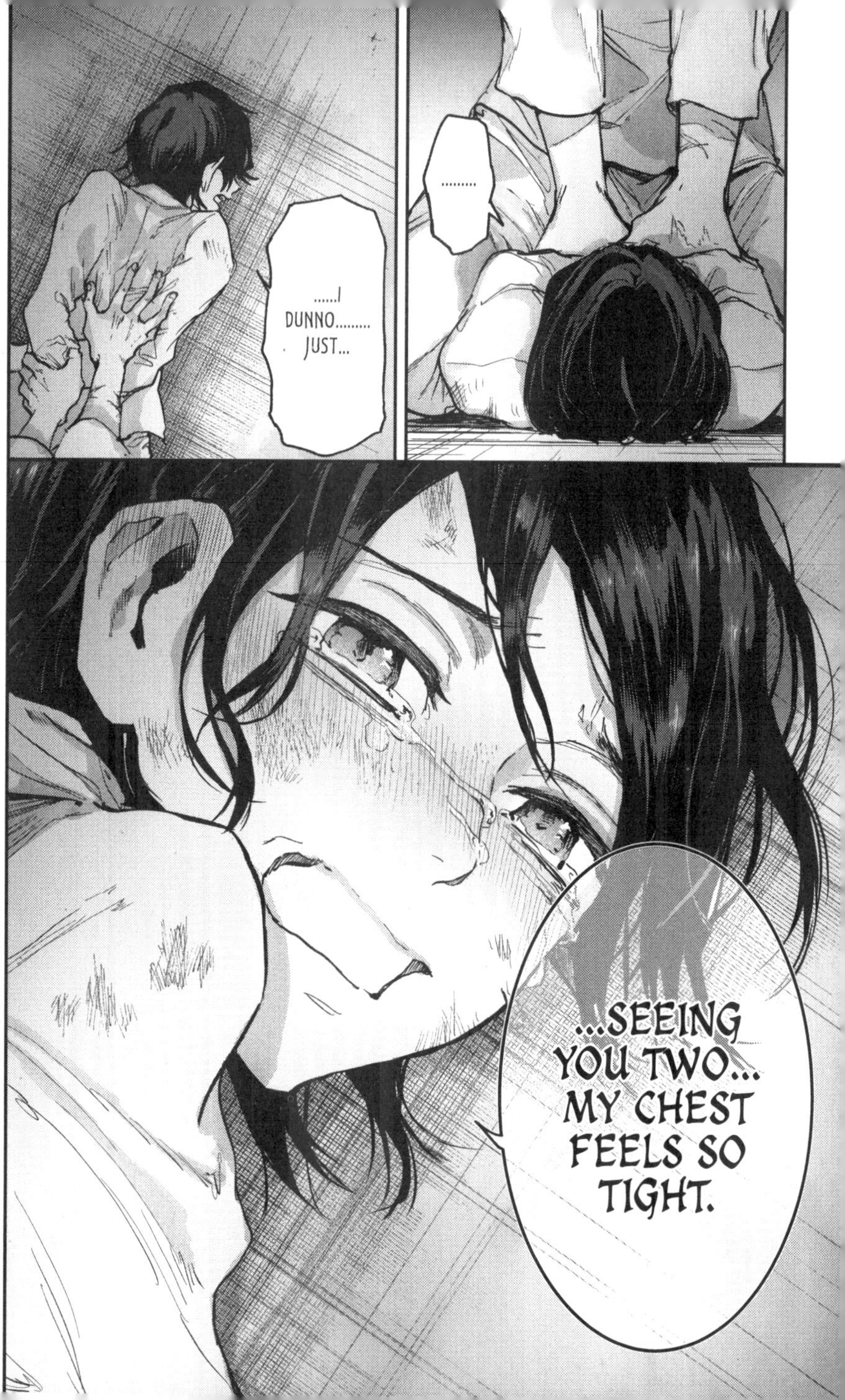
....
......I DUNNO......... JUST...
...SEEING YOU TWO... MY CHEST FEELS SO TIGHT.

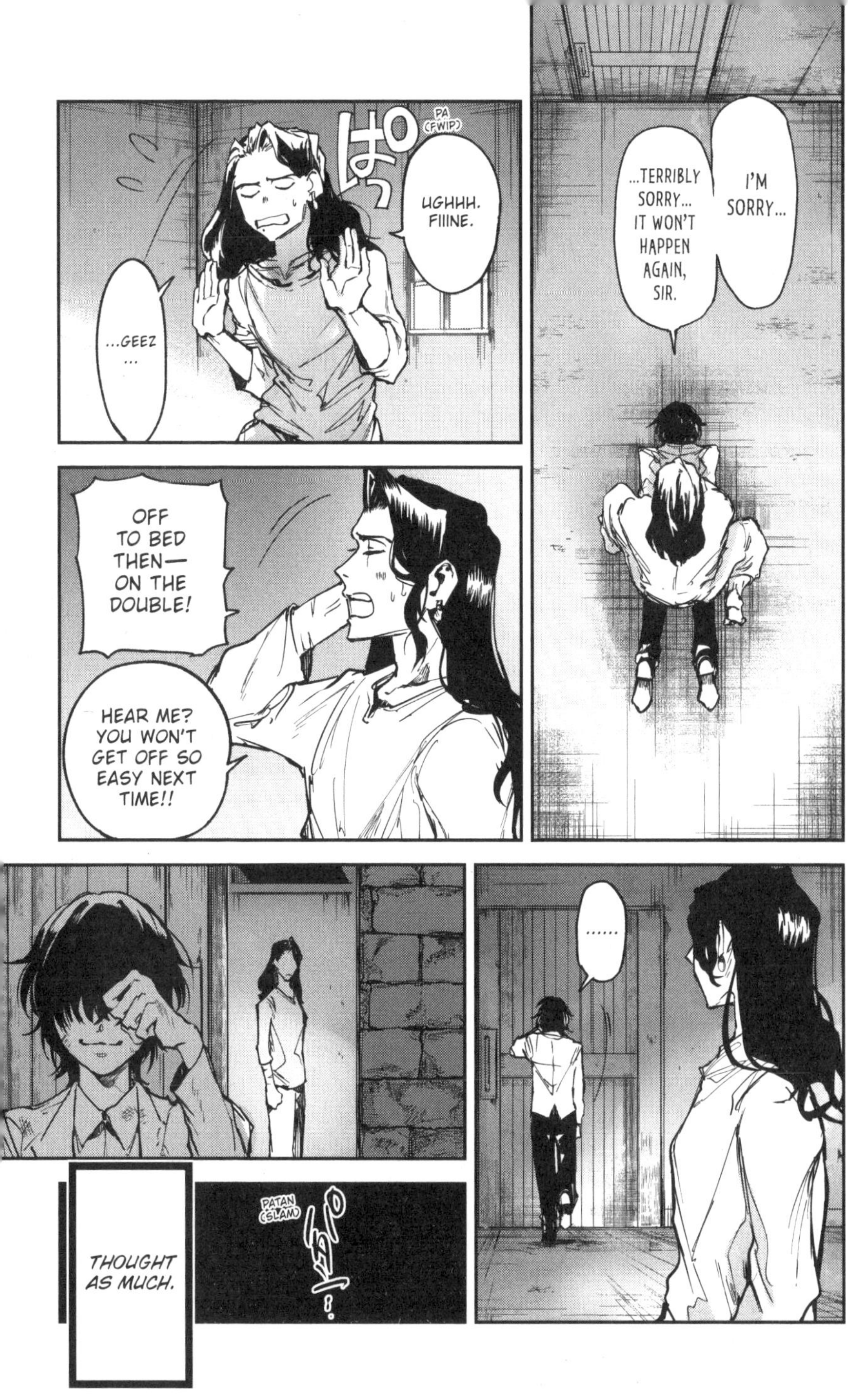
I'M SORRY...
...TERRIBLY SORRY... IT WON'T HAPPEN AGAIN, SIR.
PA (FWIP)
UGHHH. FIIINE.
...GEEZ...
OFF TO BED THEN—ON THE DOUBLE!
HEAR ME? YOU WON'T GET OFF SO EASY NEXT TIME!!
......
PATAN (SLAM)
THOUGHT AS MUCH.

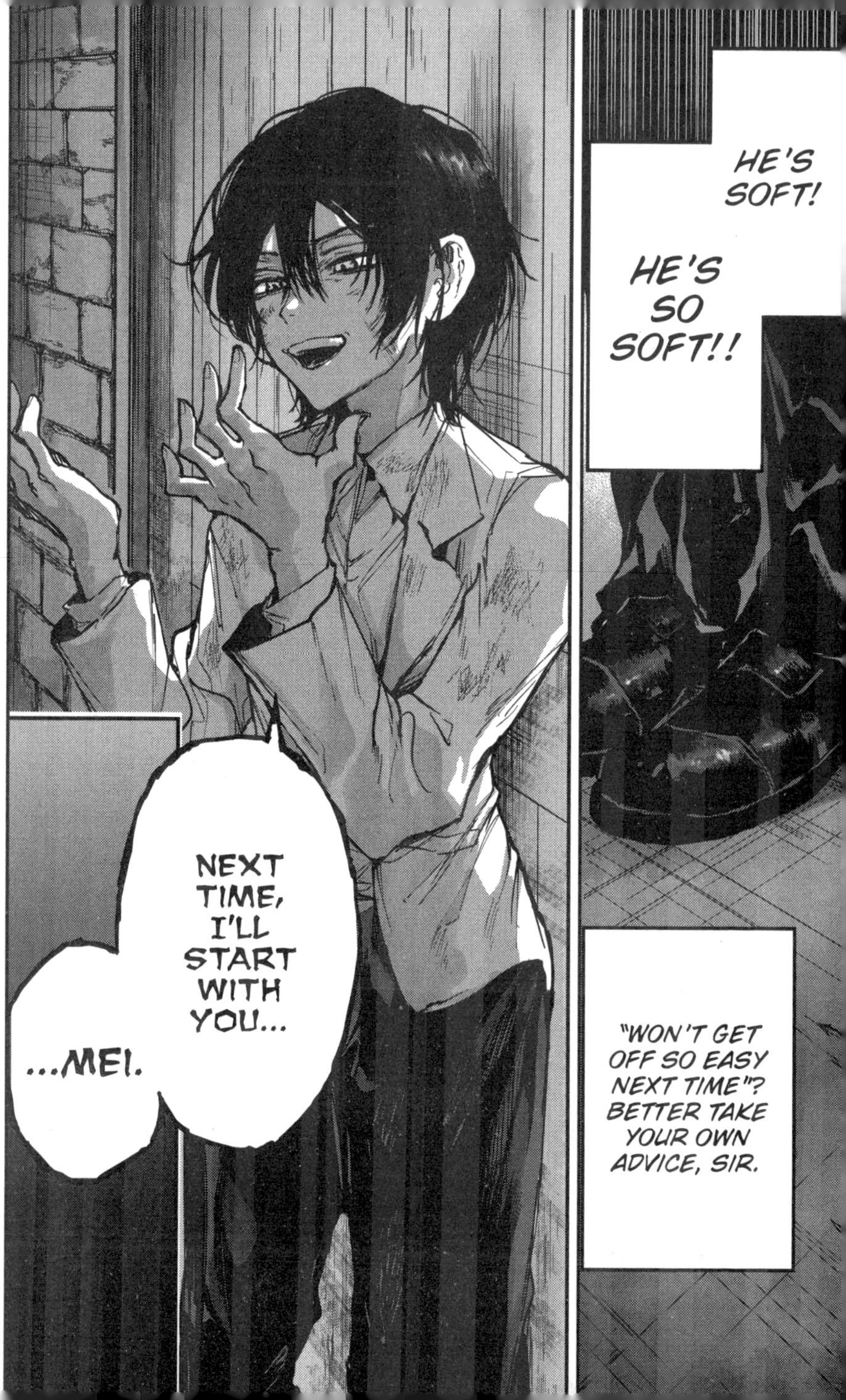
HE'S SOFT!
HE'S SO SOFT!!
"WON'T GET OFF SO EASY NEXT TIME"? BETTER TAKE YOUR OWN ADVICE, SIR.
NEXT TIME, I'LL START WITH YOU...
...MEI.

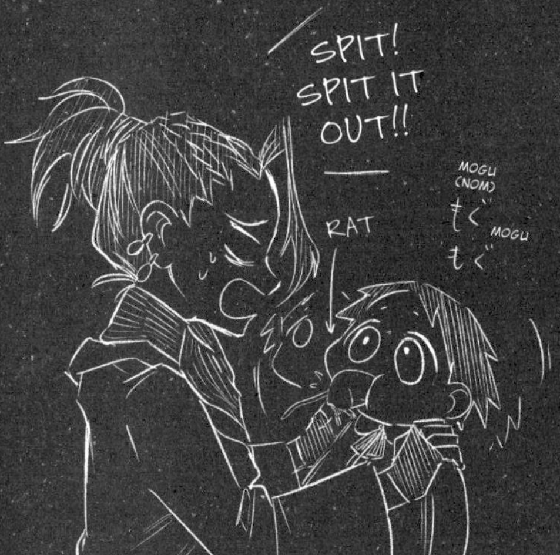
SPIT! SPIT IT OUT!!
RAT
MOGU (NOM)
もぐ
MOGU
もぐ

SCRAPPED COVER IDEAS

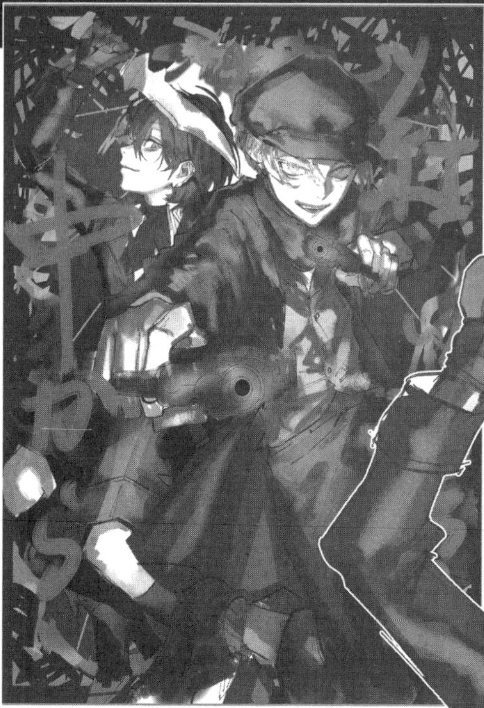

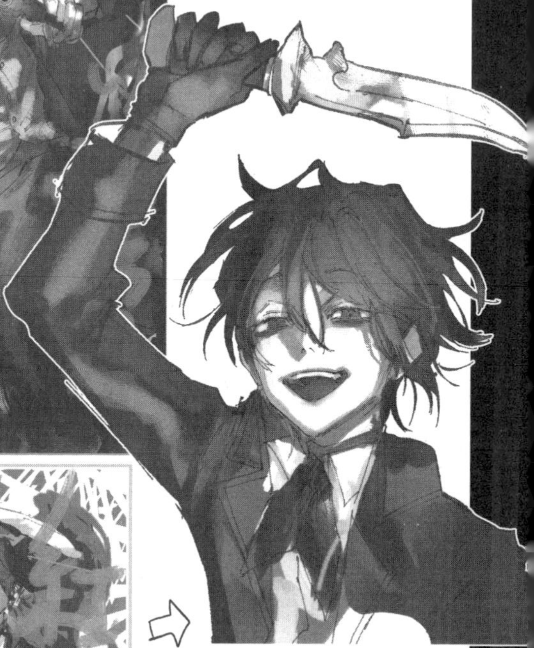

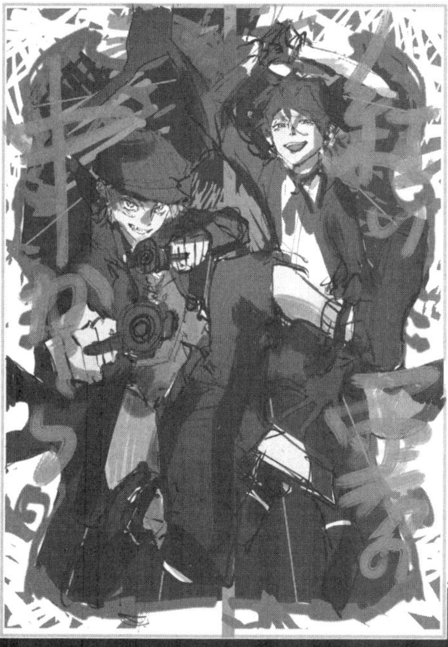

I KIND OF LOVE THE EXPRESSION ON HIS FACE HERE...

...AND YET...I DIDN'T USE IT!

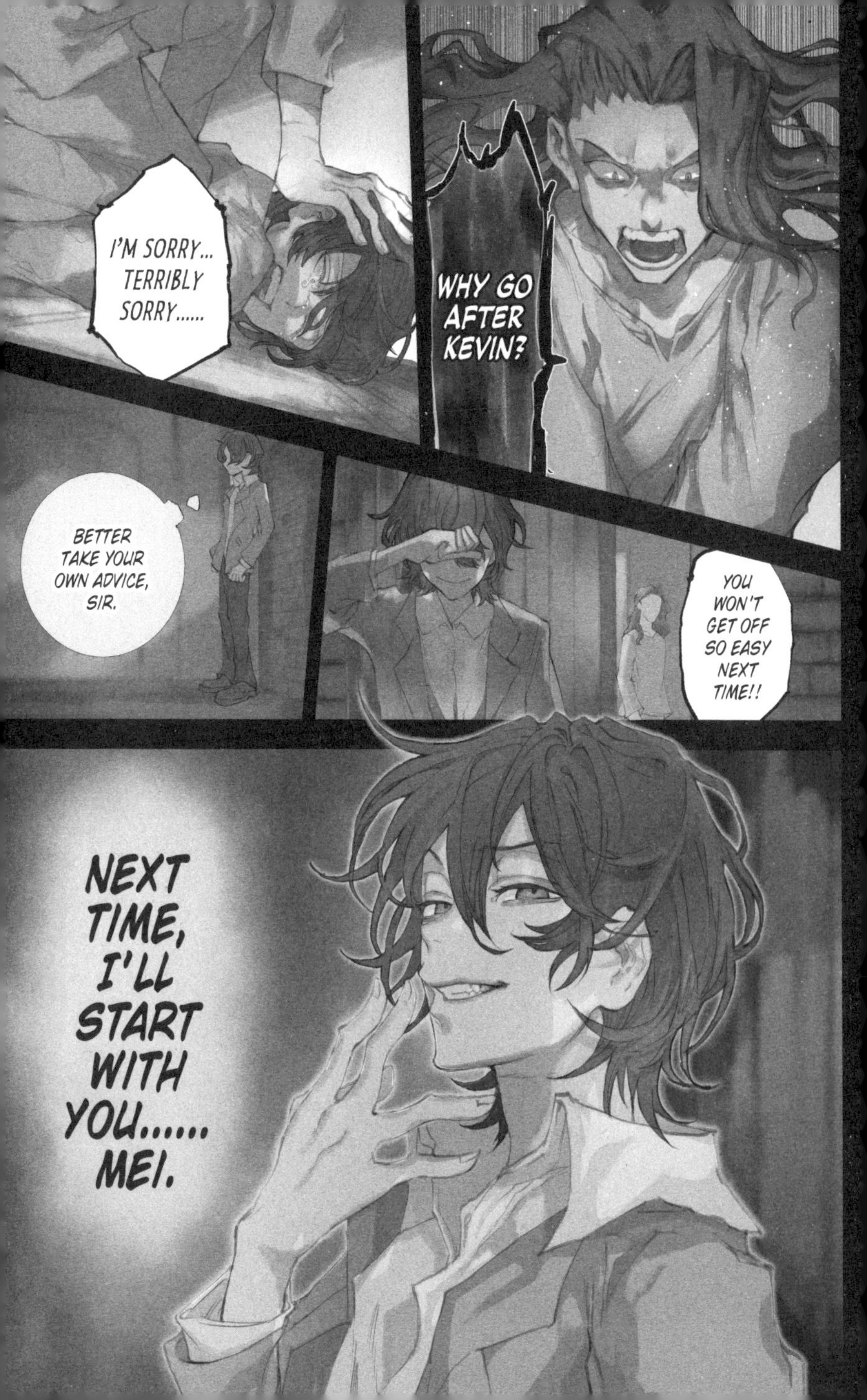
WHY GO AFTER KEVIN?
I'M SORRY... TERRIBLY SORRY......
YOU WON'T GET OFF SO EASY NEXT TIME!!
BETTER TAKE YOUR OWN ADVICE, SIR.
NEXT TIME, I'LL START WITH YOU...... MEI.

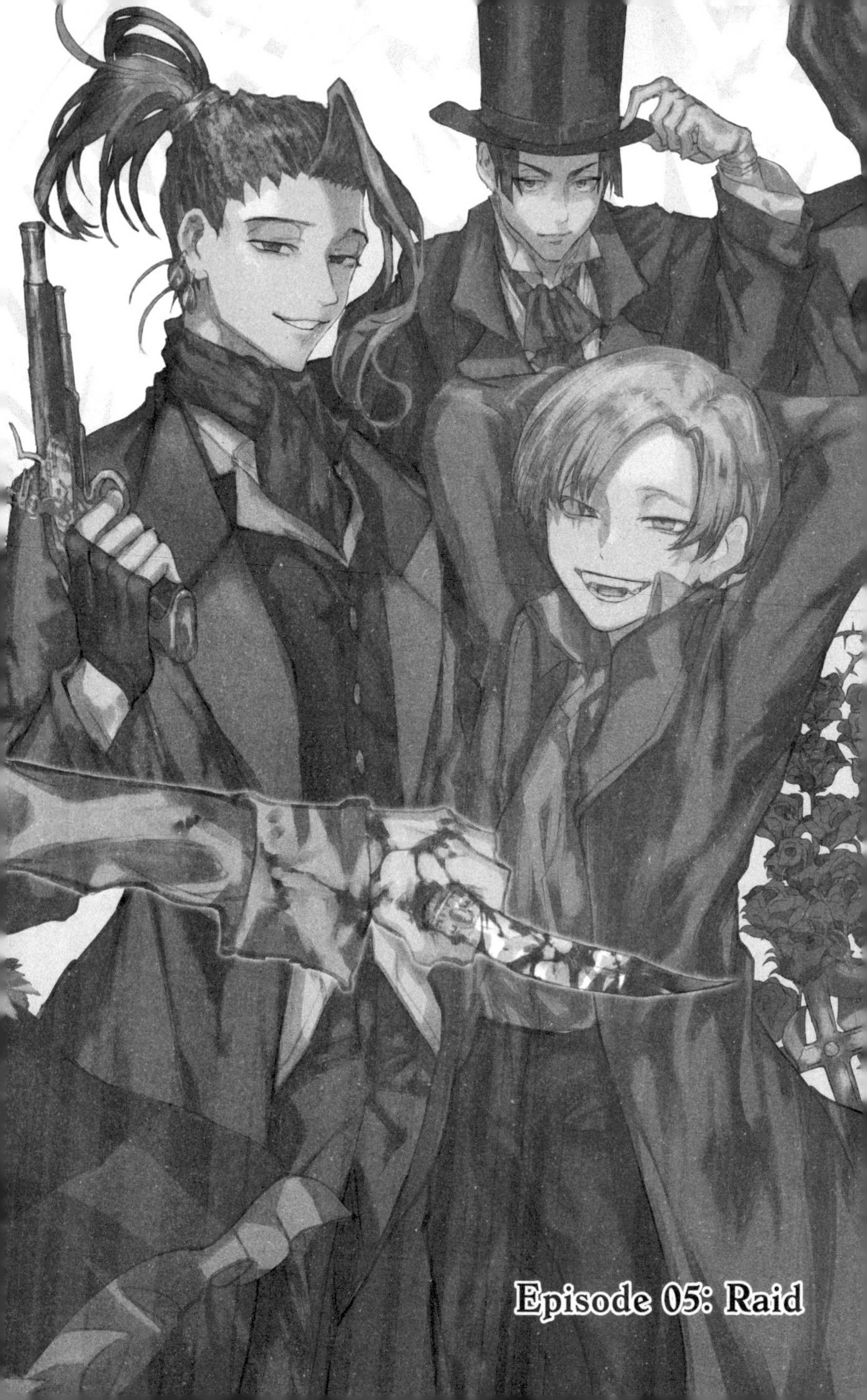

Episode 05: Raid

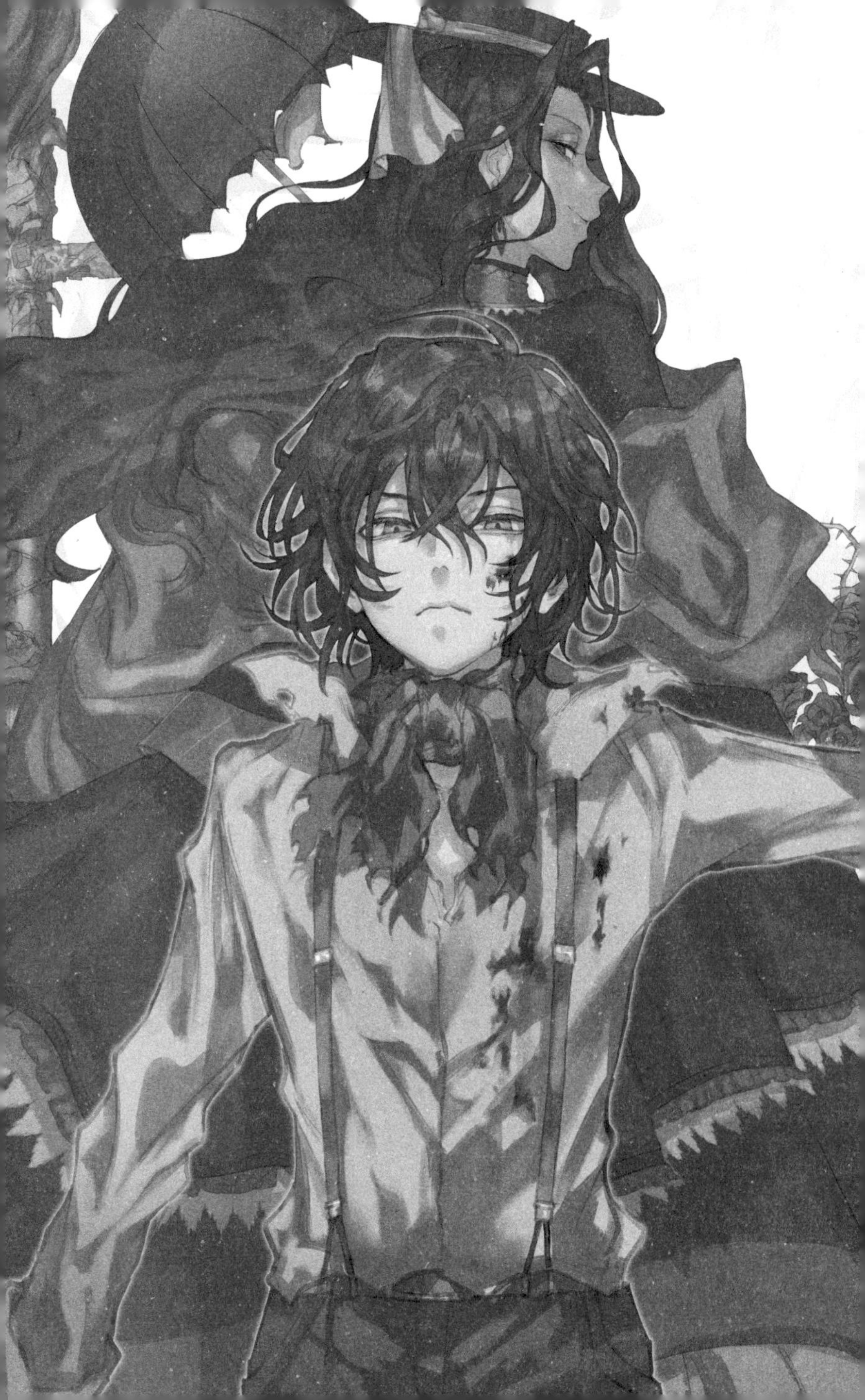

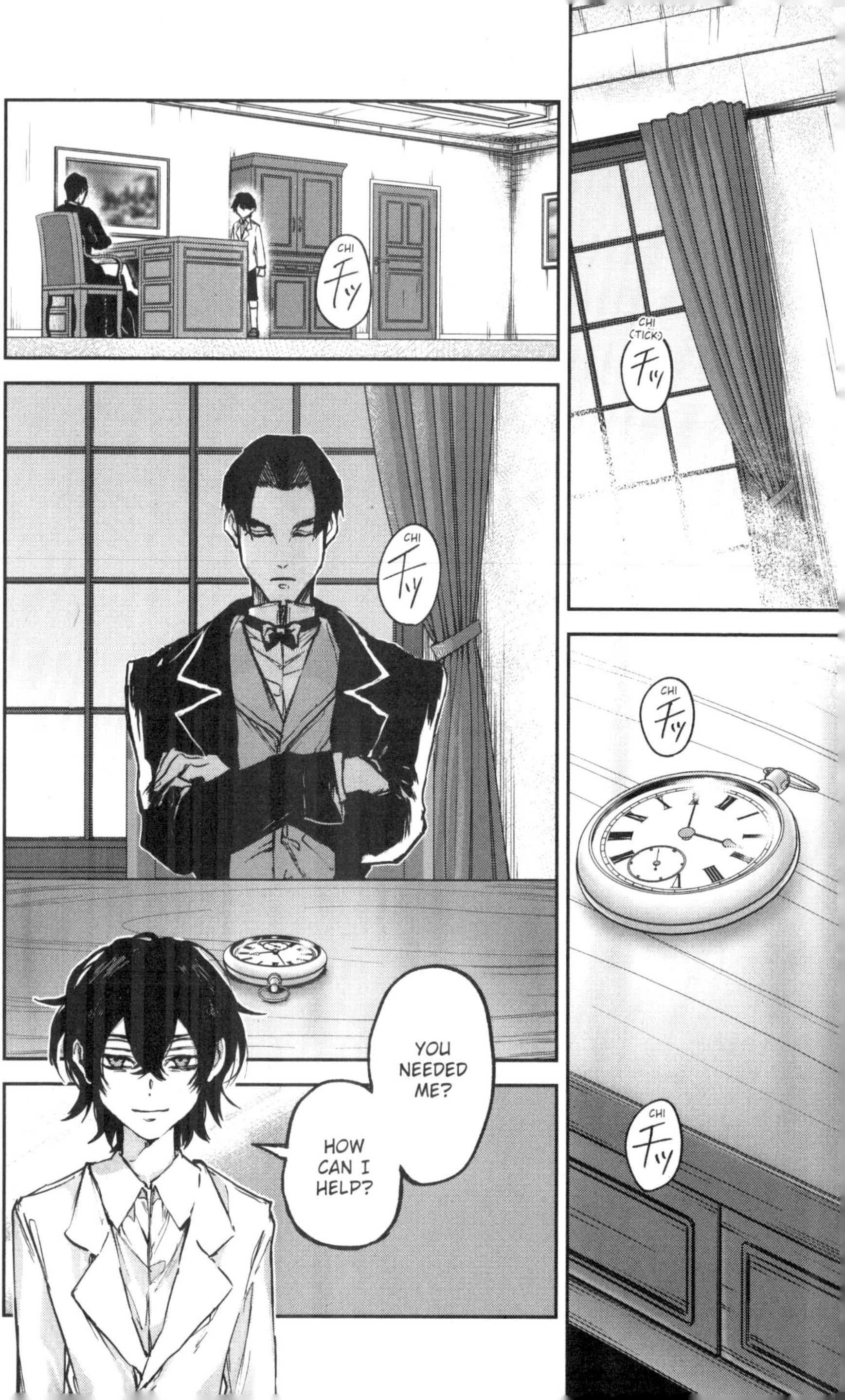

CHI (TICK) チッ
CHI チッ
CHI チッ
CHI チッ
CHI チッ
YOU NEEDED ME?
HOW CAN I HELP?

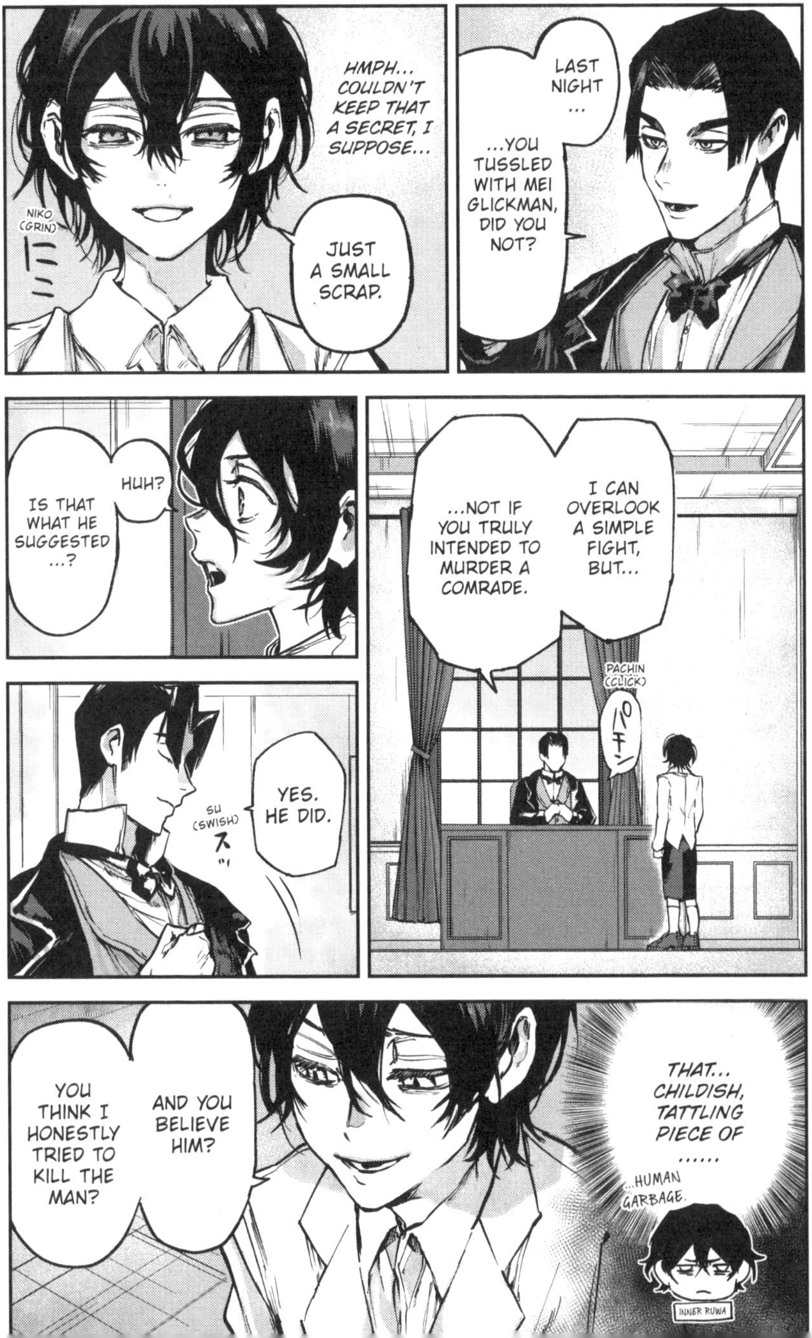
LAST NIGHT ...
...YOU TUSSLED WITH MEI GLICKMAN, DID YOU NOT?
HMPH... COULDN'T KEEP THAT A SECRET, I SUPPOSE...
JUST A SMALL SCRAP.
NIKO (GRIN)
I CAN OVERLOOK A SIMPLE FIGHT, BUT...
...NOT IF YOU TRULY INTENDED TO MURDER A COMRADE.
PACHIN (CLICK)
HUH?
IS THAT WHAT HE SUGGESTED ...?
YES. HE DID.
SU (SWISH)
THAT... CHILDISH, TATTLING PIECE OF ......
...HUMAN GARBAGE.
INNER RUWA
AND YOU BELIEVE HIM?
YOU THINK I HONESTLY TRIED TO KILL THE MAN?

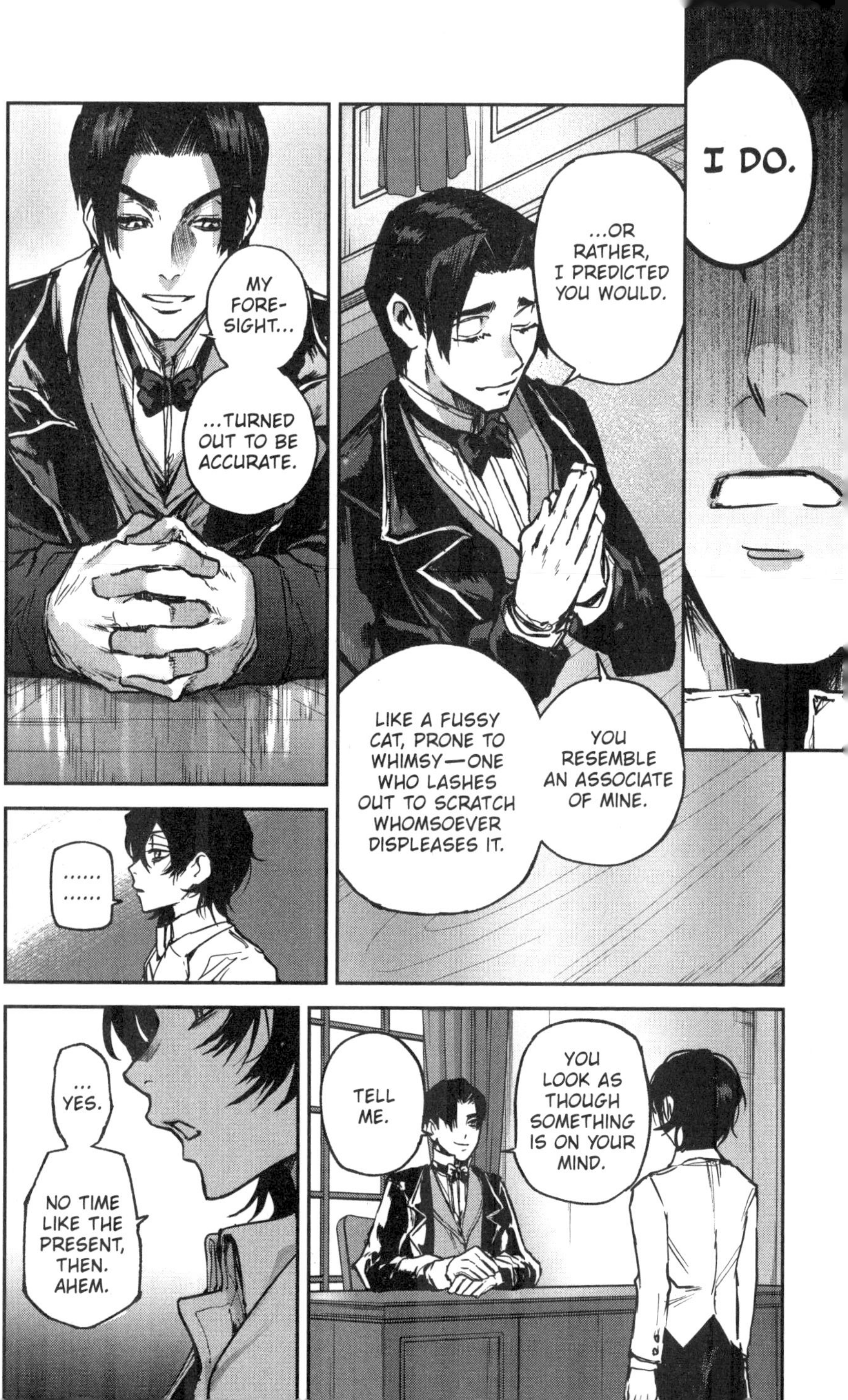
I DO.
...OR RATHER, I PREDICTED YOU WOULD.
YOU RESEMBLE AN ASSOCIATE OF MINE.
LIKE A FUSSY CAT, PRONE TO WHIMSY—ONE WHO LASHES OUT TO SCRATCH WHOMSOEVER DISPLEASES IT.
MY FORESIGHT...
...TURNED OUT TO BE ACCURATE.
......
......
YOU LOOK AS THOUGH SOMETHING IS ON YOUR MIND.
TELL ME.
... YES.
NO TIME LIKE THE PRESENT, THEN. AHEM.

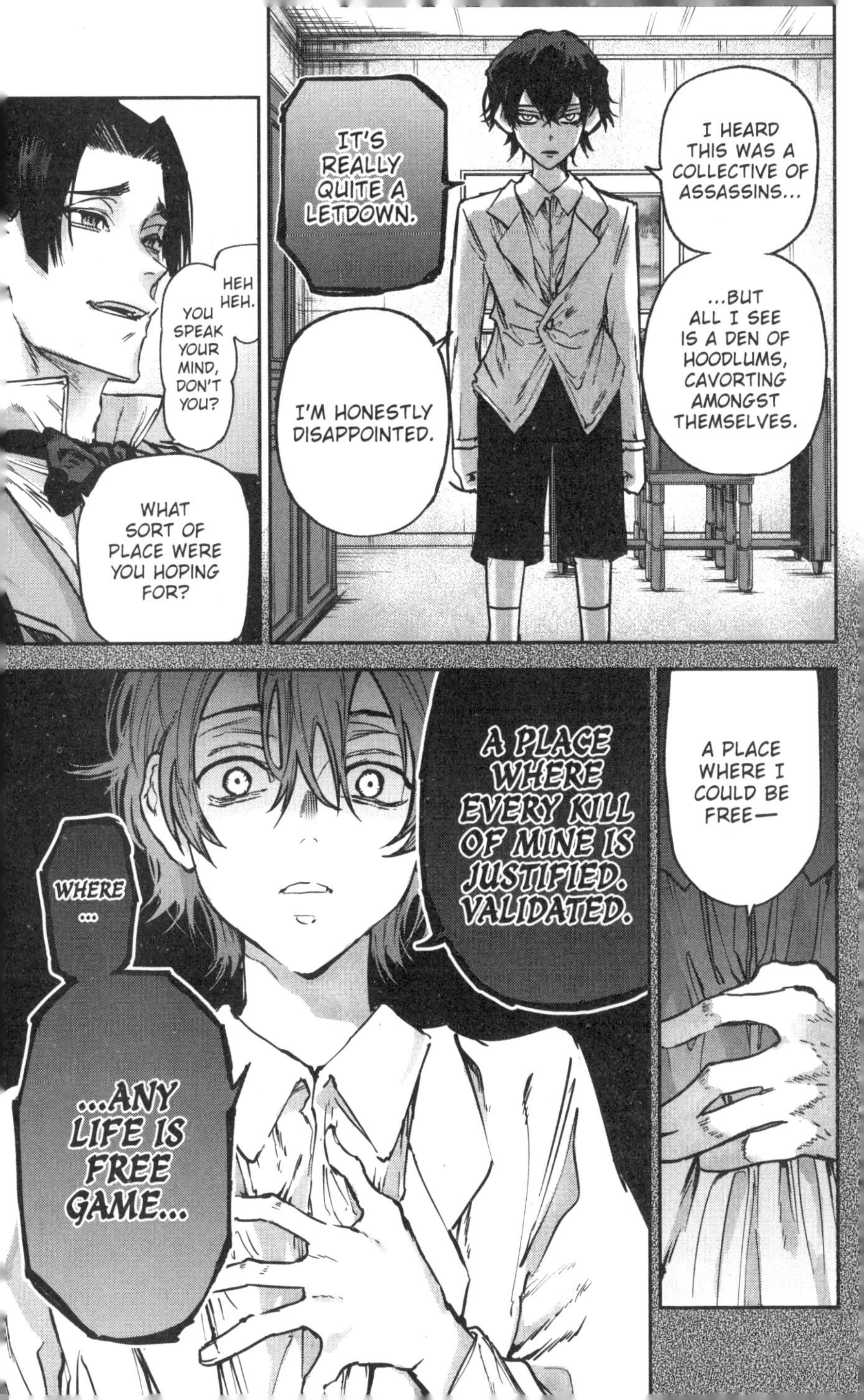
I HEARD THIS WAS A COLLECTIVE OF ASSASSINS...
...BUT ALL I SEE IS A DEN OF HOODLUMS, CAVORTING AMONGST THEMSELVES.
IT'S REALLY QUITE A LETDOWN.
I'M HONESTLY DISAPPOINTED.
HEH HEH.
YOU SPEAK YOUR MIND, DON'T YOU?
WHAT SORT OF PLACE WERE YOU HOPING FOR?
A PLACE WHERE I COULD BE FREE—
A PLACE WHERE EVERY KILL OF MINE IS JUSTIFIED. VALIDATED.
WHERE ...
...ANY LIFE IS FREE GAME...

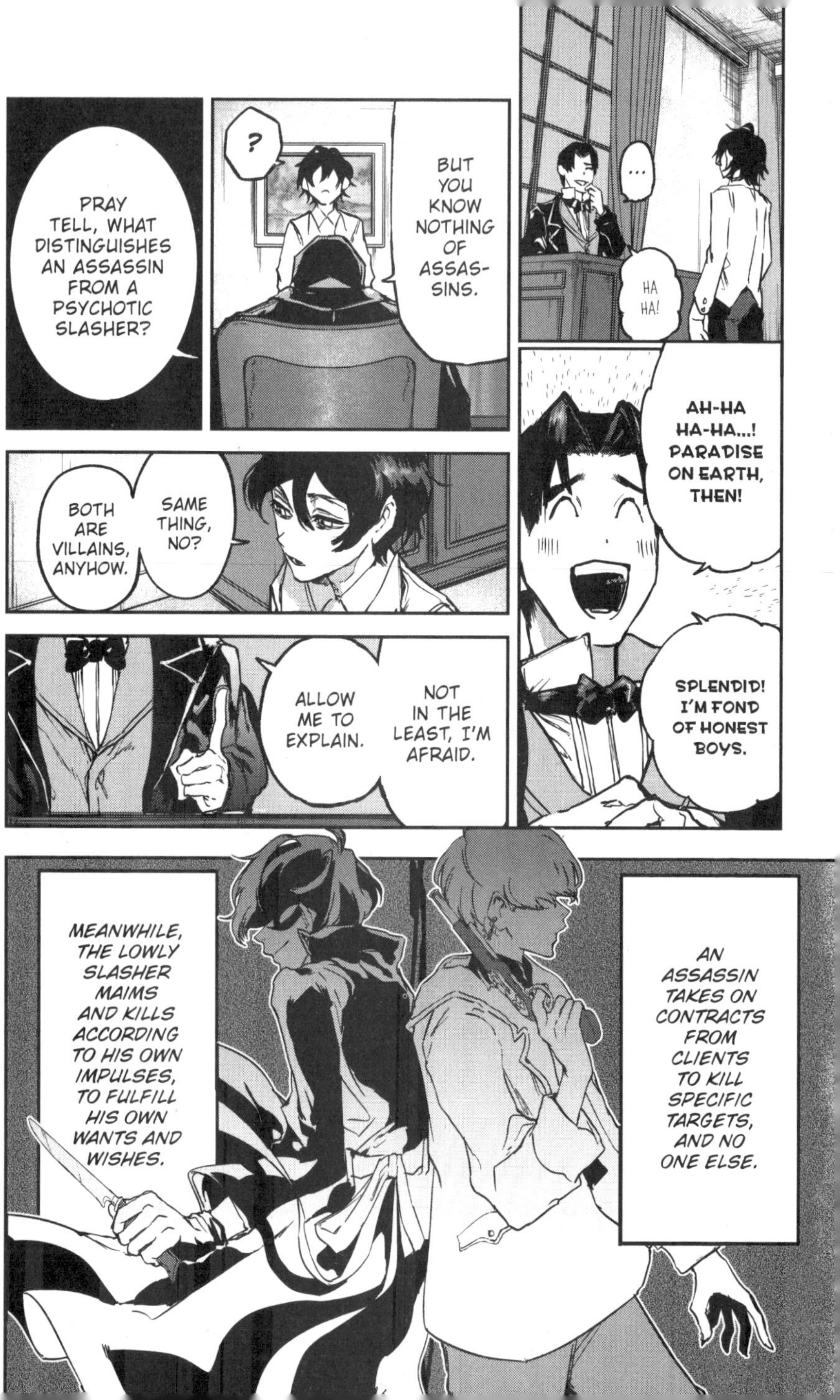
...
HA HA!
?
BUT YOU KNOW NOTHING OF ASSAS-SINS.
PRAY TELL, WHAT DISTINGUISHES AN ASSASSIN FROM A PSYCHOTIC SLASHER?
AH-HA HA-HA...! PARADISE ON EARTH, THEN!
SPLENDID! I'M FOND OF HONEST BOYS.
SAME THING, NO?
BOTH ARE VILLAINS, ANYHOW.
NOT IN THE LEAST, I'M AFRAID.
ALLOW ME TO EXPLAIN.
AN ASSASSIN TAKES ON CONTRACTS FROM CLIENTS TO KILL SPECIFIC TARGETS, AND NO ONE ELSE.
MEANWHILE, THE LOWLY SLASHER MAIMS AND KILLS ACCORDING TO HIS OWN IMPULSES, TO FULFILL HIS OWN WANTS AND WISHES.

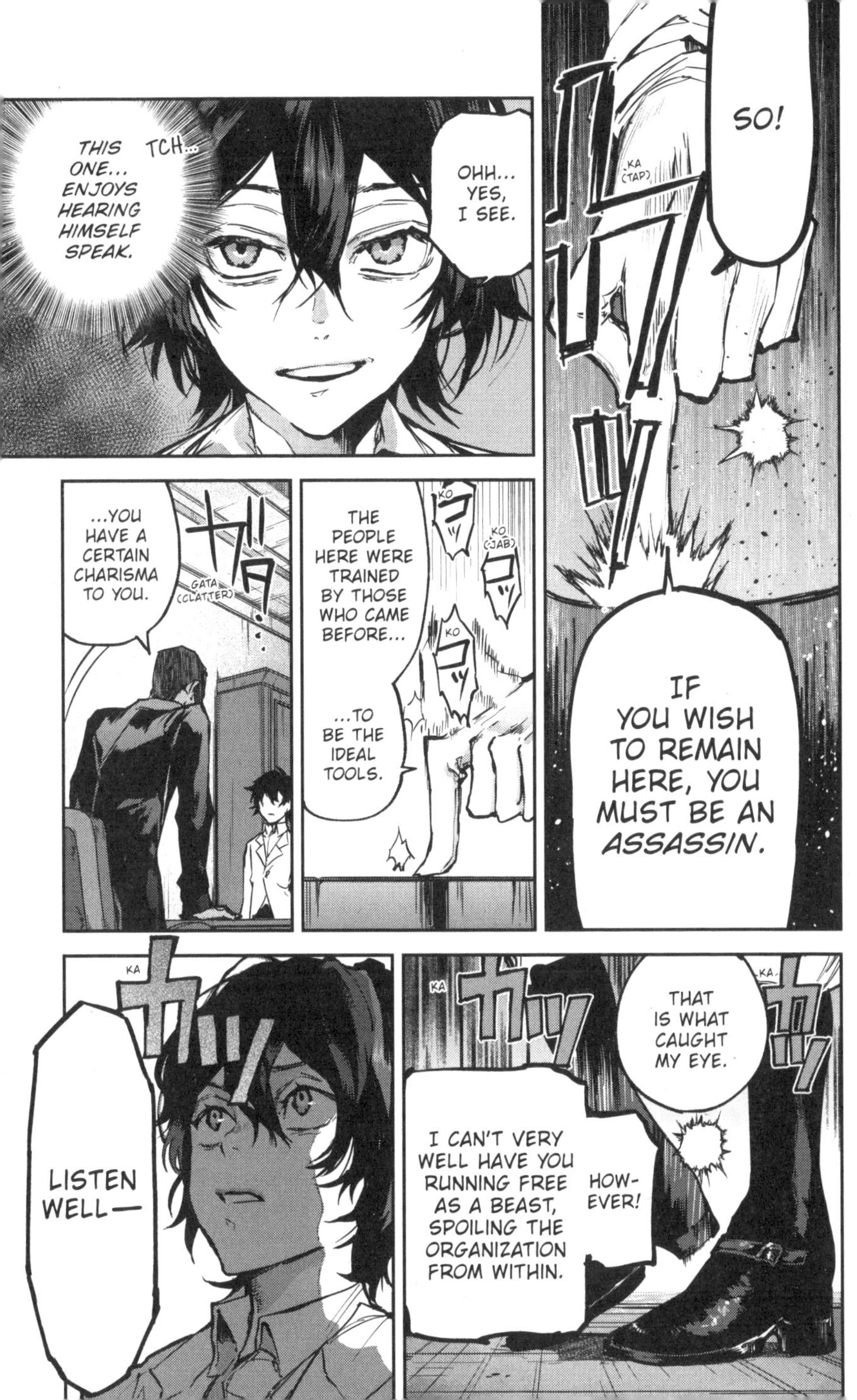
SO!
KA (TAP)
IF YOU WISH TO REMAIN HERE, YOU MUST BE AN *ASSASSIN.*
OHH... YES, I SEE.
THIS ONE... ENJOYS HEARING HIMSELF SPEAK.
TCH...
KO
KO (JAB)
KO
THE PEOPLE HERE WERE TRAINED BY THOSE WHO CAME BEFORE...
...TO BE THE IDEAL TOOLS.
GATA (CLATTER)
...YOU HAVE A CERTAIN CHARISMA TO YOU.
KA
KA
THAT IS WHAT CAUGHT MY EYE.
HOW-EVER!
I CAN'T VERY WELL HAVE YOU RUNNING FREE AS A BEAST, SPOILING THE ORGANIZATION FROM WITHIN.
KA
LISTEN WELL—

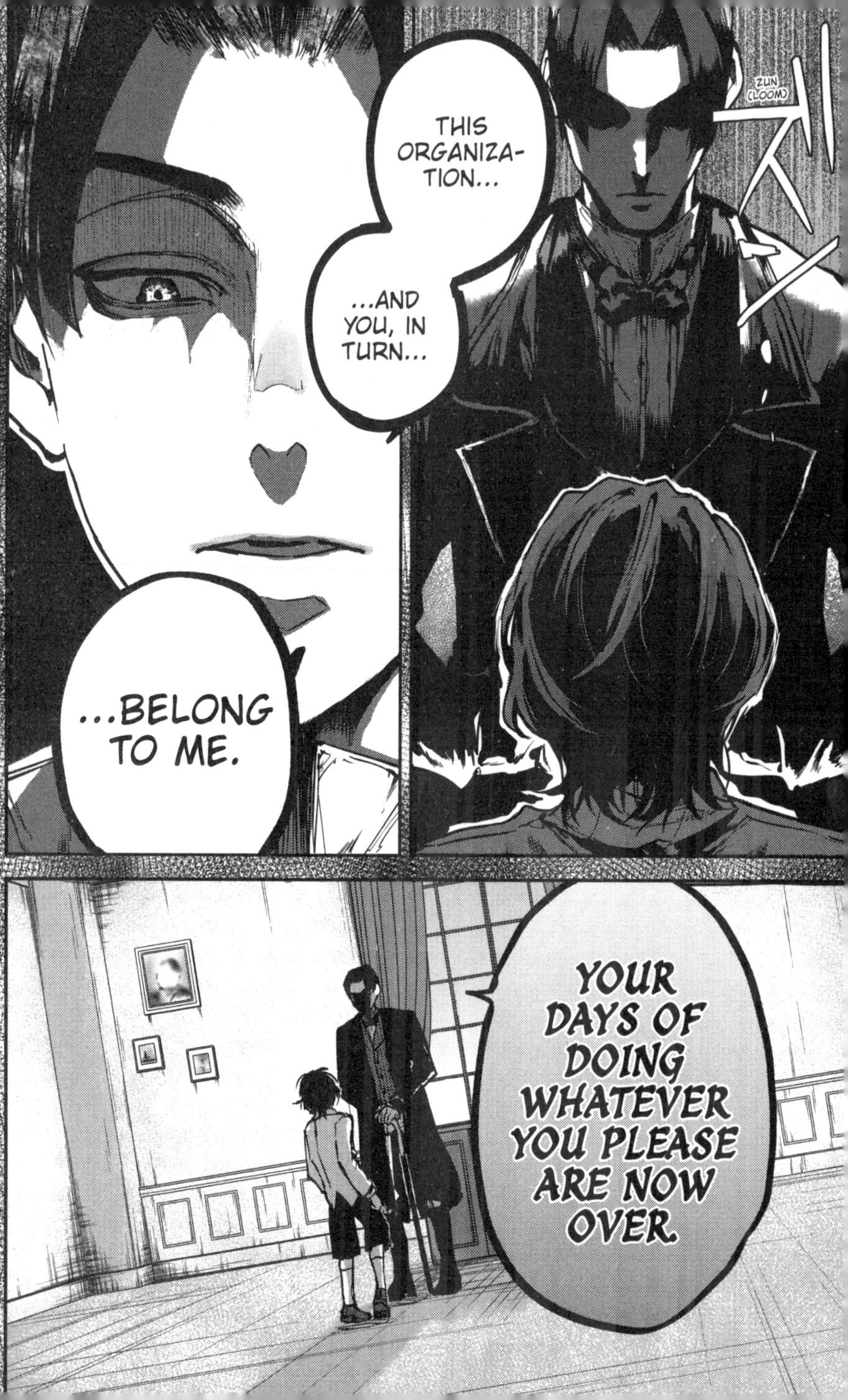
ZUN (LOOM)
THIS ORGANIZATION...
...AND YOU, IN TURN...
...BELONG TO ME.
YOUR DAYS OF DOING WHATEVER YOU PLEASE ARE NOW OVER.

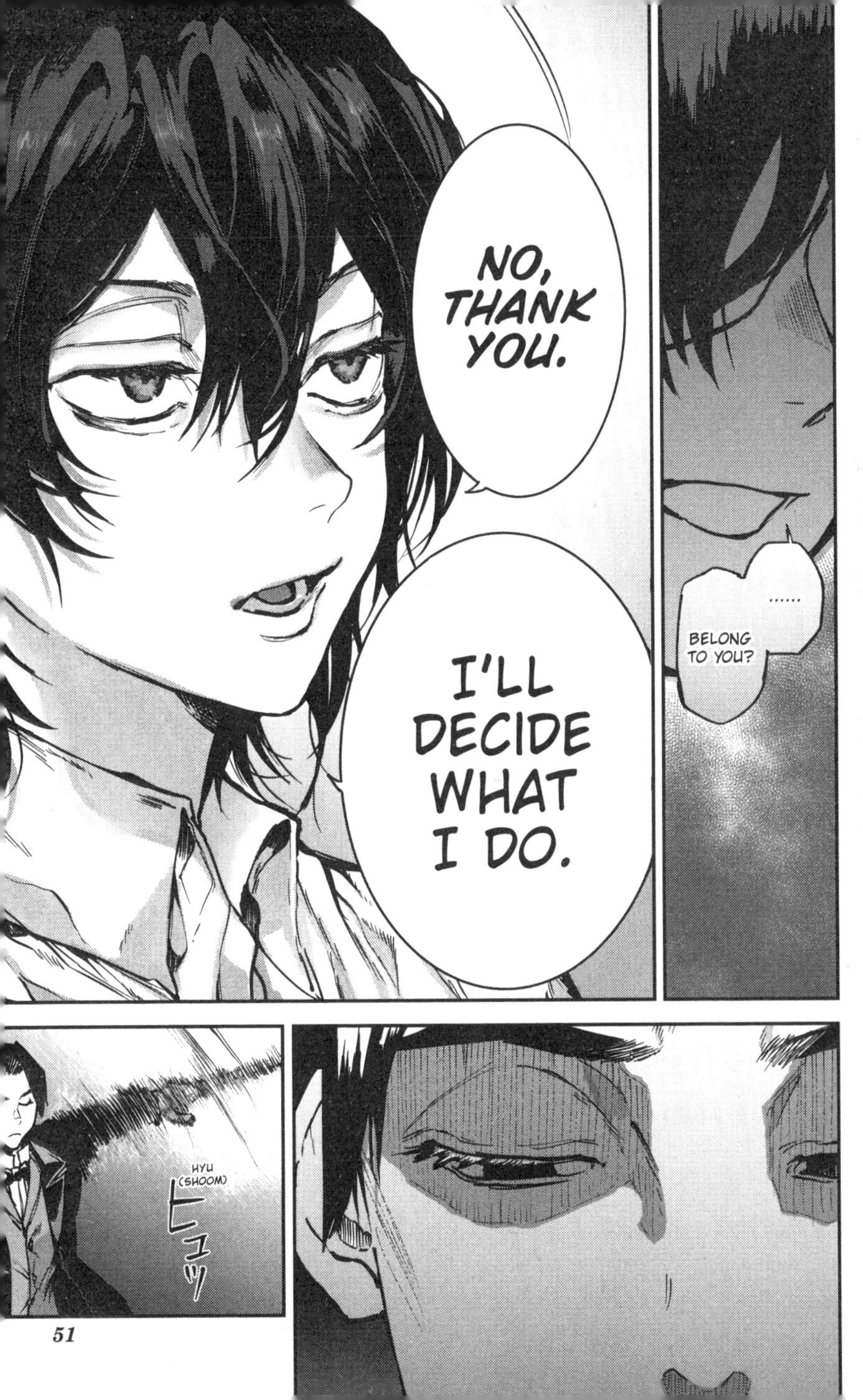
......
BELONG TO YOU?
NO, THANK YOU.
I'LL DECIDE WHAT I DO.
HYU (SHOOM)
ヒュッ

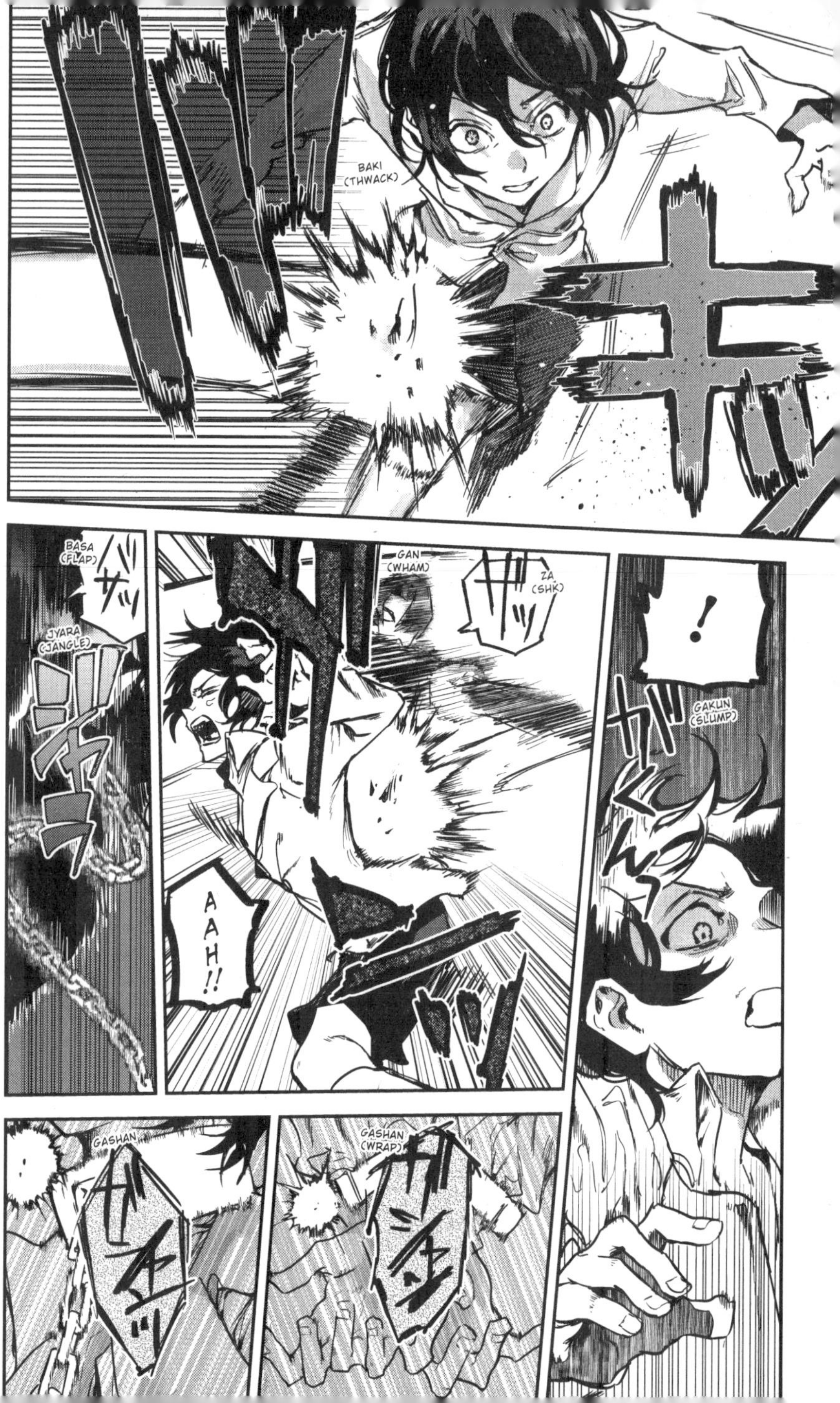
BAKI (THWACK)
!
GAKUN (SLUMP)
GAN (WHAM)
ZA (SHK)
AAH!!
BASA (FLAP)
JYARA (JANGLE)
GASHAN (WRAP)
GASHAN

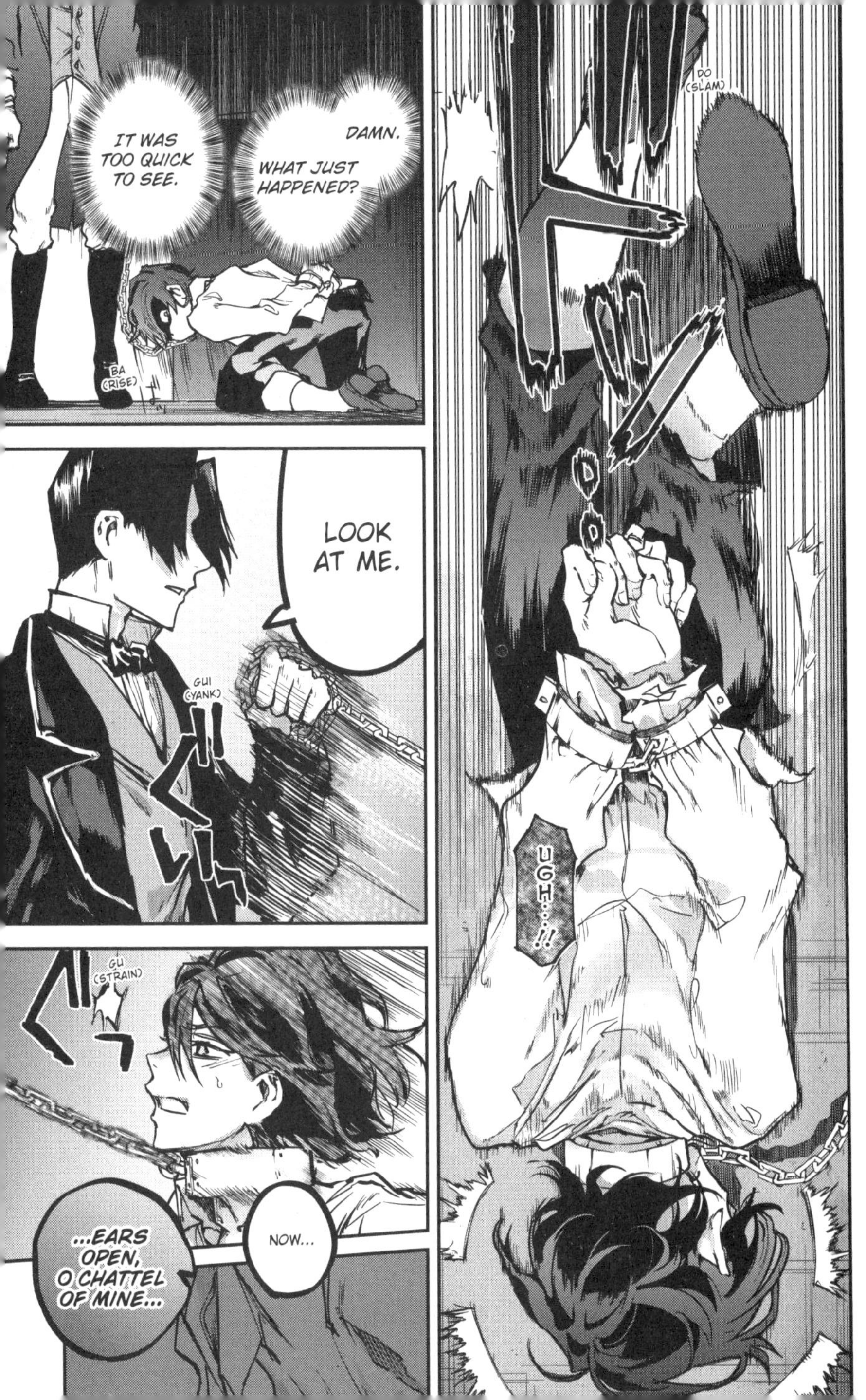
DO
(SLAM)
UGH...!!
DAMN.
WHAT JUST HAPPENED?
IT WAS TOO QUICK TO SEE.
BA
(RISE)
LOOK AT ME.
GUI
(YANK)
GU
(STRAIN)
NOW...
...EARS OPEN, O CHATTEL OF MINE...

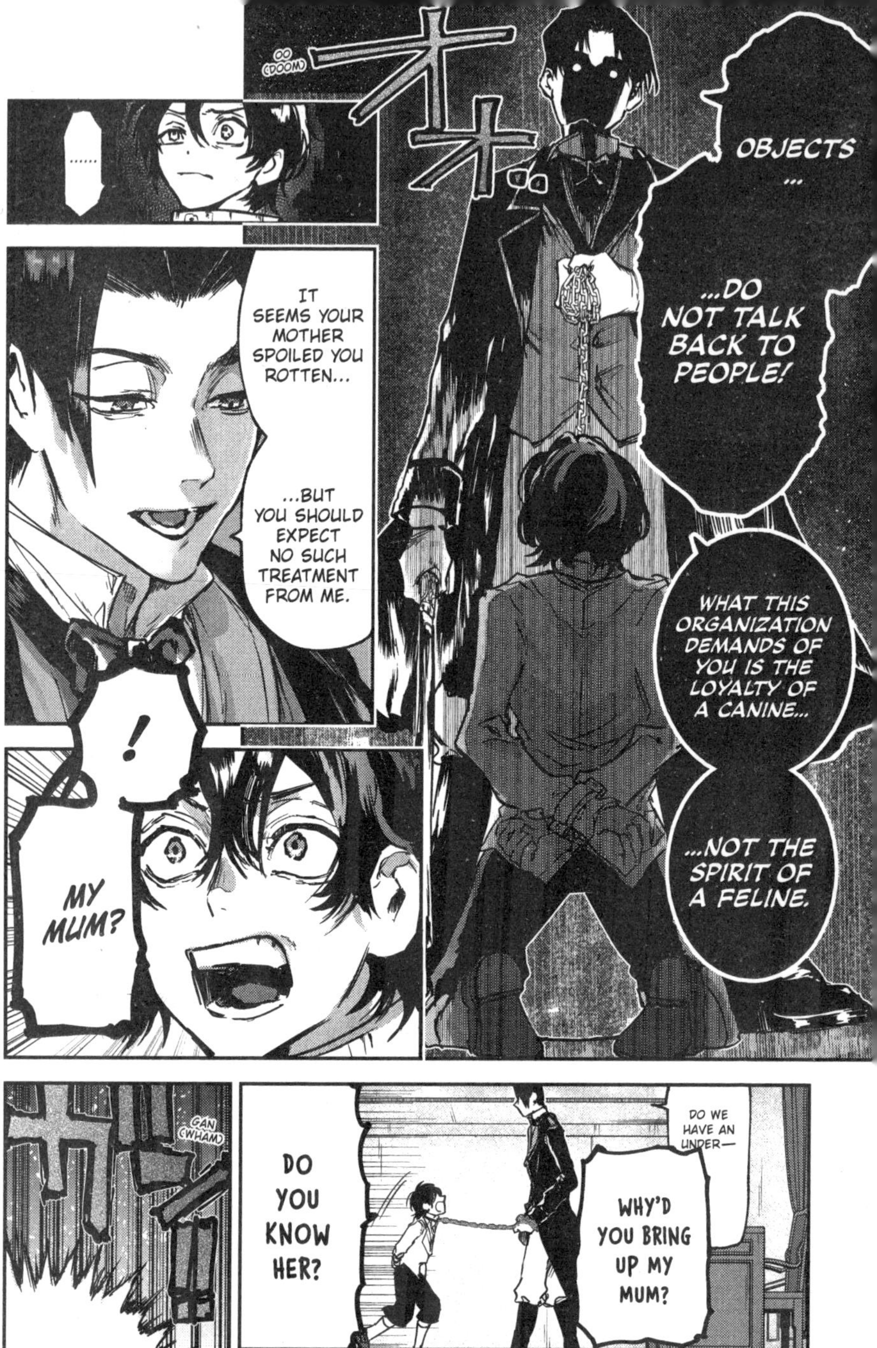
OO (DOOM)
OBJECTS ...
...DO NOT TALK BACK TO PEOPLE!
WHAT THIS ORGANIZATION DEMANDS OF YOU IS THE LOYALTY OF A CANINE...
...NOT THE SPIRIT OF A FELINE.
......
IT SEEMS YOUR MOTHER SPOILED YOU ROTTEN...
...BUT YOU SHOULD EXPECT NO SUCH TREATMENT FROM ME.
!
MY MUM?
DO WE HAVE AN UNDER—
WHY'D YOU BRING UP MY MUM?
DO YOU KNOW HER?
GAN (WHAM)

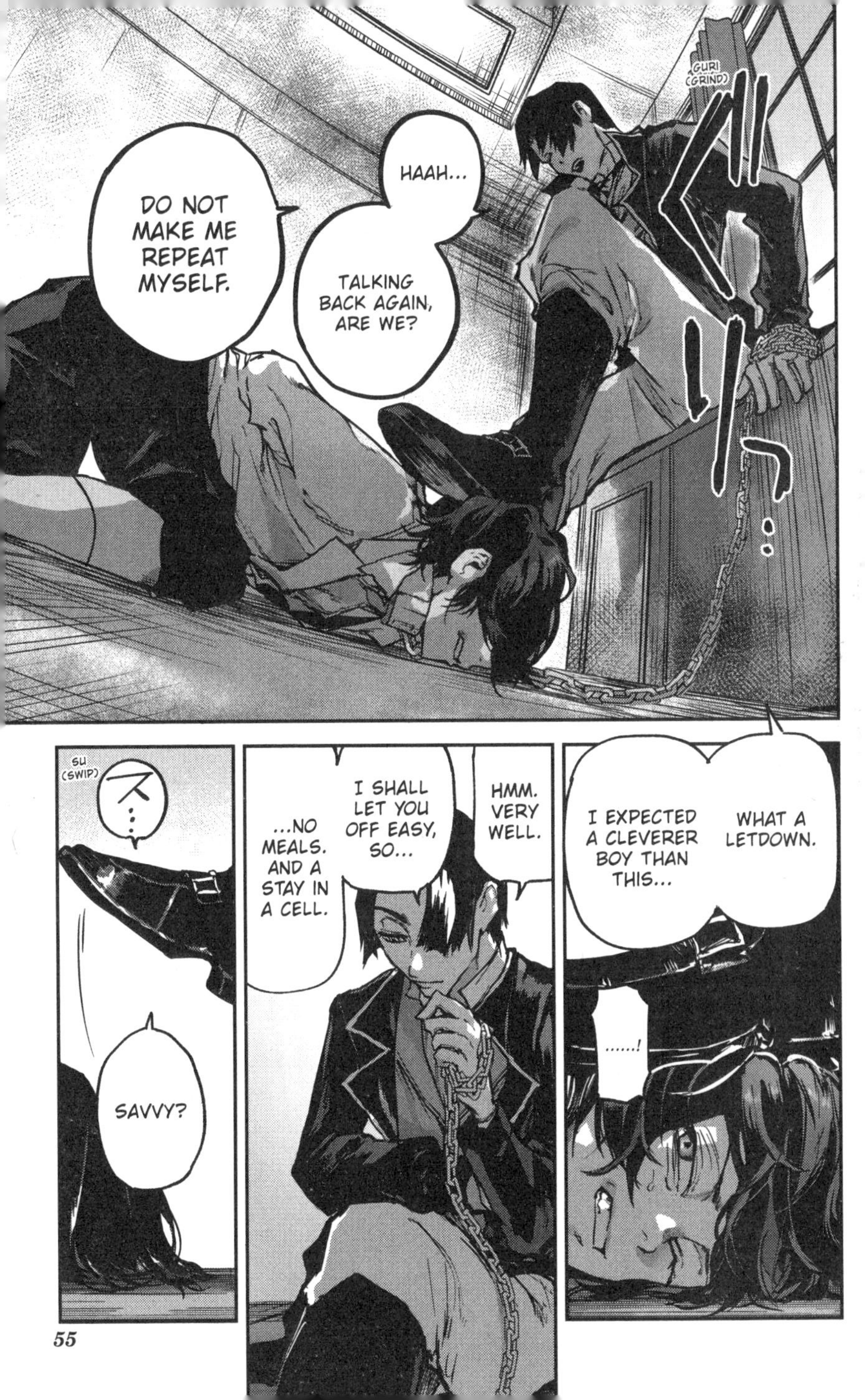
GURI (GRIND)
HAAH...
TALKING BACK AGAIN, ARE WE?
DO NOT MAKE ME REPEAT MYSELF.
WHAT A LETDOWN.
I EXPECTED A CLEVERER BOY THAN THIS...
......!
HMM. VERY WELL.
I SHALL LET YOU OFF EASY, SO...
...NO MEALS. AND A STAY IN A CELL.
SU (SWIP)
ス...
SAVVY?

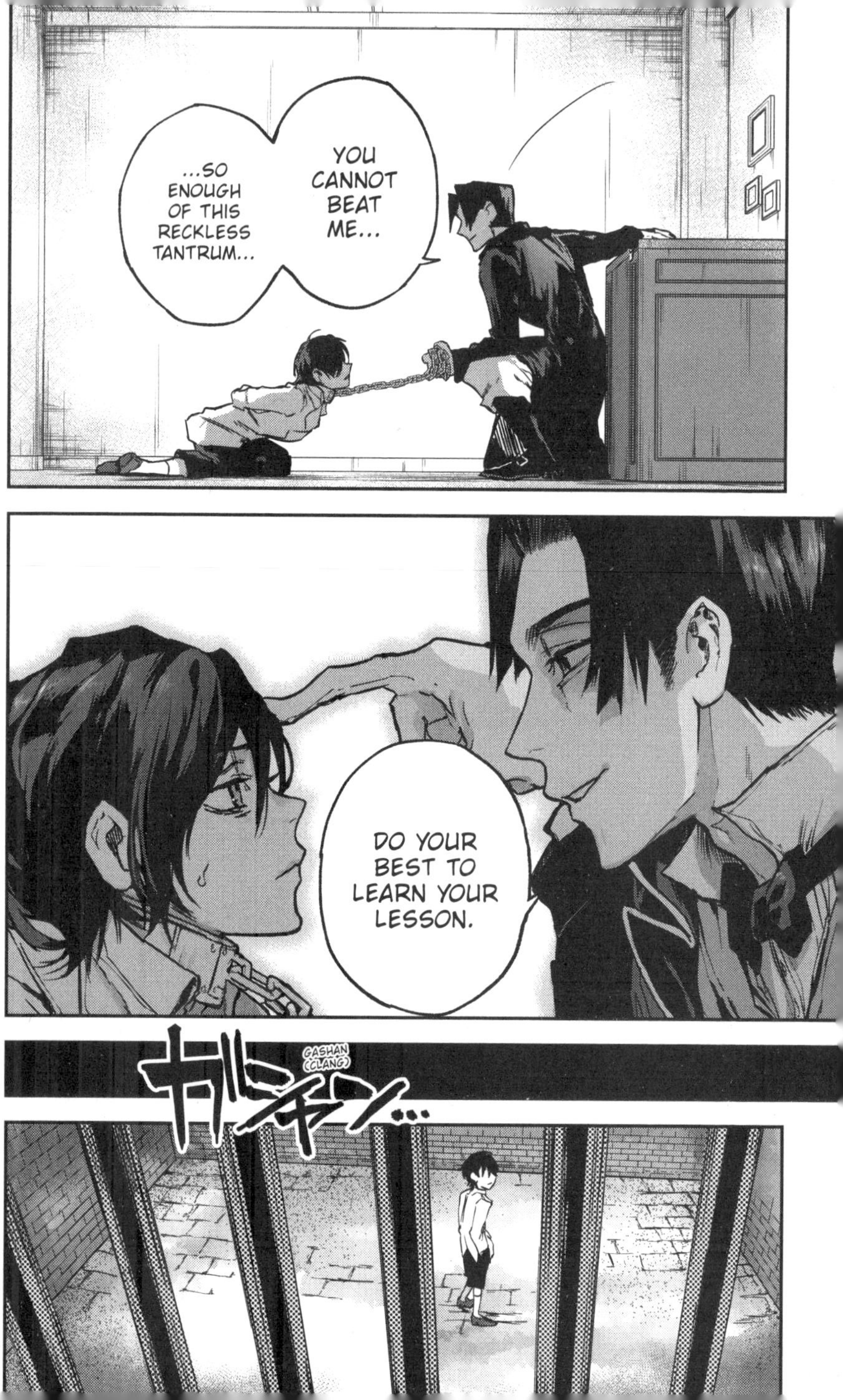
YOU CANNOT BEAT ME...
...SO ENOUGH OF THIS RECKLESS TANTRUM...
DO YOUR BEST TO LEARN YOUR LESSON.
GASHAN (CLANG)

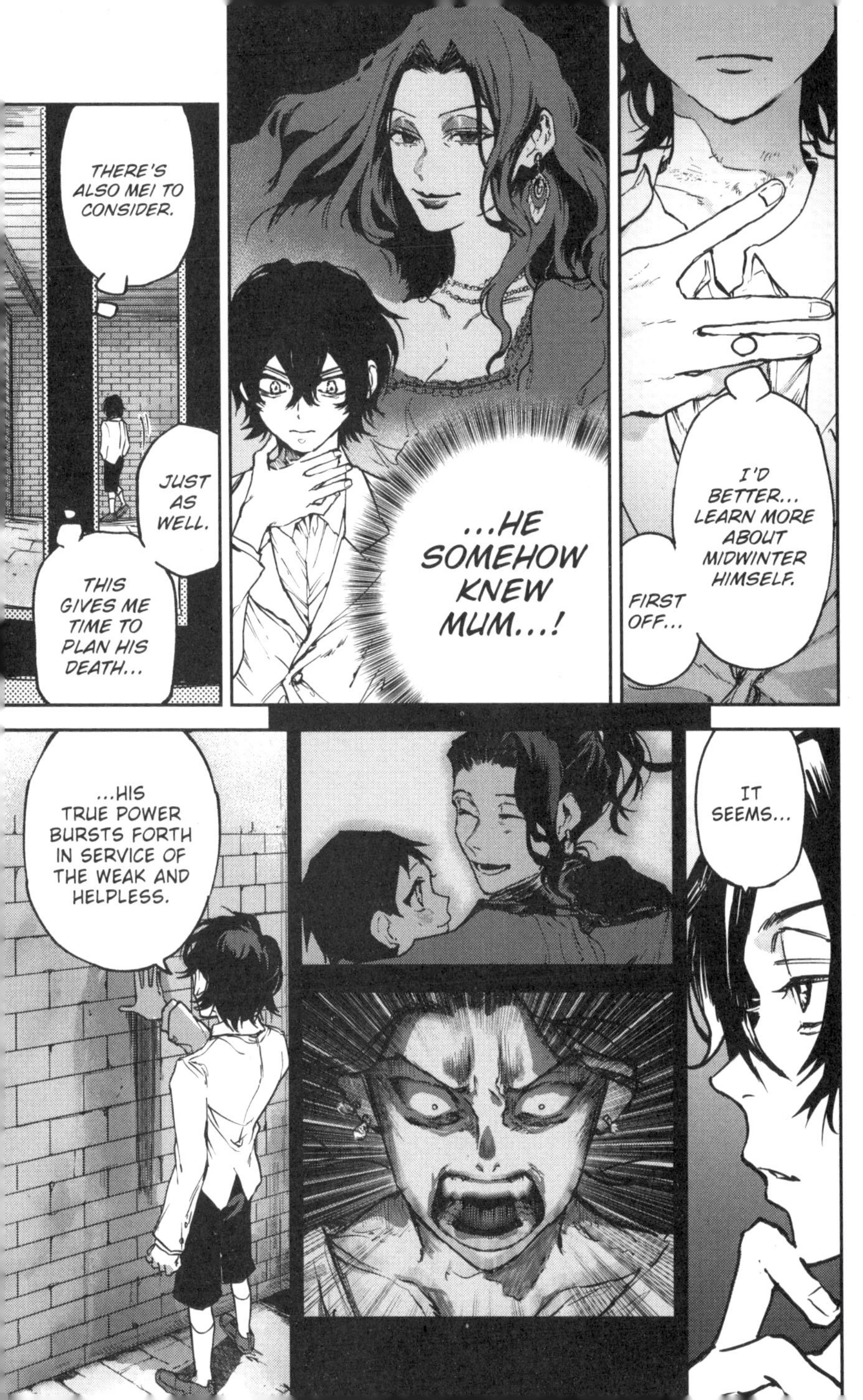

I'D BETTER... LEARN MORE ABOUT MIDWINTER HIMSELF.
FIRST OFF...
...HE SOMEHOW KNEW MUM...!
THERE'S ALSO MEI TO CONSIDER.
JUST AS WELL.
THIS GIVES ME TIME TO PLAN HIS DEATH...
IT SEEMS...
...HIS TRUE POWER BURSTS FORTH IN SERVICE OF THE WEAK AND HELPLESS.

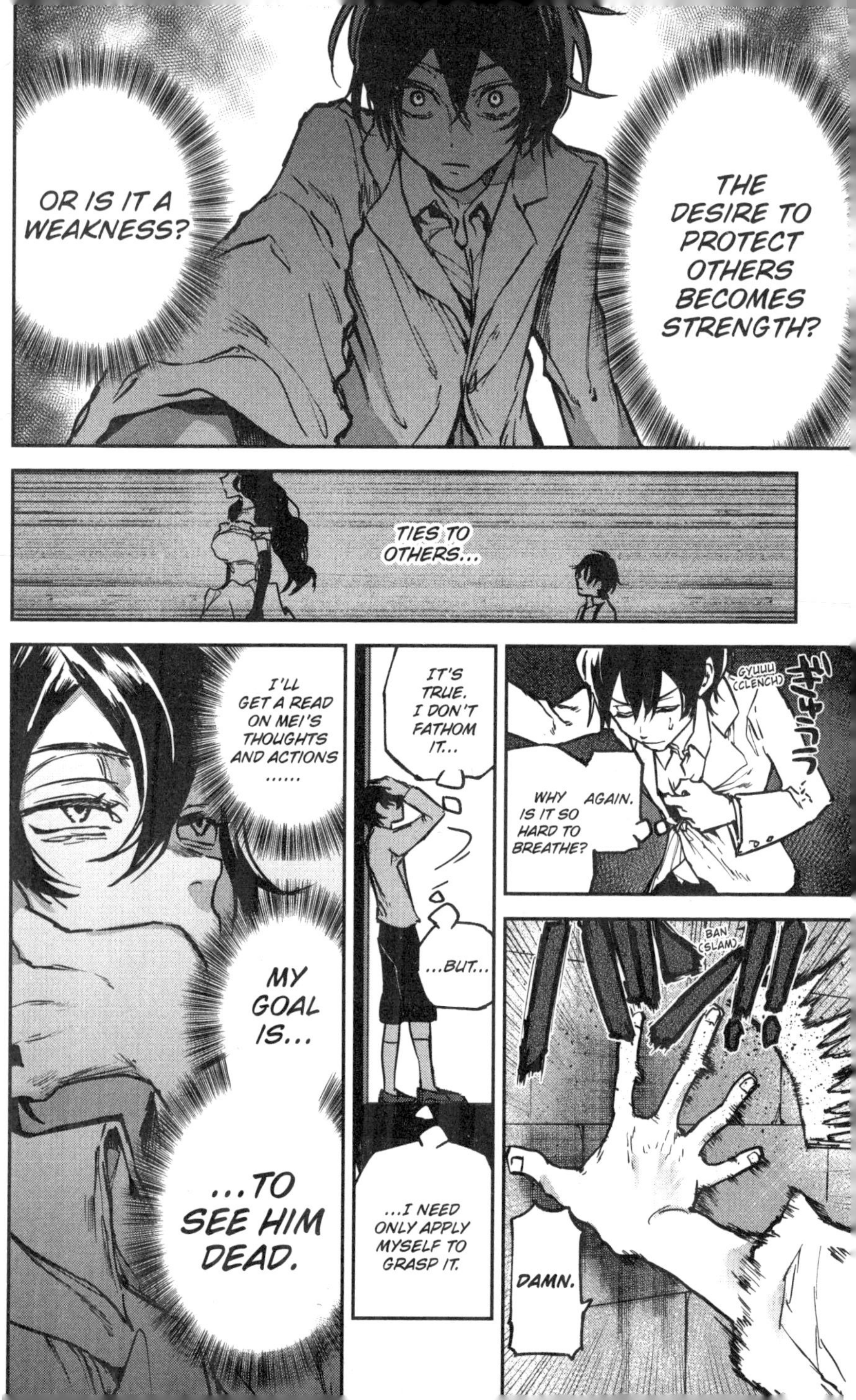
THE DESIRE TO PROTECT OTHERS BECOMES STRENGTH?
OR IS IT A WEAKNESS?
TIES TO OTHERS...
GYUUU (CLENCH)
AGAIN.
WHY IS IT SO HARD TO BREATHE?
BAN (SLAM)
DAMN.
IT'S TRUE. I DON'T FATHOM IT...
...BUT...
...I NEED ONLY APPLY MYSELF TO GRASP IT.
I'LL GET A READ ON MEI'S THOUGHTS AND ACTIONS ......
MY GOAL IS...
...TO SEE HIM DEAD.

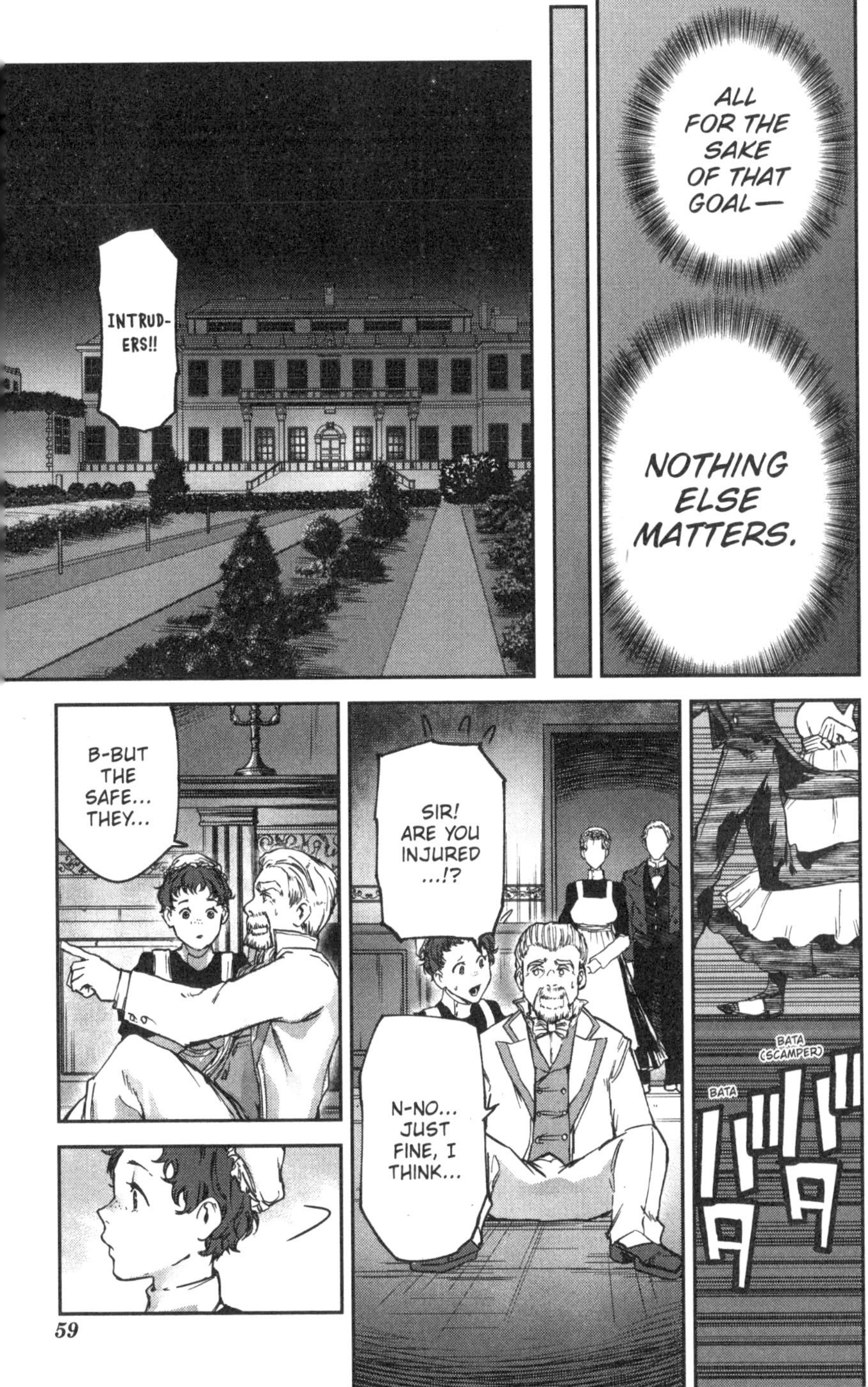
ALL FOR THE SAKE OF THAT GOAL—
NOTHING ELSE MATTERS.
INTRUD-ERS!!
BATA (SCAMPER)
BATA
SIR! ARE YOU INJURED ...!?
N-NO... JUST FINE, I THINK...
B-BUT THE SAFE... THEY...

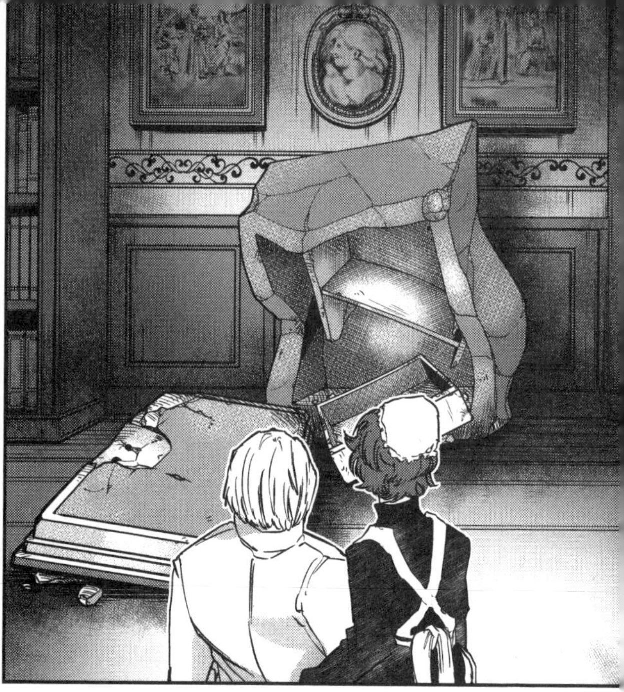

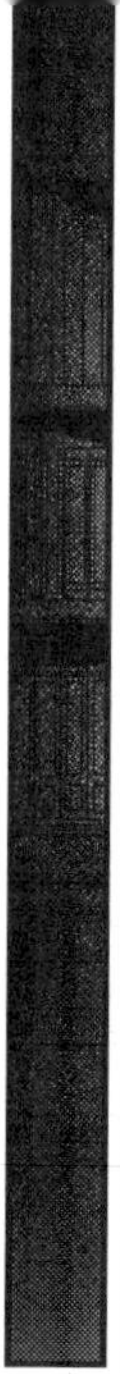

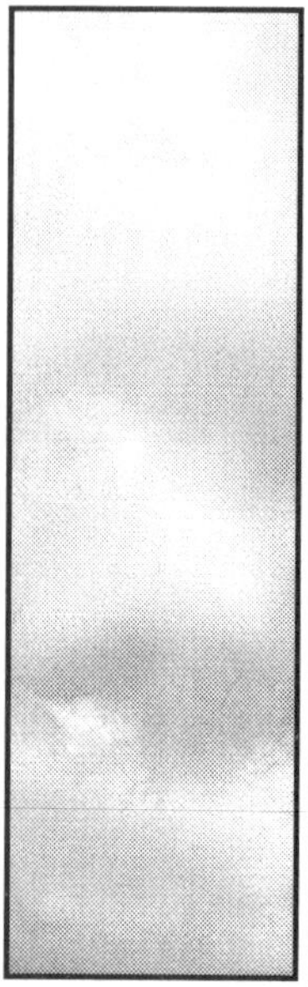

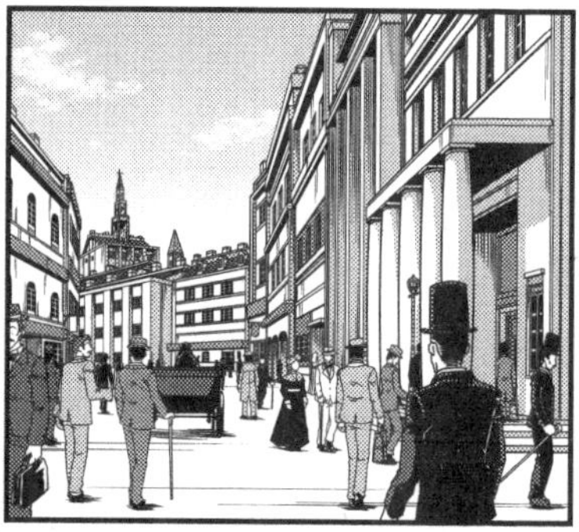

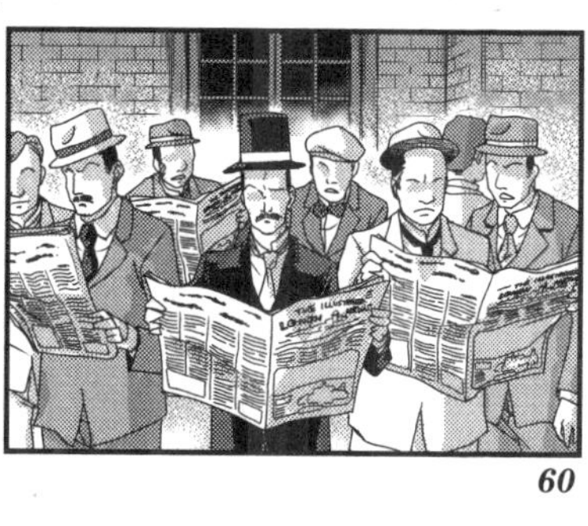

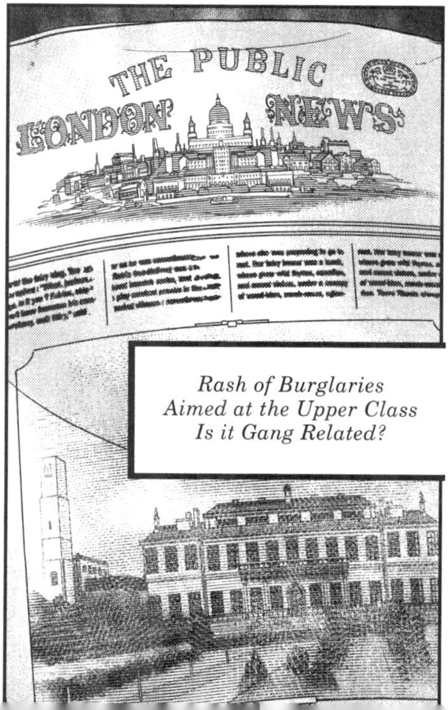
THE PUBLIC LONDON NEWS
Rash of Burglaries Aimed at the Upper Class Is it Gang Related?

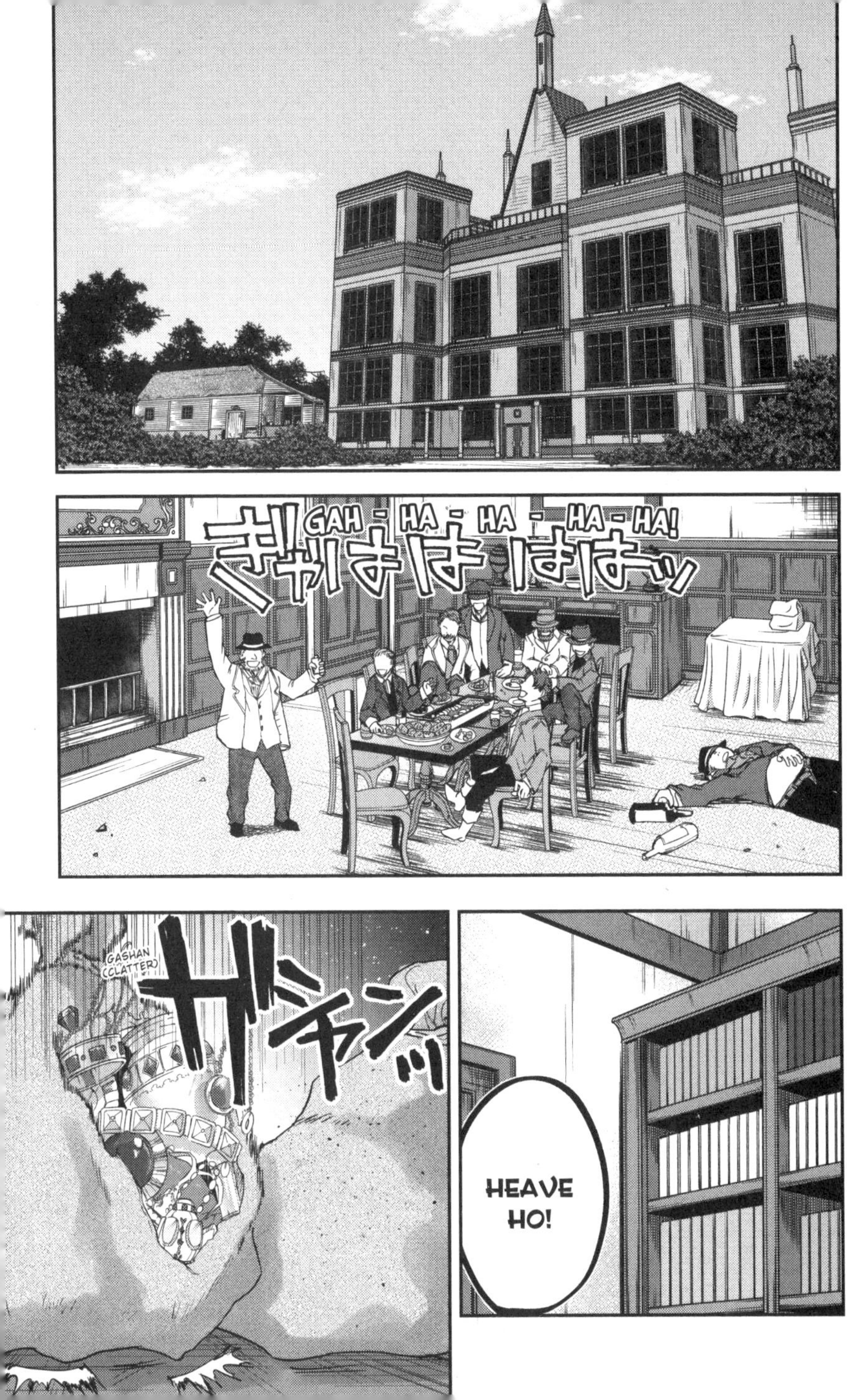
GAH-HA-HA-HA-HA!
HEAVE HO!
GASHAN (CLATTER)

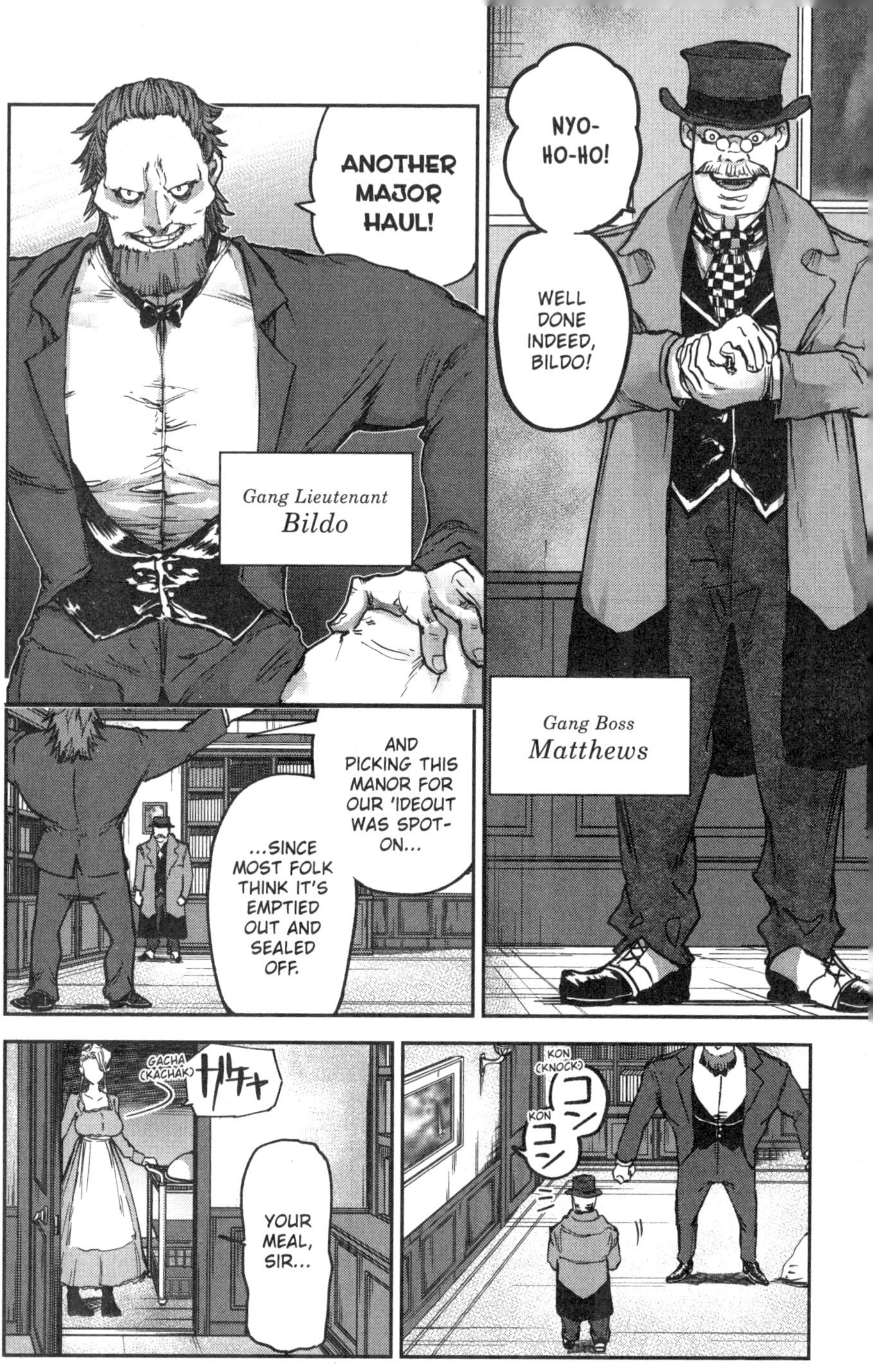
NYO-HO-HO!
WELL DONE INDEED, BILDO!
Gang Boss Matthews
ANOTHER MAJOR HAUL!
Gang Lieutenant Bildo
AND PICKING THIS MANOR FOR OUR 'IDEOUT WAS SPOT-ON...
...SINCE MOST FOLK THINK IT'S EMPTIED OUT AND SEALED OFF.
KON (KNOCK)
KON
GACHA (KACHAK)
YOUR MEAL, SIR...

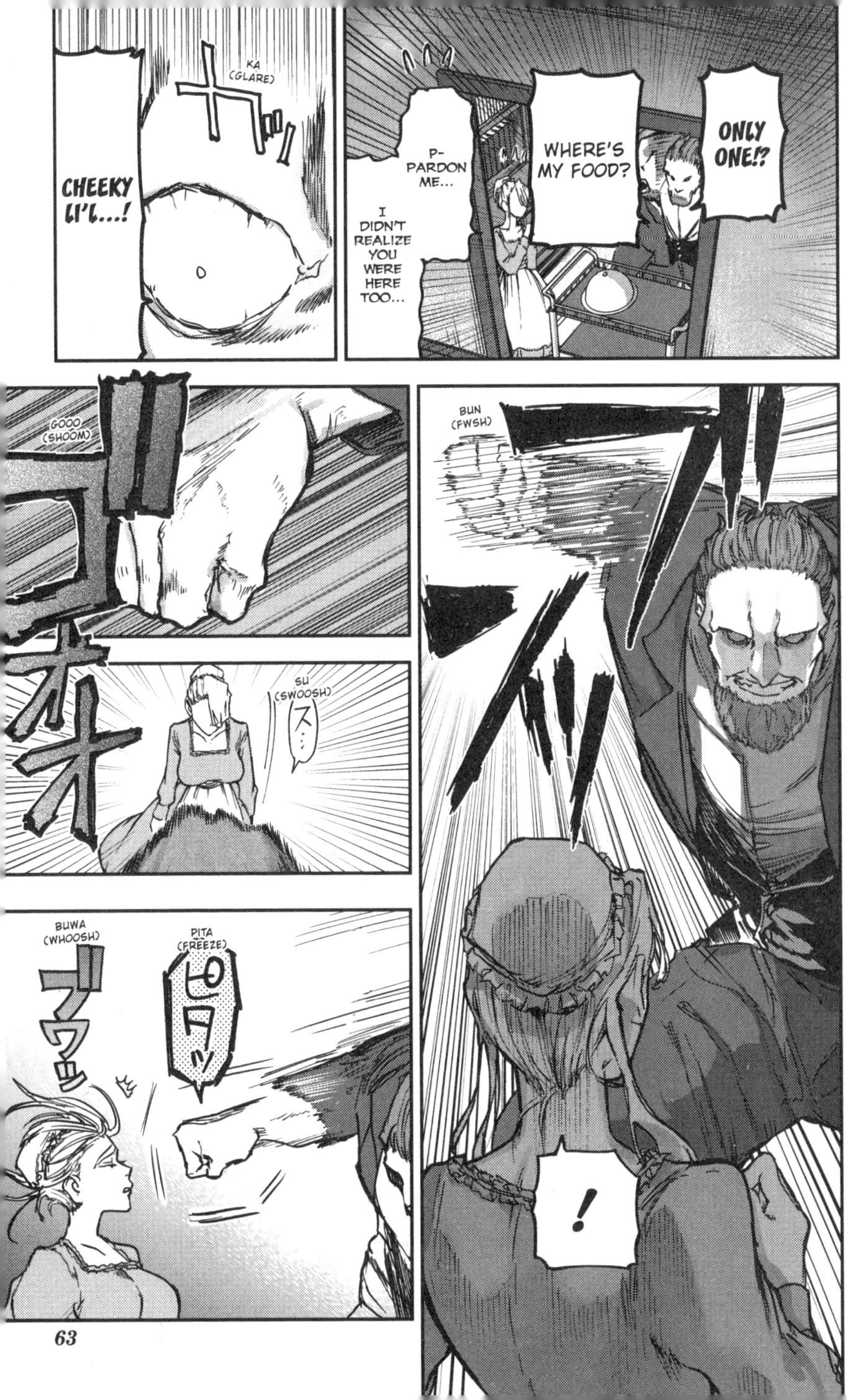

ONLY ONE!?
WHERE'S MY FOOD?
P-PARDON ME...
I DIDN'T REALIZE YOU WERE HERE TOO...
KA (GLARE)
CHEEKY LI'L...!
BUN (FWSH)
!
GOOO (SHOOM)
SU (SWOOSH)
ス…
BUWA (WHOOSH)
PITA (FREEZE)

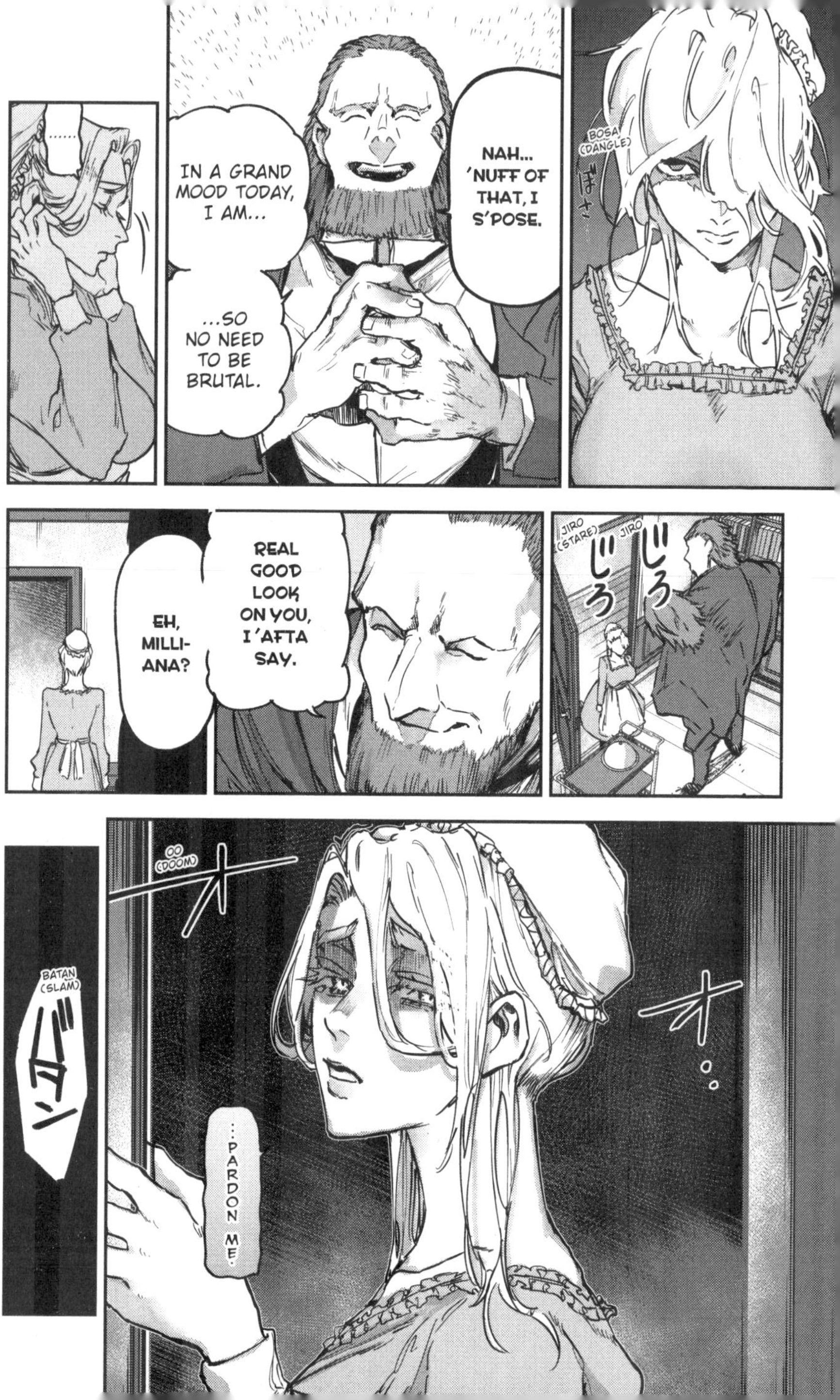
BOSA (DANGLE)
ぼさ
NAH... 'NUFF OF THAT, I S'POSE.
IN A GRAND MOOD TODAY, I AM...
...SO NO NEED TO BE BRUTAL.
......
JIRO (STARE) JIRO
じろじろ
REAL GOOD LOOK ON YOU, I'AFTA SAY.
EH, MILLI-ANA?
オ。。
OO (DOOM)
オ
BATAN (SLAM)
バタン
...PARDON ME.

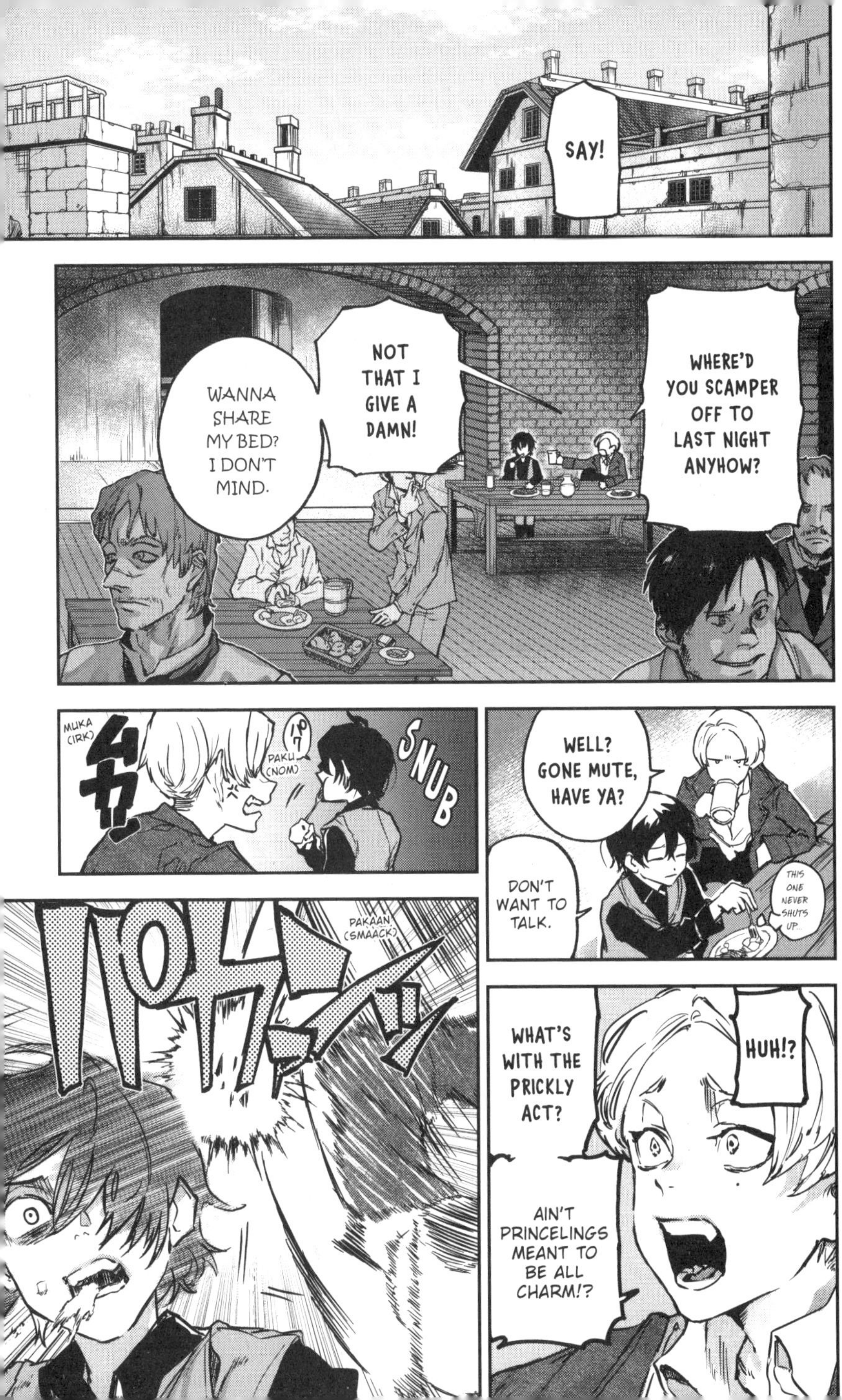
SAY!
WHERE'D YOU SCAMPER OFF TO LAST NIGHT ANYHOW?
NOT THAT I GIVE A DAMN!
WANNA SHARE MY BED? I DON'T MIND.
WELL? GONE MUTE, HAVE YA?
THIS ONE NEVER SHUTS UP...
DON'T WANT TO TALK.
SNUB
パク
PAKU (NOM)
ムカ
MUKA (IRK)
HUH!?
WHAT'S WITH THE PRICKLY ACT?
AIN'T PRINCELINGS MEANT TO BE ALL CHARM!?
PAKAAN (SMAACK)
パカーン

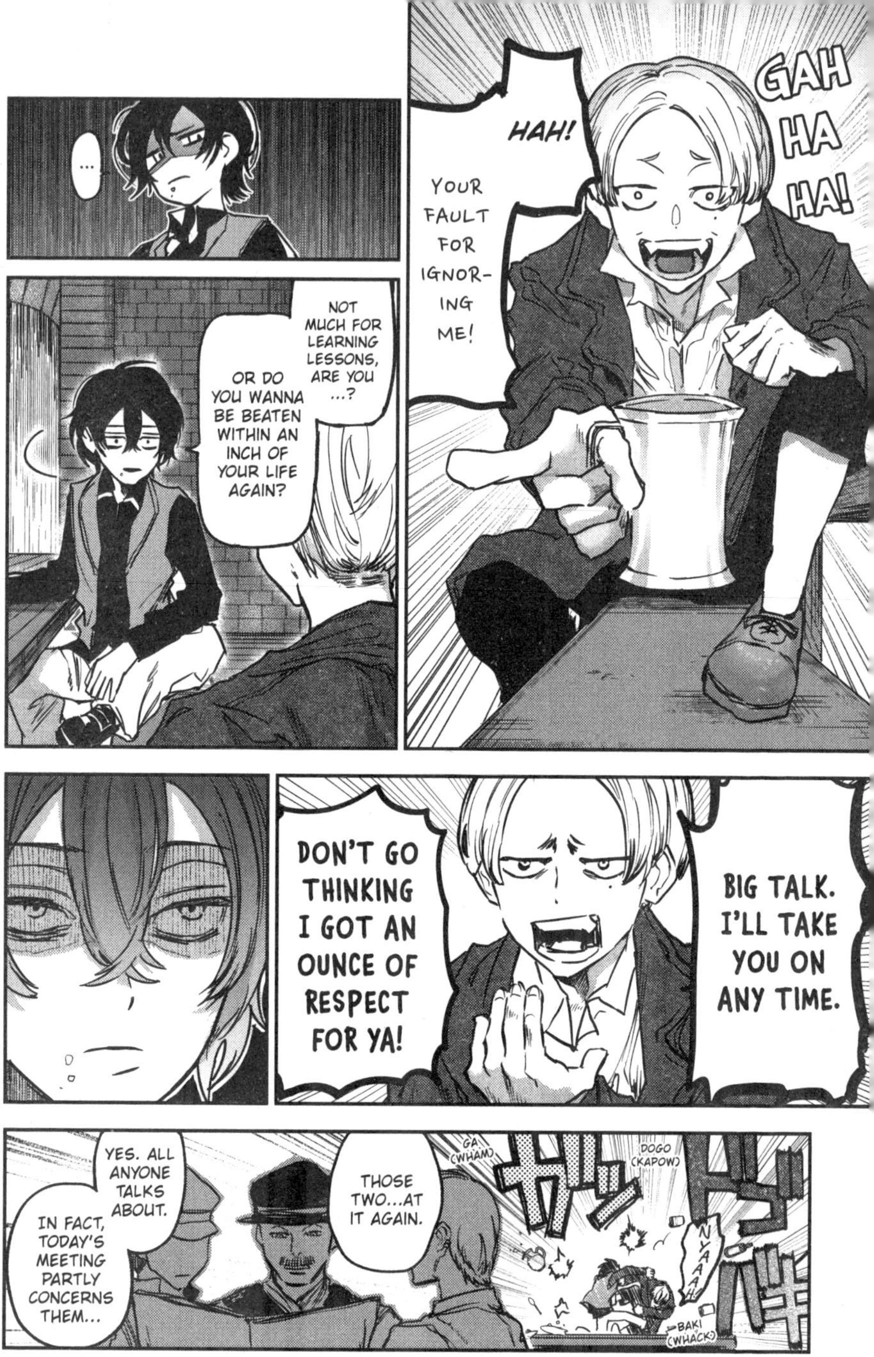
GAH HA HA!
HAH!
YOUR FAULT FOR IGNORING ME!
…
NOT MUCH FOR LEARNING LESSONS, ARE YOU …?
OR DO YOU WANNA BE BEATEN WITHIN AN INCH OF YOUR LIFE AGAIN?
BIG TALK. I'LL TAKE YOU ON ANY TIME.
DON'T GO THINKING I GOT AN OUNCE OF RESPECT FOR YA!
DOGO (KAPOW)
NYAAAAH
BAKI (WHACK)
GA (WHAM)
THOSE TWO…AT IT AGAIN.
YES. ALL ANYONE TALKS ABOUT.
IN FACT, TODAY'S MEETING PARTLY CONCERNS THEM…

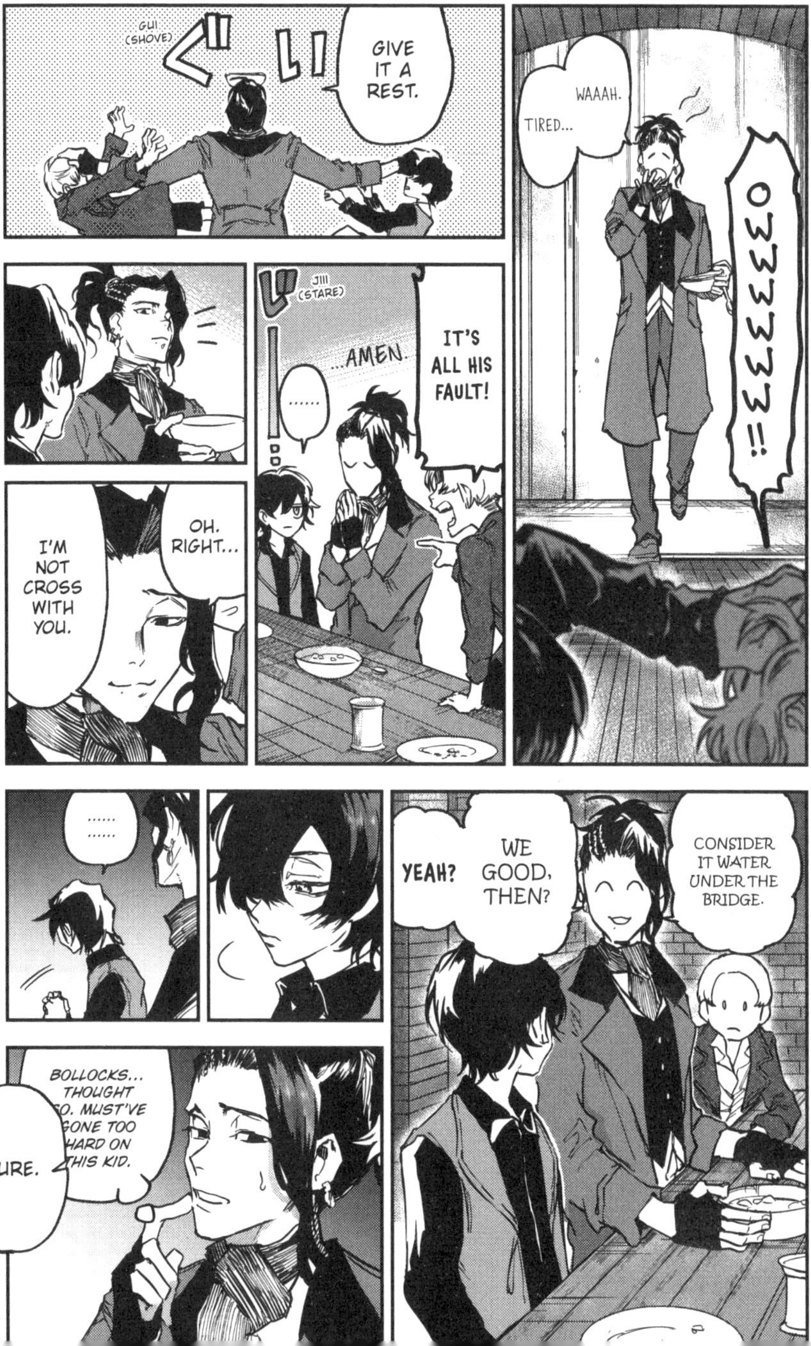
WAAAH. TIRED...
OWWWWWW!!
GIVE IT A REST.
GUI (SHOVE)
IT'S ALL HIS FAULT!
JIII (STARE)
...AMEN.
......
OH. RIGHT...
I'M NOT CROSS WITH YOU.
CONSIDER IT WATER UNDER THE BRIDGE.
WE GOOD, THEN?
YEAH?
....
BOLLOCKS... THOUGHT SO. MUST'VE GONE TOO HARD ON THIS KID.
SURE.

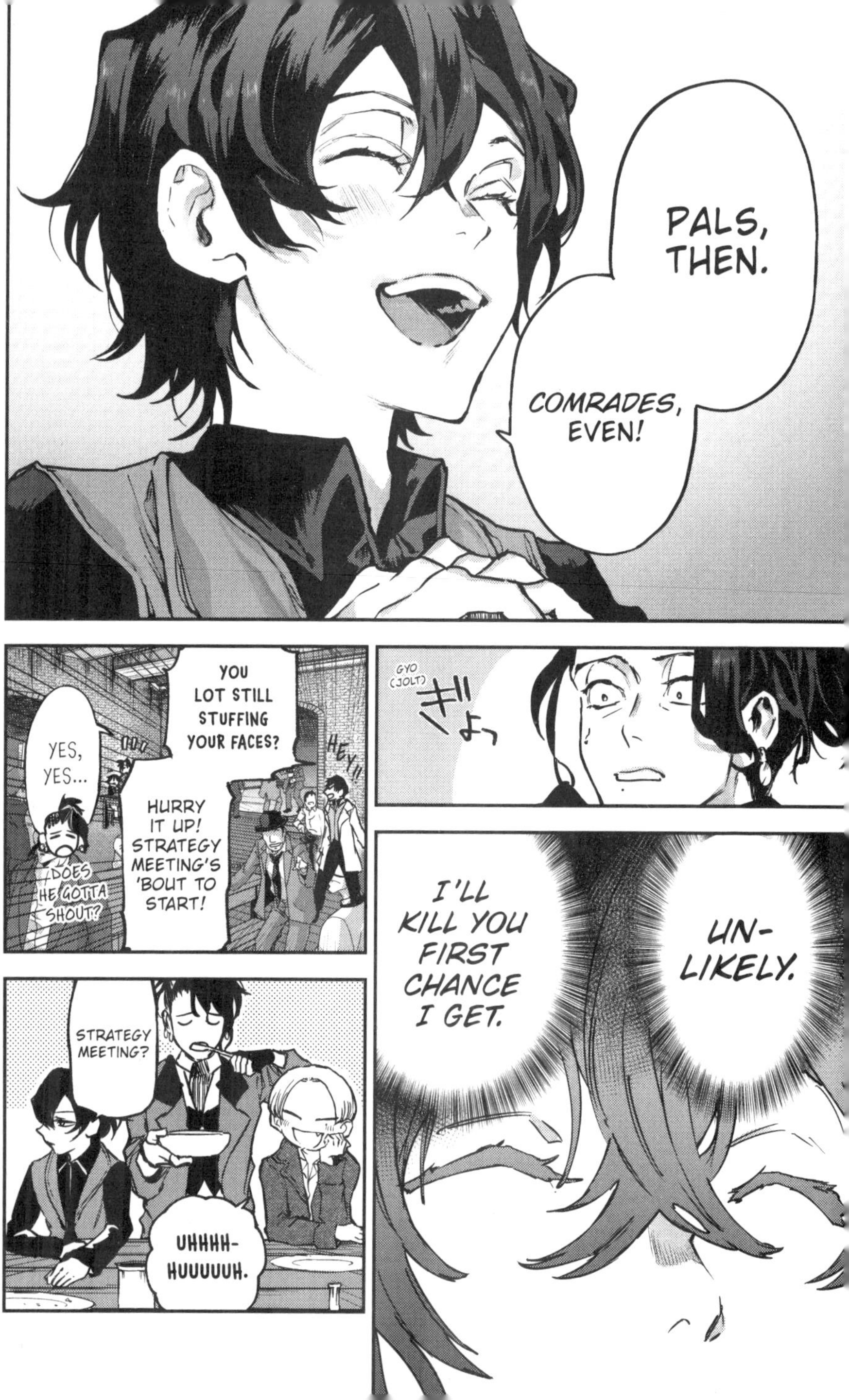
PALS, THEN.
COMRADES, EVEN!
GYO (JOLT)
ぎょっ
I'LL KILL YOU FIRST CHANCE I GET.
UN-LIKELY.
YOU LOT STILL STUFFING YOUR FACES?
HEY!!
HURRY IT UP! STRATEGY MEETING'S 'BOUT TO START!
YES, YES...
DOES HE GOTTA SHOUT?
STRATEGY MEETING?
UHHHH-HUUUUUH.

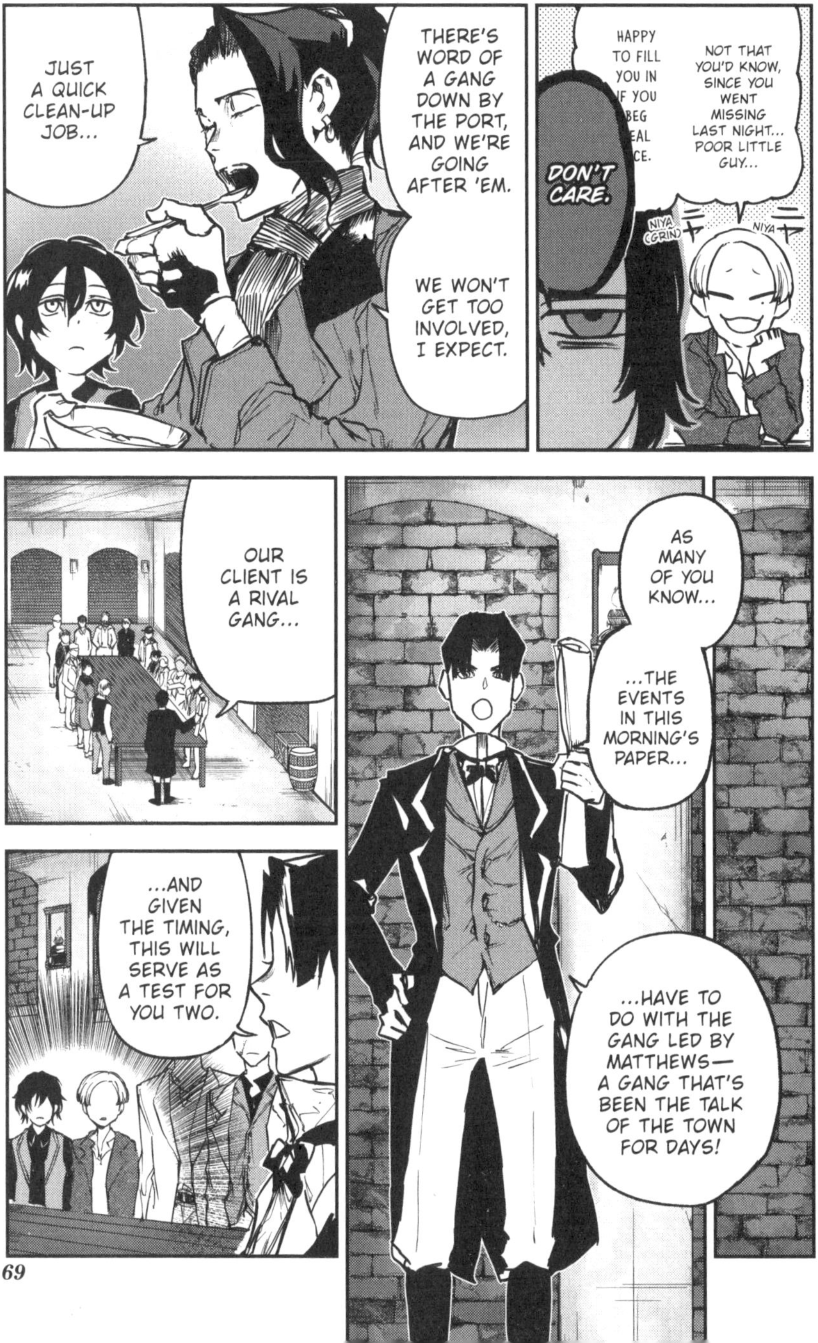

NOT THAT YOU'D KNOW, SINCE YOU WENT MISSING LAST NIGHT... POOR LITTLE GUY...
HAPPY TO FILL YOU IN IF YOU BEG
DON'T CARE.
NIYA
NIYA (GRIN)
THERE'S WORD OF A GANG DOWN BY THE PORT, AND WE'RE GOING AFTER 'EM.
WE WON'T GET TOO INVOLVED, I EXPECT.
JUST A QUICK CLEAN-UP JOB...
AS MANY OF YOU KNOW...
...THE EVENTS IN THIS MORNING'S PAPER...
...HAVE TO DO WITH THE GANG LED BY MATTHEWS—A GANG THAT'S BEEN THE TALK OF THE TOWN FOR DAYS!
OUR CLIENT IS A RIVAL GANG...
...AND GIVEN THE TIMING, THIS WILL SERVE AS A TEST FOR YOU TWO.

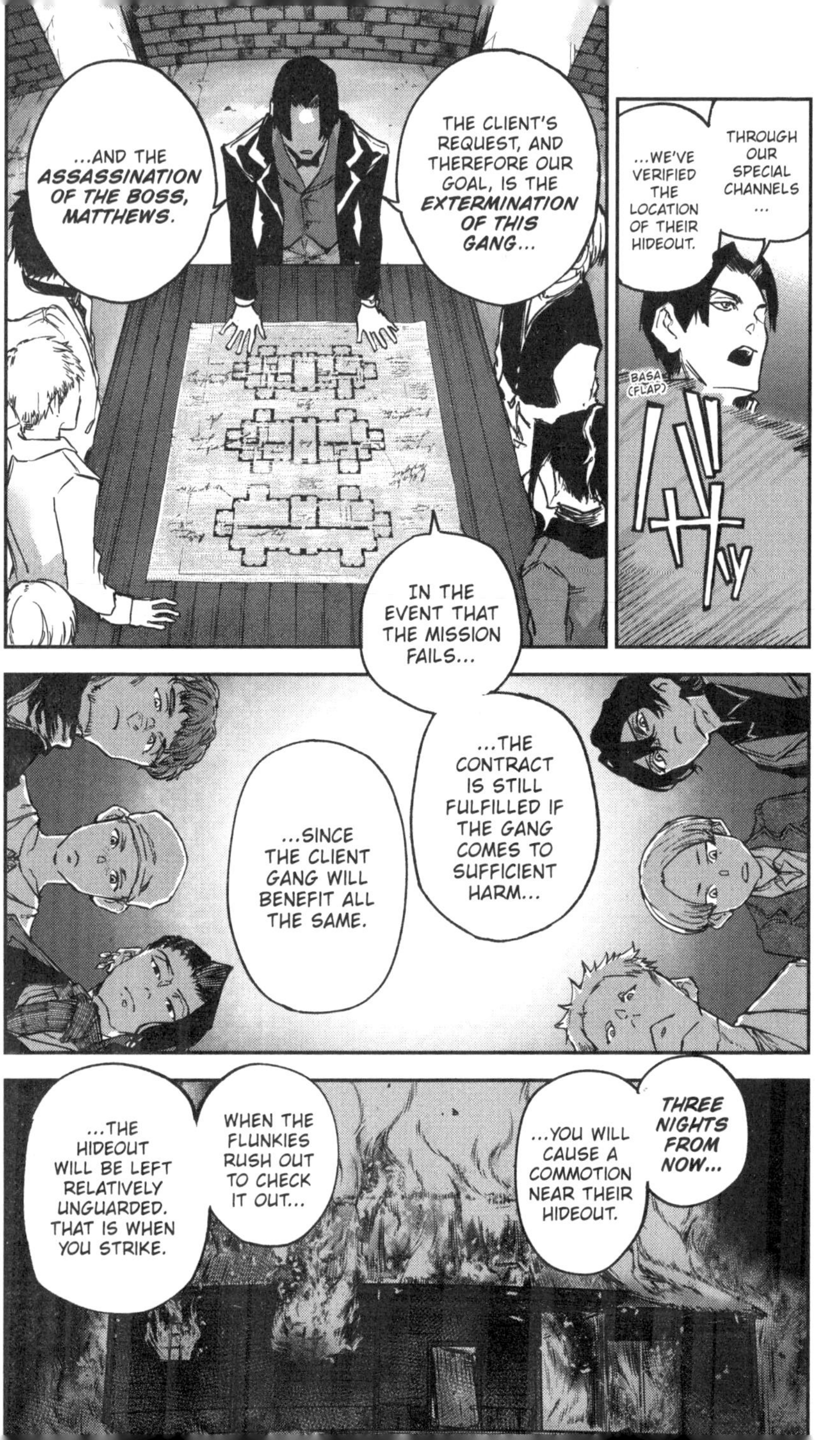
THROUGH OUR SPECIAL CHANNELS...
...WE'VE VERIFIED THE LOCATION OF THEIR HIDEOUT.
BASA (FLAP)
THE CLIENT'S REQUEST, AND THEREFORE OUR GOAL, IS THE *EXTERMINATION OF THIS GANG*...
...AND THE *ASSASSINATION OF THE BOSS, MATTHEWS.*
IN THE EVENT THAT THE MISSION FAILS...
...THE CONTRACT IS STILL FULFILLED IF THE GANG COMES TO SUFFICIENT HARM...
...SINCE THE CLIENT GANG WILL BENEFIT ALL THE SAME.
THREE NIGHTS FROM NOW...
...YOU WILL CAUSE A COMMOTION NEAR THEIR HIDEOUT.
WHEN THE FLUNKIES RUSH OUT TO CHECK IT OUT...
...THE HIDEOUT WILL BE LEFT RELATIVELY UNGUARDED. THAT IS WHEN YOU STRIKE.

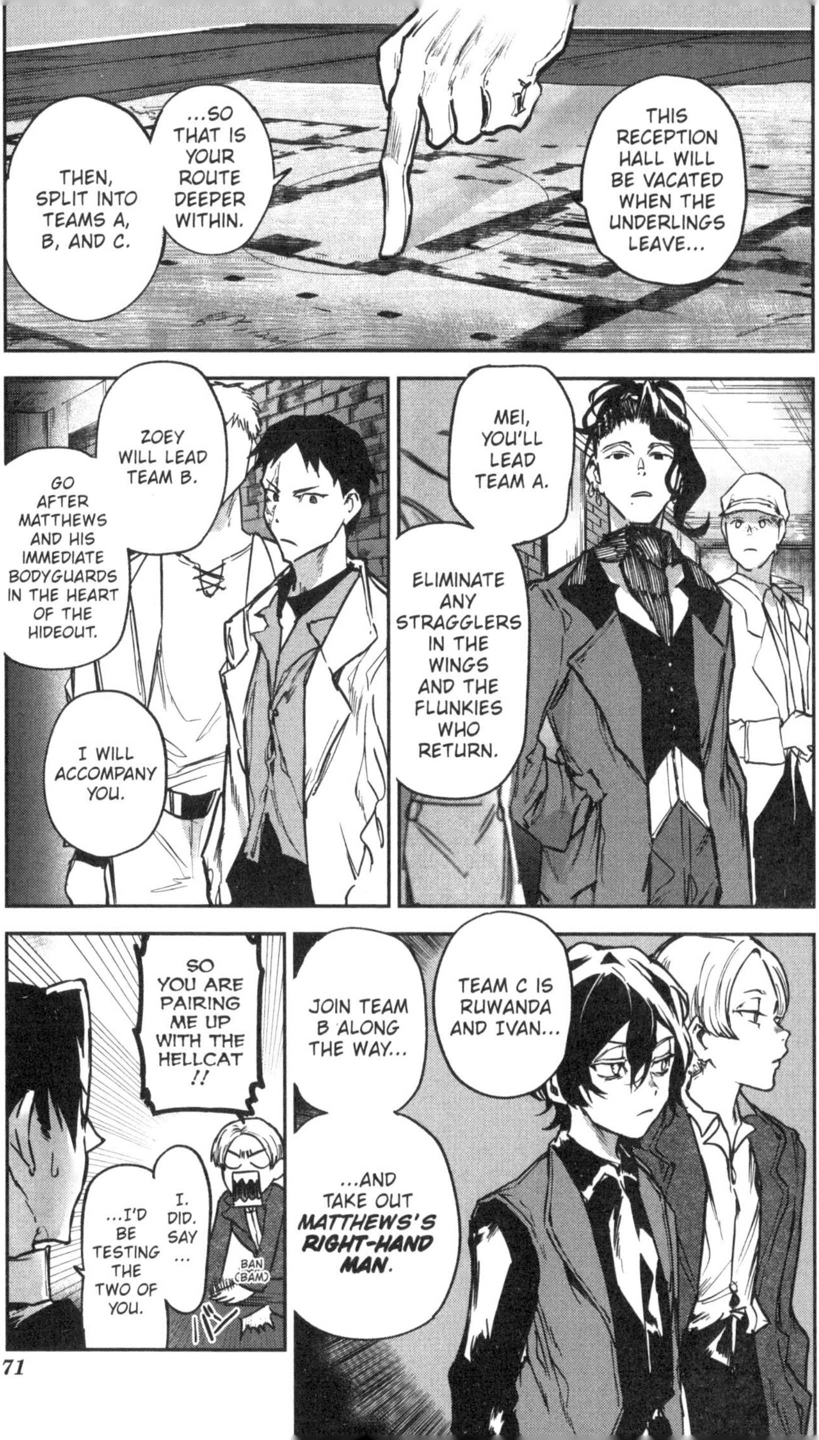
THIS RECEPTION HALL WILL BE VACATED WHEN THE UNDERLINGS LEAVE...
...SO THAT IS YOUR ROUTE DEEPER WITHIN.
THEN, SPLIT INTO TEAMS A, B, AND C.
MEI, YOU'LL LEAD TEAM A.
ELIMINATE ANY STRAGGLERS IN THE WINGS AND THE FLUNKIES WHO RETURN.
ZOEY WILL LEAD TEAM B.
GO AFTER MATTHEWS AND HIS IMMEDIATE BODYGUARDS IN THE HEART OF THE HIDEOUT.
I WILL ACCOMPANY YOU.
TEAM C IS RUWANDA AND IVAN...
JOIN TEAM B ALONG THE WAY...
...AND TAKE OUT ***MATTHEWS'S RIGHT-HAND MAN***.
SO YOU ARE PAIRING ME UP WITH THE HELLCAT!!
I. DID. SAY...
...I'D BE TESTING THE TWO OF YOU.
BAN (BAM)

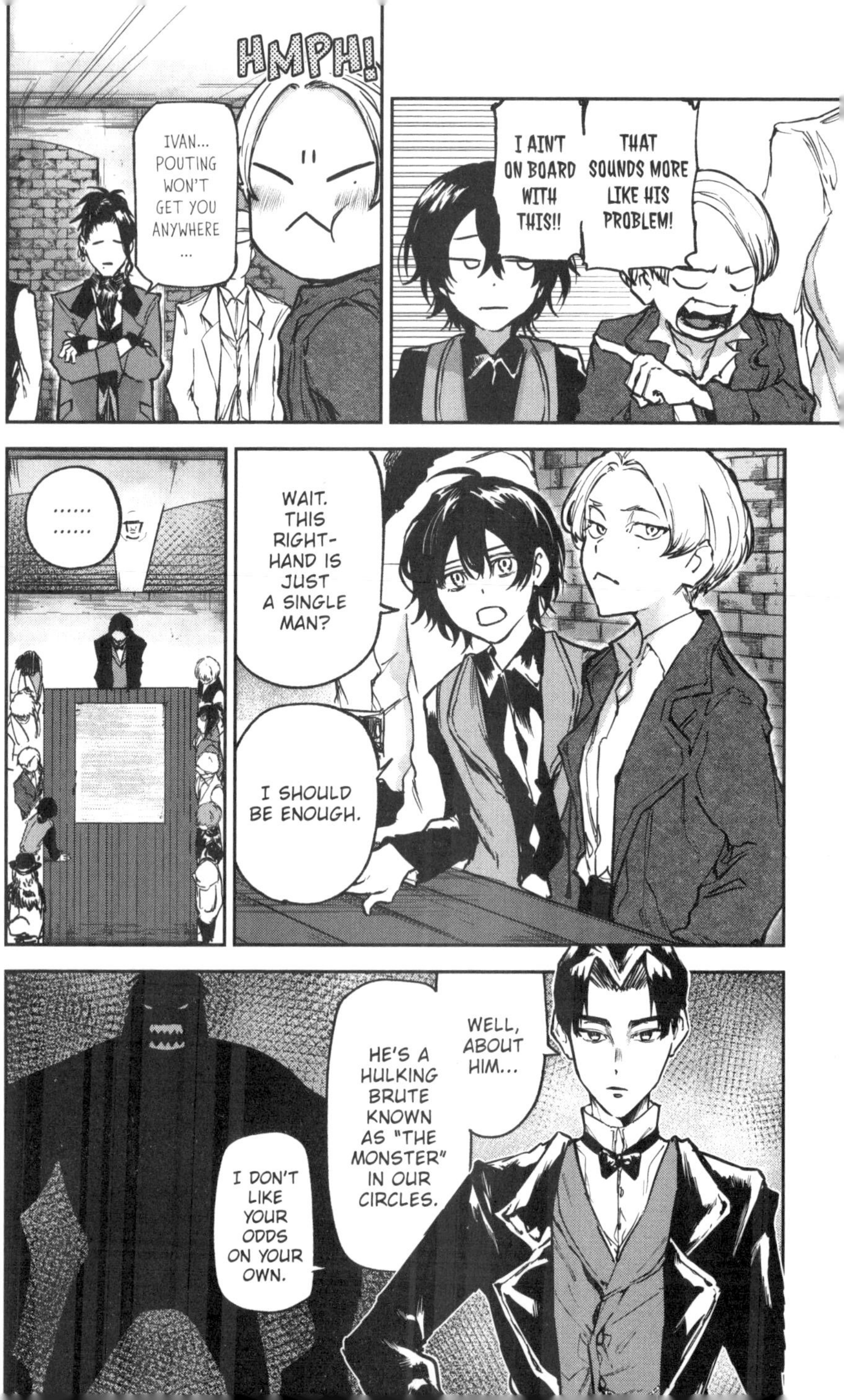
THAT SOUNDS MORE LIKE HIS PROBLEM!
I AIN'T ON BOARD WITH THIS!!
HMPH!
IVAN... POUTING WON'T GET YOU ANYWHERE ...
WAIT. THIS RIGHT-HAND IS JUST A SINGLE MAN?
I SHOULD BE ENOUGH.
....
WELL, ABOUT HIM...
HE'S A HULKING BRUTE KNOWN AS "THE MONSTER" IN OUR CIRCLES.
I DON'T LIKE YOUR ODDS ON YOUR OWN.

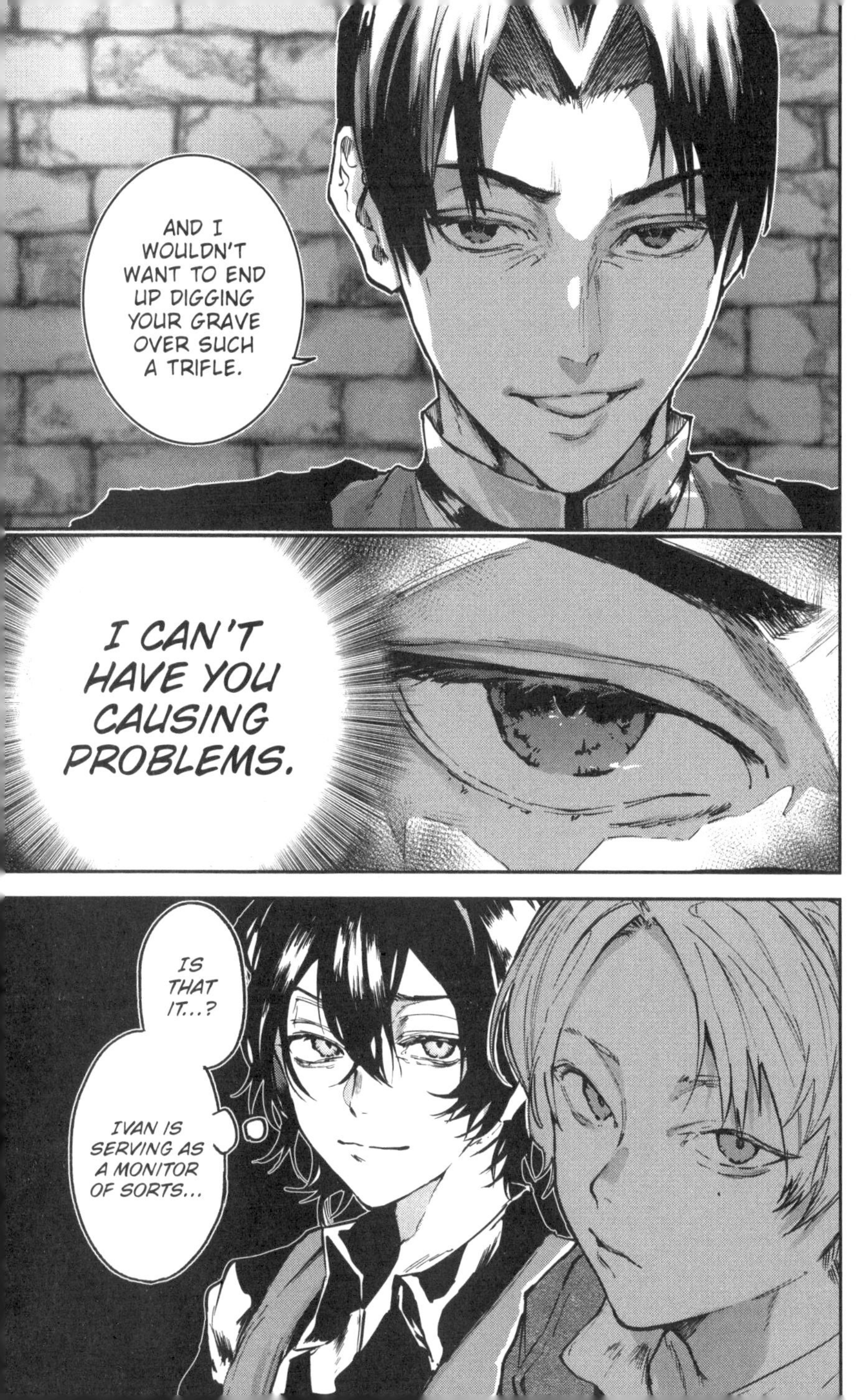
AND I WOULDN'T WANT TO END UP DIGGING YOUR GRAVE OVER SUCH A TRIFLE.
I CAN'T HAVE YOU CAUSING PROBLEMS.
IS THAT IT...?
IVAN IS SERVING AS A MONITOR OF SORTS...

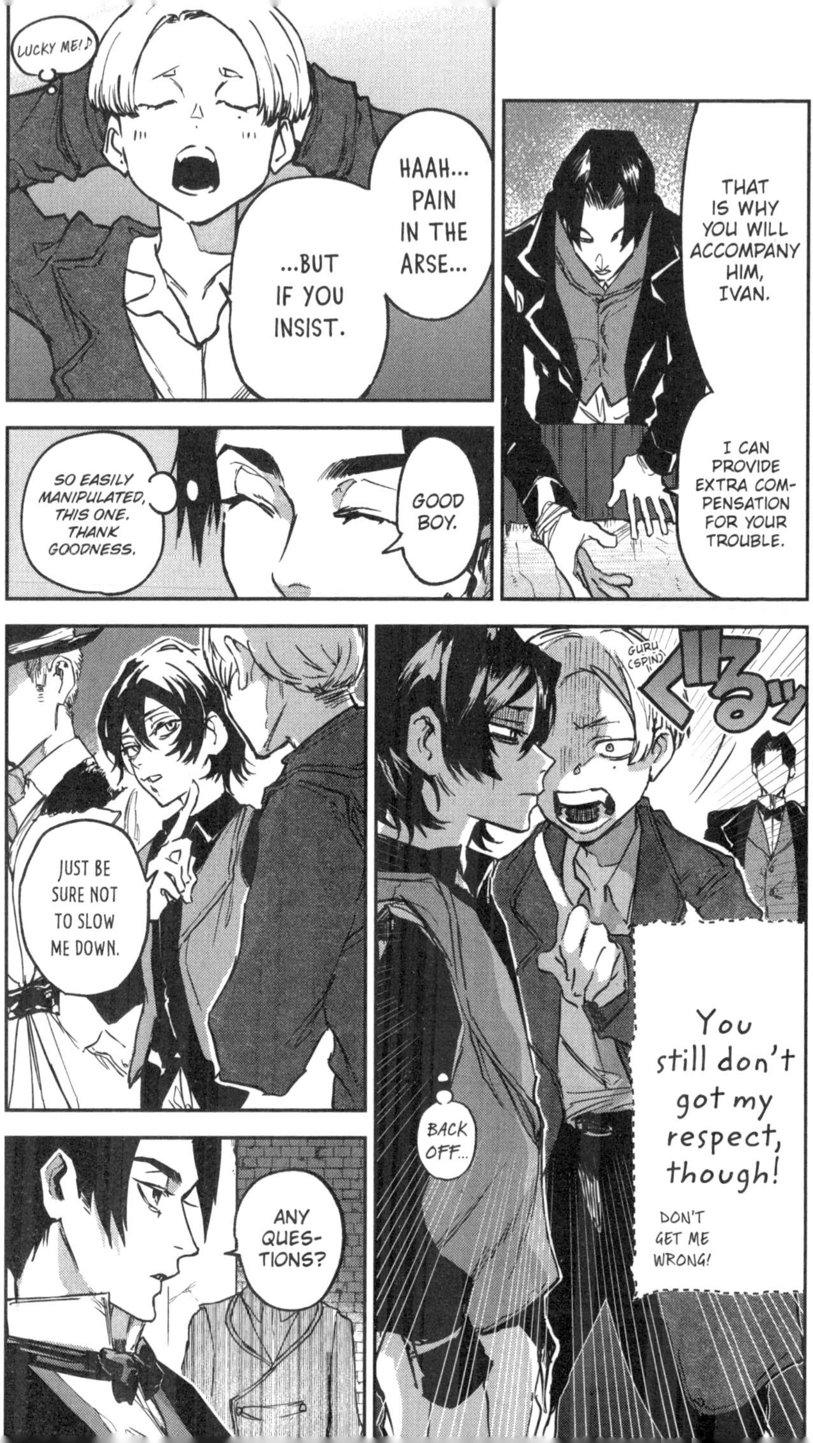
THAT IS WHY YOU WILL ACCOMPANY HIM, IVAN.
I CAN PROVIDE EXTRA COMPENSATION FOR YOUR TROUBLE.
HAAH... PAIN IN THE ARSE...
...BUT IF YOU INSIST.
LUCKY ME!♪
GOOD BOY.
SO EASILY MANIPULATED, THIS ONE. THANK GOODNESS.
GURU (SPIN)
You still don't got my respect, though!
DON'T GET ME WRONG!
BACK OFF...
JUST BE SURE NOT TO SLOW ME DOWN.
ANY QUESTIONS?

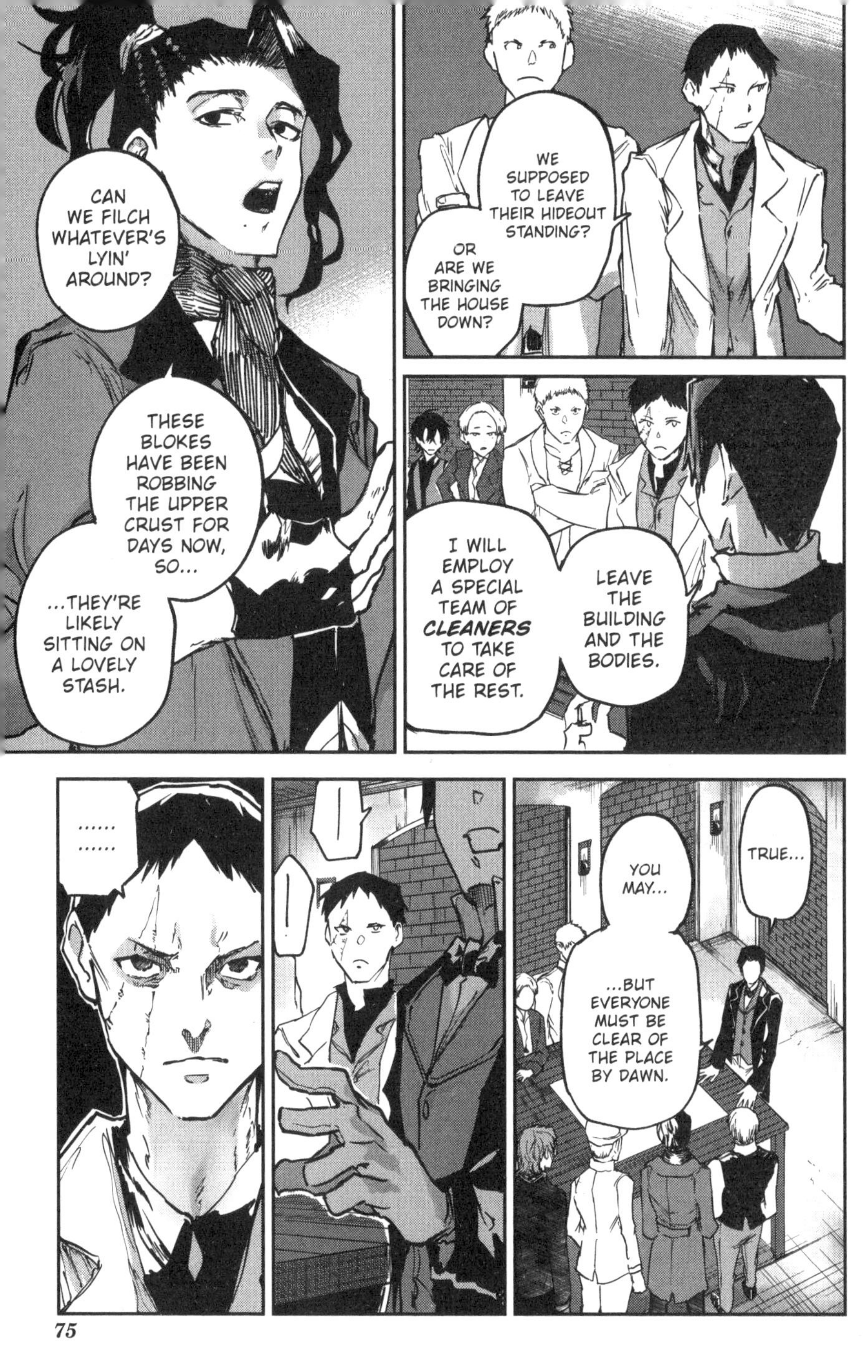
WE SUPPOSED TO LEAVE THEIR HIDEOUT STANDING?
OR ARE WE BRINGING THE HOUSE DOWN?
LEAVE THE BUILDING AND THE BODIES.
I WILL EMPLOY A SPECIAL TEAM OF CLEANERS TO TAKE CARE OF THE REST.
CAN WE FILCH WHATEVER'S LYIN' AROUND?
THESE BLOKES HAVE BEEN ROBBING THE UPPER CRUST FOR DAYS NOW, SO...
...THEY'RE LIKELY SITTING ON A LOVELY STASH.
TRUE...
YOU MAY...
...BUT EVERYONE MUST BE CLEAR OF THE PLACE BY DAWN.
!
......
......

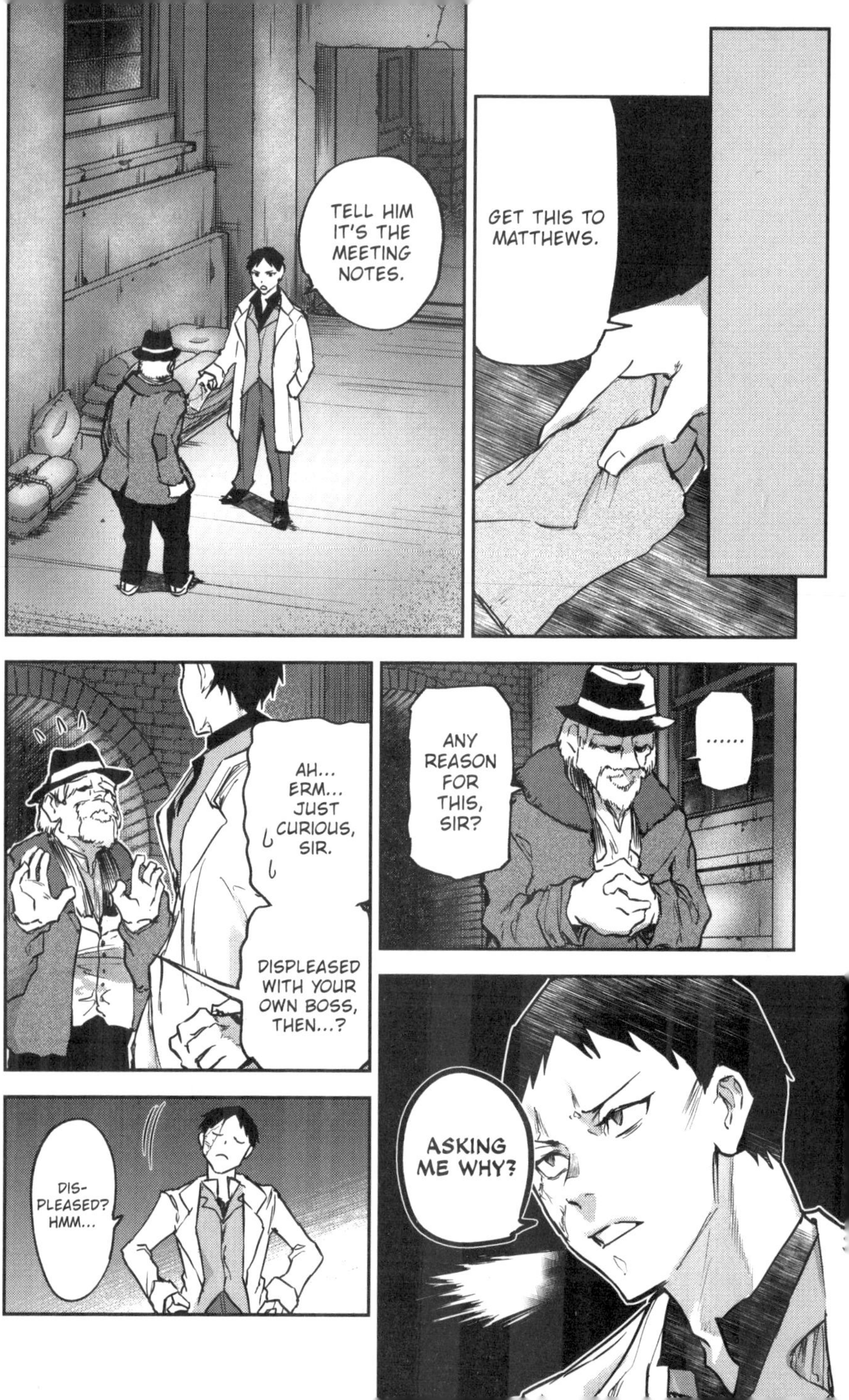
GET THIS TO MATTHEWS.
TELL HIM IT'S THE MEETING NOTES.
ANY REASON FOR THIS, SIR?
......
AH... ERM... JUST CURIOUS, SIR.
DISPLEASED WITH YOUR OWN BOSS, THEN...?
DIS-PLEASED? HMM...
ASKING ME WHY?

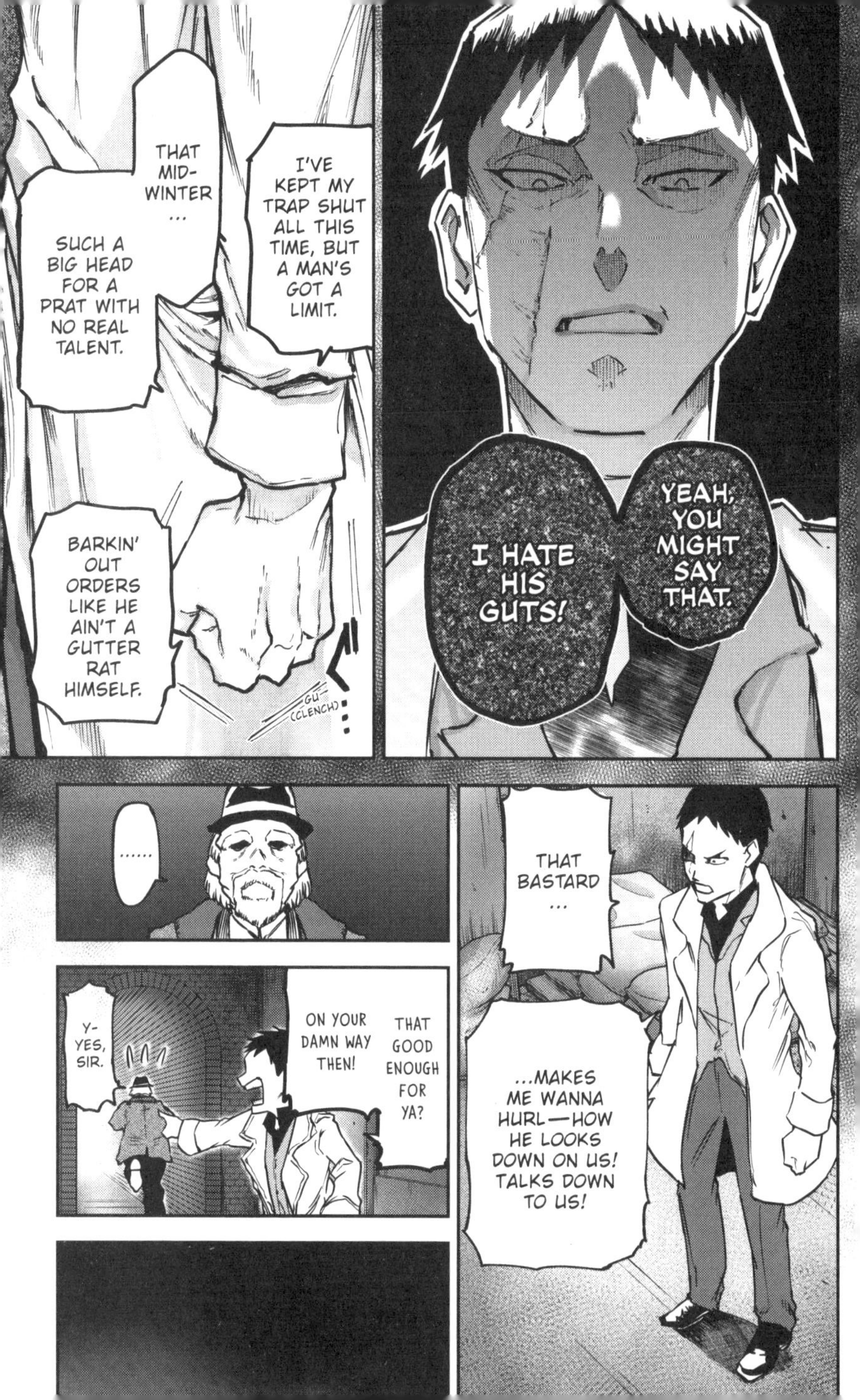
YEAH, YOU MIGHT SAY THAT.
I HATE HIS GUTS!
I'VE KEPT MY TRAP SHUT ALL THIS TIME, BUT A MAN'S GOT A LIMIT.
THAT MID-WINTER ...
SUCH A BIG HEAD FOR A PRAT WITH NO REAL TALENT.
BARKIN' OUT ORDERS LIKE HE AIN'T A GUTTER RAT HIMSELF.
GU- (CLENCH)
THAT BASTARD ...
...MAKES ME WANNA HURL—HOW HE LOOKS DOWN ON US! TALKS DOWN TO US!
......
THAT GOOD ENOUGH FOR YA?
ON YOUR DAMN WAY THEN!
Y-YES, SIR.

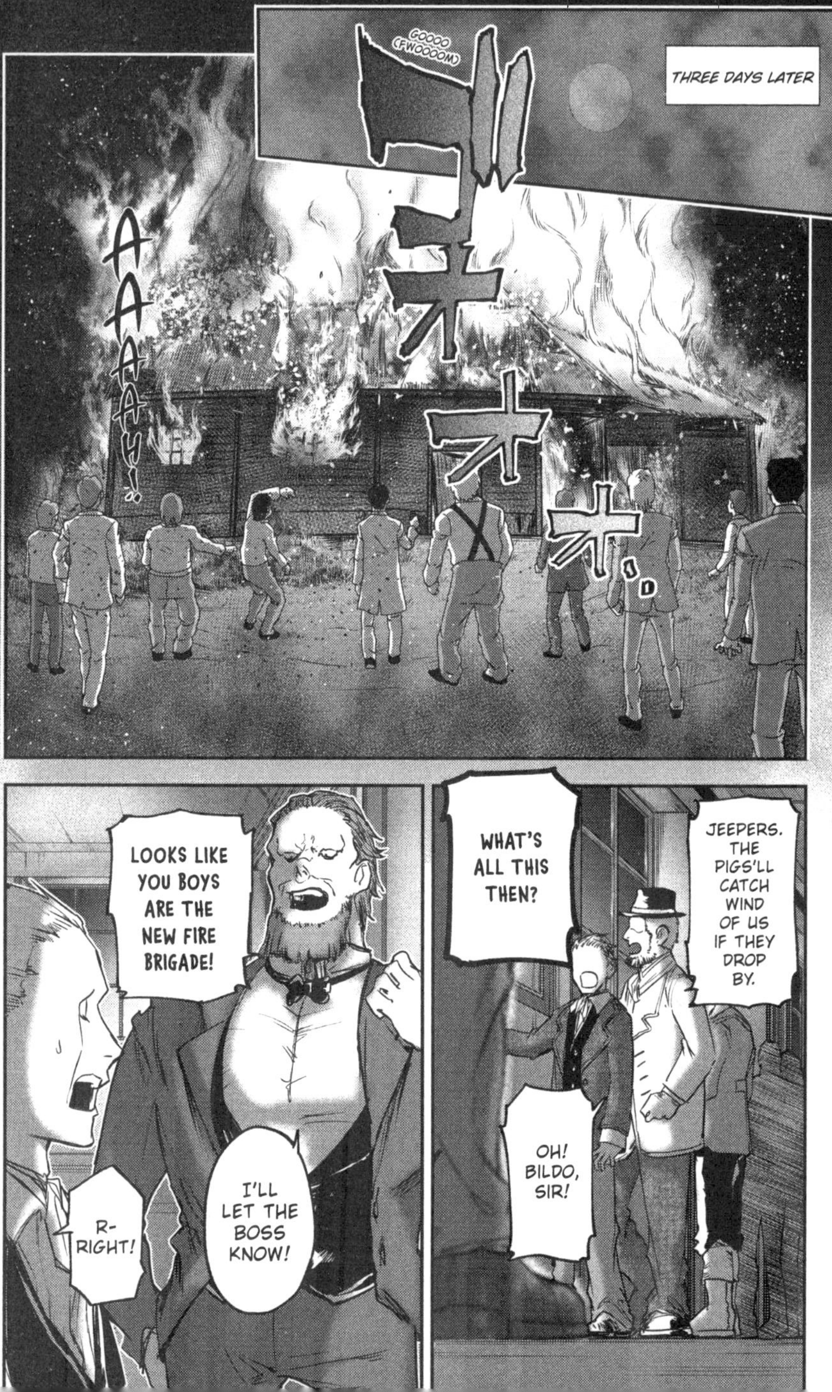
THREE DAYS LATER
GOOOO (FWOOOOM)
AAAAAH!!
JEEPERS. THE PIGS'LL CATCH WIND OF US IF THEY DROP BY.
WHAT'S ALL THIS THEN?
OH! BILDO, SIR!
LOOKS LIKE YOU BOYS ARE THE NEW FIRE BRIGADE!
I'LL LET THE BOSS KNOW!
R-RIGHT!

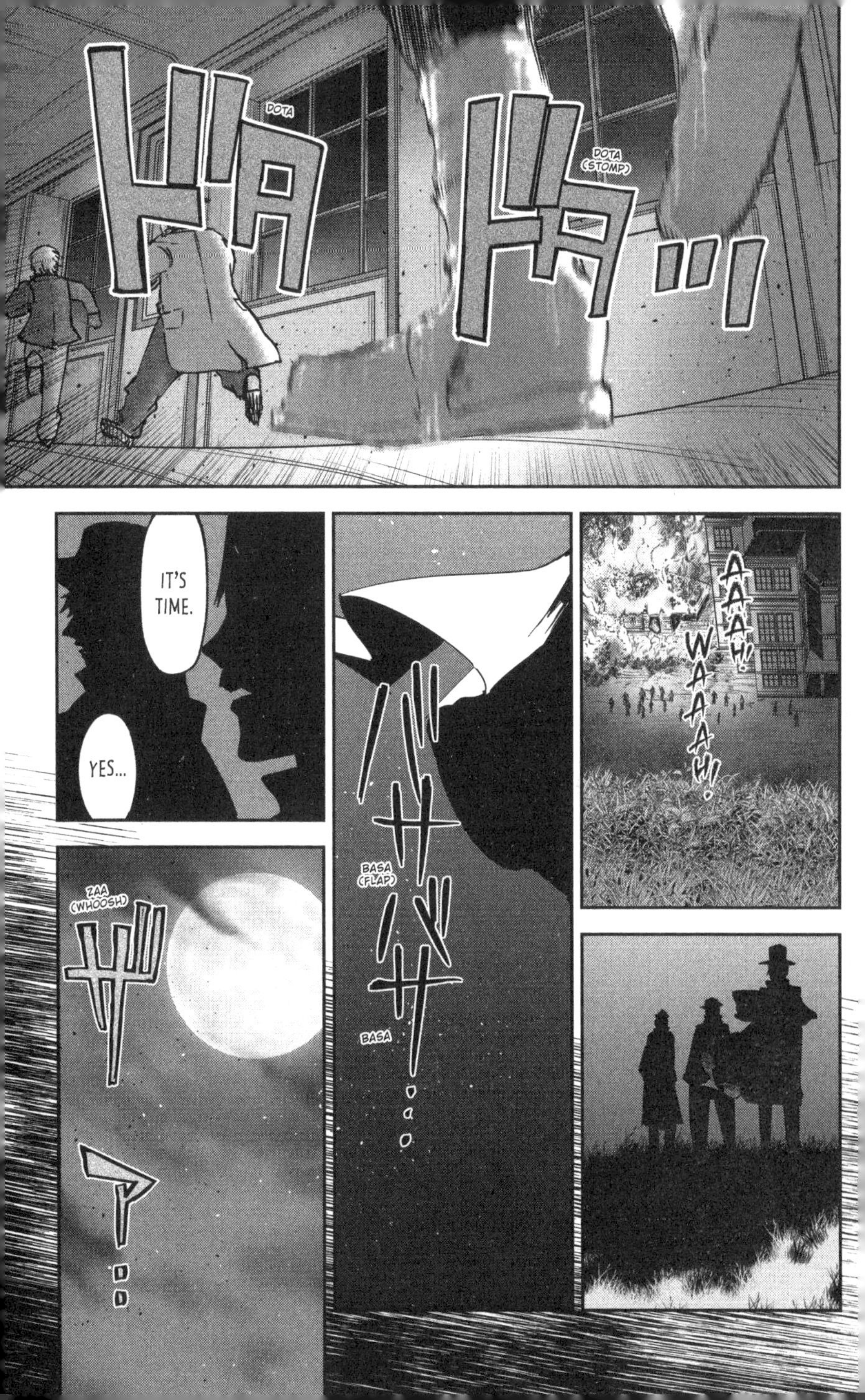
DOTA (STOMP)
DOTA
AAAAH! WAAAAH!
BASA (FLAP)
BASA
IT'S TIME.
YES...
ZAA (WHOOSH)

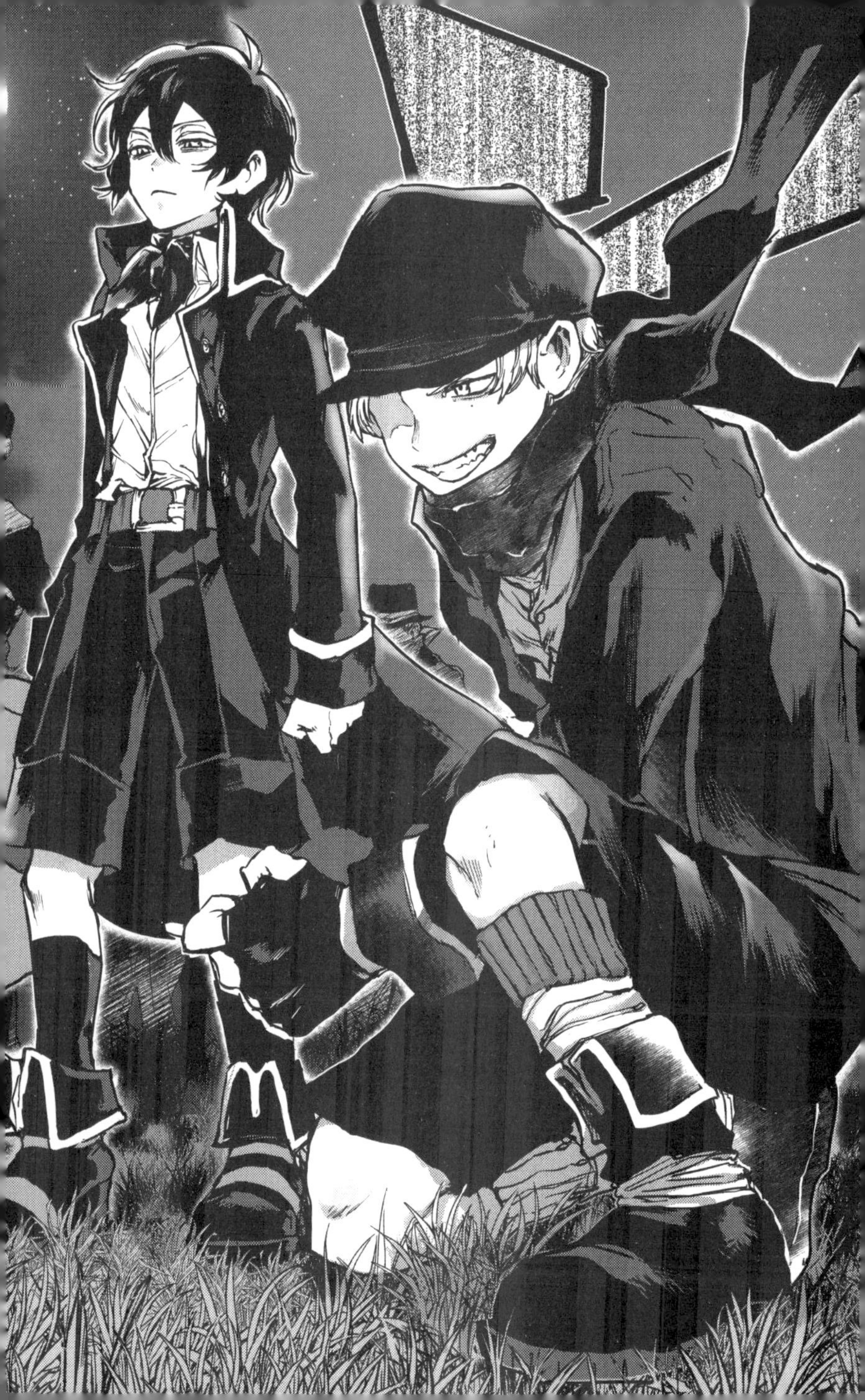

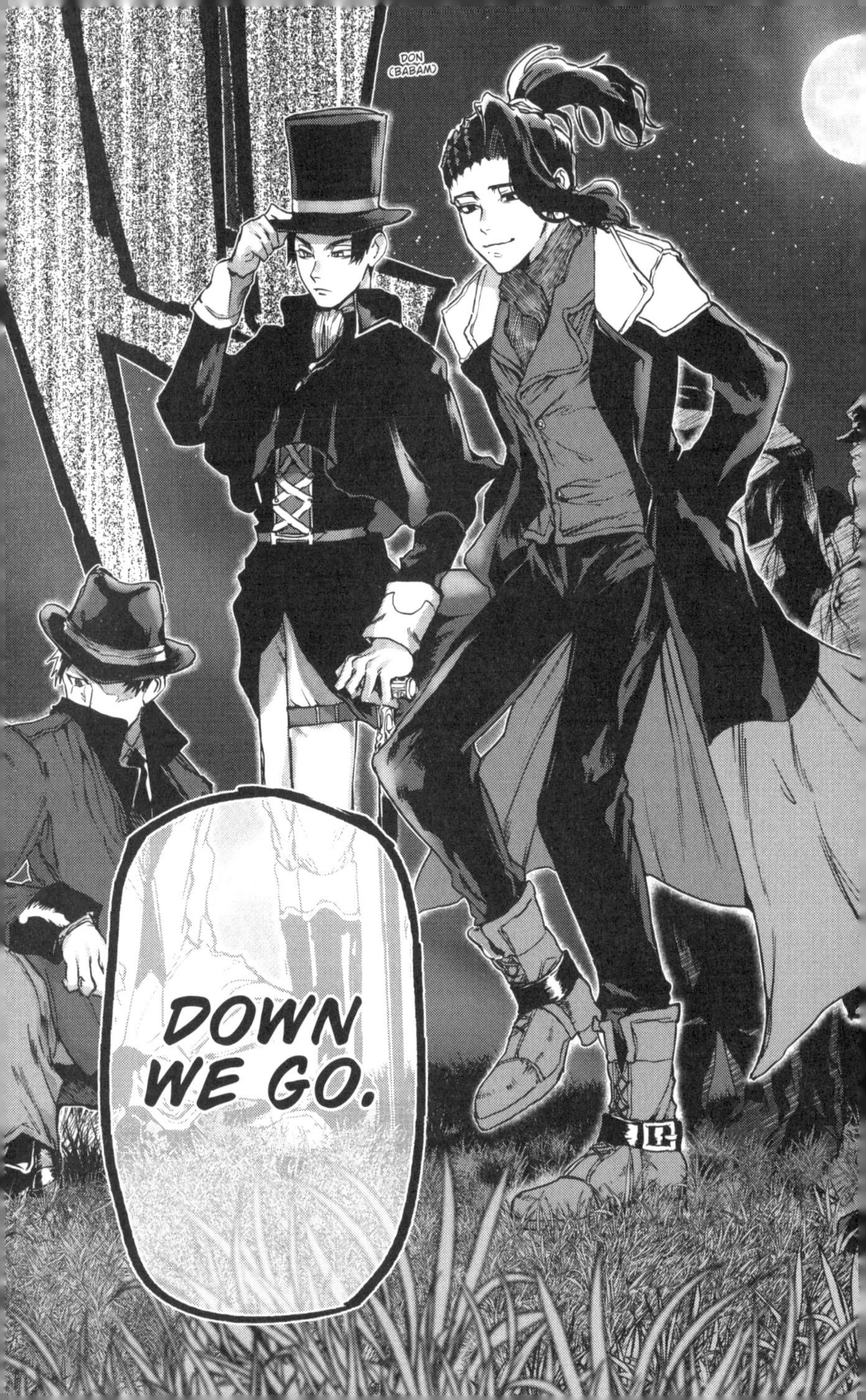
DON (BABAM)
DOWN WE GO.

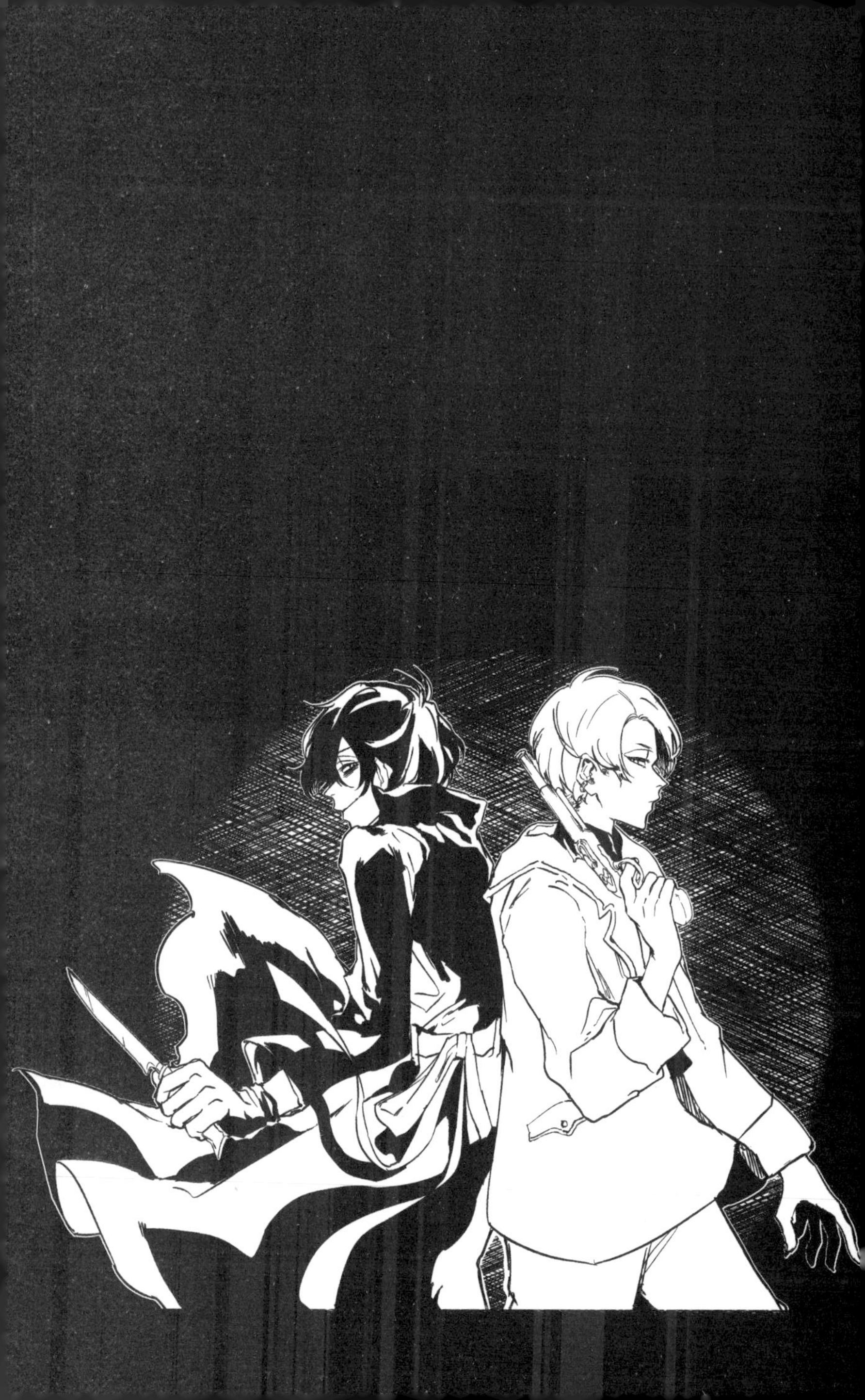

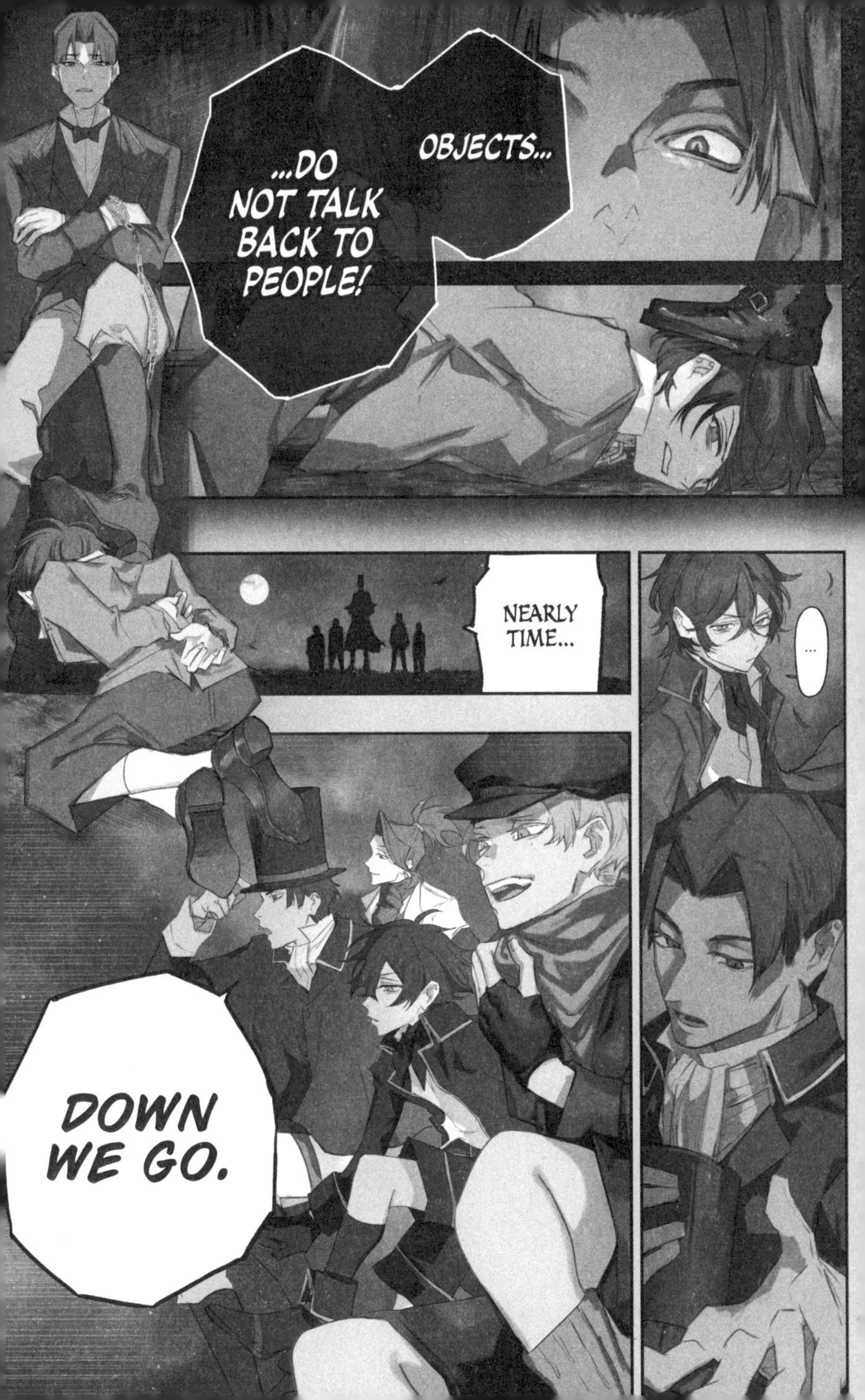
OBJECTS...
...DO NOT TALK BACK TO PEOPLE!
...
NEARLY TIME...
DOWN WE GO.

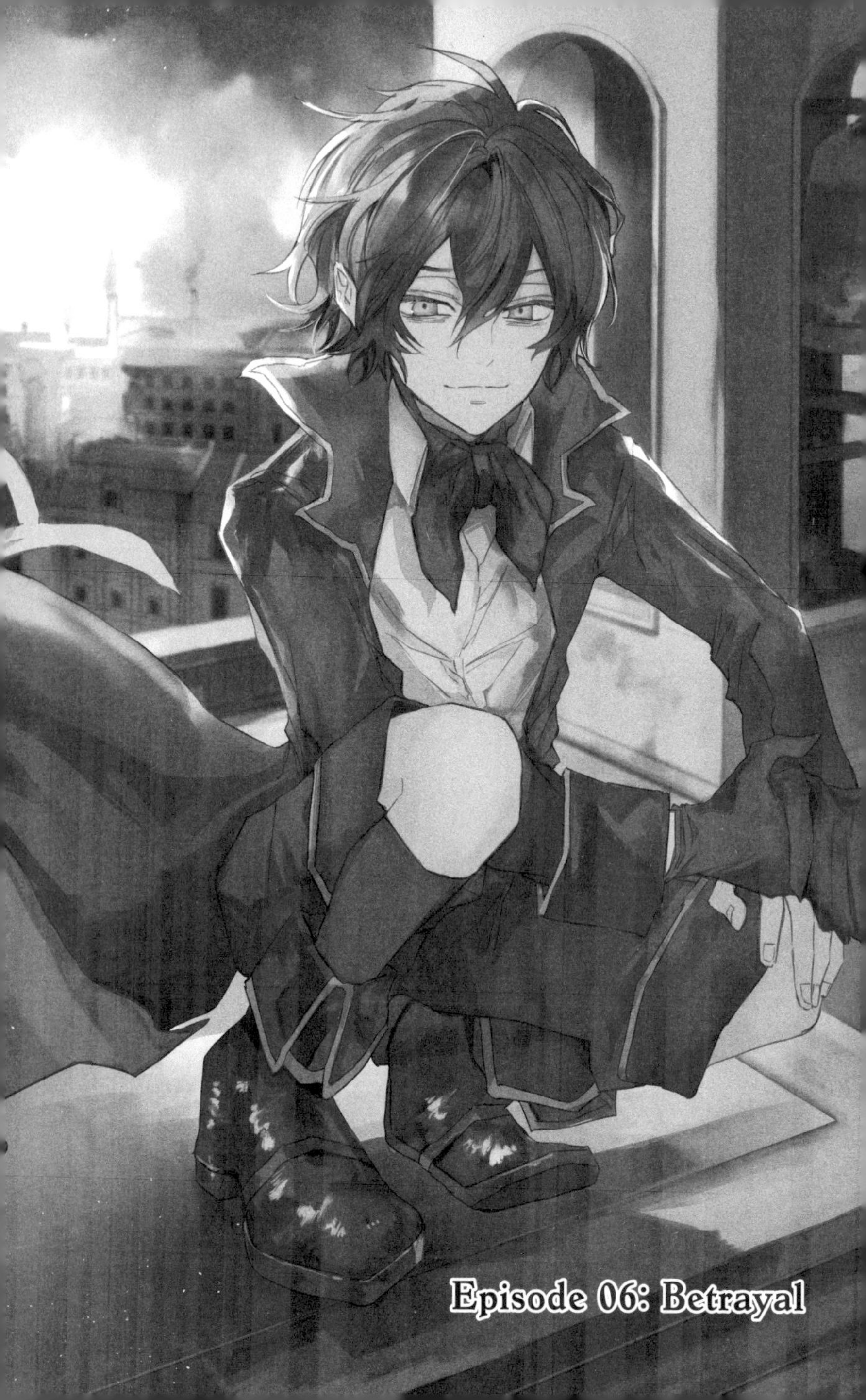

Episode 06: Betrayal

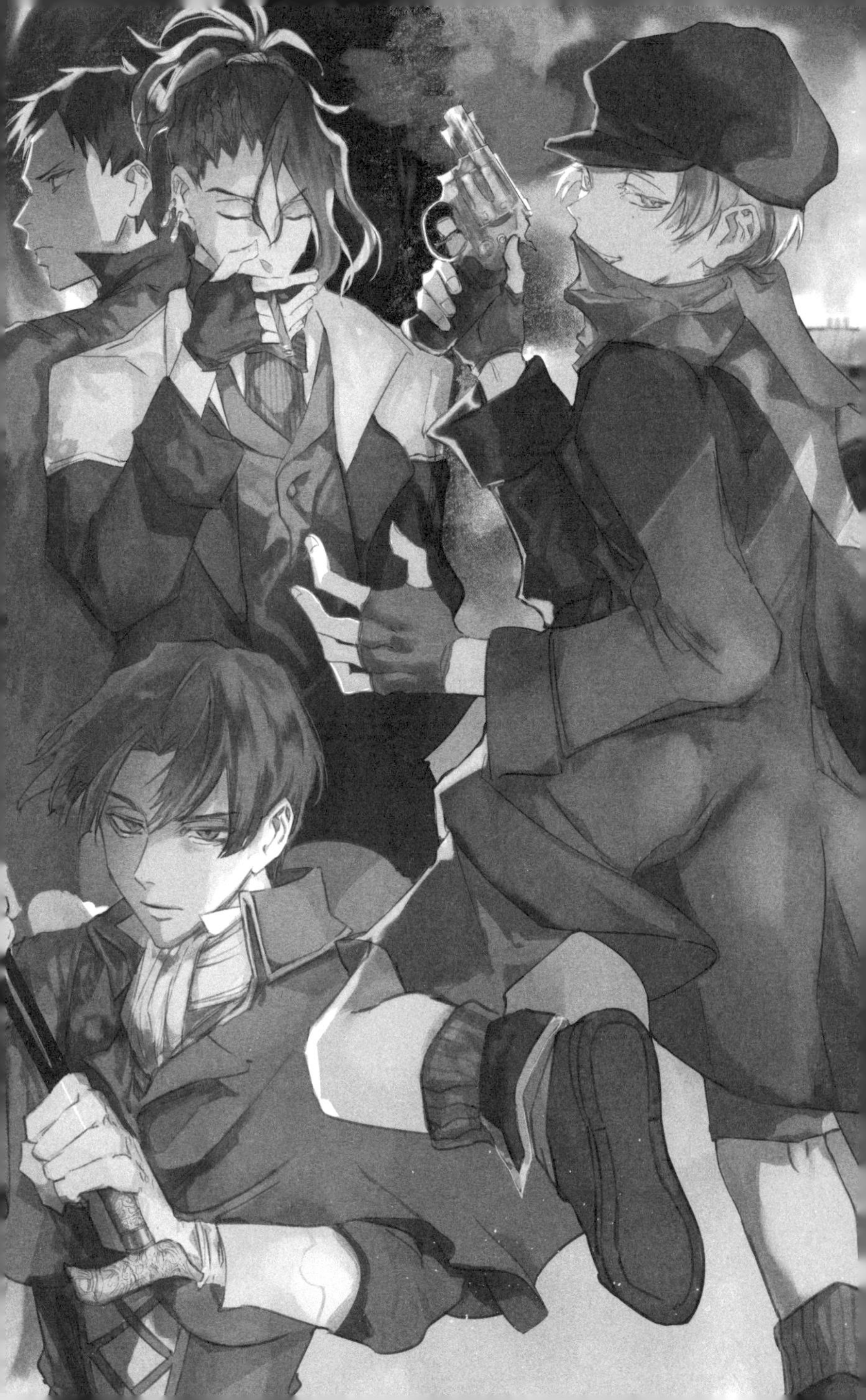

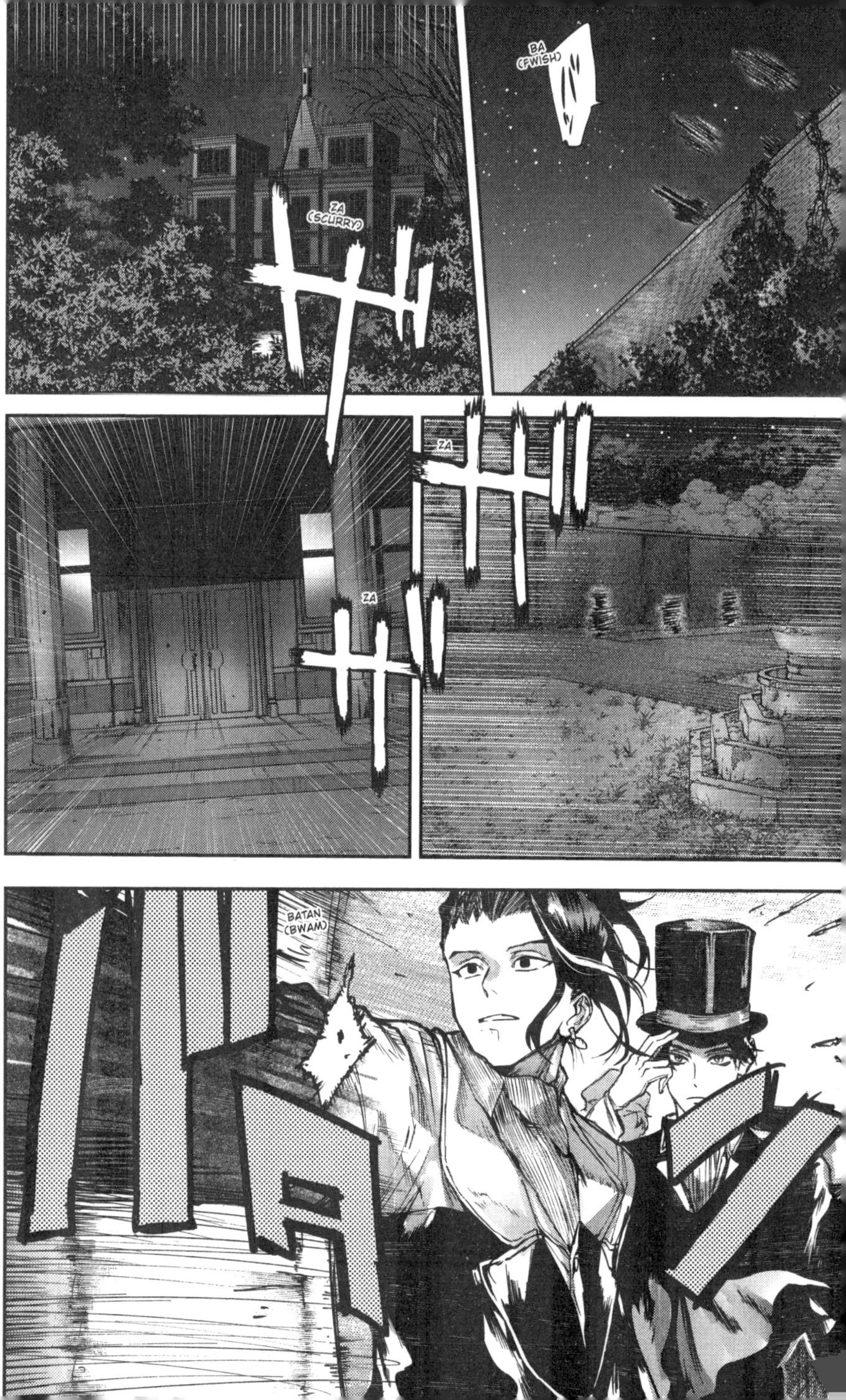
BA (FWISH)
ZA (SCURRY)
ZA
ZA
BATAN (BWAM)

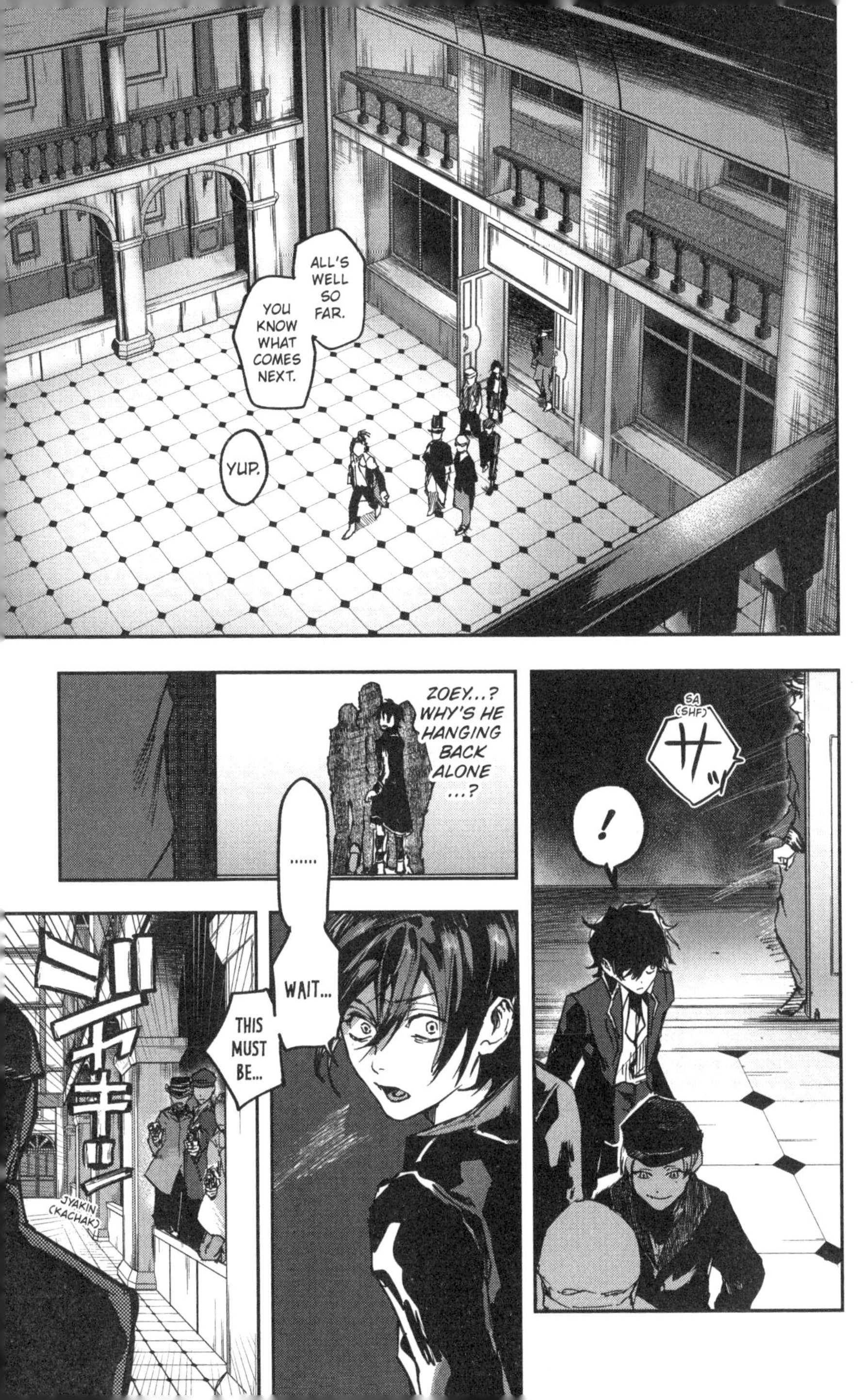
ALL'S WELL SO FAR.
YOU KNOW WHAT COMES NEXT.
YUP.
SA (SHF)
!
ZOEY...? WHY'S HE HANGING BACK ALONE ...?
......
WAIT...
THIS MUST BE...
JYAKIN (KACHAK)

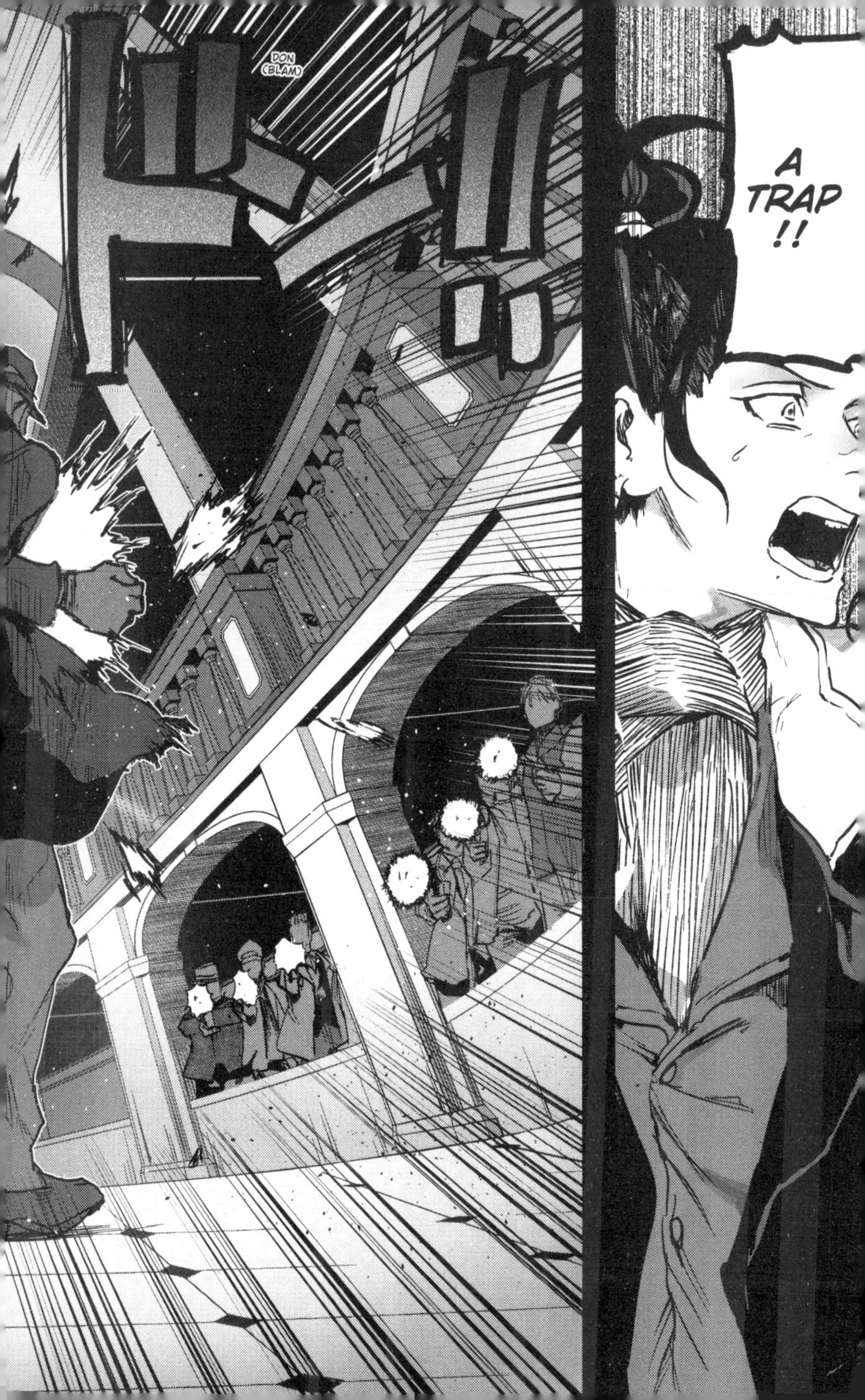
A TRAP !!
DON (BLAM)

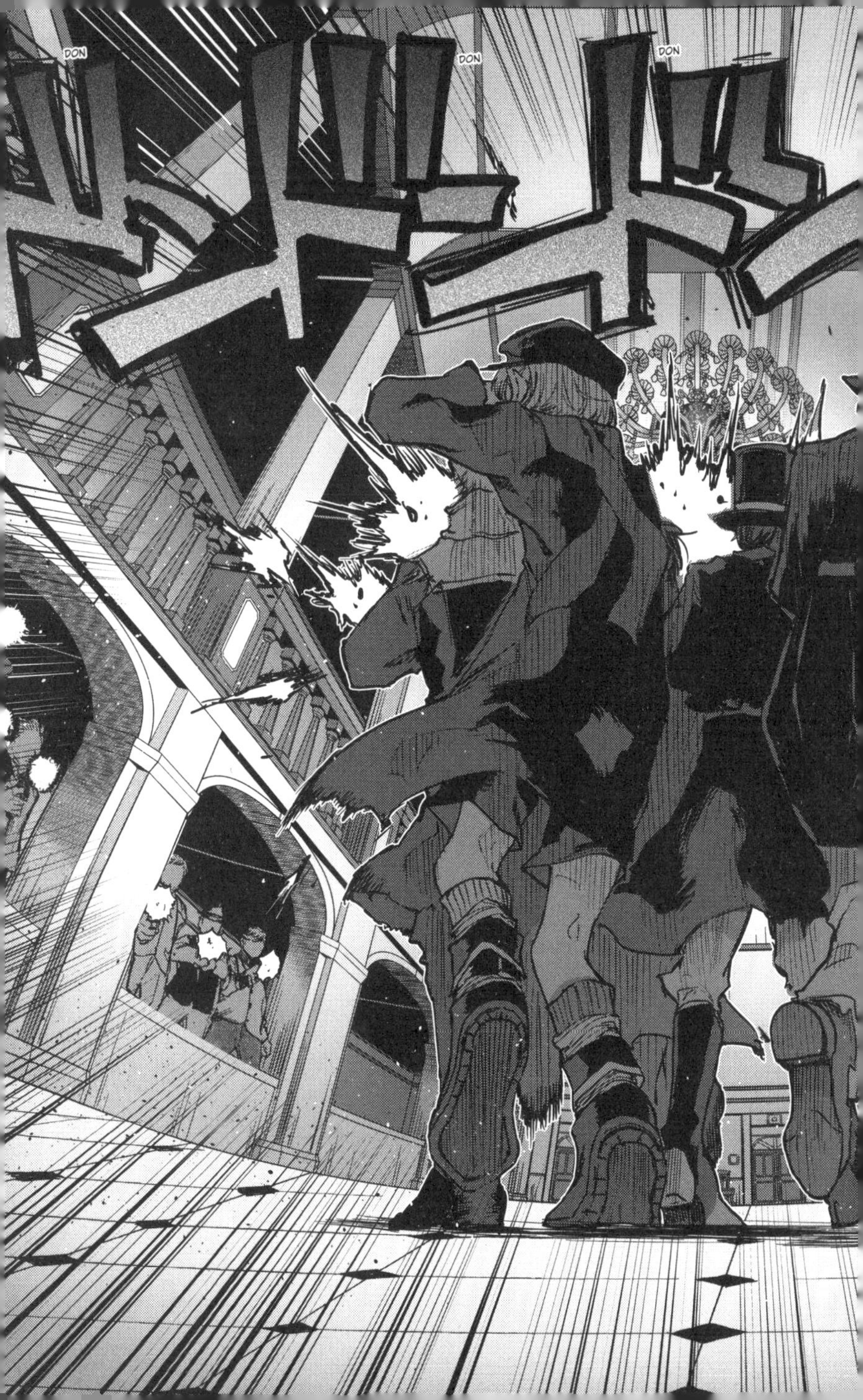
DON
DON
DON

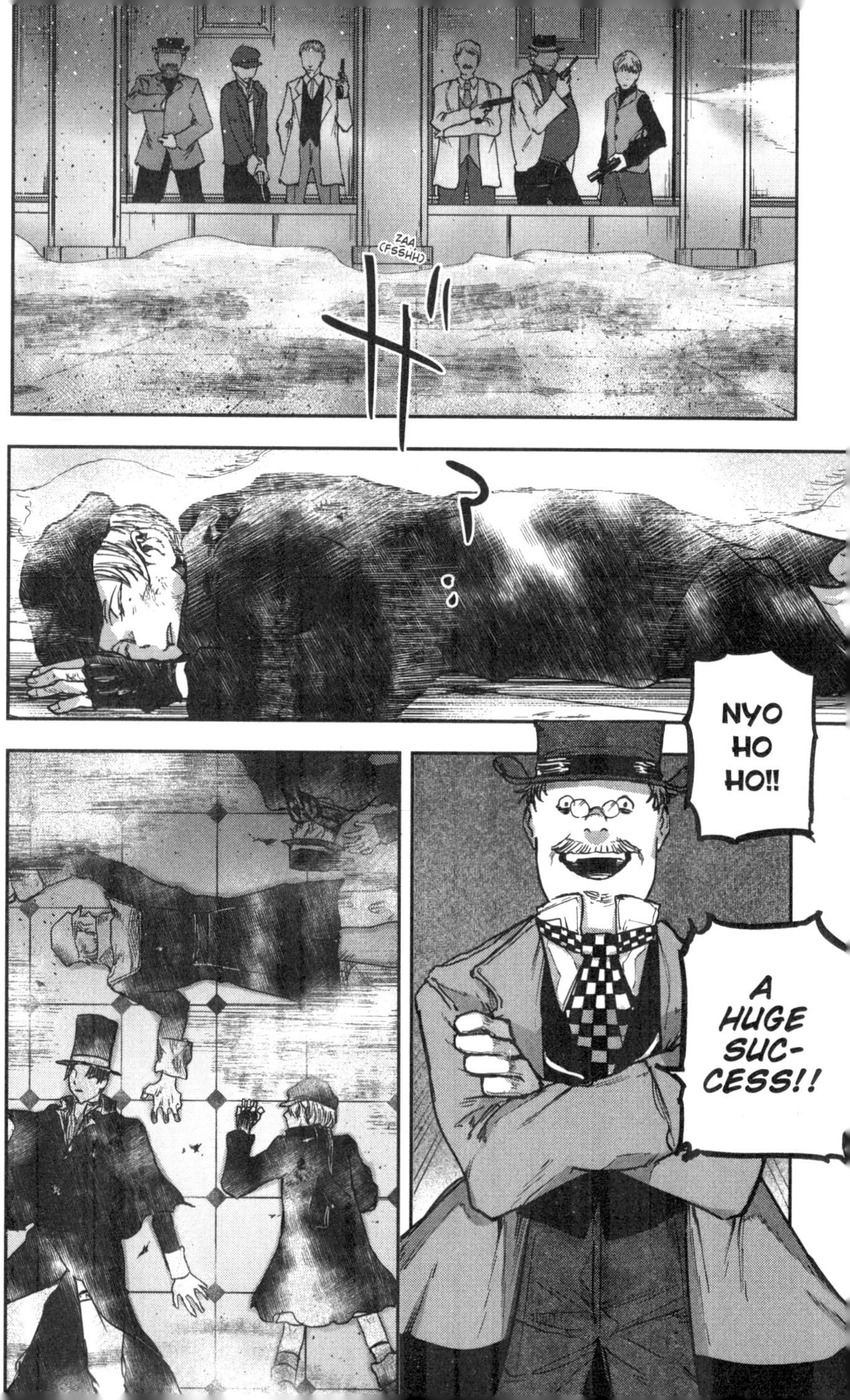
ZAA
(FSSHH)
NYO HO HO!!
A HUGE SUC-CESS!!

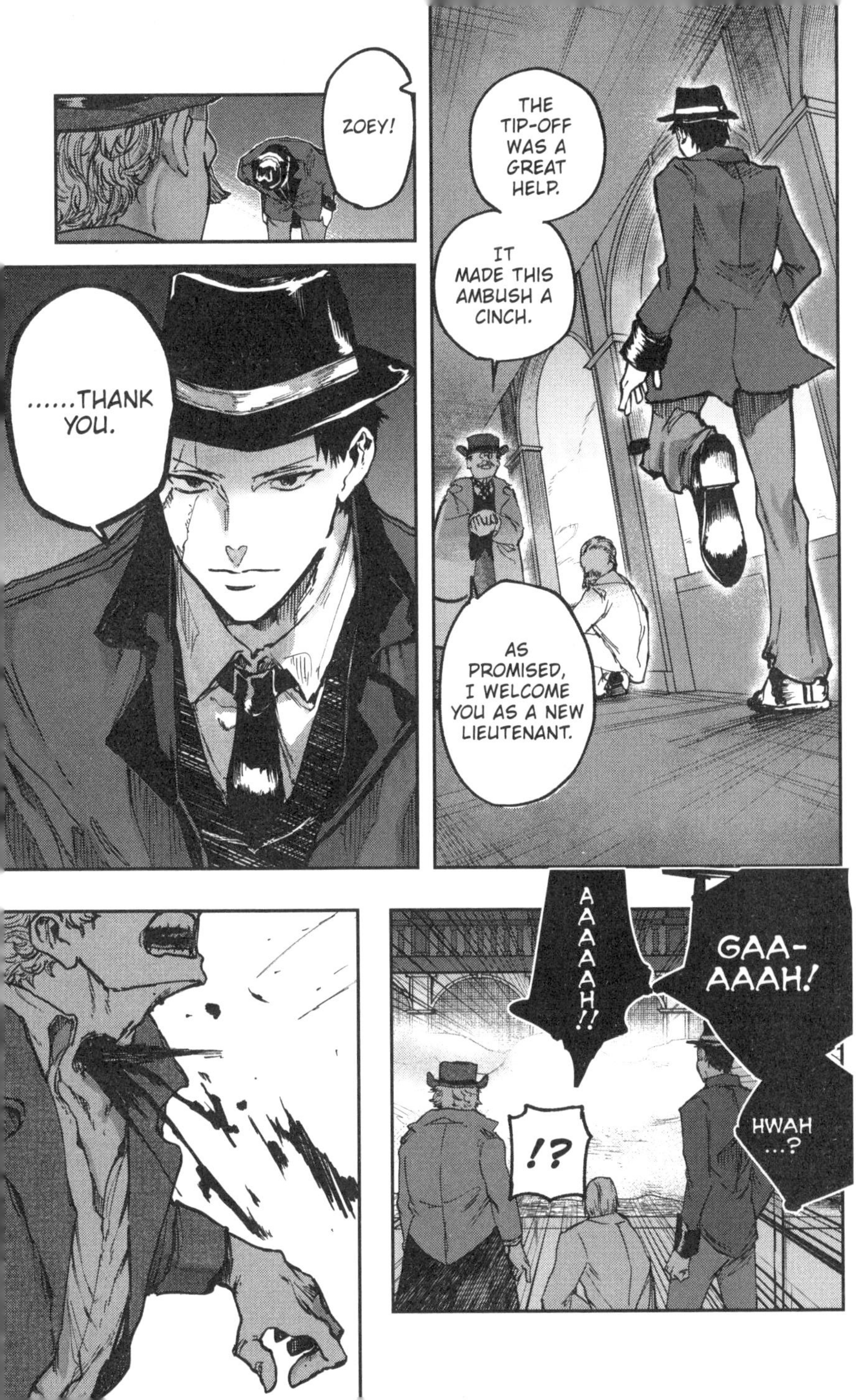
THE TIP-OFF WAS A GREAT HELP.
IT MADE THIS AMBUSH A CINCH.
AS PROMISED, I WELCOME YOU AS A NEW LIEUTENANT.
ZOEY!
......THANK YOU.
GAA-AAAH!
AAAAAH!!
HWAH ...?
!?

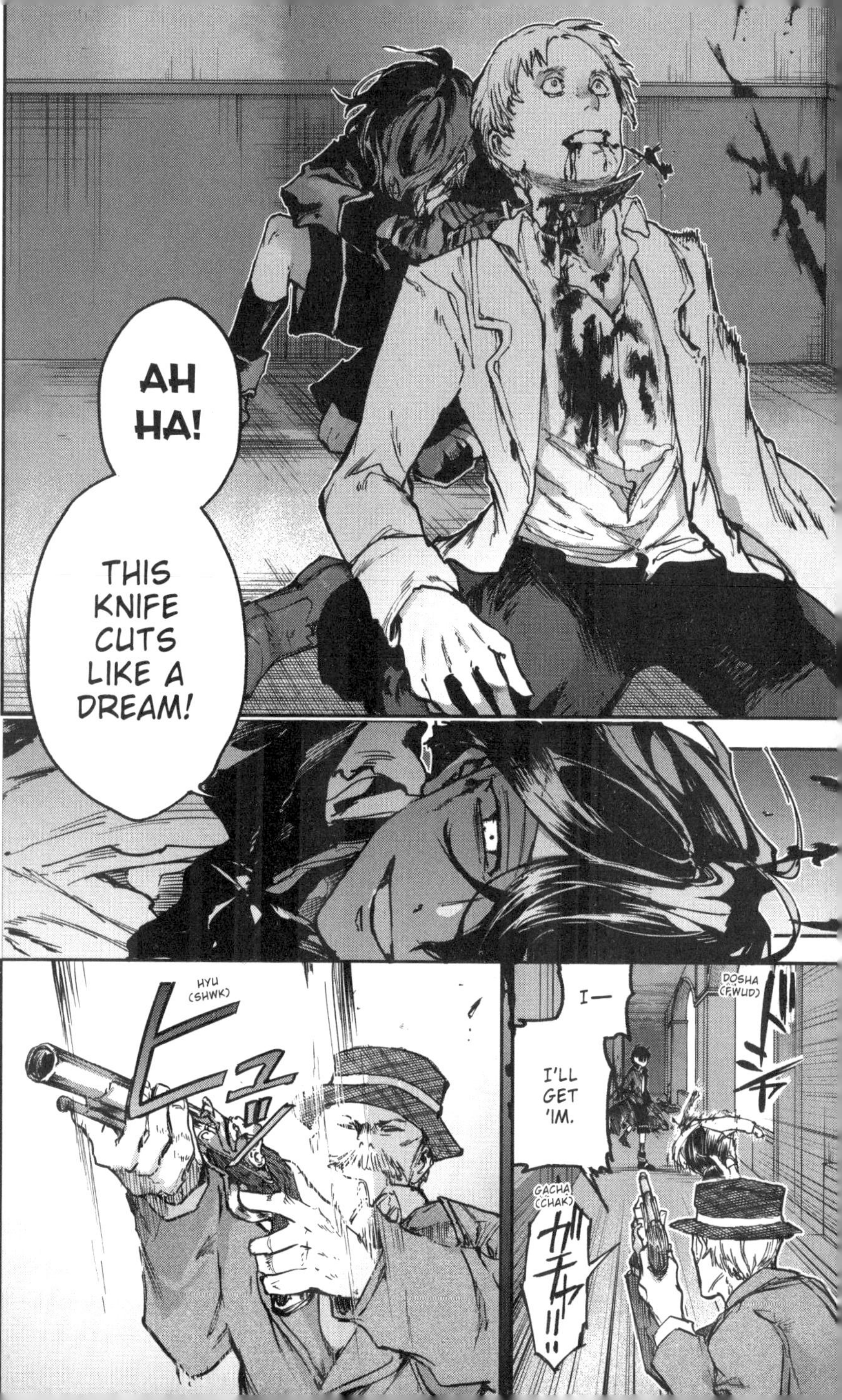
AH HA! THIS KNIFE CUTS LIKE A DREAM!
DOSHA (FWUD)
I— I'LL GET 'IM.
GACHA (CHAK)
HYU (SHWK)

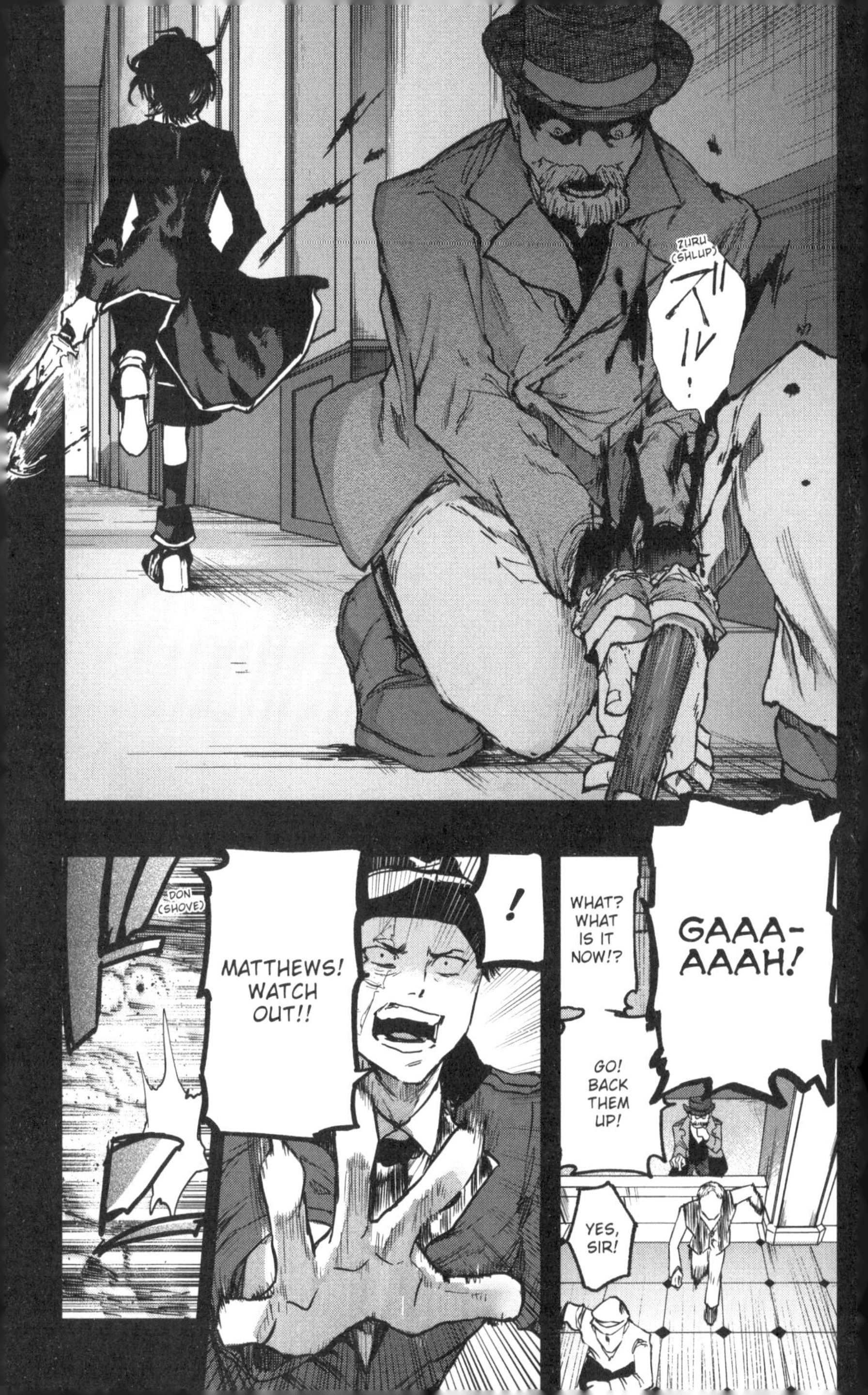
ZURU (SHLUP)
GAAAA-AAAH!
WHAT? WHAT IS IT NOW!?
GO! BACK THEM UP!
YES, SIR!
!
MATTHEWS! WATCH OUT!!
DON (SHOVE)

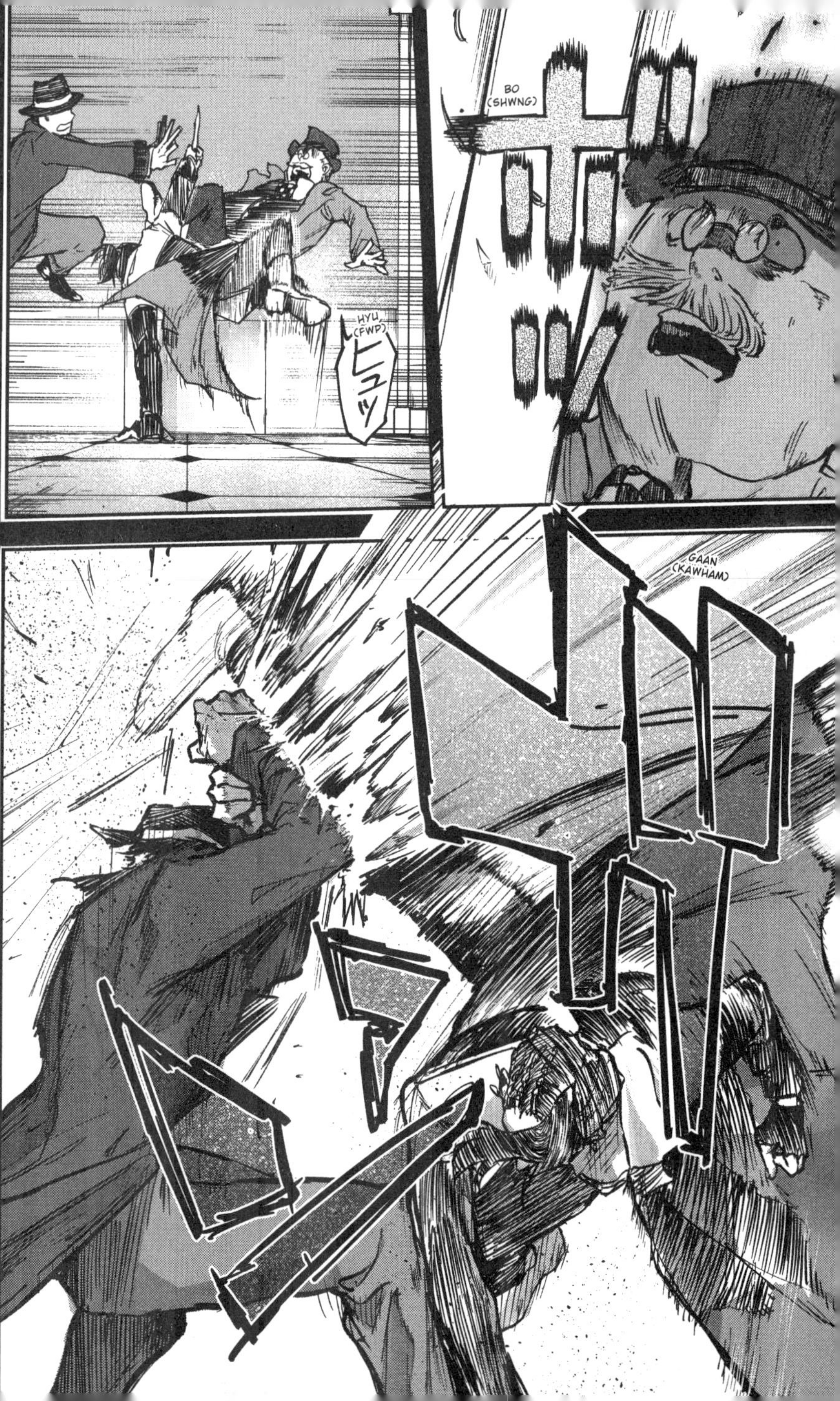
BO
(SHWNG)
HYU
(FWP)
ヒュッ
GAAN
(KAWHAM)

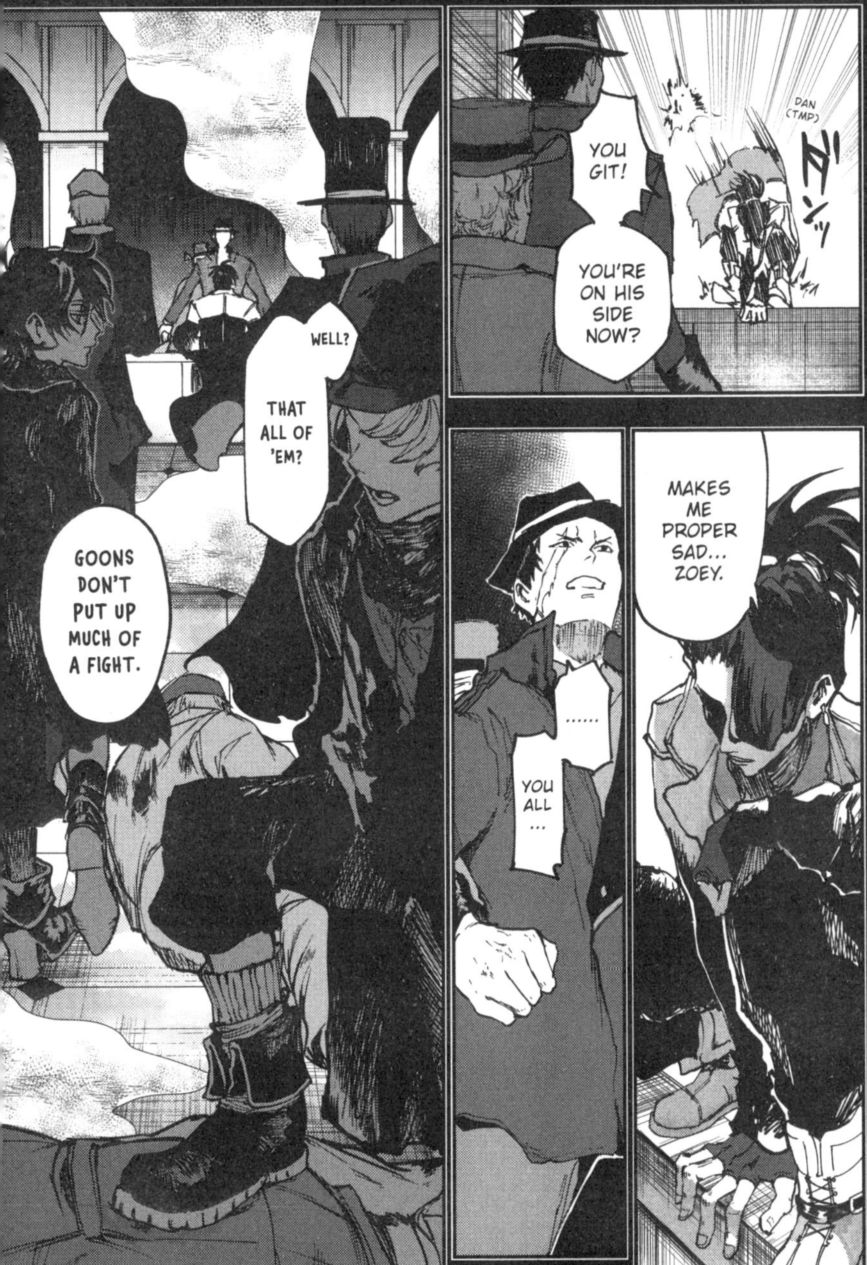
DAN (TMP)
ダンッ
YOU GIT!
YOU'RE ON HIS SIDE NOW?
MAKES ME PROPER SAD... ZOEY.
......
YOU ALL ...
WELL?
THAT ALL OF 'EM?
GOONS DON'T PUT UP MUCH OF A FIGHT.

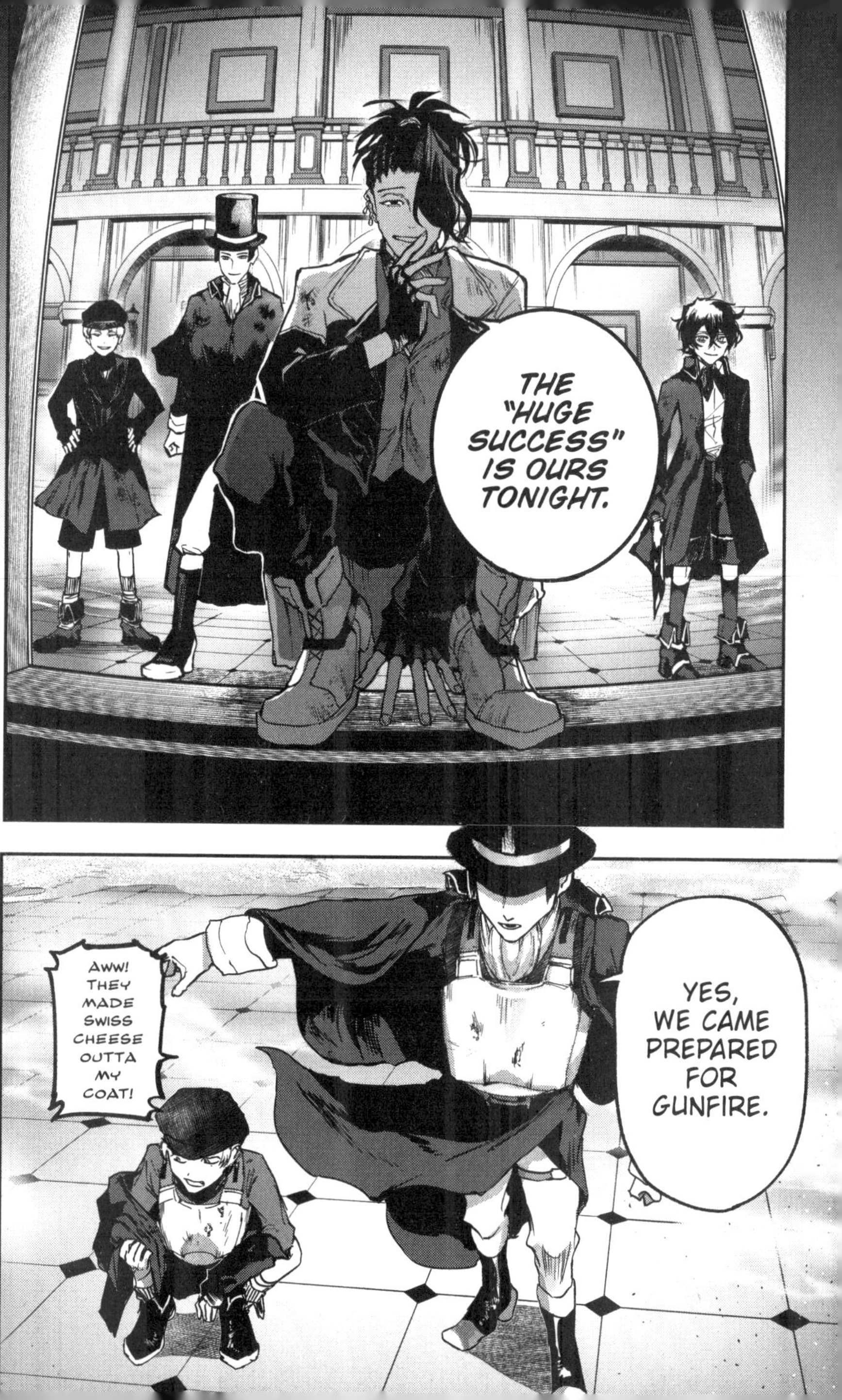
THE "HUGE SUCCESS" IS OURS TONIGHT.
YES, WE CAME PREPARED FOR GUNFIRE.
AWW! THEY MADE SWISS CHEESE OUTTA MY COAT!

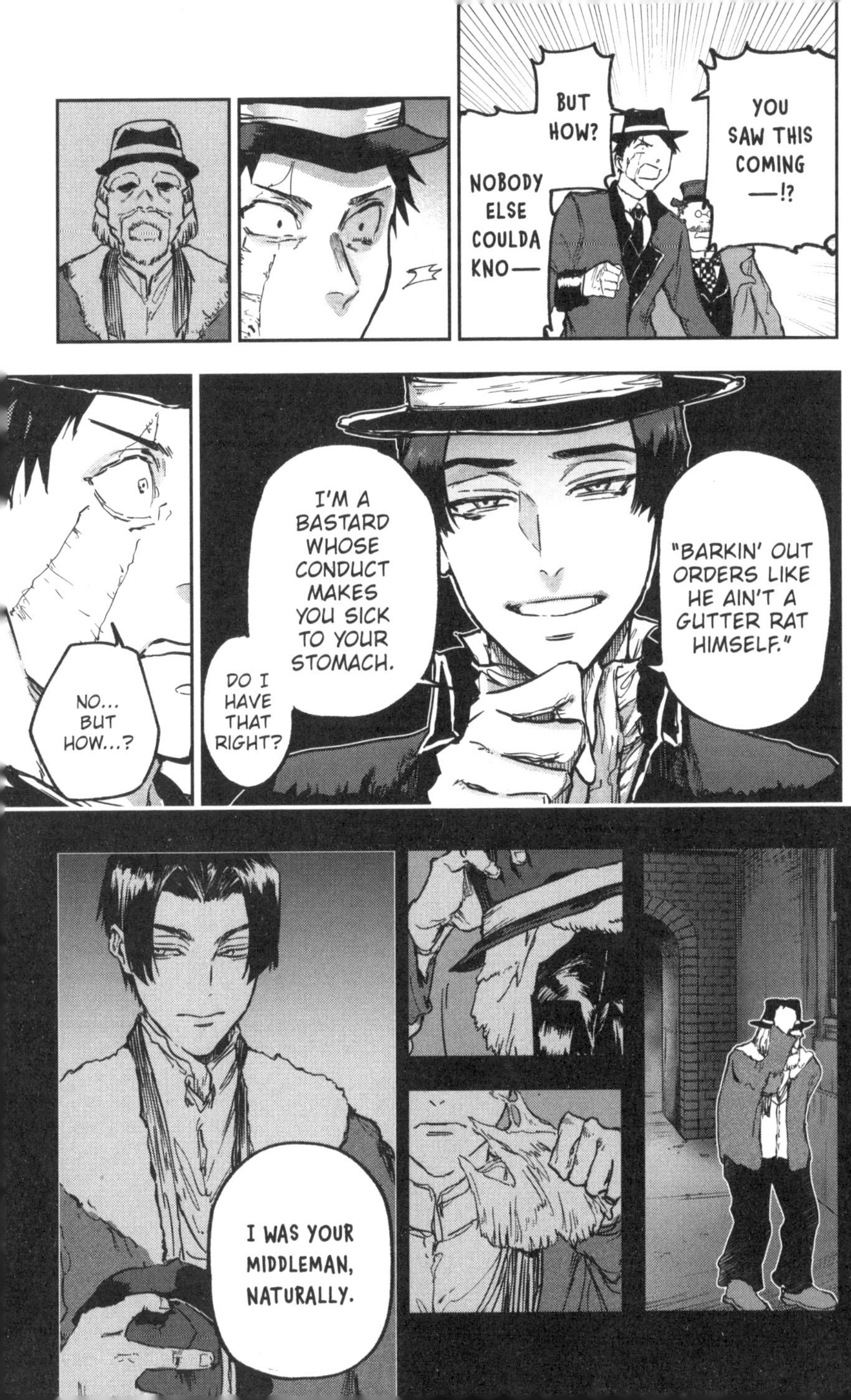
YOU SAW THIS COMING —!?
BUT HOW?
NOBODY ELSE COULDA KNO—
"BARKIN' OUT ORDERS LIKE HE AIN'T A GUTTER RAT HIMSELF."
I'M A BASTARD WHOSE CONDUCT MAKES YOU SICK TO YOUR STOMACH.
DO I HAVE THAT RIGHT?
NO... BUT HOW...?
I WAS YOUR MIDDLEMAN, NATURALLY.

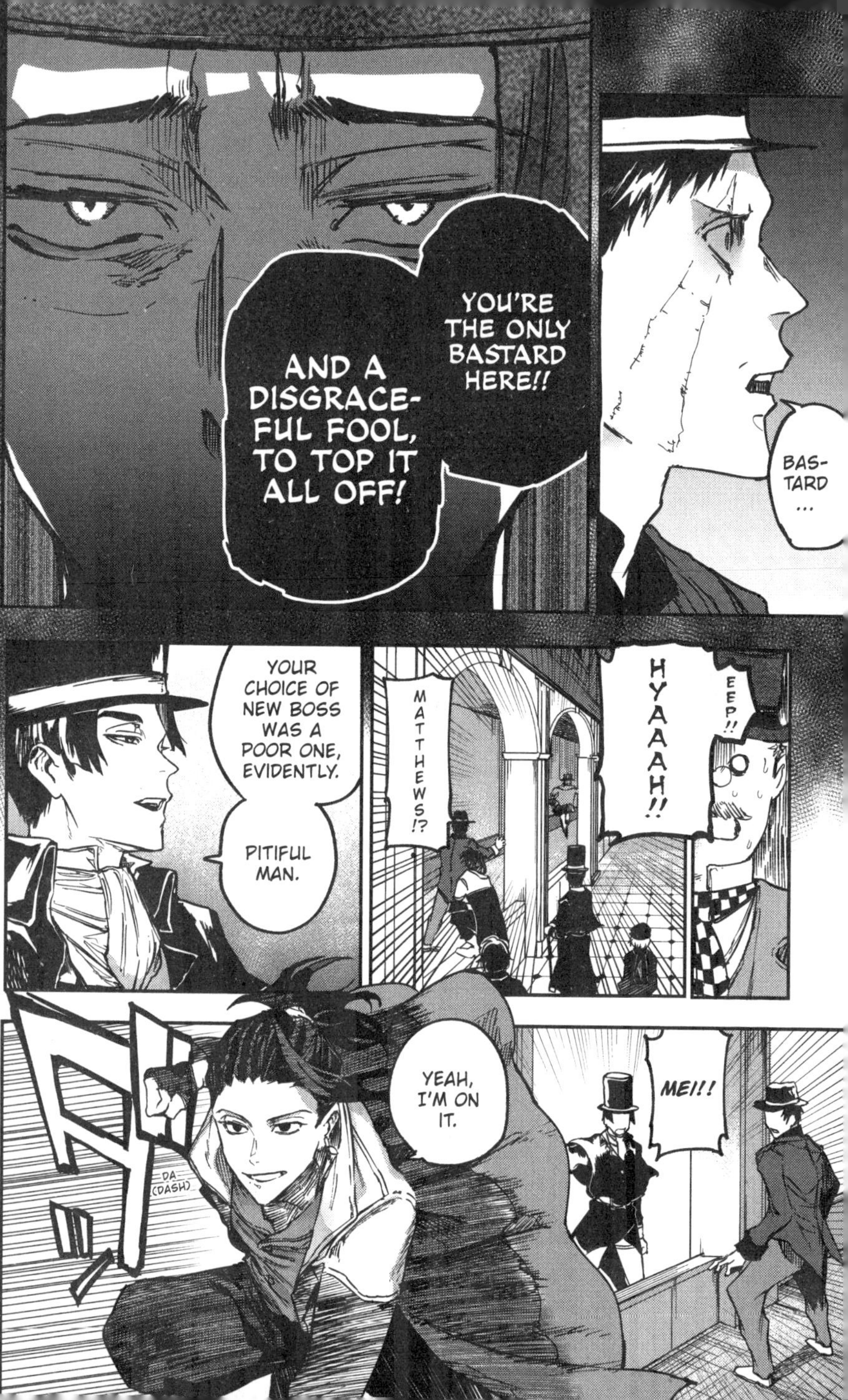
BAS-TARD...
YOU'RE THE ONLY BASTARD HERE!!
AND A DISGRACE-FUL FOOL, TO TOP IT ALL OFF!
EEP!!
HYAAAH!!
MATTHEWS!?
YOUR CHOICE OF NEW BOSS WAS A POOR ONE, EVIDENTLY.
PITIFUL MAN.
MEI!!
YEAH, I'M ON IT.
DA (DASH)

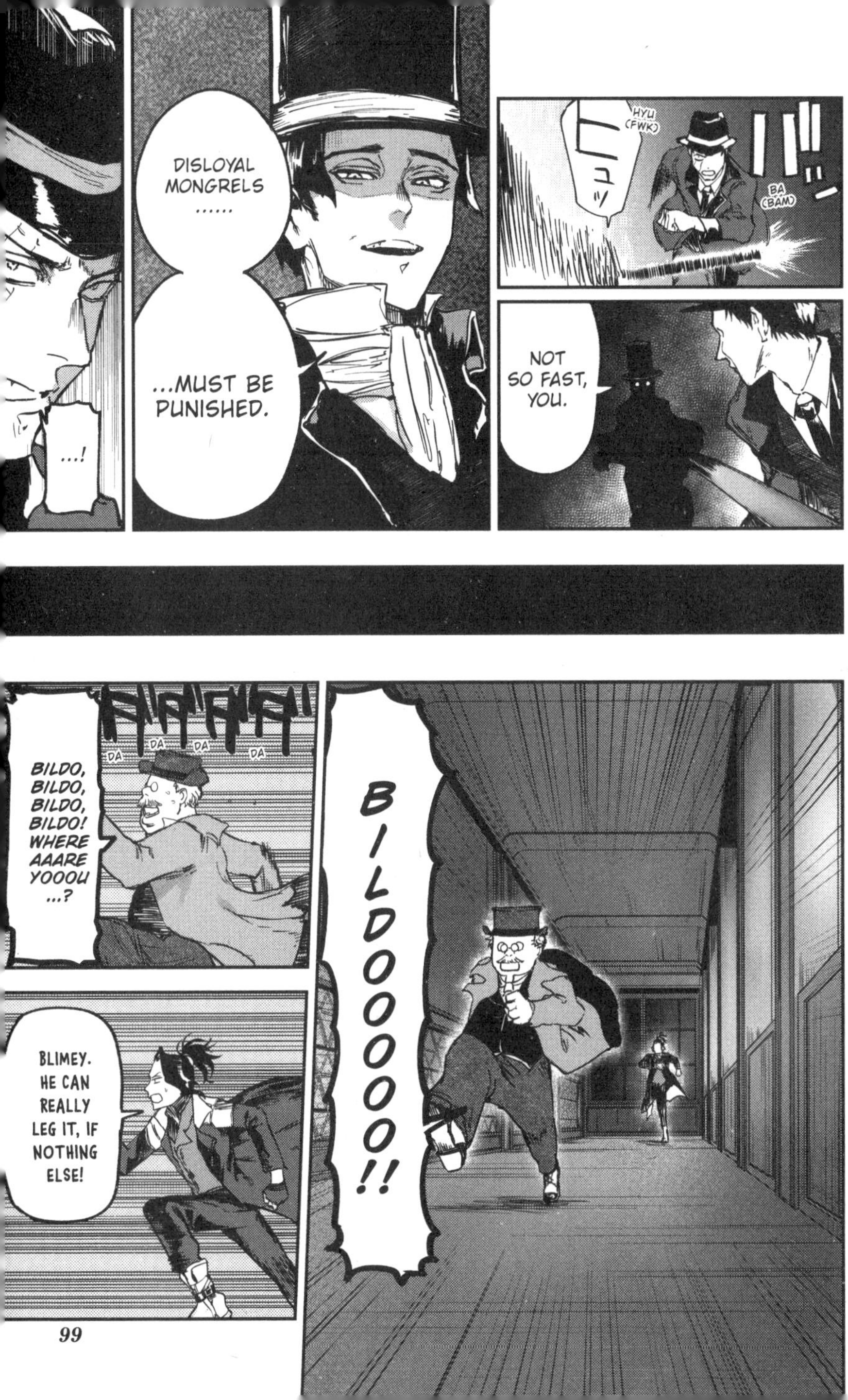
BA (BAM)
HYU (FWK)
ヒュッ
NOT SO FAST, YOU.
DISLOYAL MONGRELS ......
...MUST BE PUNISHED.
...!
BILDOOOOOOOOO!!
DA DA DA DA
BILDO, BILDO, BILDO, BILDO! WHERE AAARE YOOOU ...?
BLIMEY. HE CAN REALLY LEG IT, IF NOTHING ELSE!

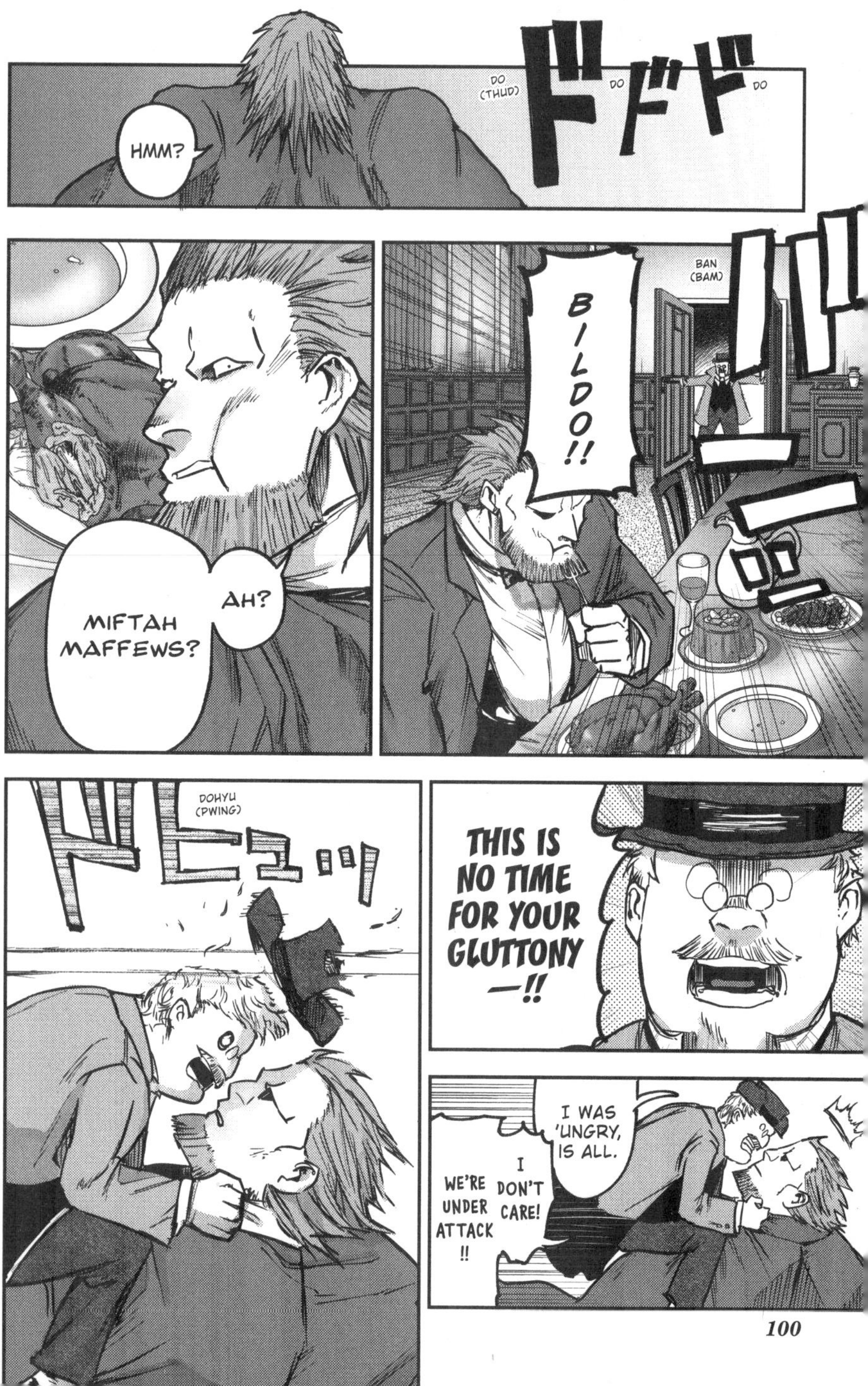
DO (THUD)
DO
DO
HMM?
BAN (BAM)
BILDOO!!
AH?
MIFTAH MAFFEWS?
THIS IS NO TIME FOR YOUR GLUTTONY—!!
I WAS 'UNGRY, IS ALL.
I DON'T CARE!
WE'RE UNDER ATTACK!!
DOHYU (PWING)

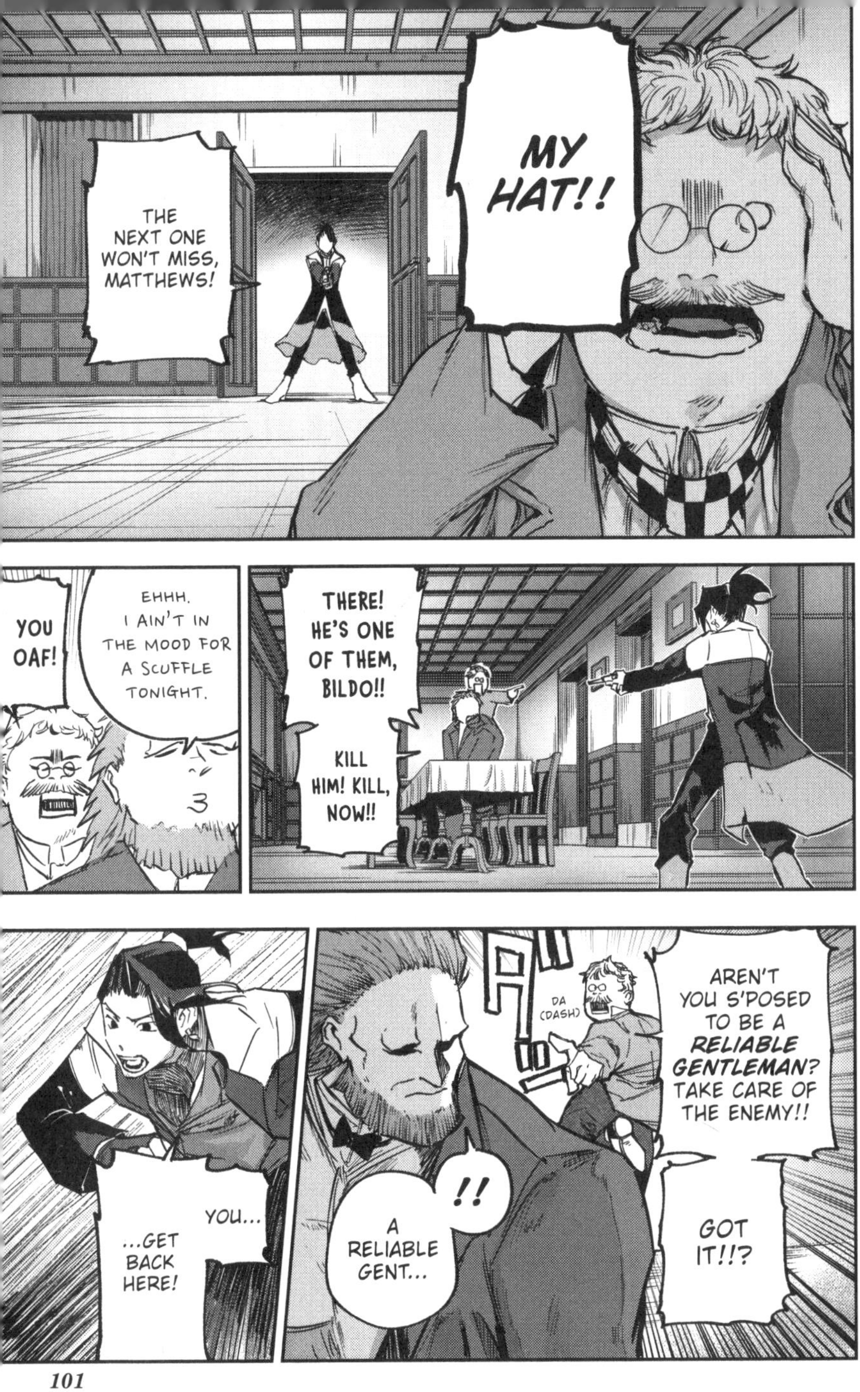
MY HAT!!
THE NEXT ONE WON'T MISS, MATTHEWS!
THERE! HE'S ONE OF THEM, BILDO!!
KILL HIM! KILL, NOW!!
EHHH. I AIN'T IN THE MOOD FOR A SCUFFLE TONIGHT.
YOU OAF!
AREN'T YOU S'POSED TO BE A RELIABLE GENTLEMAN? TAKE CARE OF THE ENEMY!!
DA (DASH)
GOT IT!!?
!!
A RELIABLE GENT...
YOU...
...GET BACK HERE!

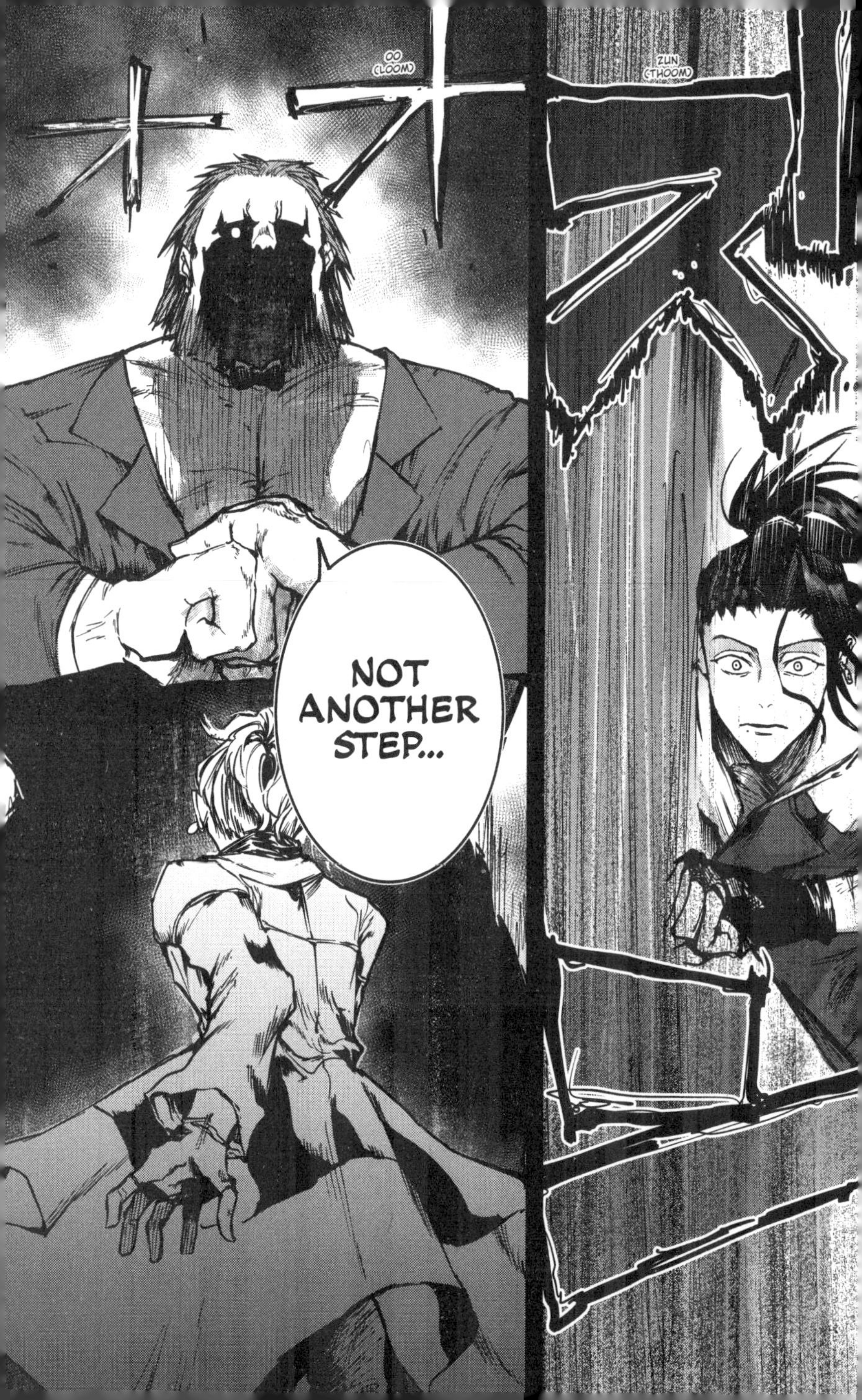
ZUN (THOOM)
OO (LOOM)
NOT ANOTHER STEP...

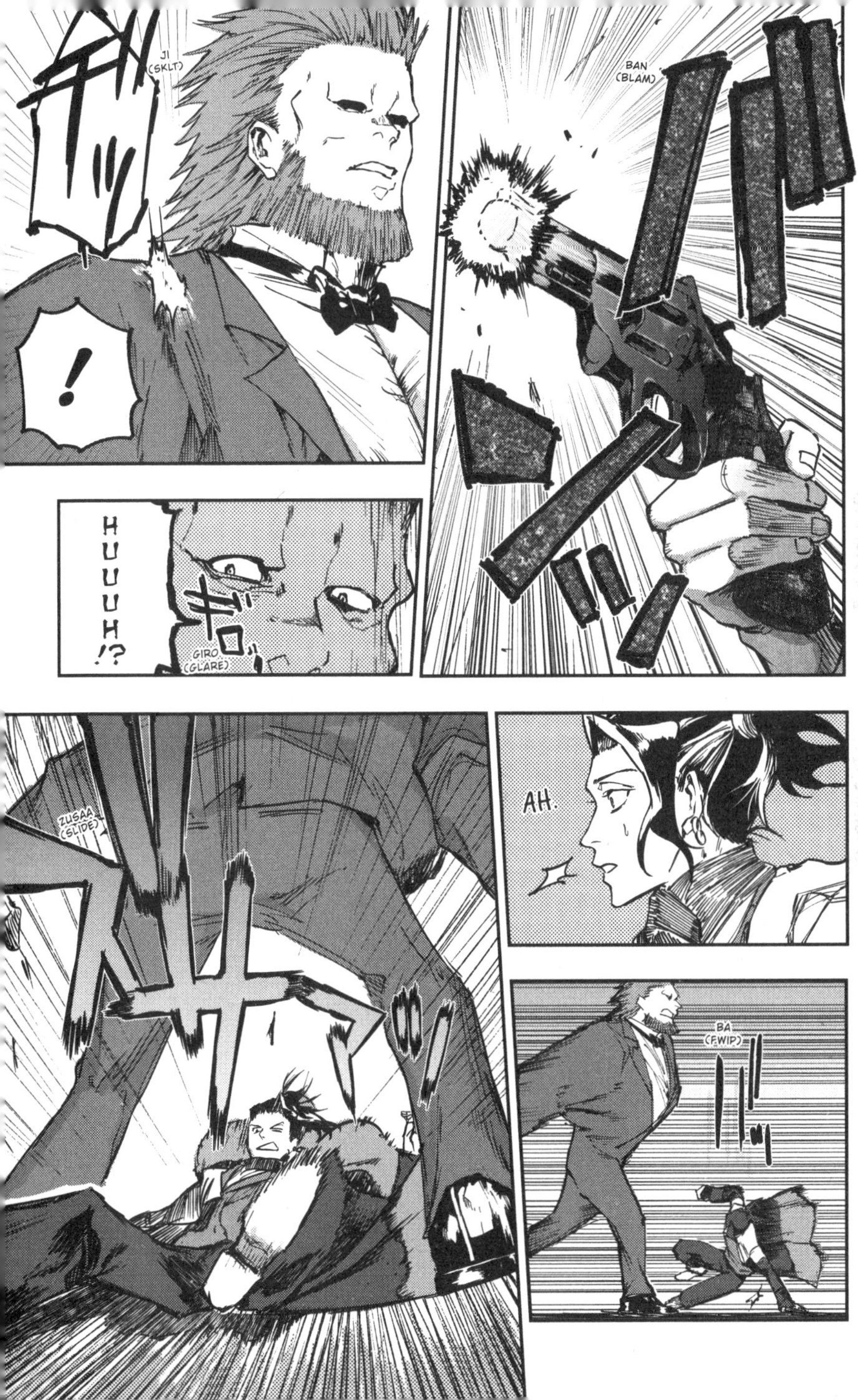
BAN
(BLAM)
JI
(SKLT)
!
HUUUUH!?
GIRO
(GLARE)
AH.
BA
(FWIP)
ZUSAA
(SLIDE)

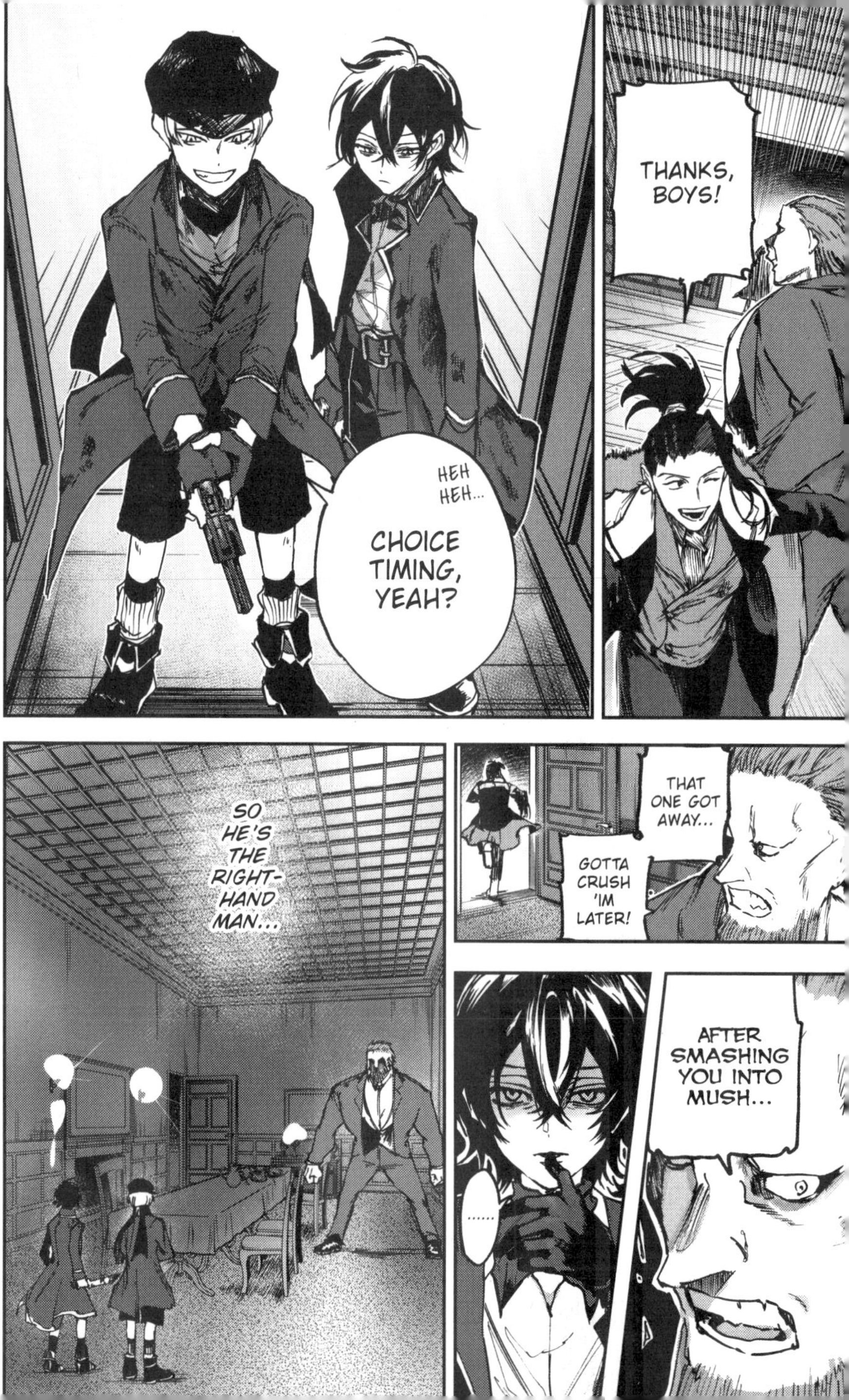
THANKS, BOYS!
HEH HEH...
CHOICE TIMING, YEAH?
THAT ONE GOT AWAY...
GOTTA CRUSH 'IM LATER!
AFTER SMASHING YOU INTO MUSH...
......
SO HE'S THE RIGHT-HAND MAN...

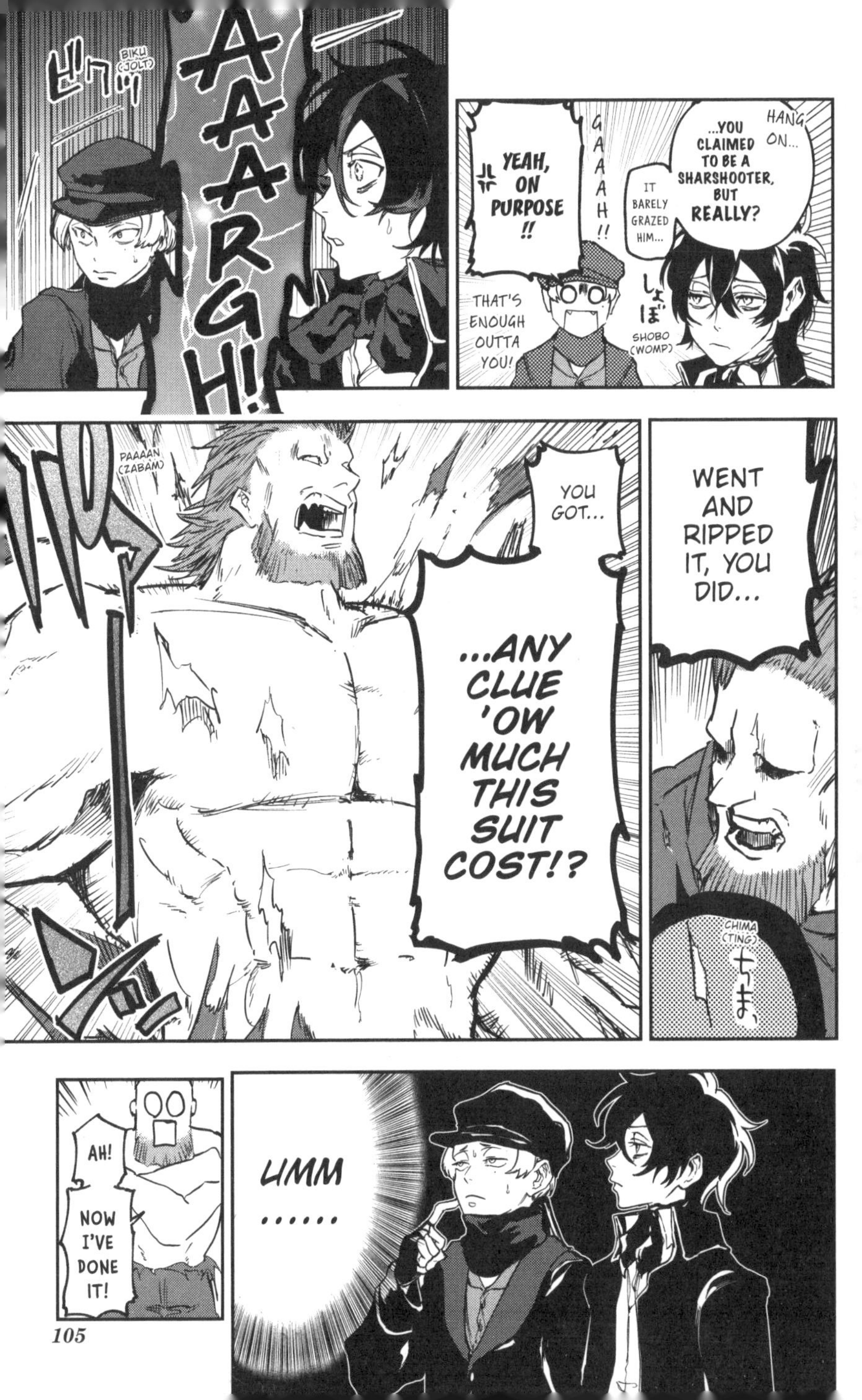
HANG ON...
...YOU CLAIMED TO BE A SHARSHOOTER, BUT REALLY?
IT BARELY GRAZED HIM...
しょぼ
SHOBO (WOMP)
GAAAAH!!
YEAH, ON PURPOSE!!
THAT'S ENOUGH OUTTA YOU!
AAAARGH!
ビクッ
BIKU (JOLT)
WENT AND RIPPED IT, YOU DID...
ちま、
CHIMA (TING)
YOU GOT...
...ANY CLUE 'OW MUCH THIS SUIT COST!?
PAAAAN (ZABAM)
UMM......
AH!
NOW I'VE DONE IT!

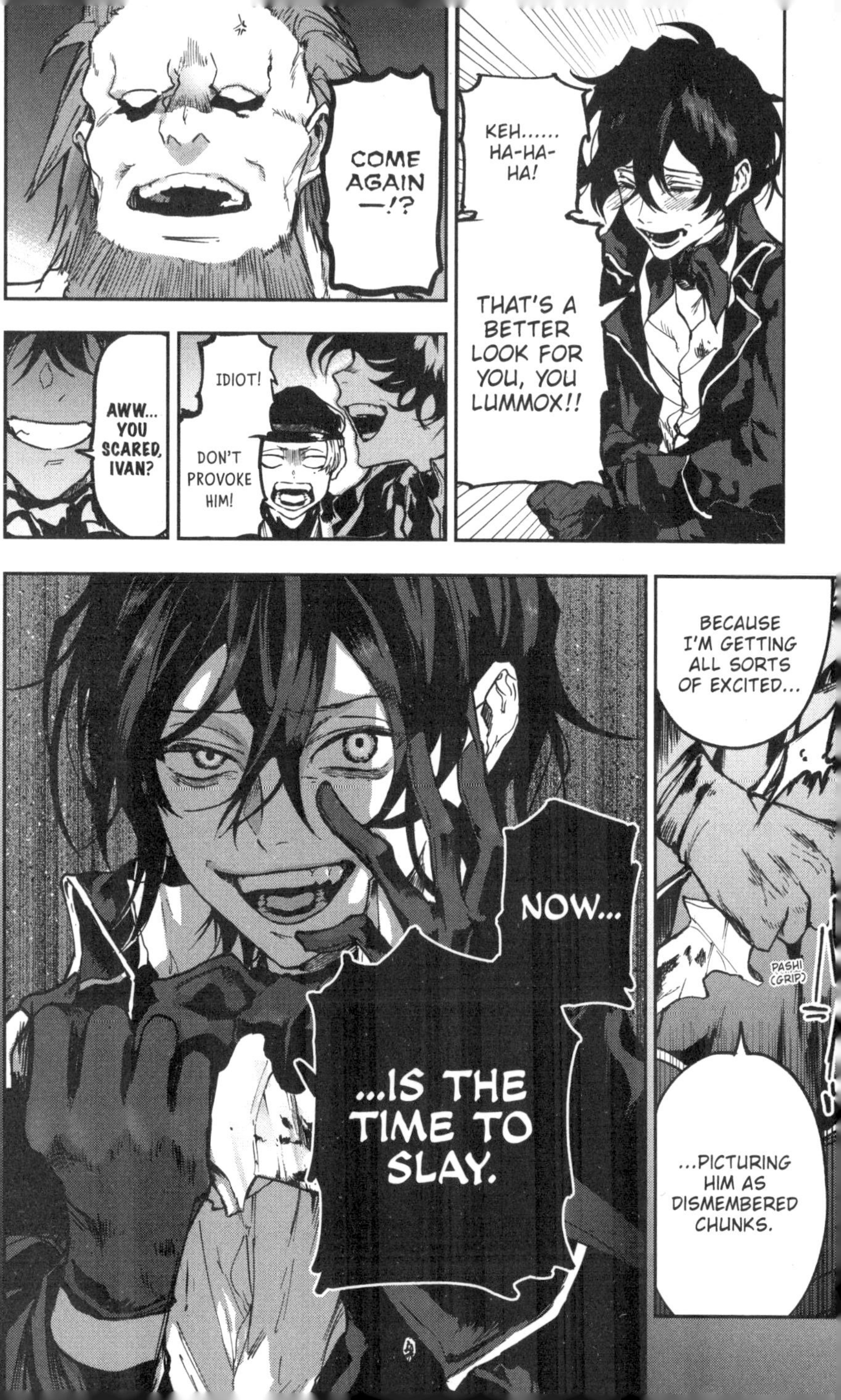
KEH...... HA-HA-HA!
THAT'S A BETTER LOOK FOR YOU, YOU LUMMOX!!
COME AGAIN—!?
IDIOT!
DON'T PROVOKE HIM!
AWW... YOU SCARED, IVAN?
BECAUSE I'M GETTING ALL SORTS OF EXCITED...
PASHI (GRIP)
...PICTURING HIM AS DISMEMBERED CHUNKS.
NOW...
...IS THE TIME TO SLAY.

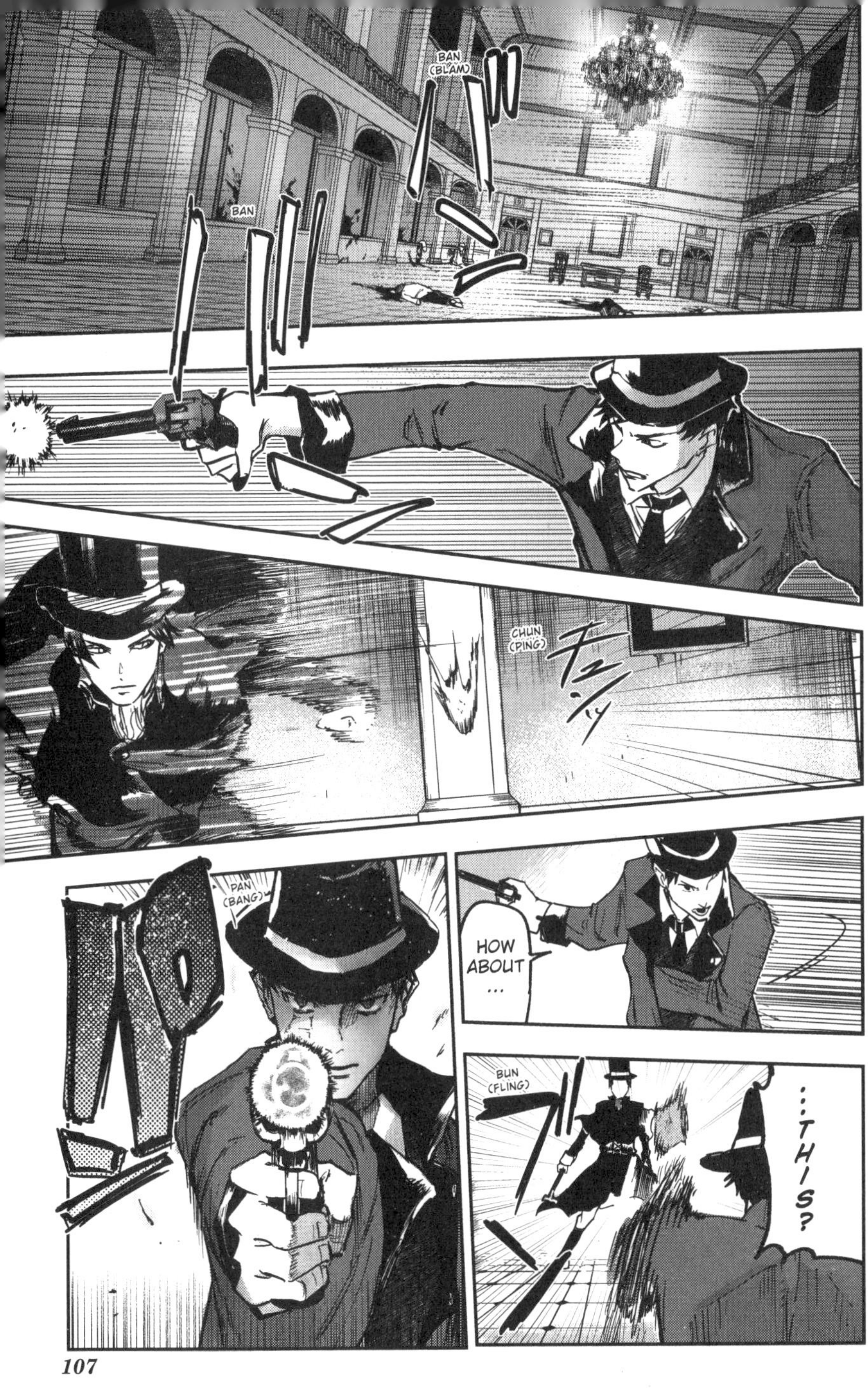
BAN (BLAM)
BAN
CHUN (PING)
HOW ABOUT ...
...THIS?
BUN (FLING)
PAN (BANG)

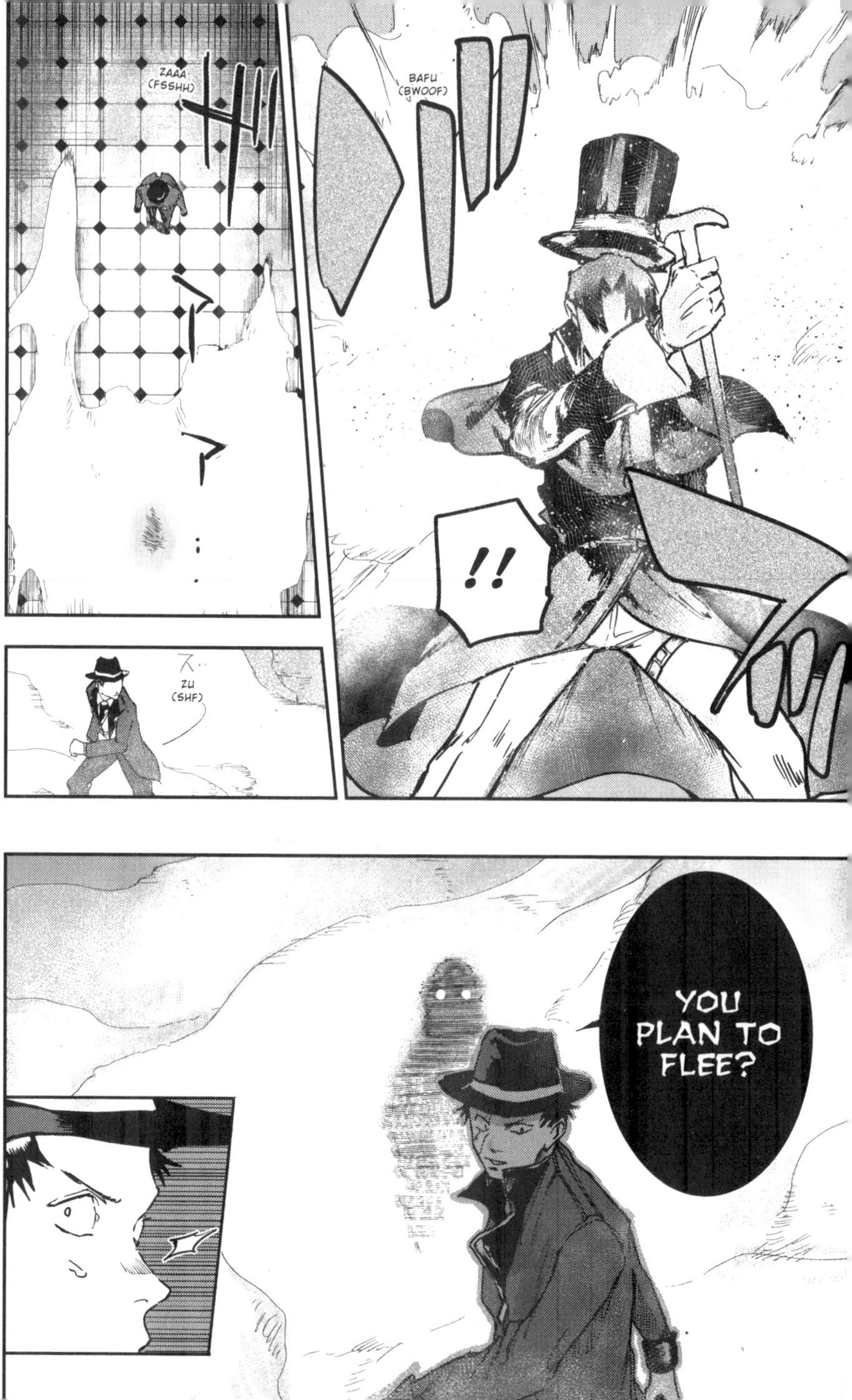
BAFU (BWOOF)
!!
ZAAA (FSSHH)
ZU (SHF)
YOU PLAN TO FLEE?

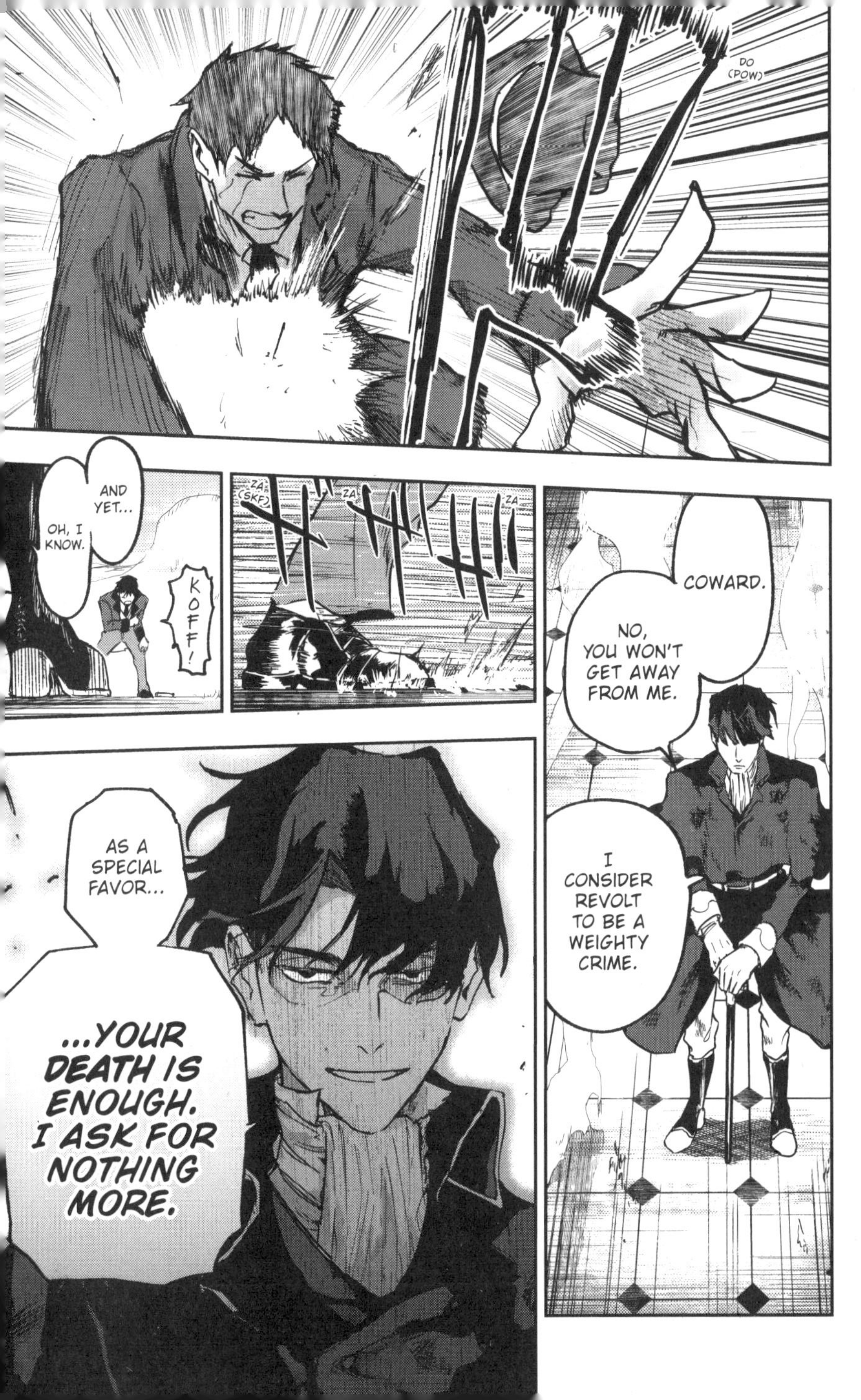
DO (POW)
COWARD.
NO, YOU WON'T GET AWAY FROM ME.
I CONSIDER REVOLT TO BE A WEIGHTY CRIME.
ZA (SKF)
ZA
ZA
AND YET...
OH, I KNOW.
KOFF!
AS A SPECIAL FAVOR...
...YOUR DEATH IS ENOUGH. I ASK FOR NOTHING MORE.

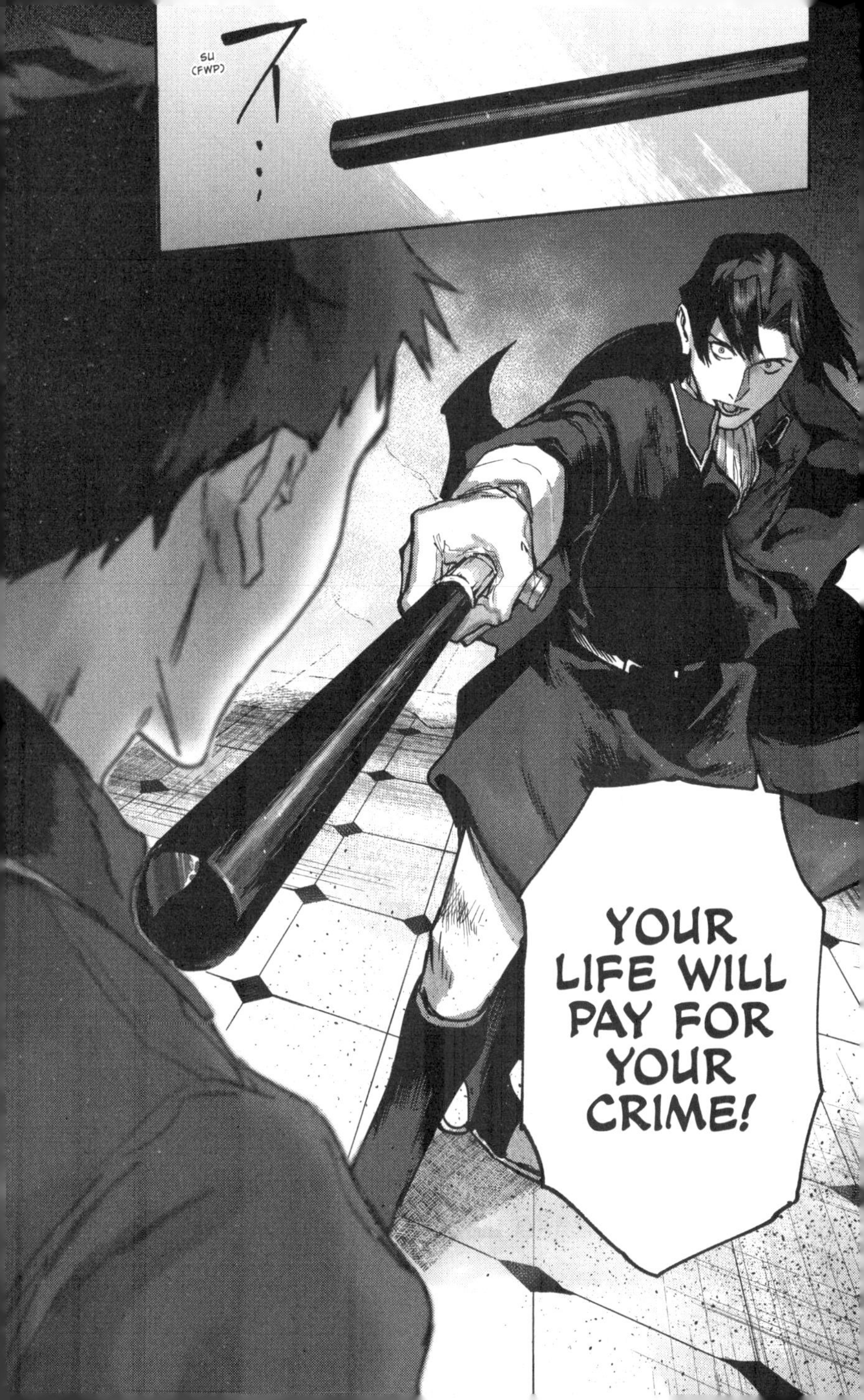
SU (FWP)
YOUR LIFE WILL PAY FOR YOUR CRIME!

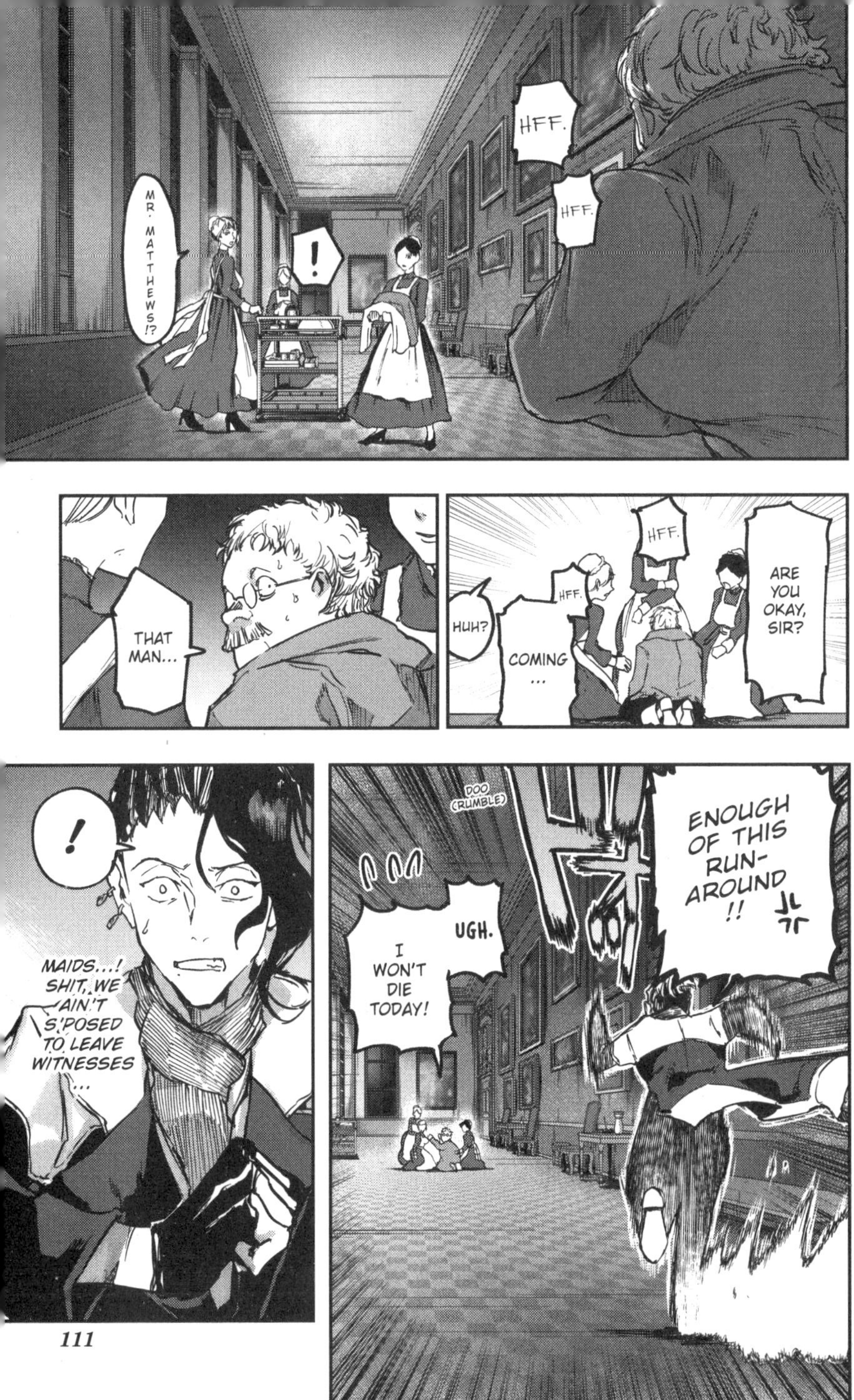
HFF.
HFF.
!
MR. MATTHEWS!?
ARE YOU OKAY, SIR?
HFF.
HFF.
COMING...
HUH?
THAT MAN...
DOO (RUMBLE)
ENOUGH OF THIS RUN-AROUND!!
UGH.
I WON'T DIE TODAY!
!
MAIDS...! SHIT, WE AIN'T S'POSED TO LEAVE WITNESSES...

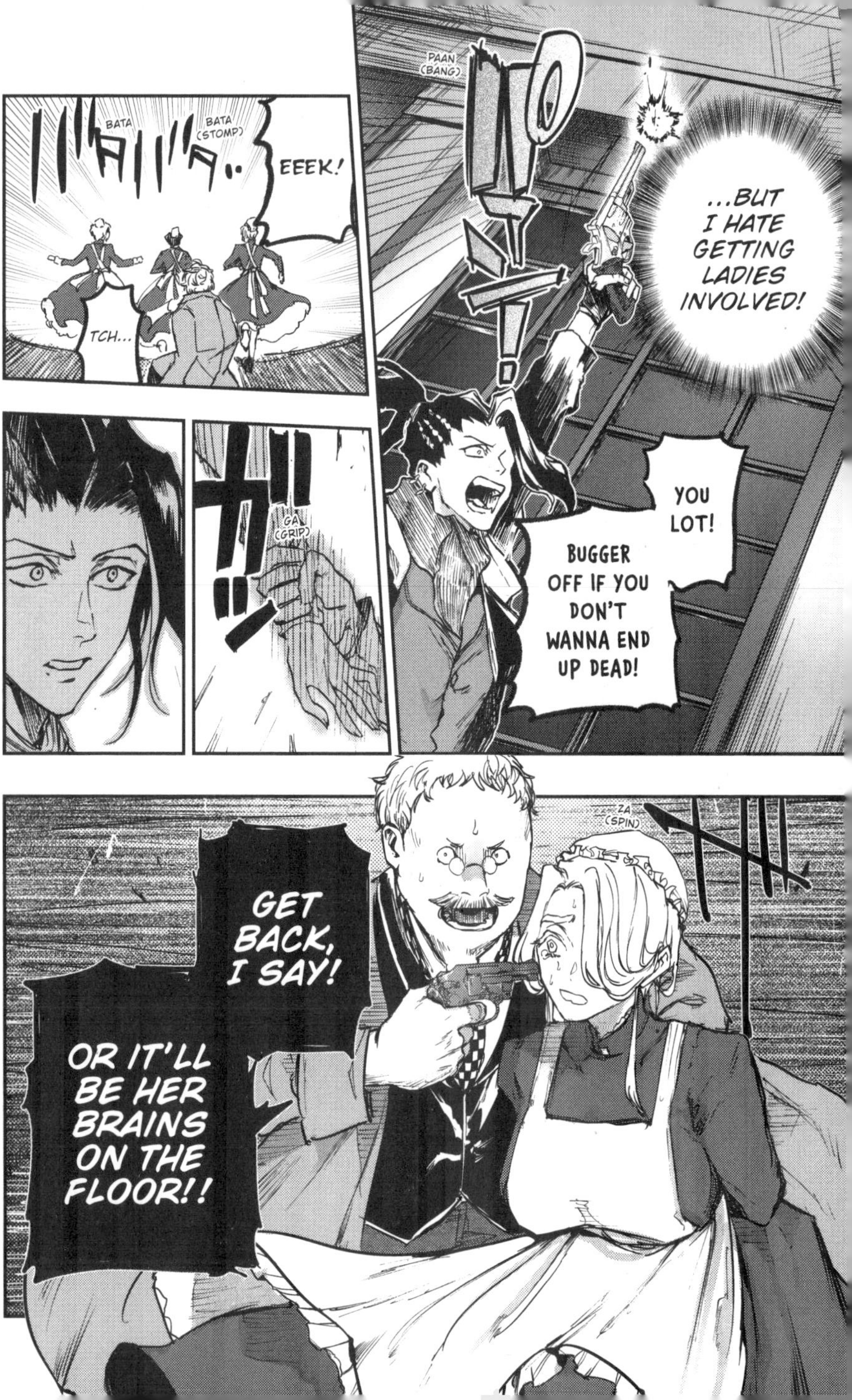
PAAN (BANG)
...BUT I HATE GETTING LADIES INVOLVED!
YOU LOT!
BUGGER OFF IF YOU DON'T WANNA END UP DEAD!
BATA BATA (STOMP)
EEEK!
TCH...
GA (GRIP)
ZA (SPIN)
GET BACK, I SAY!
OR IT'LL BE HER BRAINS ON THE FLOOR!!

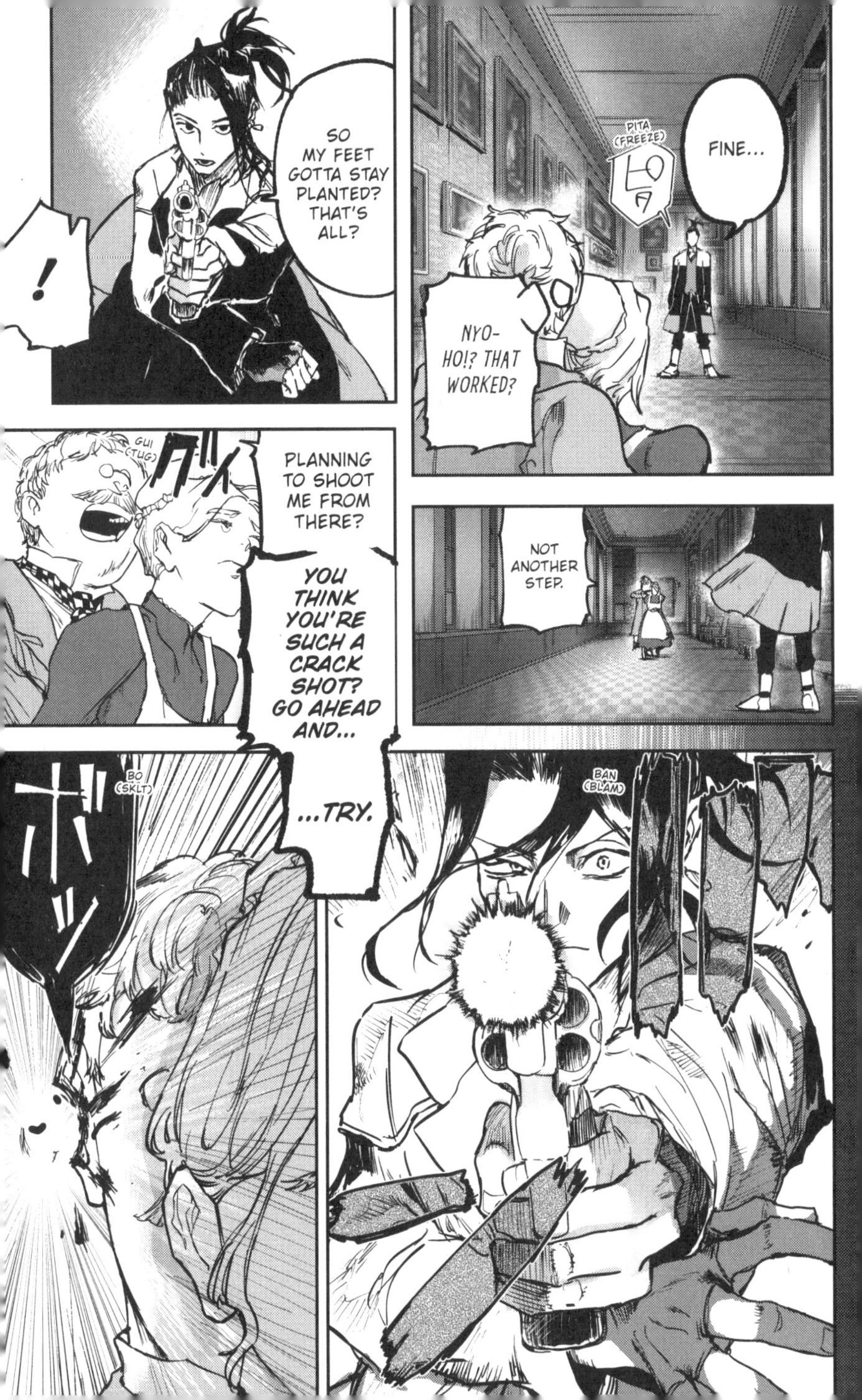
FINE...
PITA (FREEZE)
NYO-HO!? THAT WORKED?
SO MY FEET GOTTA STAY PLANTED? THAT'S ALL?
!
NOT ANOTHER STEP.
PLANNING TO SHOOT ME FROM THERE?
GUI (TUG)
YOU THINK YOU'RE SUCH A CRACK SHOT? GO AHEAD AND...
BAN (BLAM)
...TRY.
BO (SKLT)

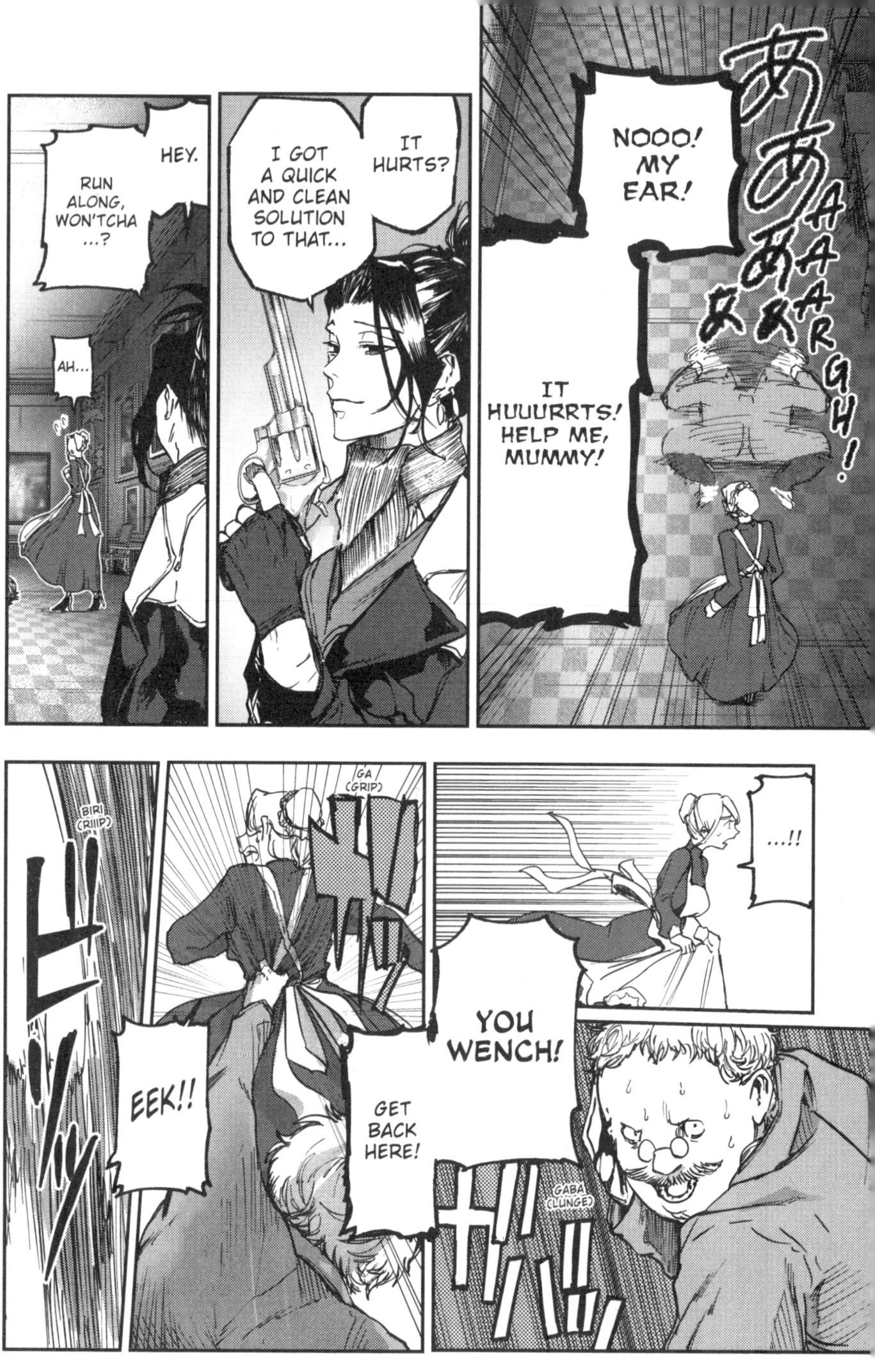
AAAARGH!
NOOO! MY EAR!
IT HUUURRTS! HELP ME, MUMMY!
IT HURTS?
I GOT A QUICK AND CLEAN SOLUTION TO THAT...
HEY.
RUN ALONG, WON'TCHA ...?
AH...
...!!
YOU WENCH!
GET BACK HERE!
GABA (LUNGE)
GA (GRIP)
BIRI (RIIIP)
EEK!!

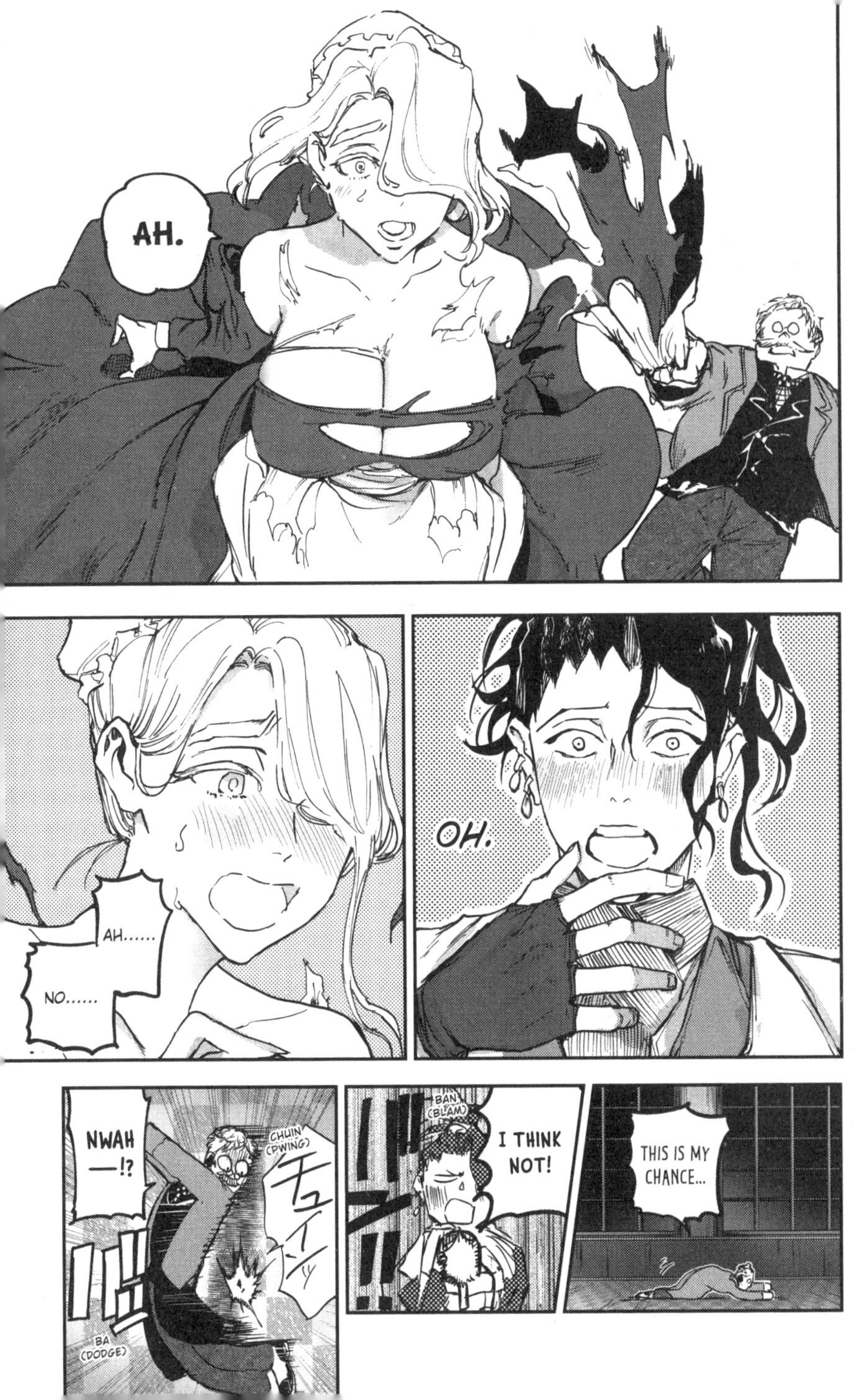
AH.
OH.
AH......
NO......
THIS IS MY CHANCE...
BAN (BLAM)
I THINK NOT!
CHUIN (PWING)
NWAH —!?
BA (DODGE)

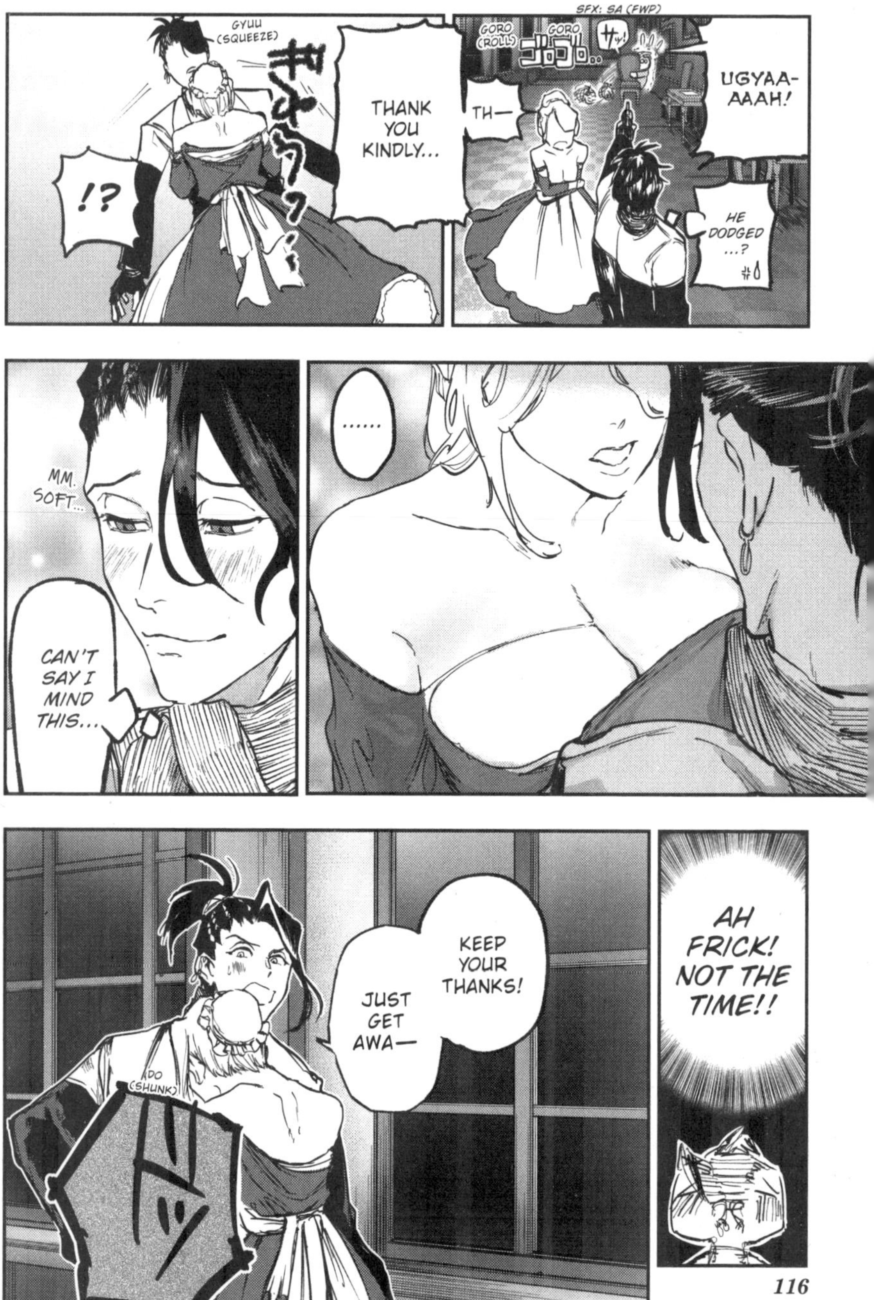
SFX: SA (FWP)
UGYAA-AAAH!
GORO (ROLL) GORO
TH—
HE DODGED ...?
GYUU (SQUEEZE)
THANK YOU KINDLY...
!?
......
MM. SOFT...
CAN'T SAY I MIND THIS...
AH FRICK! NOT THE TIME!!
KEEP YOUR THANKS!
JUST GET AWA—
DO (SHUNK)

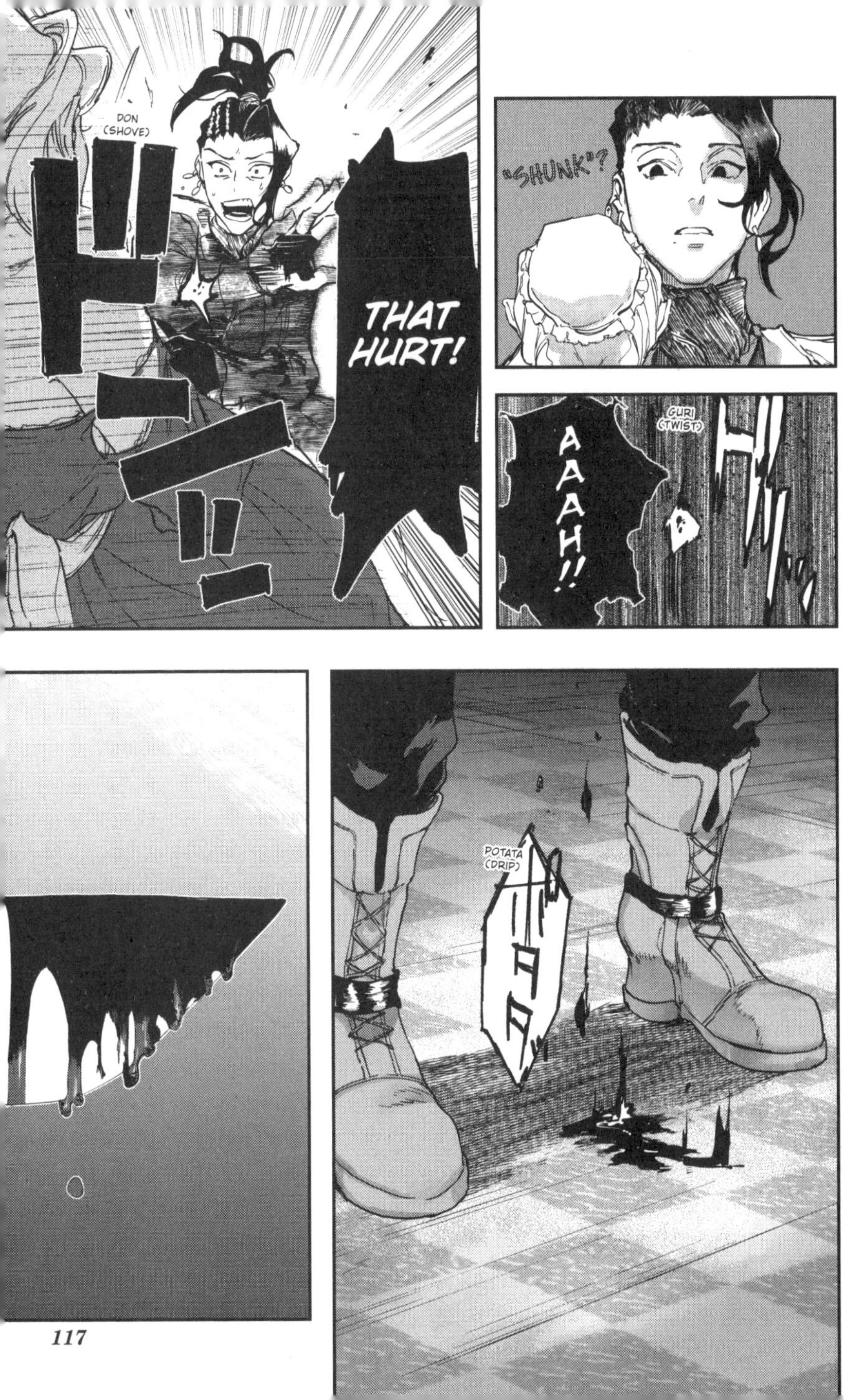
"SHUNK"?
GURI (TWIST)
AAAAH!!
DON (SHOVE)
THAT HURT!
POTATA (DRIP)

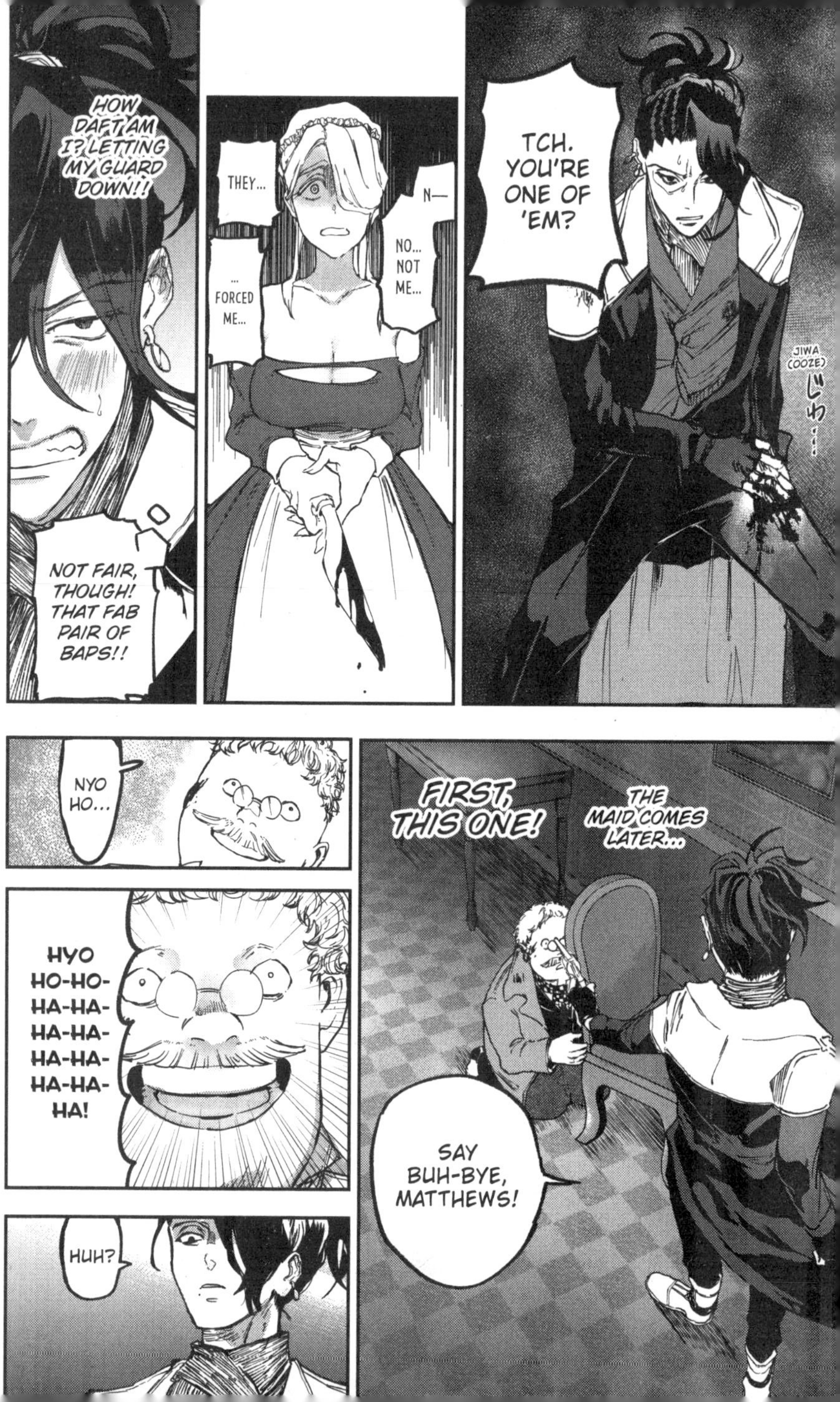
TCH. YOU'RE ONE OF 'EM?
JIWA (OOZE)
じわ…
N—
NO... NOT ME...
THEY...
... FORCED ME...
HOW DAFT AM I? LETTING MY GUARD DOWN!!
NOT FAIR, THOUGH! THAT FAB PAIR OF BAPS!!
THE MAID COMES LATER...
FIRST, THIS ONE!
SAY BUH-BYE, MATTHEWS!
NYO HO...
HYO HO-HO-HA-HA-HA-HA-HA-HA-HA-HA-HA!
HUH?

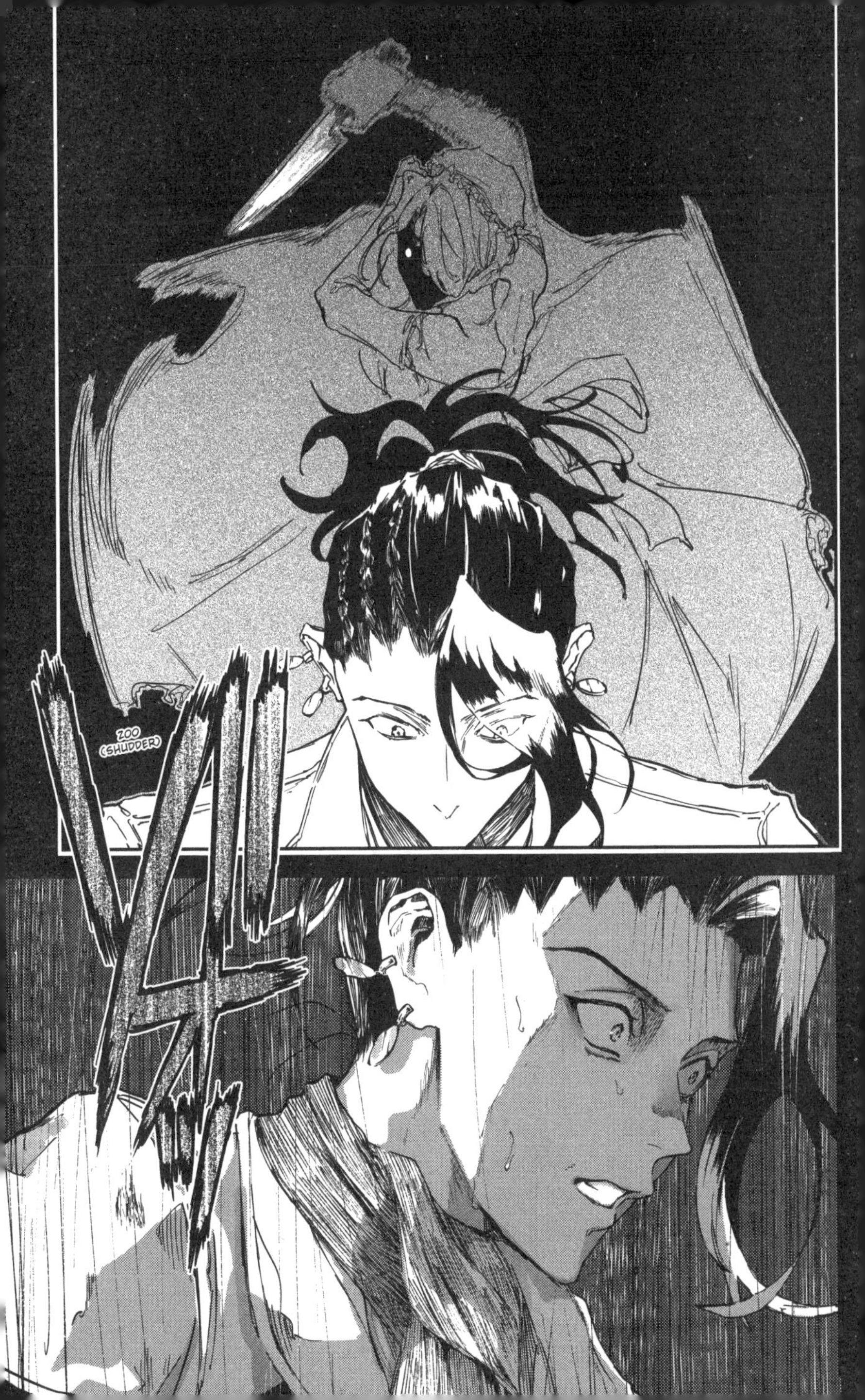
ZOO
(SHUDDER)

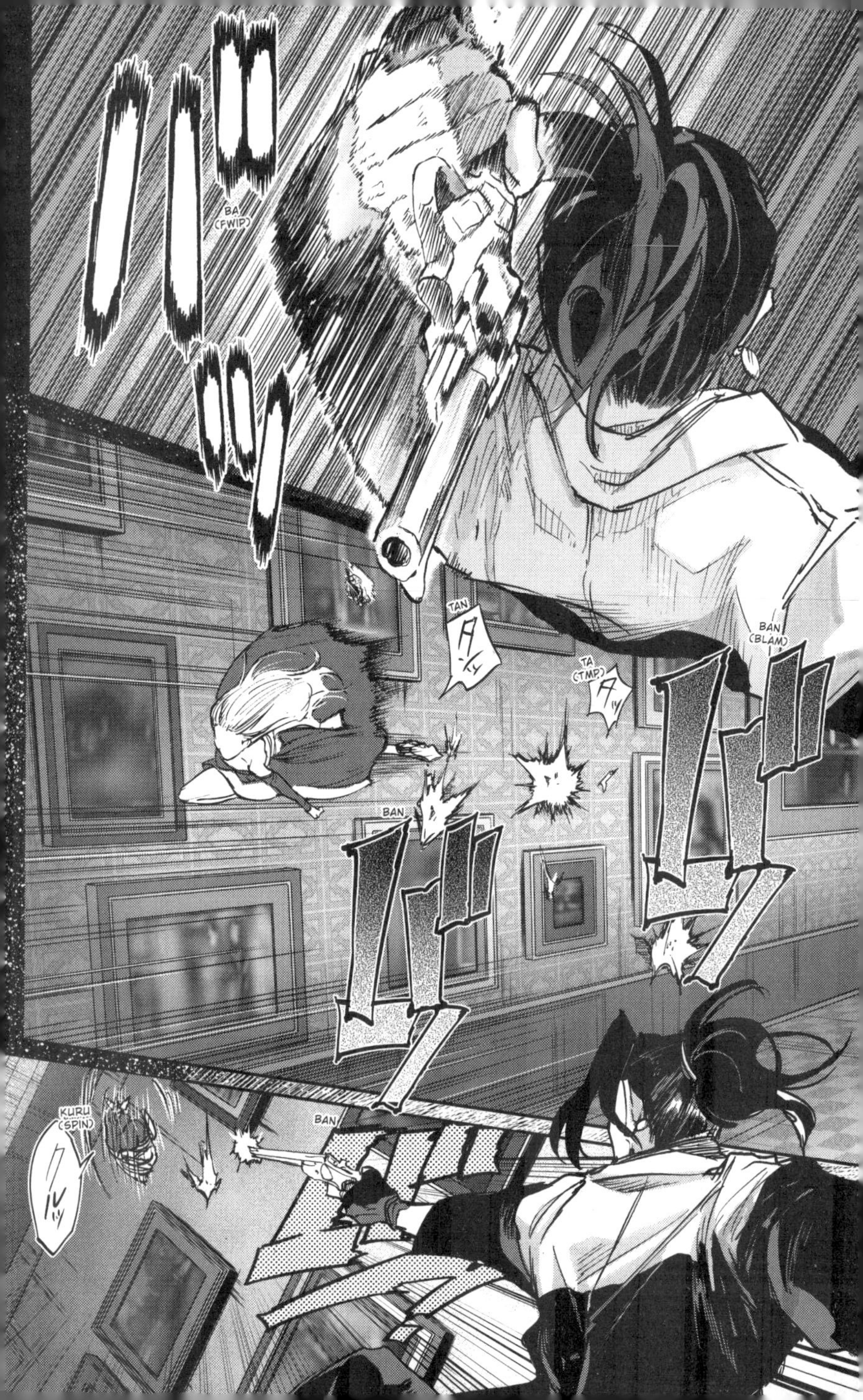
BA (FWIP)
BAN (BLAM)
TA (TMP)
TAN
BAN
BAN
KURU (SPIN)

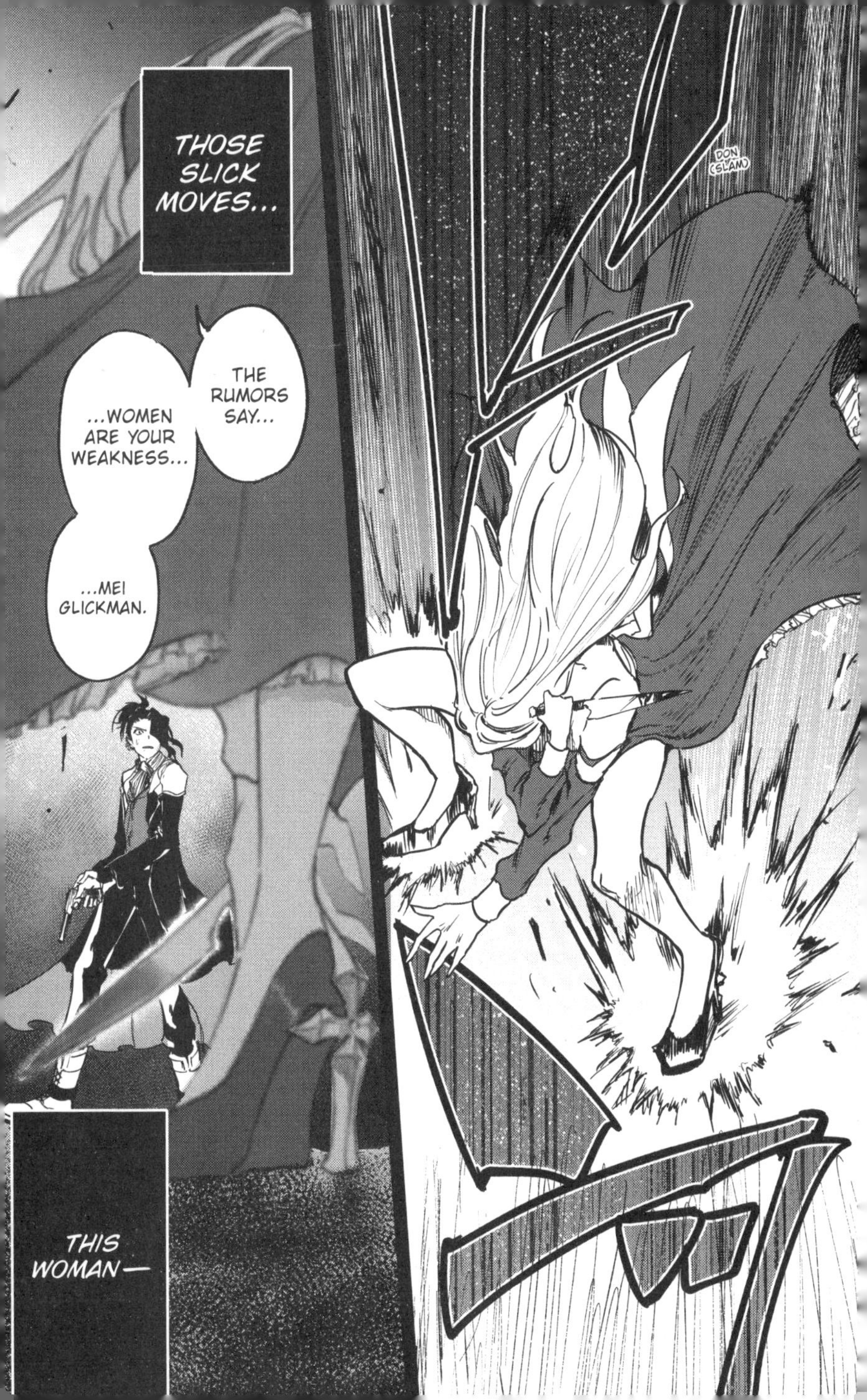
DON (SLAM)
THOSE SLICK MOVES...
THE RUMORS SAY...
...WOMEN ARE YOUR WEAKNESS...
...MEI GLICKMAN.
THIS WOMAN—

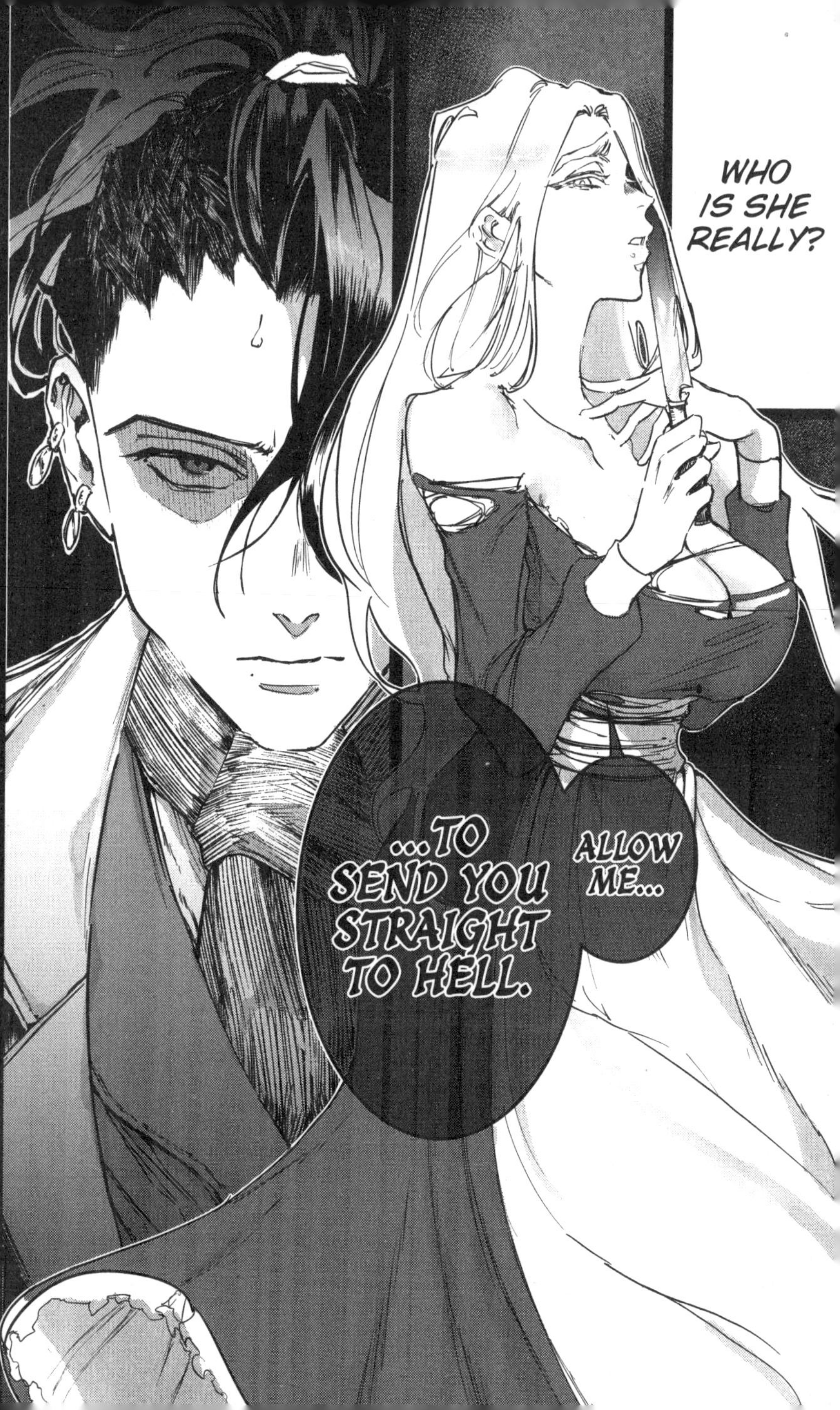
WHO IS SHE REALLY?
ALLOW ME...
...TO SEND YOU STRAIGHT TO HELL.

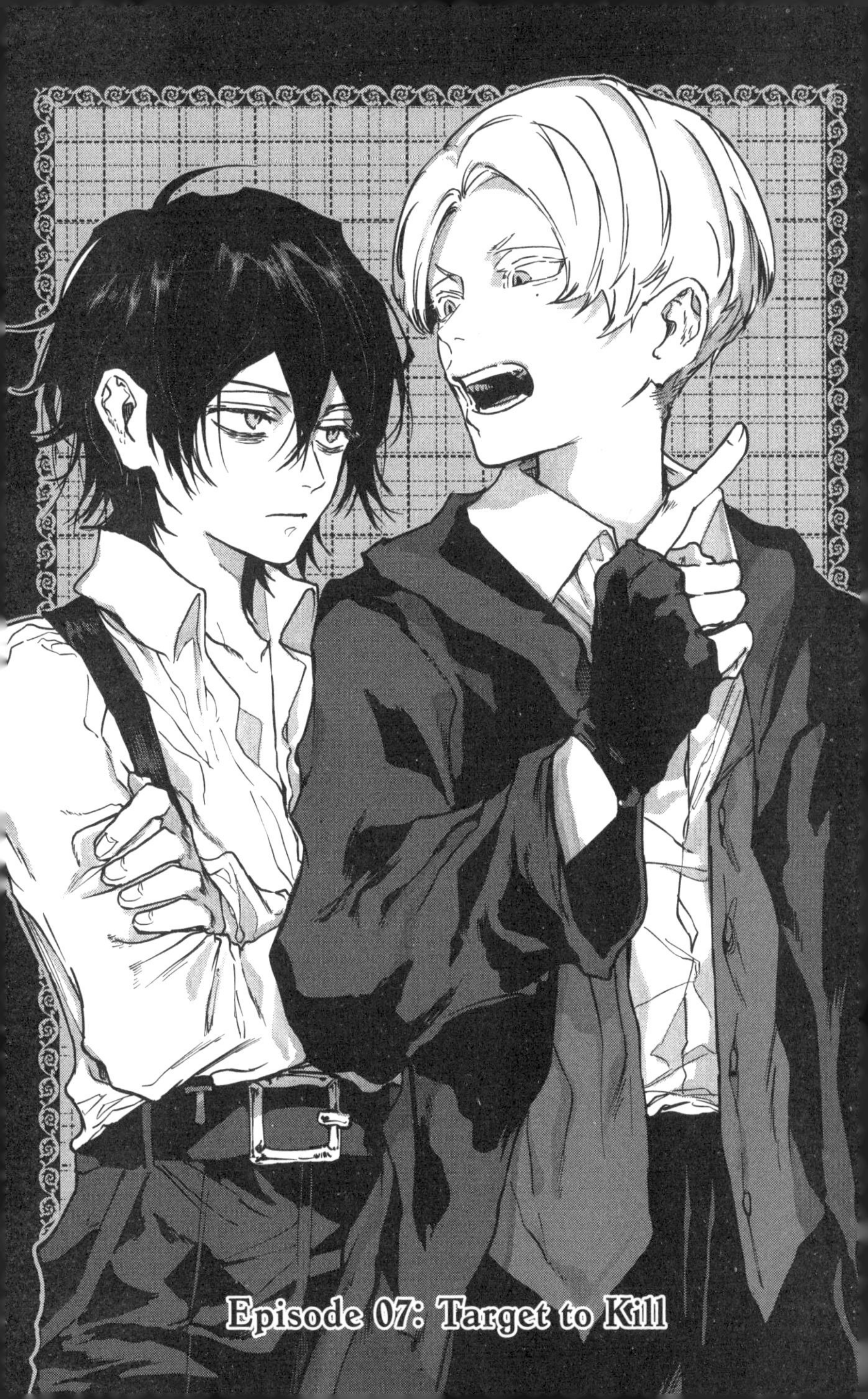
Episode 07: Target to Kill

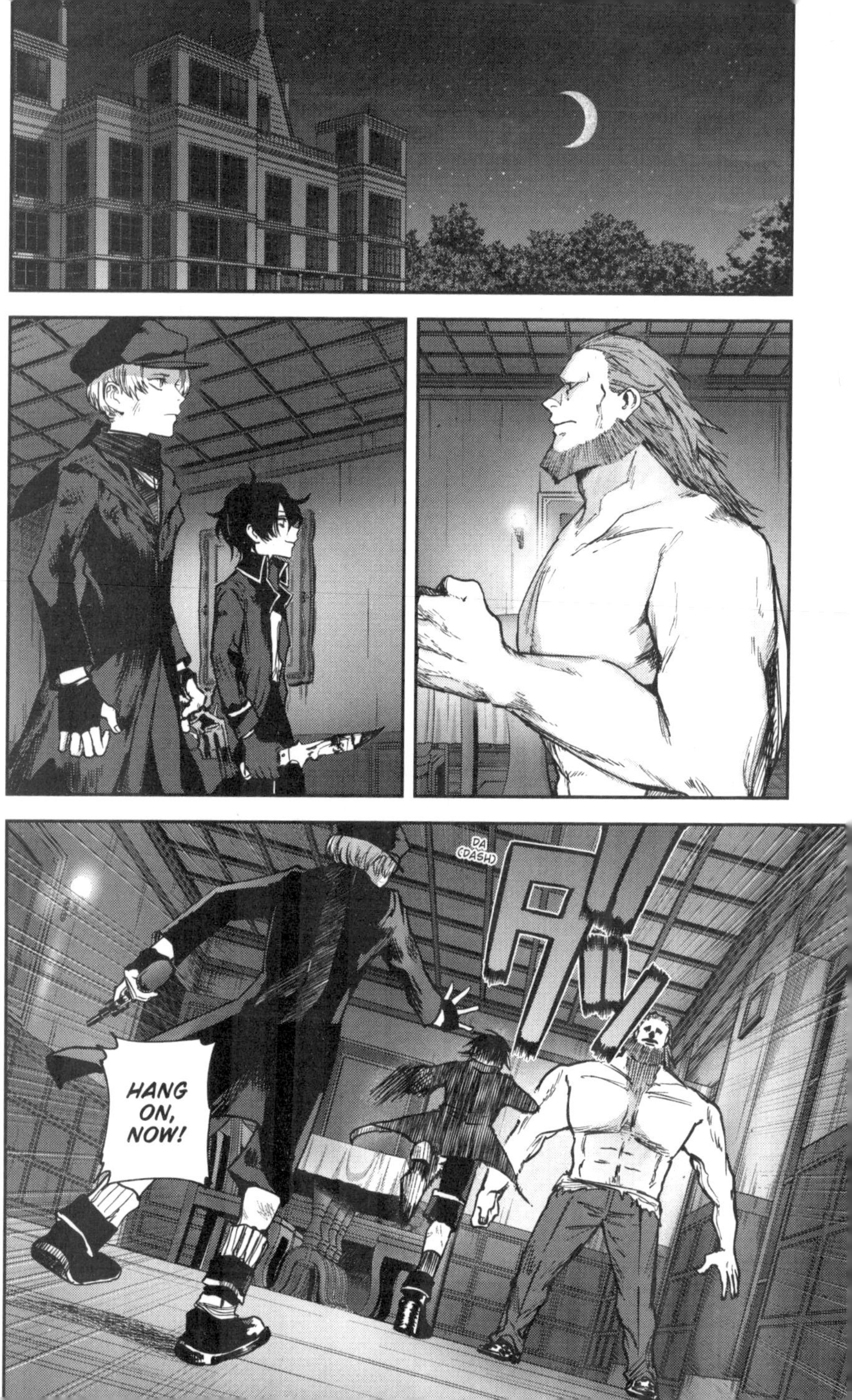
DA (DASH)
HANG ON, NOW!

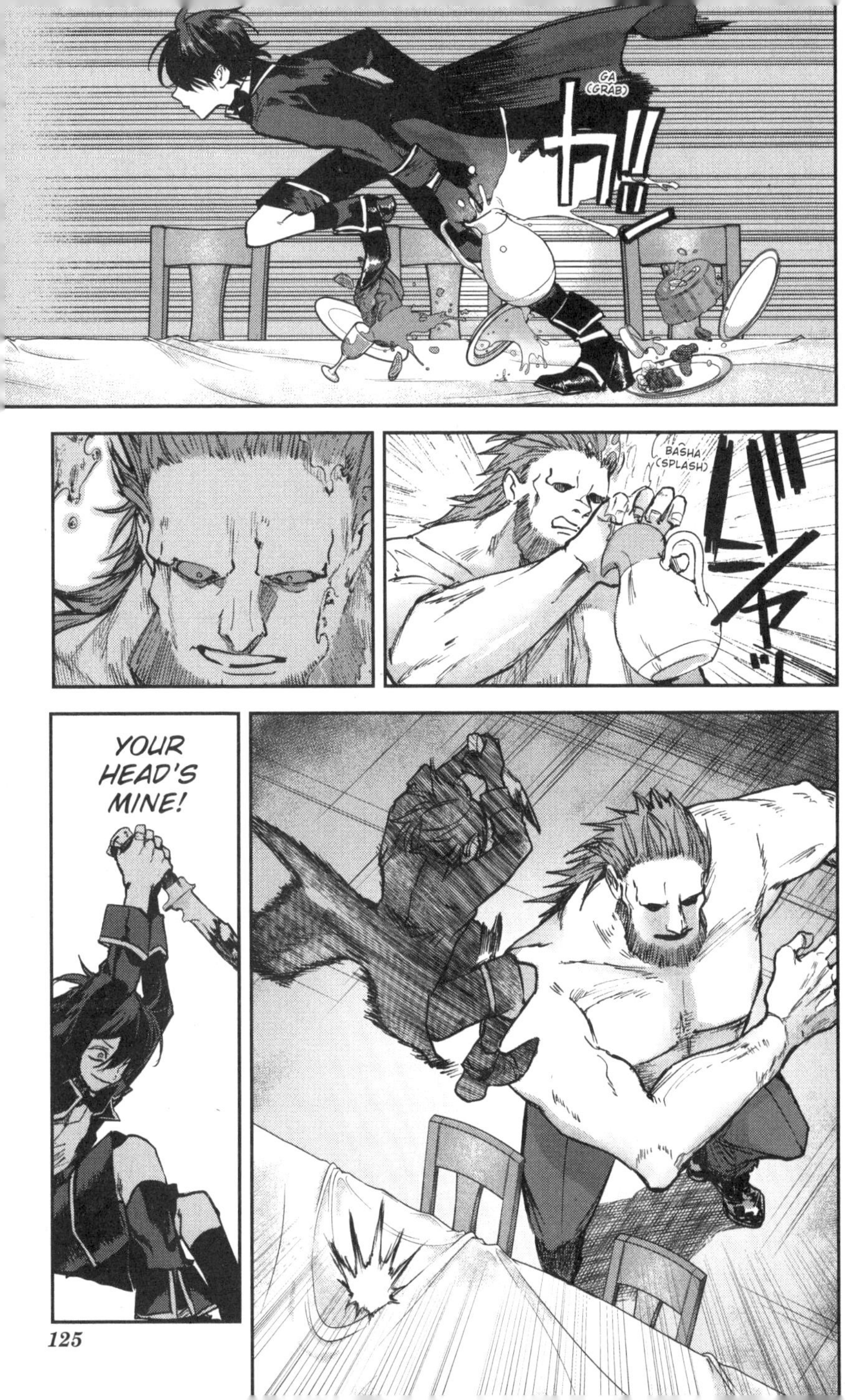
GA (GRAB)
BASHA (SPLASH)
YOUR HEAD'S MINE!

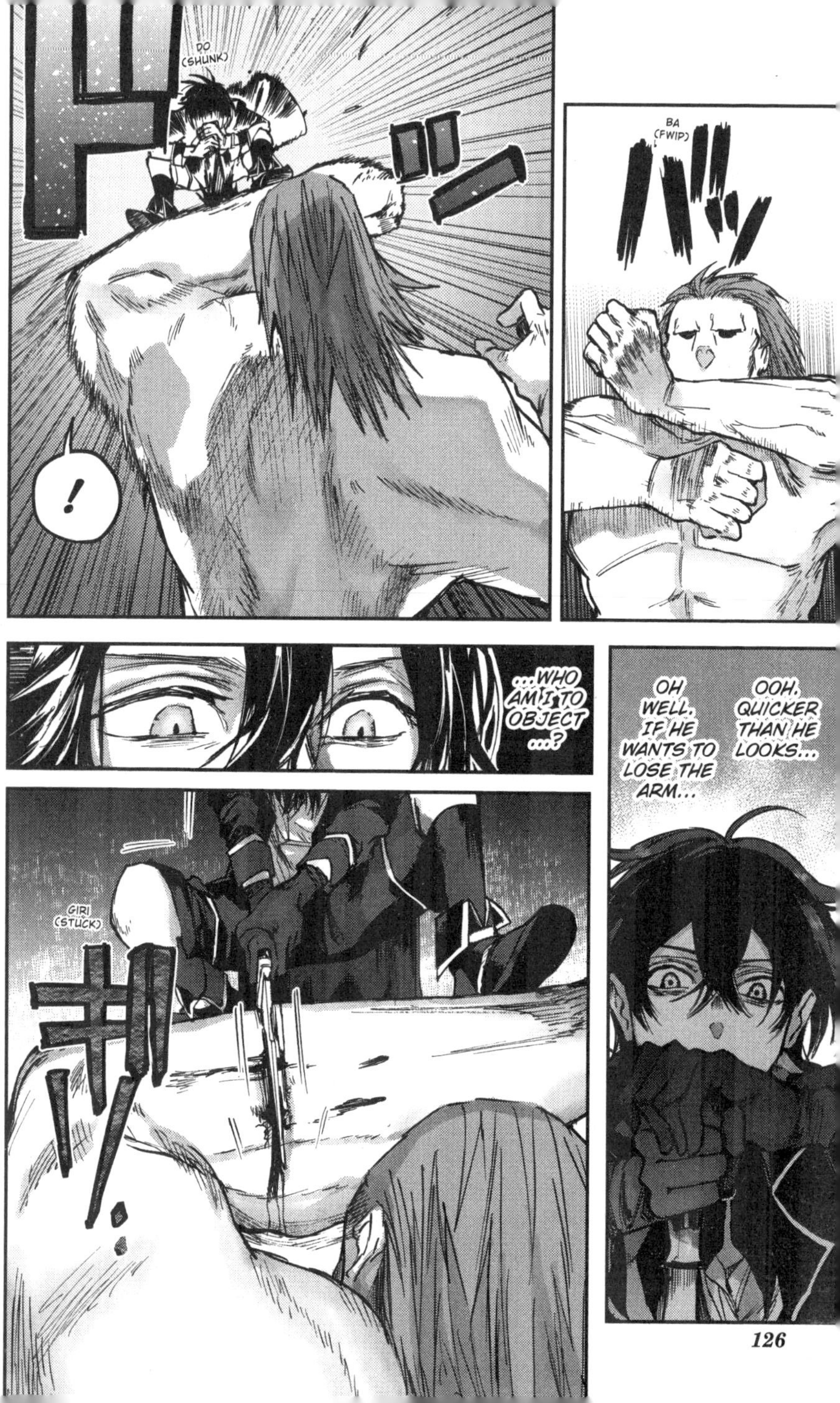
BA (FWIP)
DO (SHUNK)
!
OOH. QUICKER THAN HE LOOKS...
OH WELL. IF HE WANTS TO LOSE THE ARM...
...WHO AM I TO OBJECT ...?
GIRI (STUCK)

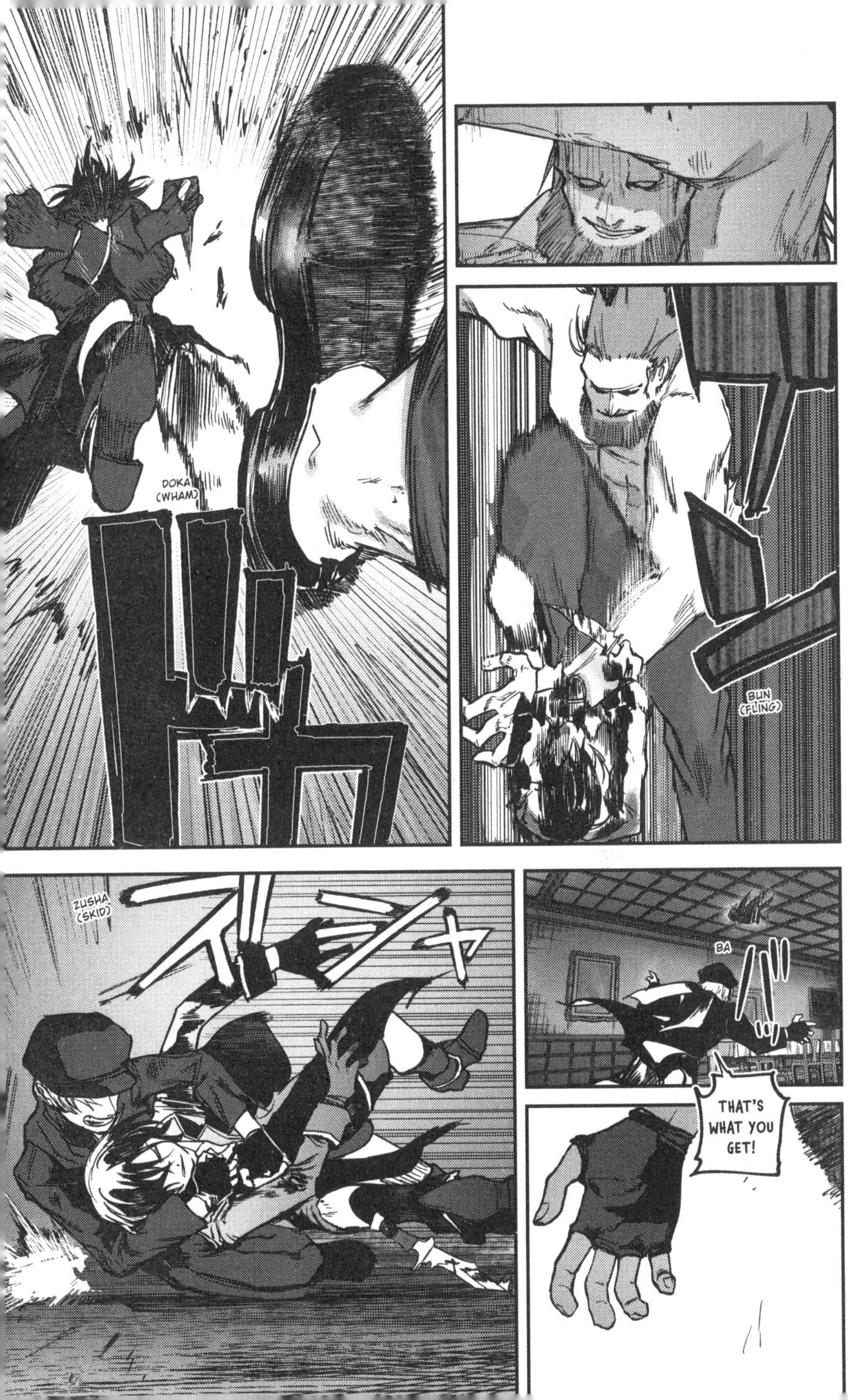
BUN
(FLING)
DOKA
(WHAM)
BA
THAT'S WHAT YOU GET!
ZUSHA
(SKID)

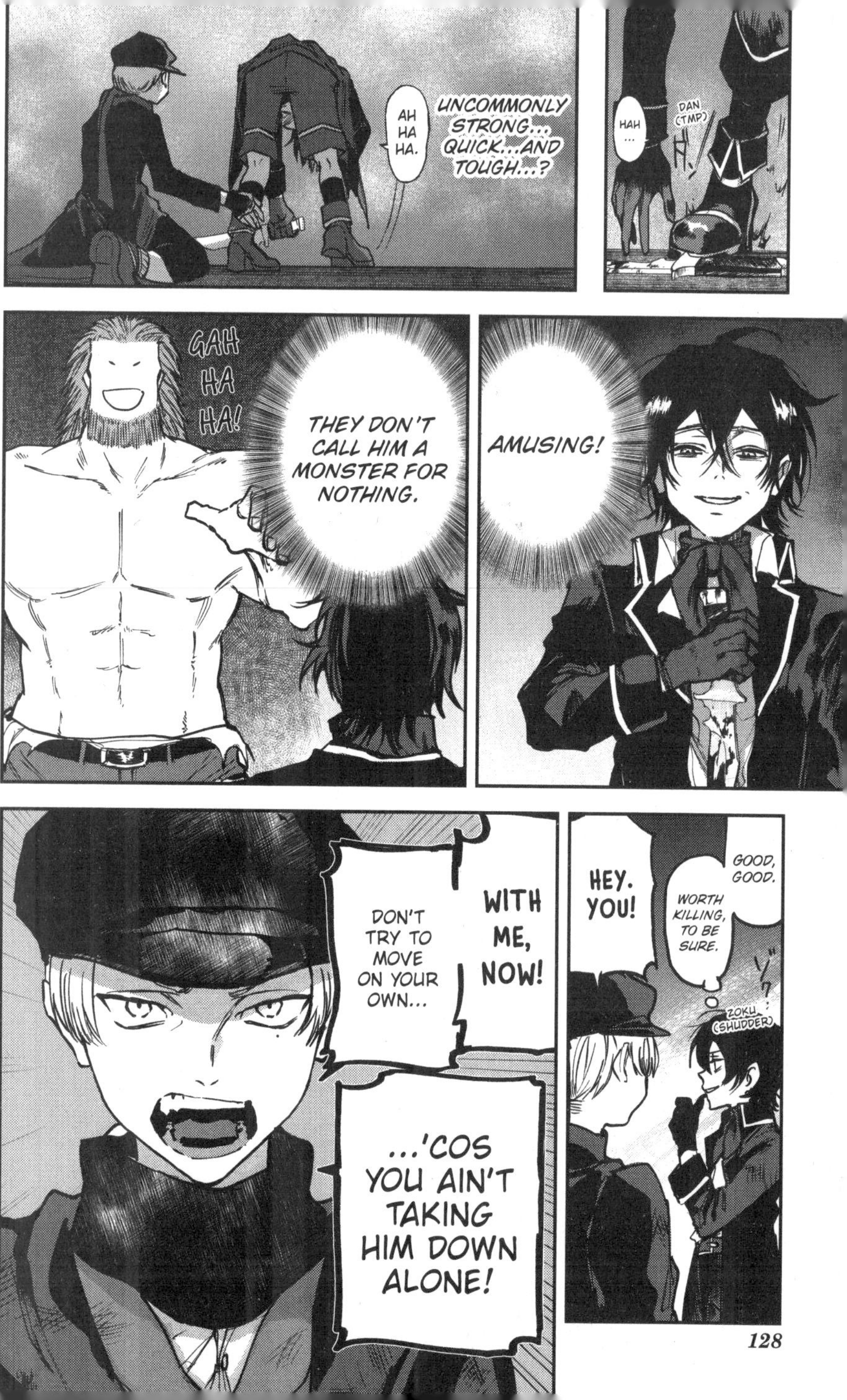

HAH ...
DAN (TMP)
UNCOMMONLY STRONG... QUICK...AND TOUGH...?
AH HA HA.
AMUSING!
THEY DON'T CALL HIM A MONSTER FOR NOTHING.
GAH HA HA!
GOOD, GOOD.
WORTH KILLING, TO BE SURE.
HEY. YOU!
ZOKU (SHUDDER)
WITH ME, NOW!
DON'T TRY TO MOVE ON YOUR OWN...
...'COS YOU AIN'T TAKING HIM DOWN ALONE!

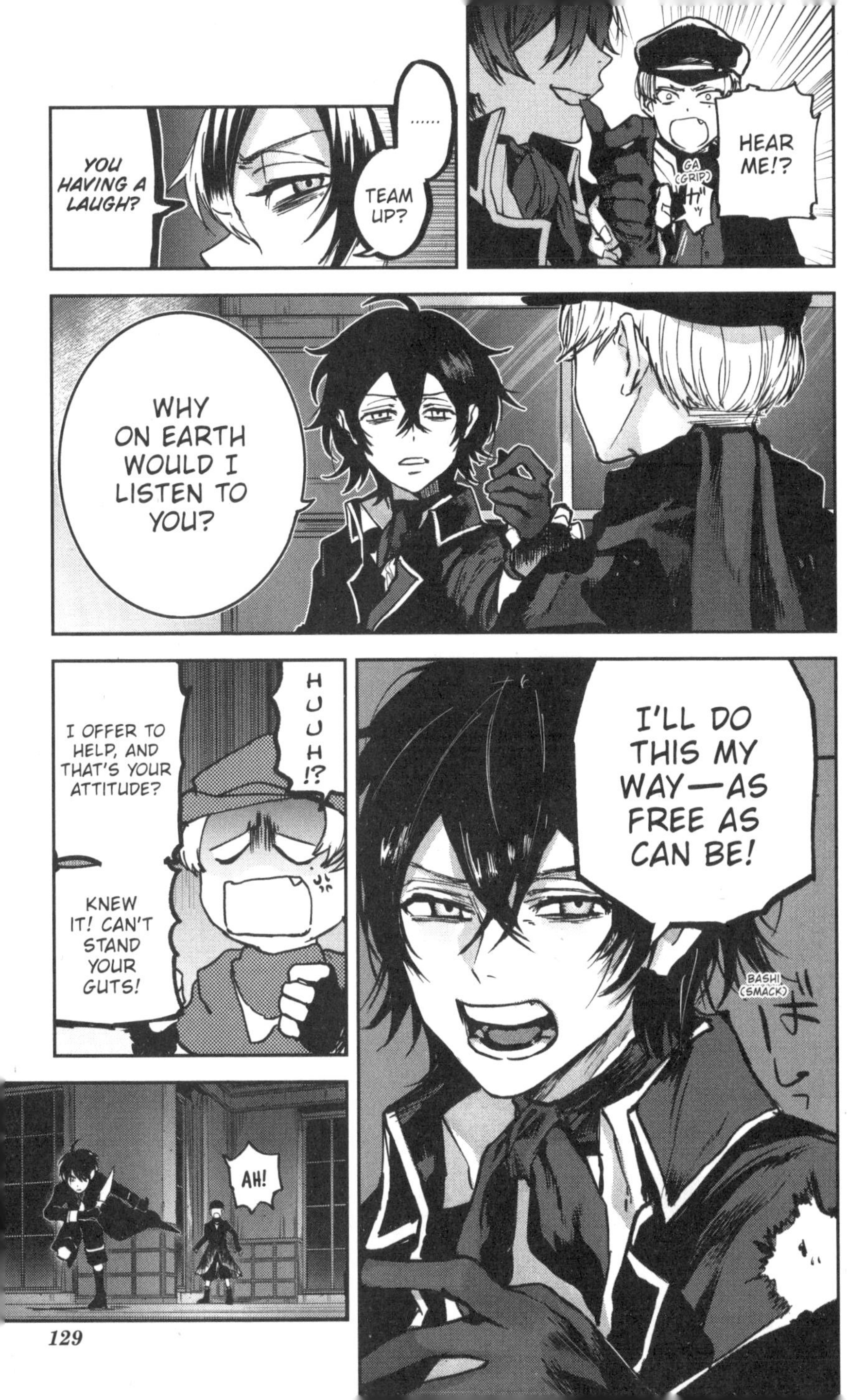
HEAR ME!?
GA (GRIP)
......
TEAM UP?
YOU HAVING A LAUGH?
WHY ON EARTH WOULD I LISTEN TO YOU?
I'LL DO THIS MY WAY—AS FREE AS CAN BE!
BASHI (SMACK)
HUUH!?
I OFFER TO HELP, AND THAT'S YOUR ATTITUDE?
KNEW IT! CAN'T STAND YOUR GUTS!
AH!

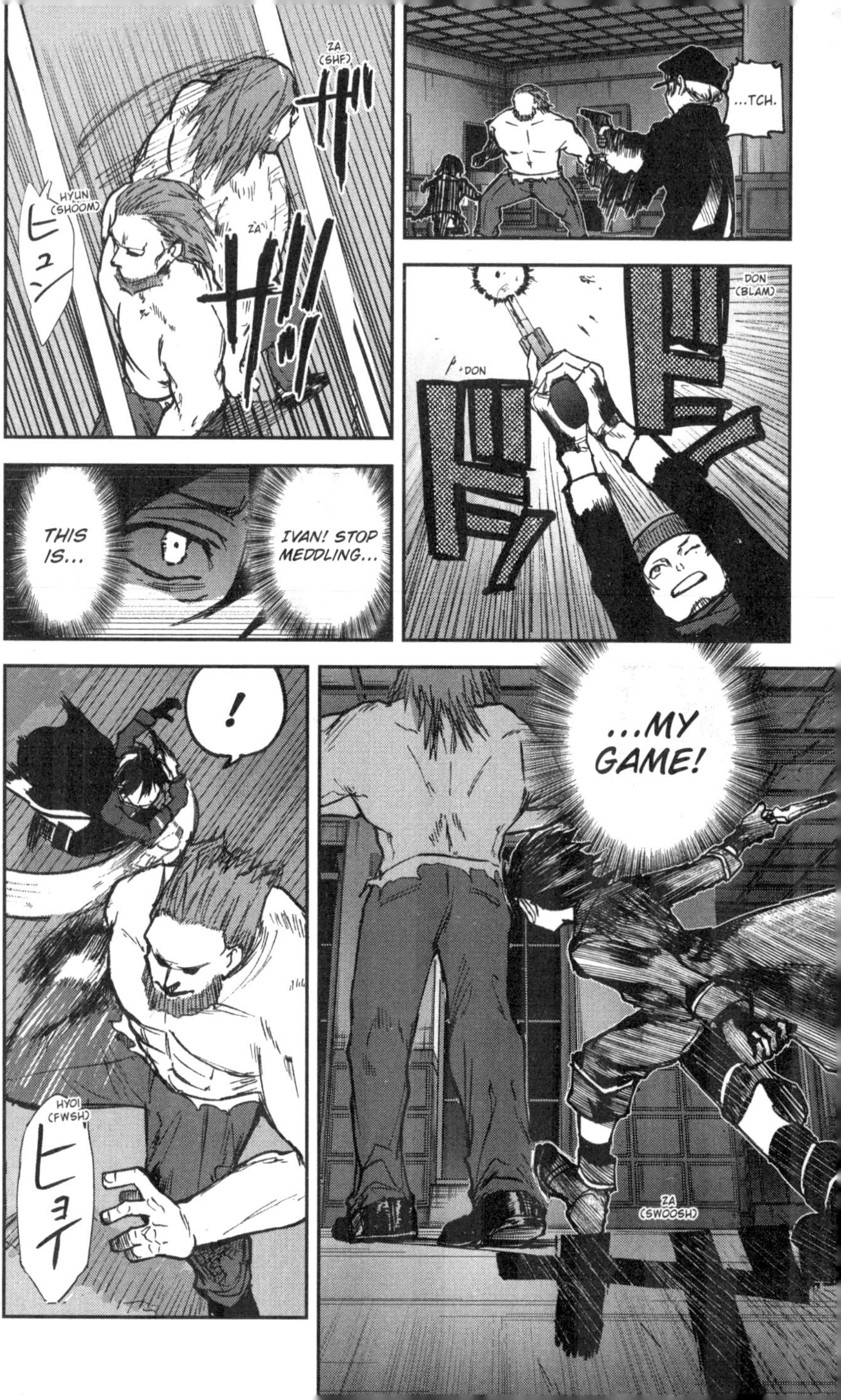
...TCH.
ZA (SHF)
ザ
HYUN (SHOOM)
ヒュン
ZA
ザ!!
DON (BLAM)
DON
ドン
ドン
THIS IS...
IVAN! STOP MEDDLING...
...MY GAME!
ZA (SWOOSH)
!
HYOI (FWSH)
ヒョイ

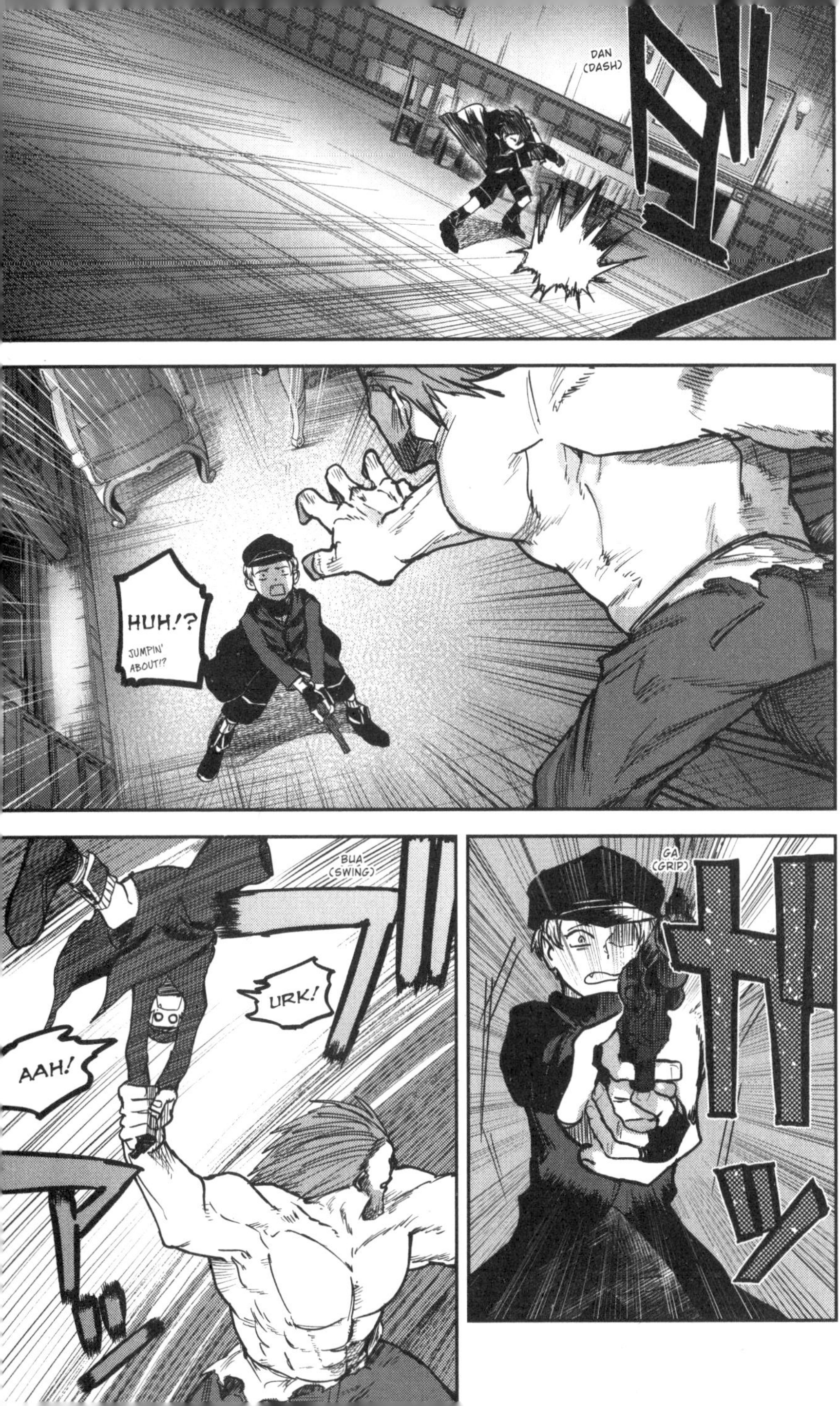
DAN (DASH)
HUH!? JUMPIN' ABOUT!?
GA (GRIP)
BUA (SWING)
URK!
AAH!

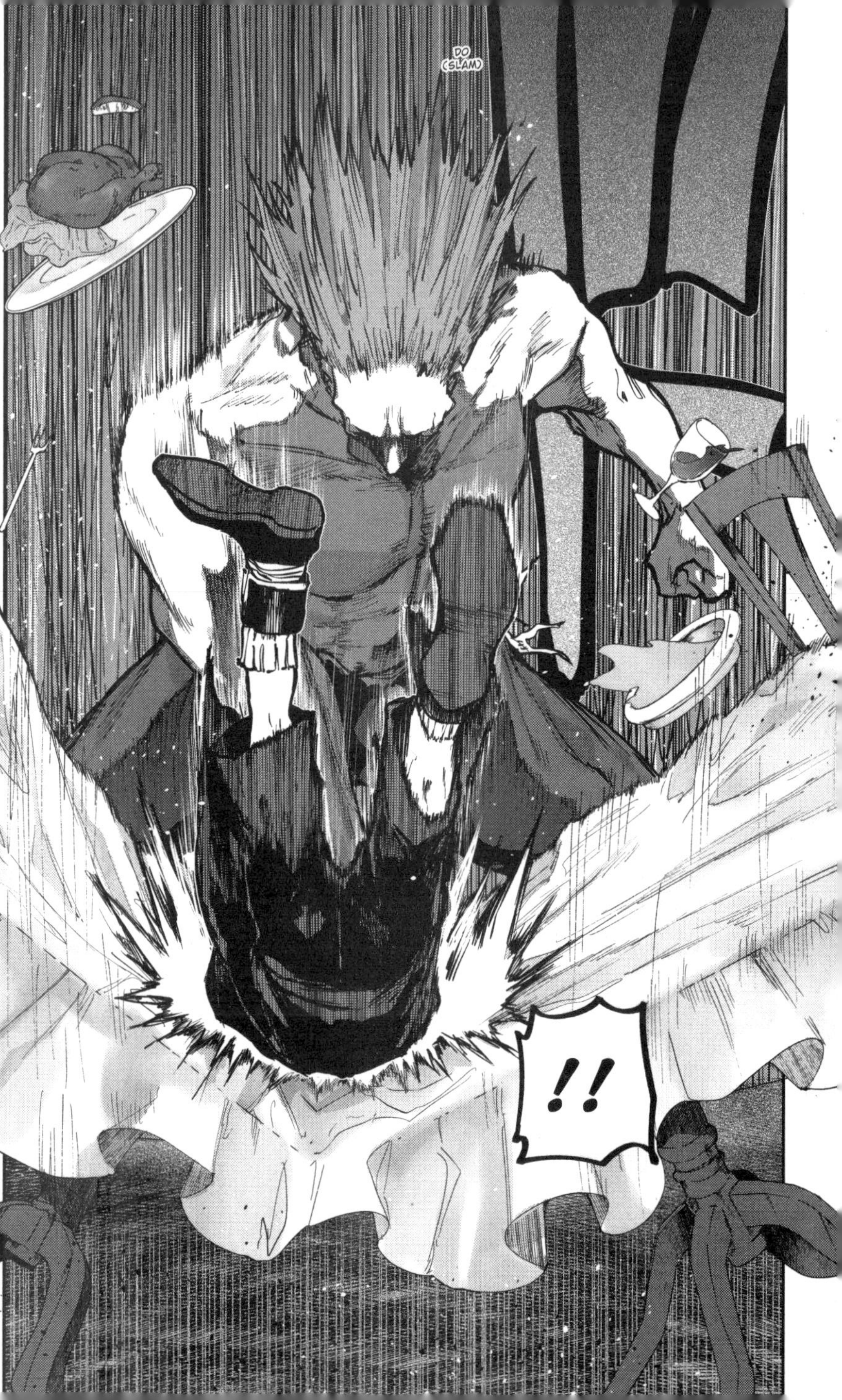
DO (SLAM)
!!

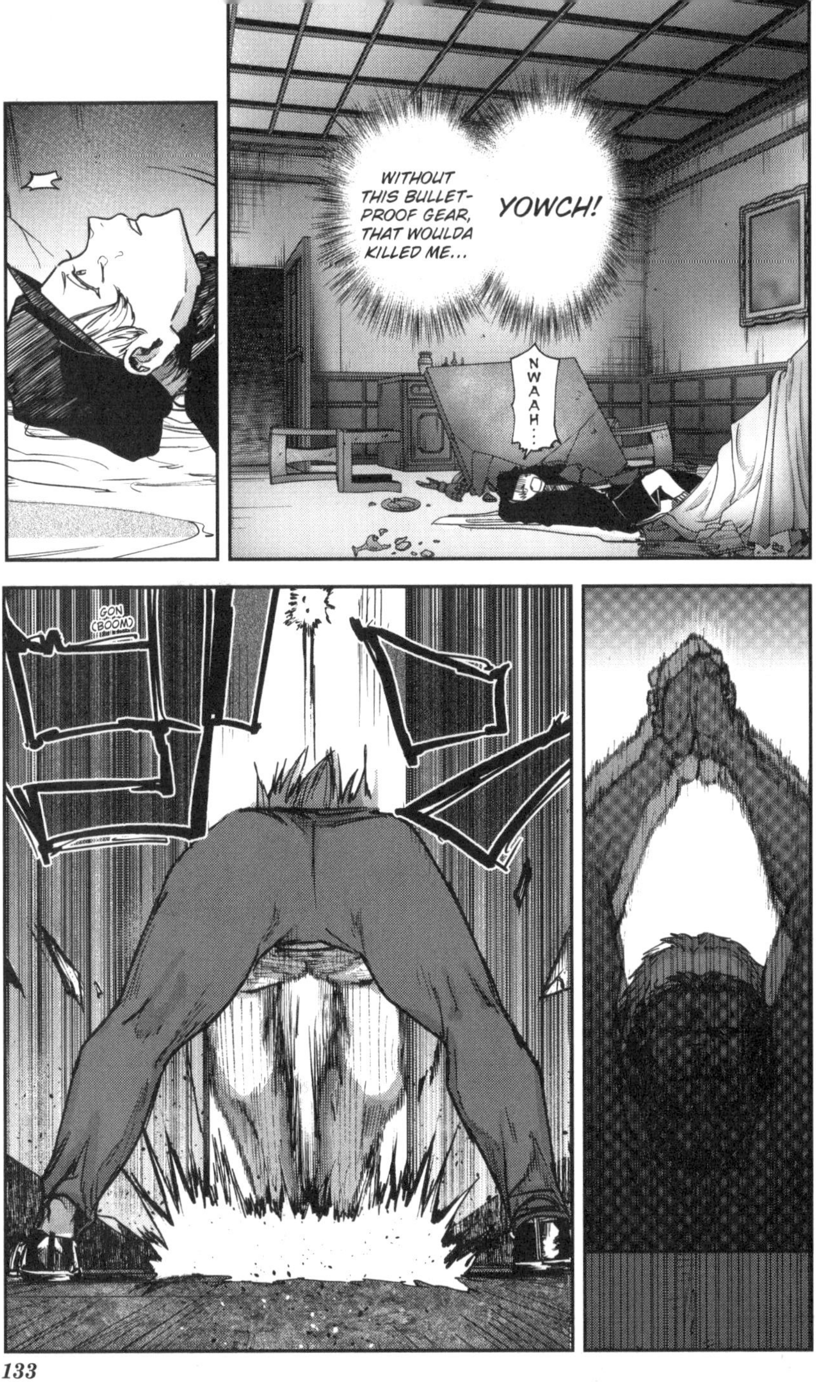
YOWCH!
WITHOUT THIS BULLET-PROOF GEAR, THAT WOULDA KILLED ME...
NWAAH...
GON (BOOM)

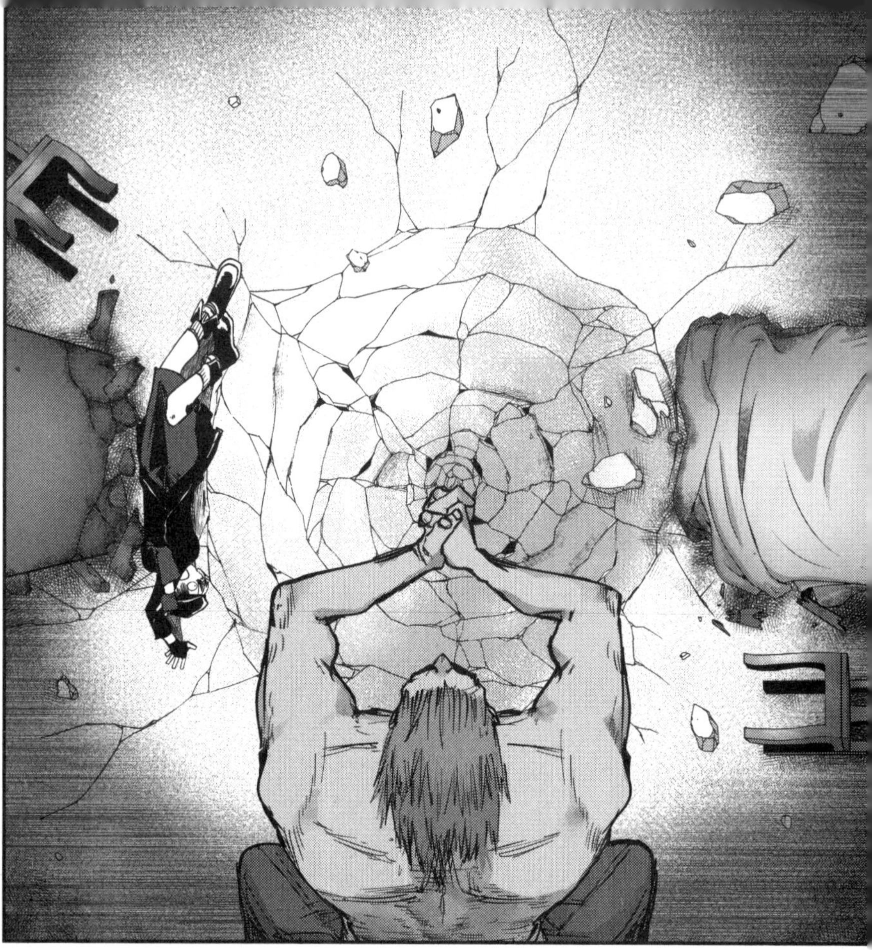

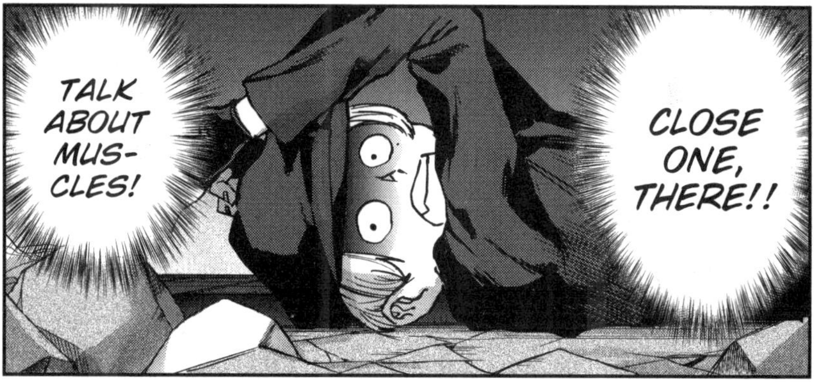
CLOSE ONE, THERE!!
TALK ABOUT MUS- CLES!

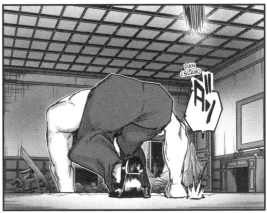

DAN
(SLAM)

MINE
NOW—

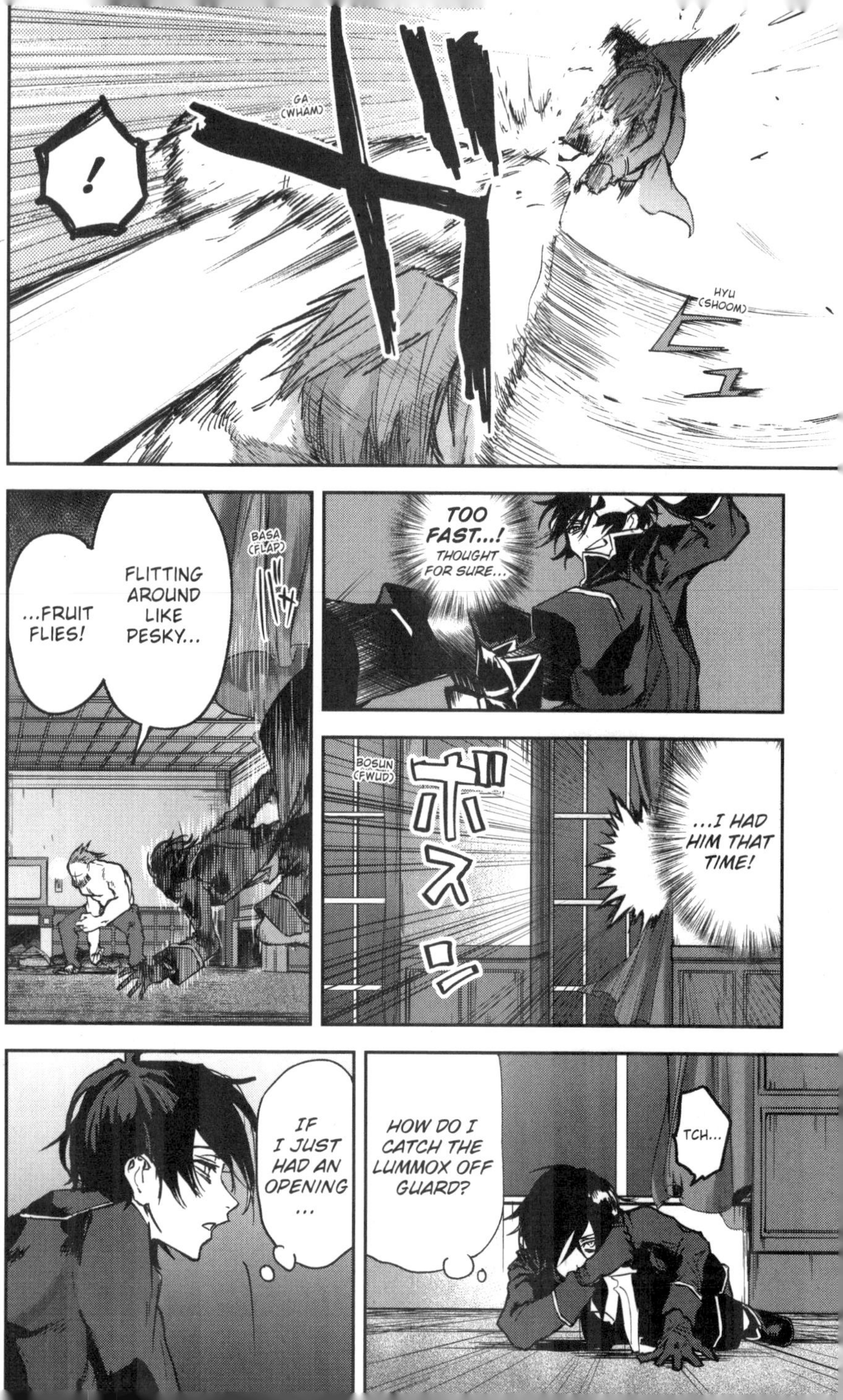

HYU (SHOOM)
GA (WHAM)
!
TOO FAST...! THOUGHT FOR SURE...
BASA (FLAP)
FLITTING AROUND LIKE PESKY...
...FRUIT FLIES!
BOSUN (FWUD)
...I HAD HIM THAT TIME!
TCH...
HOW DO I CATCH THE LUMMOX OFF GUARD?
IF I JUST HAD AN OPENING...

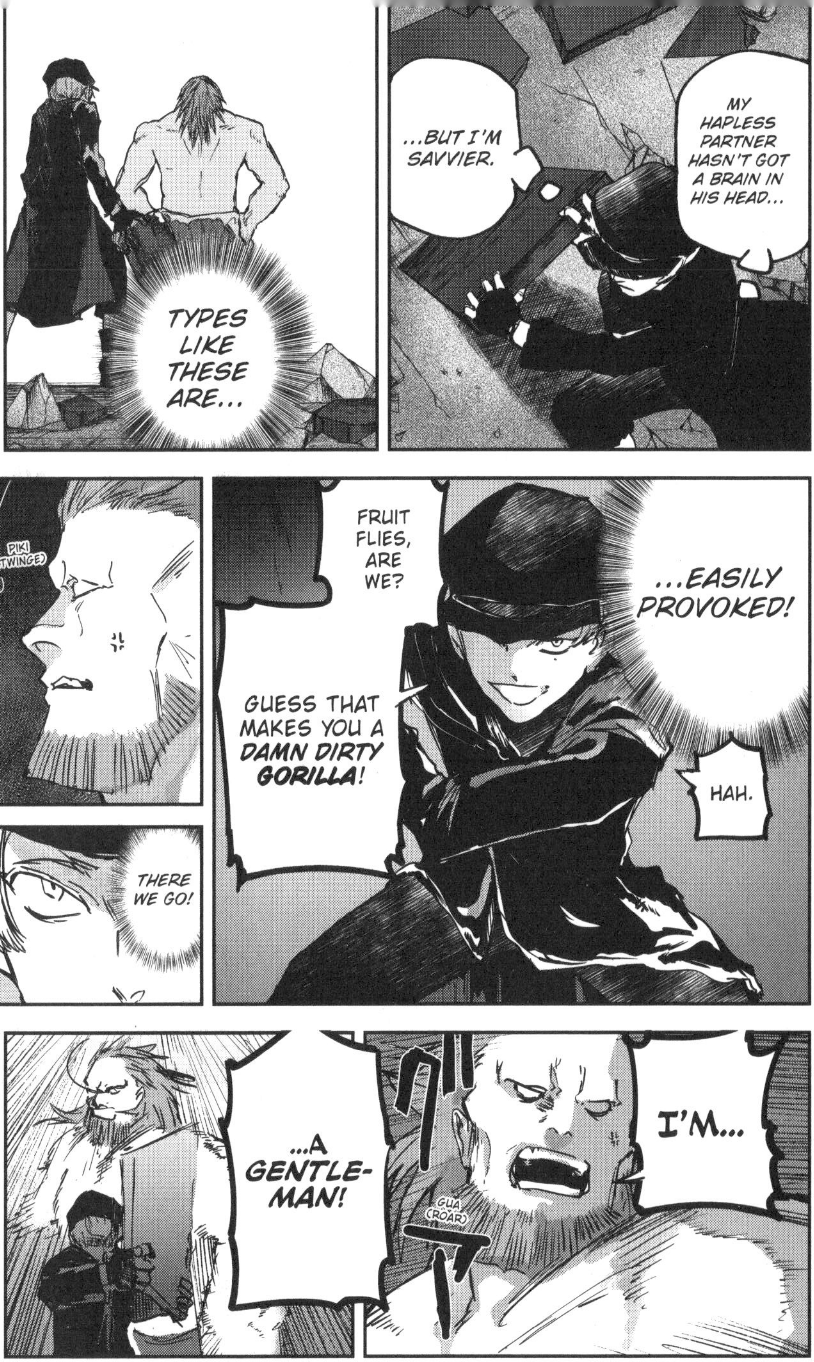
MY HAPLESS PARTNER HASN'T GOT A BRAIN IN HIS HEAD...
...BUT I'M SAVVIER.
TYPES LIKE THESE ARE...
...EASILY PROVOKED!
FRUIT FLIES, ARE WE?
HAH.
GUESS THAT MAKES YOU A *DAMN DIRTY* ***GORILLA***!
PIKI (TWINGE)
THERE WE GO!
I'M...
GUA (ROAR)
...A GENTLE-MAN!

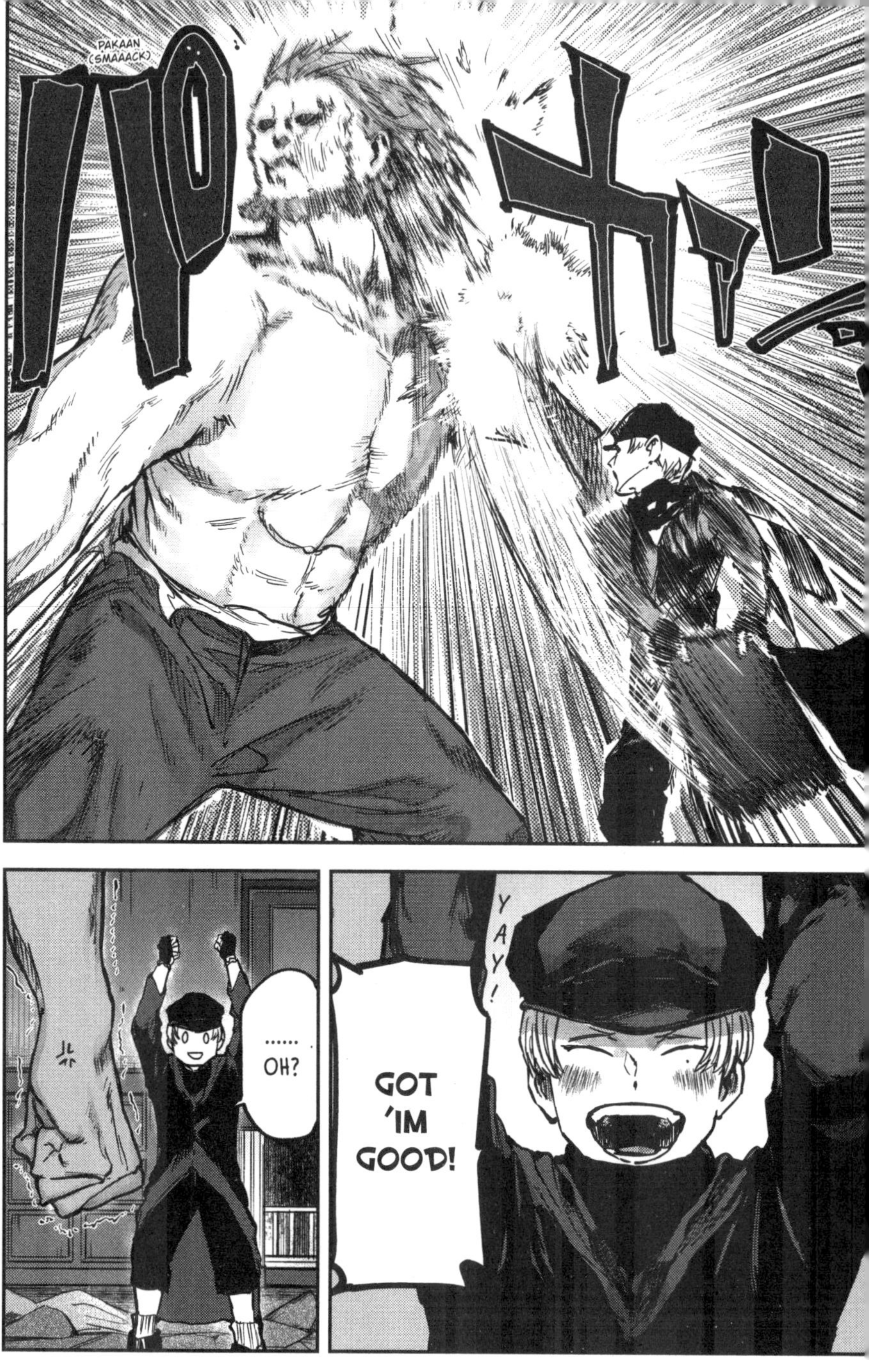
PAKAAN
(SMAAACK)
YAY!
GOT 'IM GOOD!
...... OH?

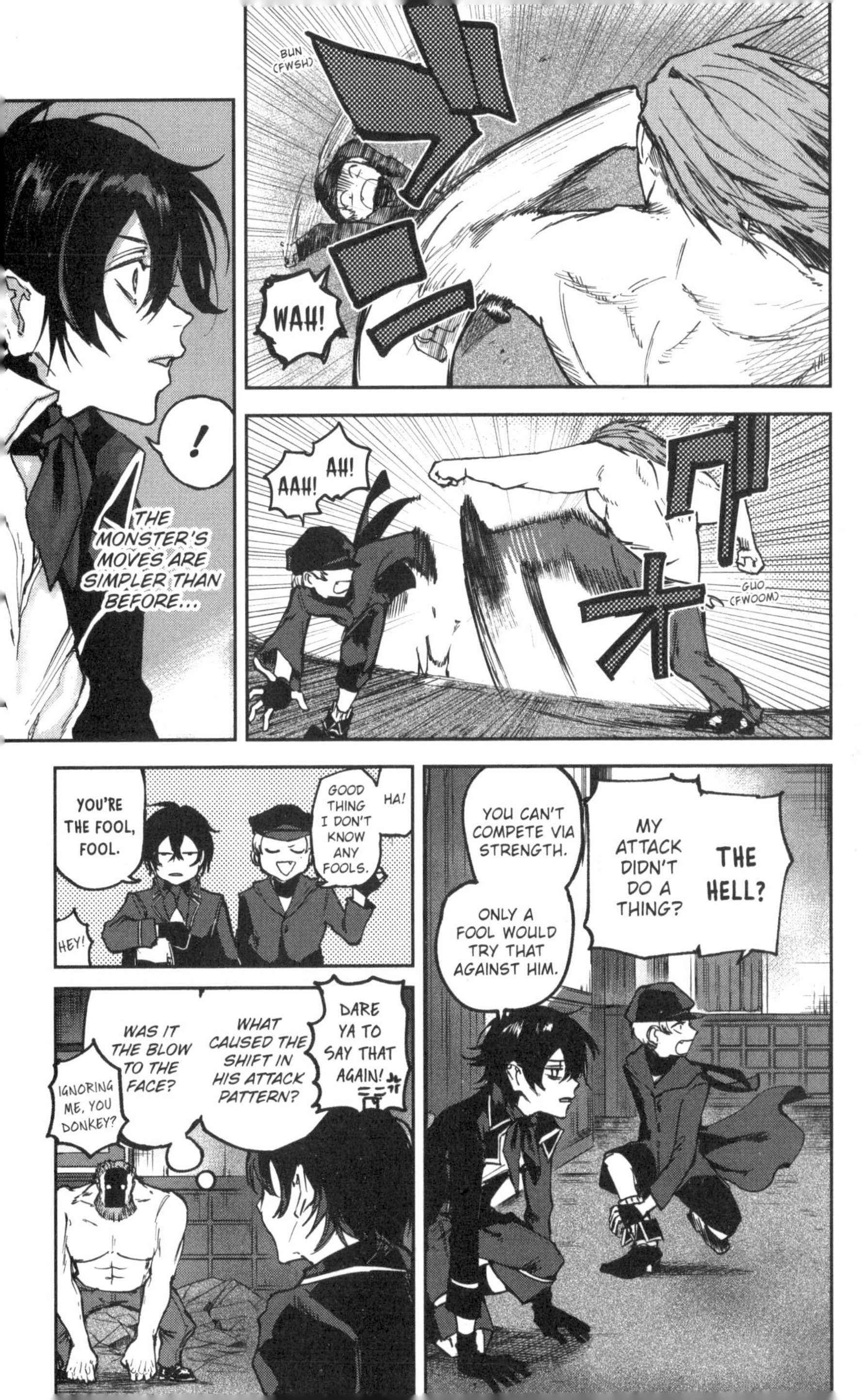
BUN (FWSH)
WAH!
AH!
AAH!
GUO (FWOOM)
!
THE MONSTER'S MOVES ARE SIMPLER THAN BEFORE...
THE HELL?
MY ATTACK DIDN'T DO A THING?
YOU CAN'T COMPETE VIA STRENGTH.
ONLY A FOOL WOULD TRY THAT AGAINST HIM.
HA!
GOOD THING I DON'T KNOW ANY FOOLS.
YOU'RE THE FOOL, FOOL.
HEY!
DARE YA TO SAY THAT AGAIN!
WHAT CAUSED THE SHIFT IN HIS ATTACK PATTERN?
WAS IT THE BLOW TO THE FACE?
IGNORING ME, YOU DONKEY?

HEY!

PAY ATTENTION TO ME!

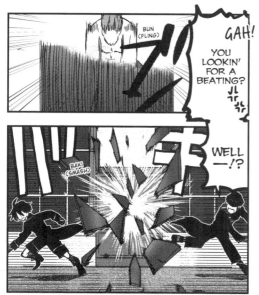

BUN (FLING)

GAH!

YOU LOOKIN' FOR A BEATING?

BAKI (SMASH)

WELL—!?

YOU INFANT...

← YOUNGER   OLDER →

PARIN (SHATTER)

ZA (SHF)

!

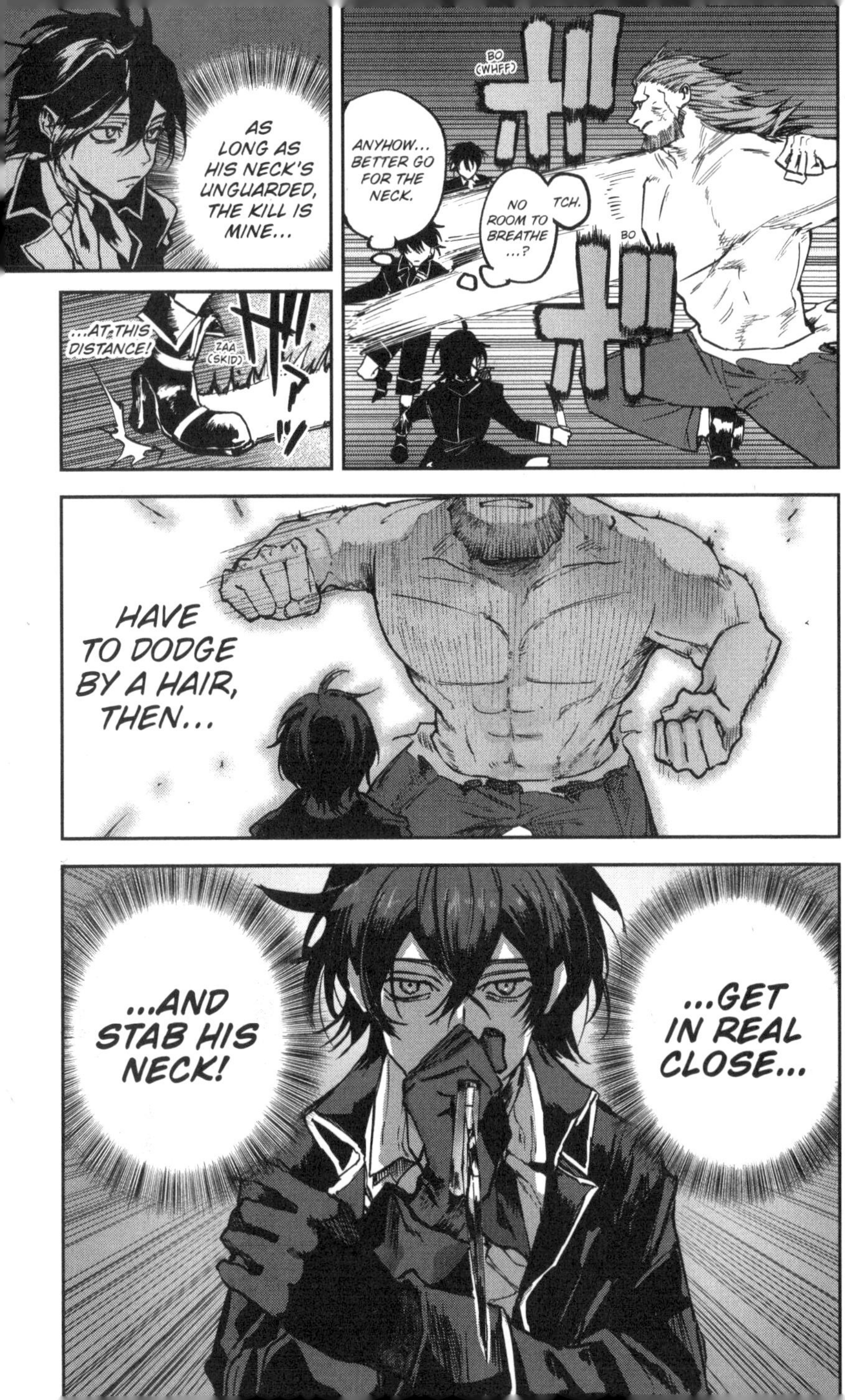
BO (WHFF)
TCH.
NO ROOM TO BREATHE ...?
BO
ANYHOW... BETTER GO FOR THE NECK.
AS LONG AS HIS NECK'S UNGUARDED, THE KILL IS MINE...
...AT THIS DISTANCE!
ZAA (SKID)
HAVE TO DODGE BY A HAIR, THEN...
...GET IN REAL CLOSE...
...AND STAB HIS NECK!

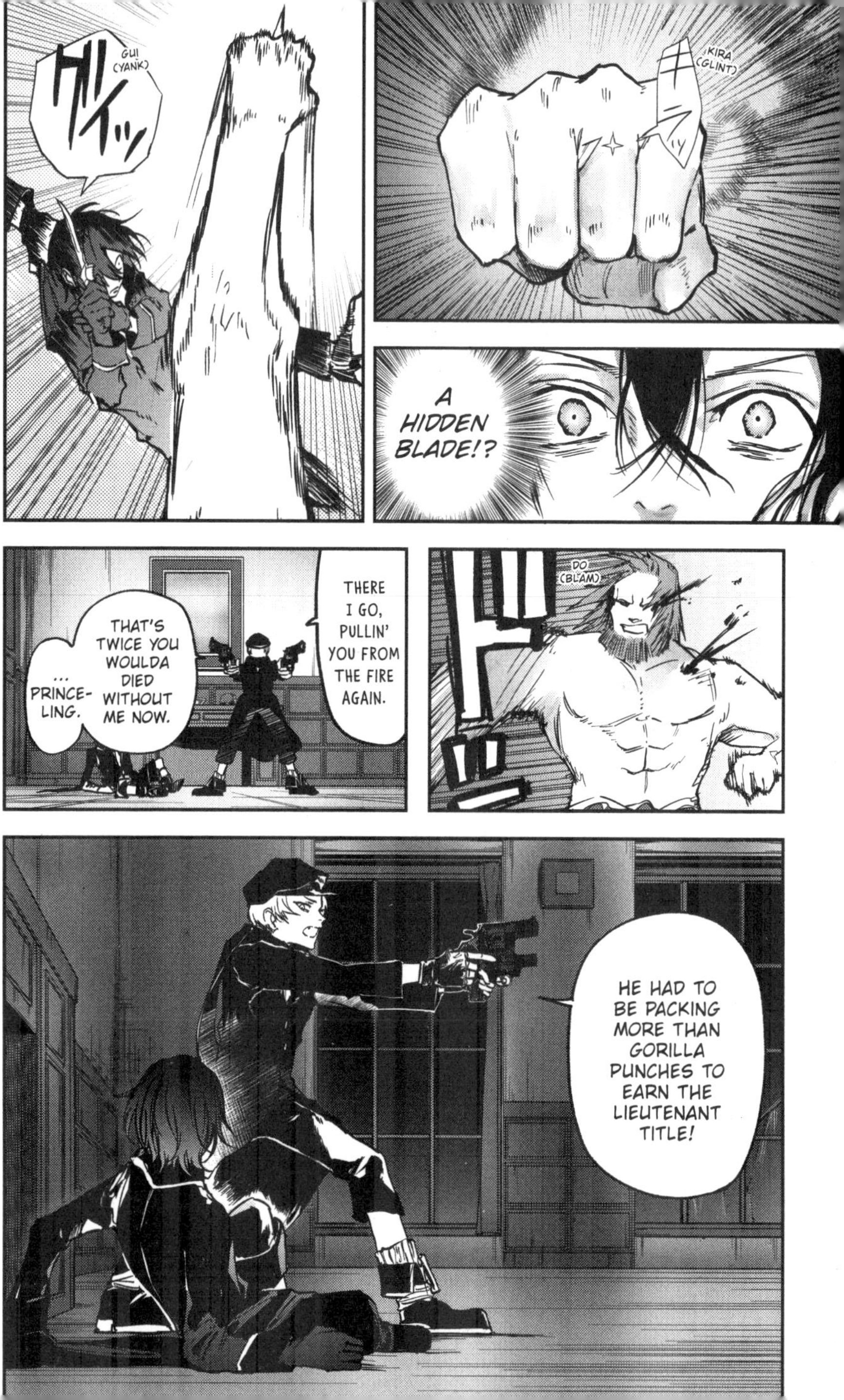
KIRA (GLINT)
A HIDDEN BLADE!?
グイッ
GUI (YANK)
DO (BLAM)
THERE I GO, PULLIN' YOU FROM THE FIRE AGAIN.
THAT'S TWICE YOU WOULDA DIED WITHOUT ME NOW.
... PRINCE-LING.
HE HAD TO BE PACKING MORE THAN GORILLA PUNCHES TO EARN THE LIEUTENANT TITLE!

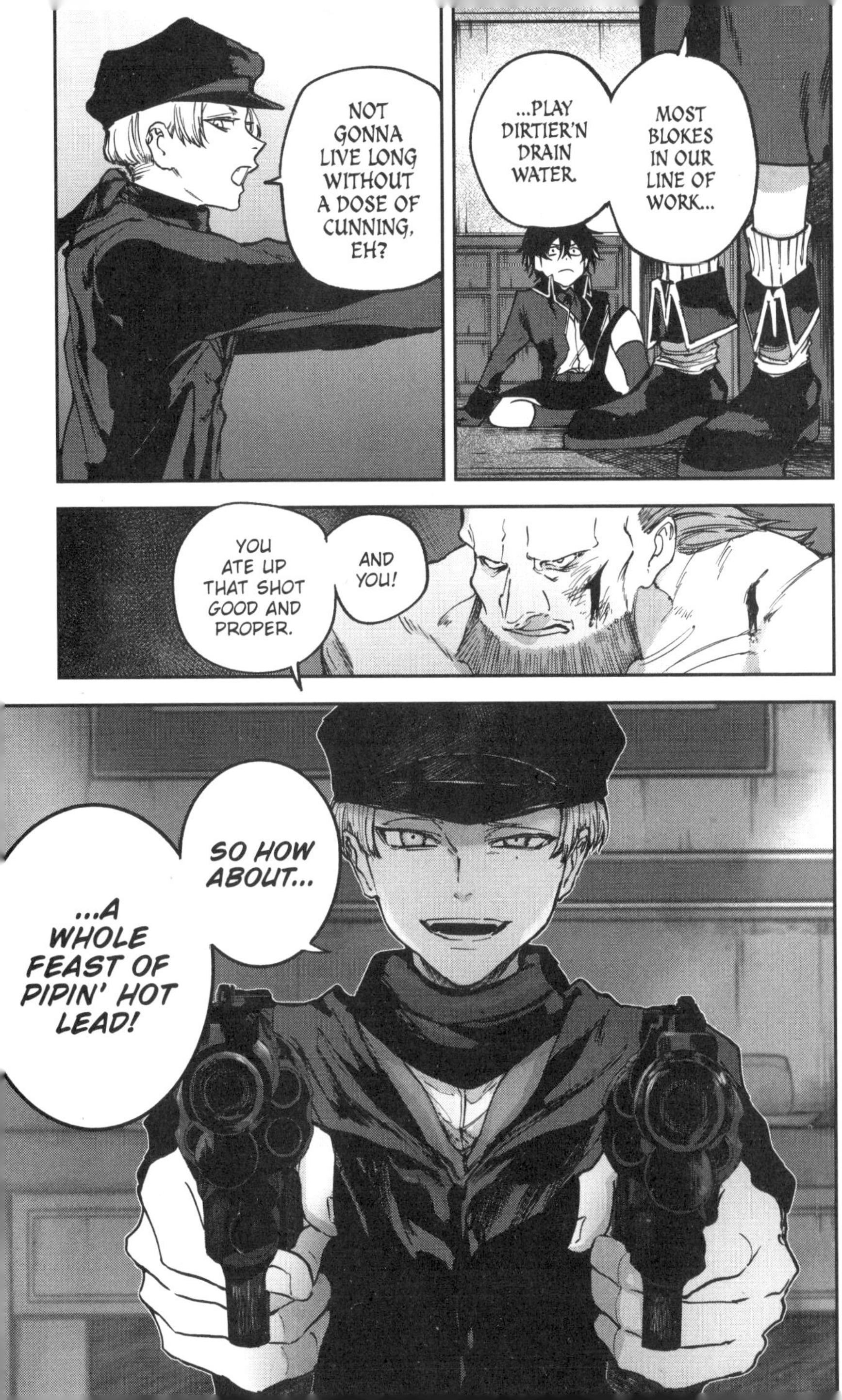
MOST BLOKES IN OUR LINE OF WORK...
...PLAY DIRTIER'N DRAIN WATER.
NOT GONNA LIVE LONG WITHOUT A DOSE OF CUNNING, EH?
AND YOU!
YOU ATE UP THAT SHOT GOOD AND PROPER.
SO HOW ABOUT...
...A WHOLE FEAST OF PIPIN' HOT LEAD!

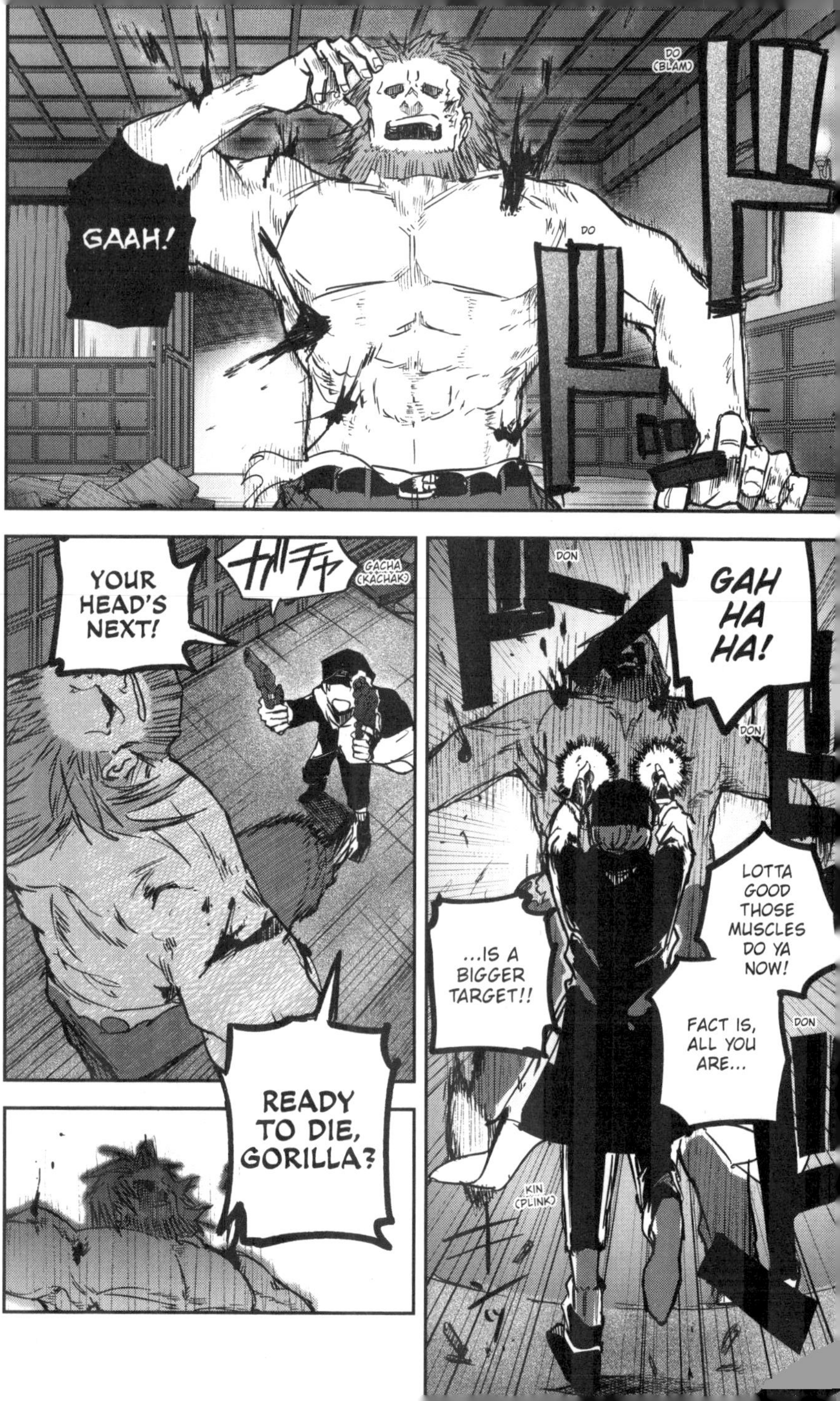
DO (BLAM)
DO
GAAH!
DON
GAH HA HA!
DON
LOTTA GOOD THOSE MUSCLES DO YA NOW!
DON
FACT IS, ALL YOU ARE...
...IS A BIGGER TARGET!!
KIN (PLINK)
ガチャ
GACHA (KACHAK)
YOUR HEAD'S NEXT!
READY TO DIE, GORILLA?

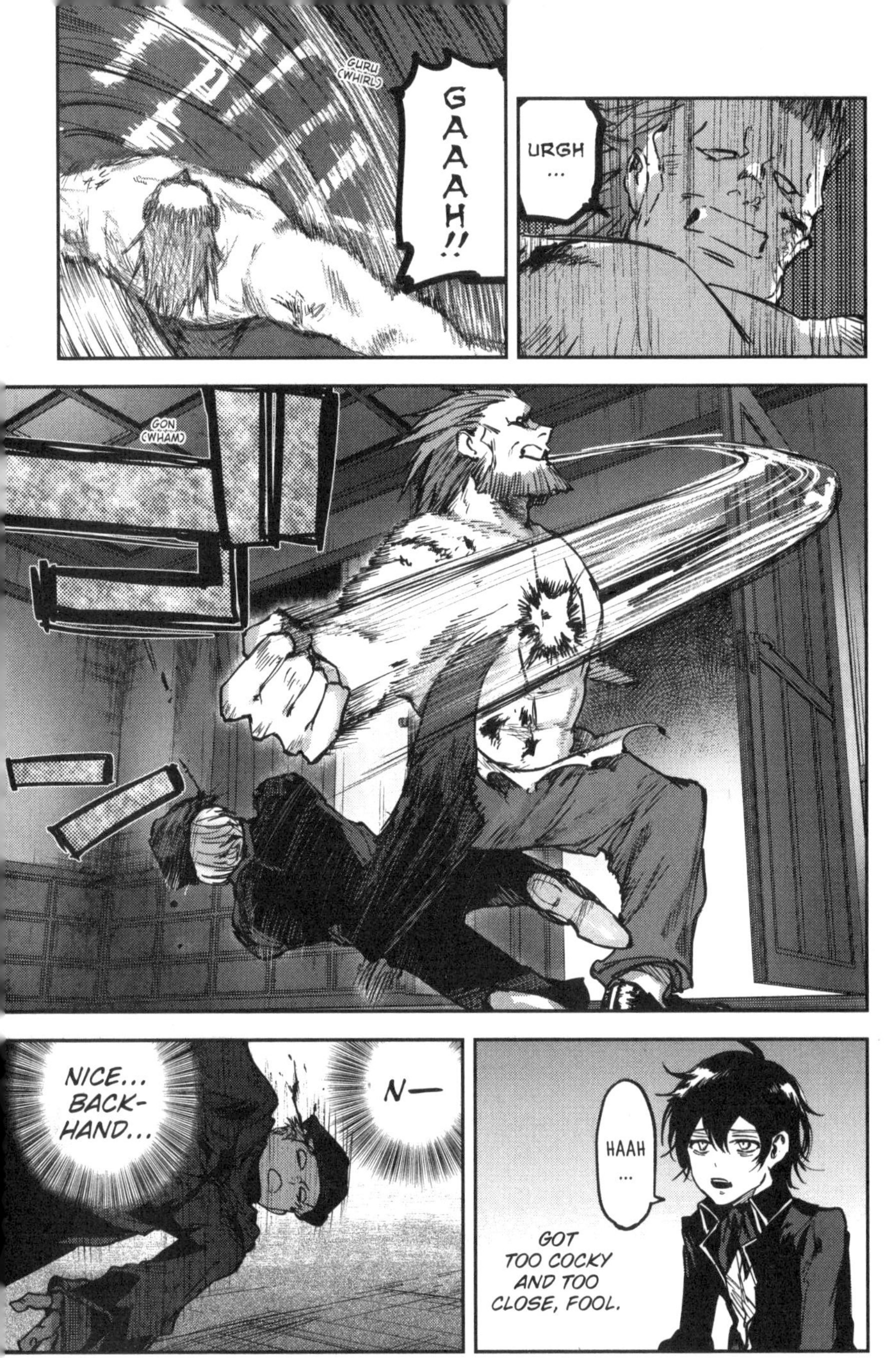
URGH ...
GURU (WHIRL)
GAAAH!!
GON (WHAM)
HAAH ...
GOT TOO COCKY AND TOO CLOSE, FOOL.
N—
NICE... BACK-HAND...

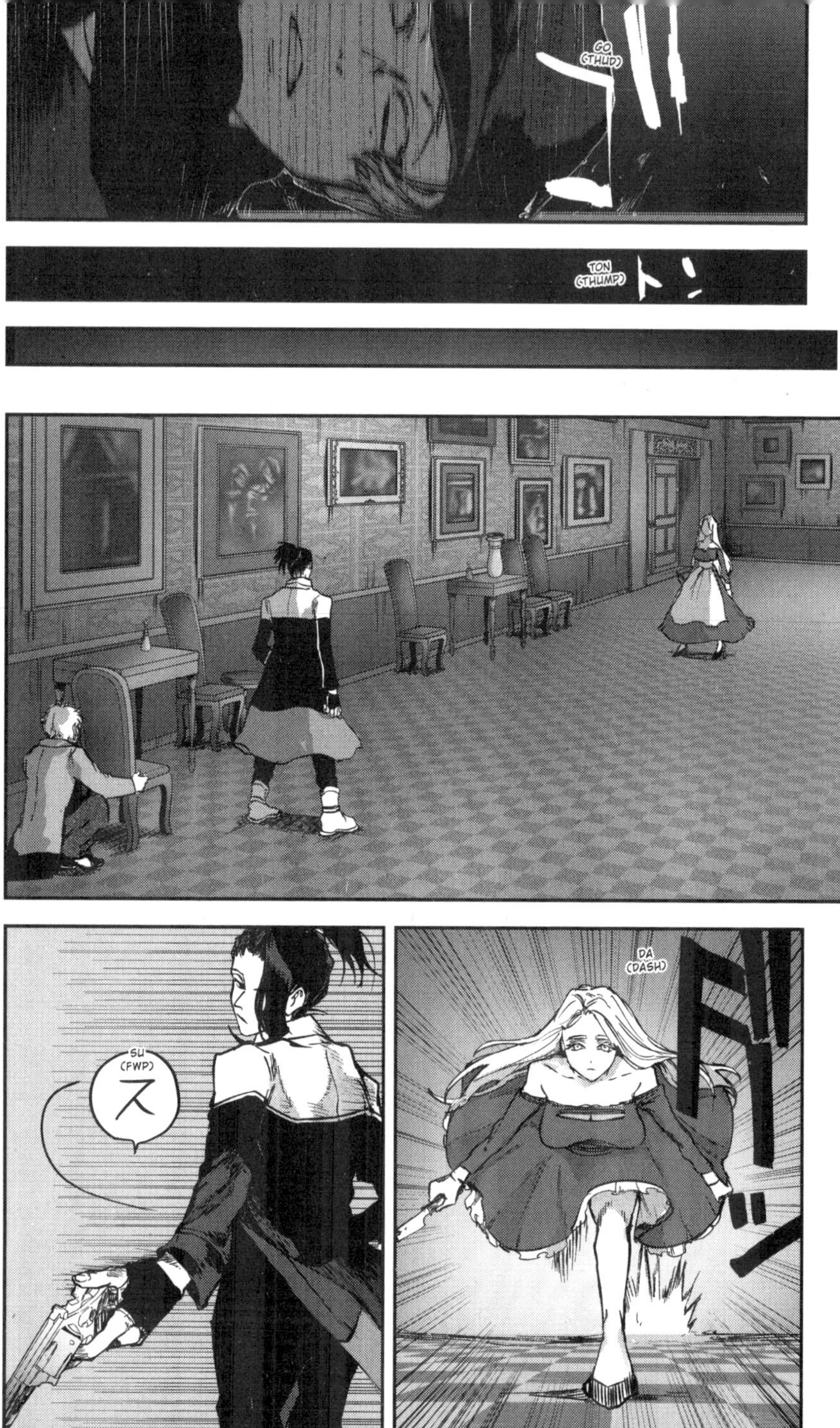
GO
(THUD)
TON
(THUMP)
DA
(DASH)
SU
(FWP)
ス

PAN
(BANG)

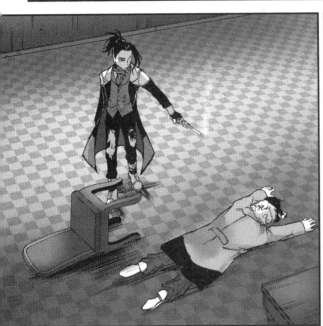

GATA
(CLATTER)

THERE.
NO REASON
LEFT FOR US
TO SCRAP.

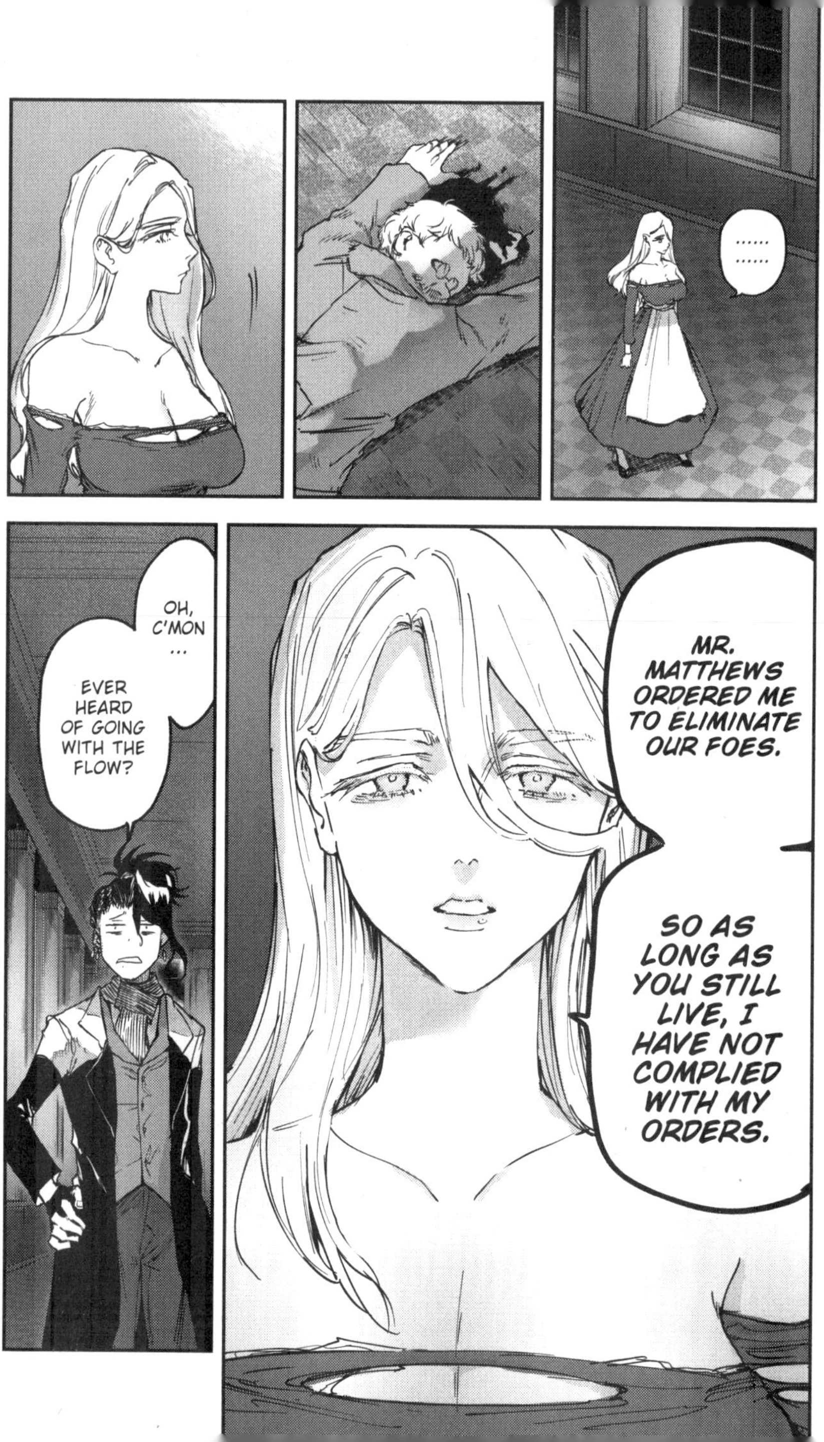
……
……
MR. MATTHEWS ORDERED ME TO ELIMINATE OUR FOES.
SO AS LONG AS YOU STILL LIVE, I HAVE NOT COMPLIED WITH MY ORDERS.
OH, C'MON …
EVER HEARD OF GOING WITH THE FLOW?

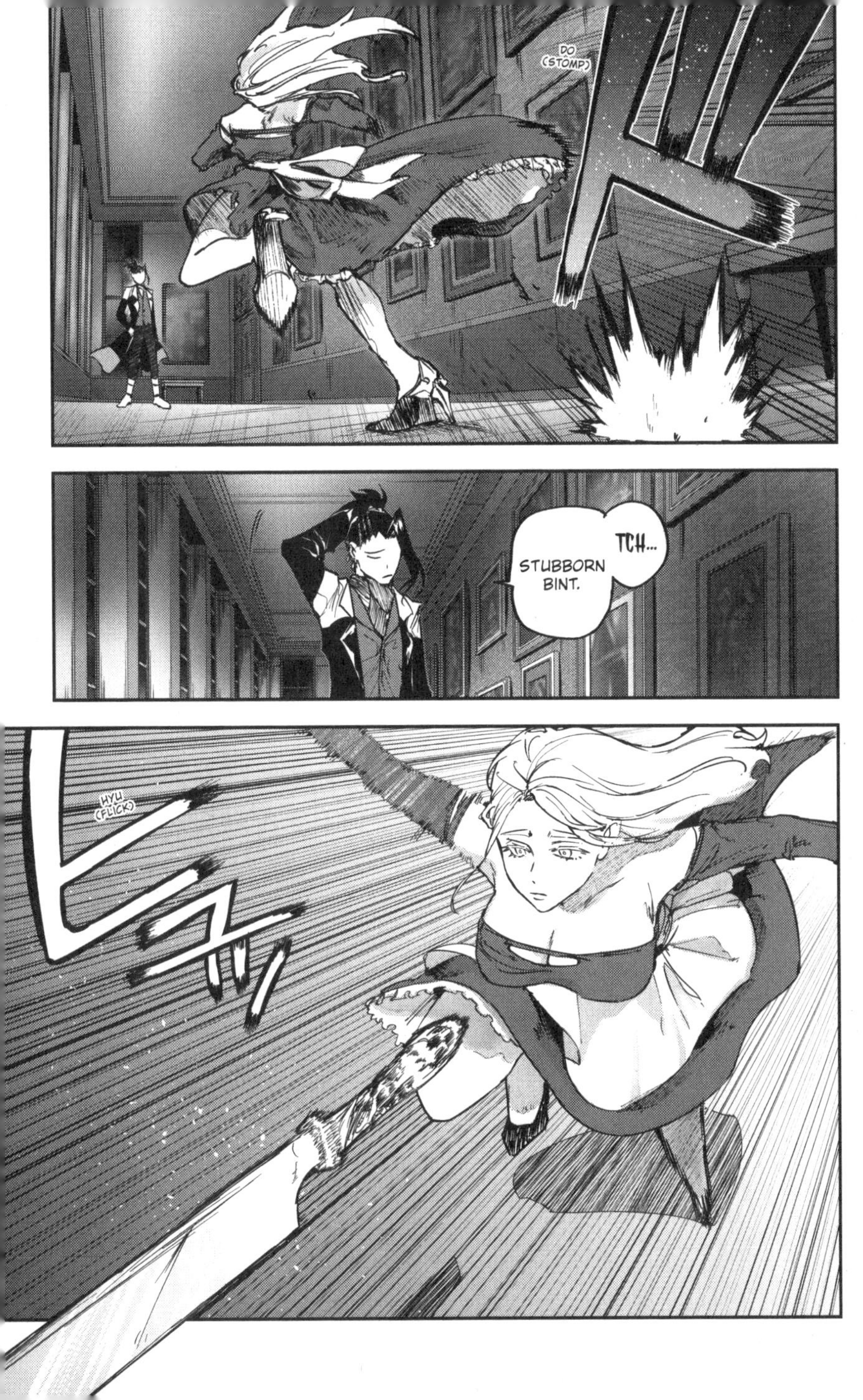
DO
(STOMP)
TCH...
STUBBORN
BINT.
HYU
(FLICK)

ZA
(ZOOSH)
GA
(GRIP)
BAN
(BANG)
BAN
BA
(FWAP)
KIN
(PLINK)
KIN
HYUPA
(FWOOSH)
!

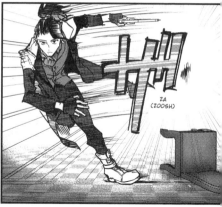

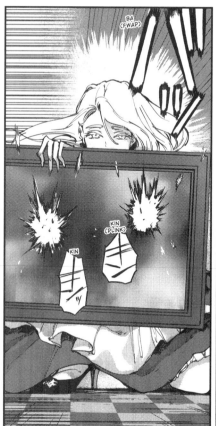

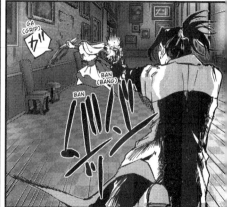

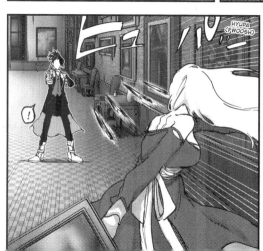

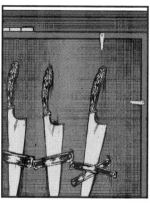

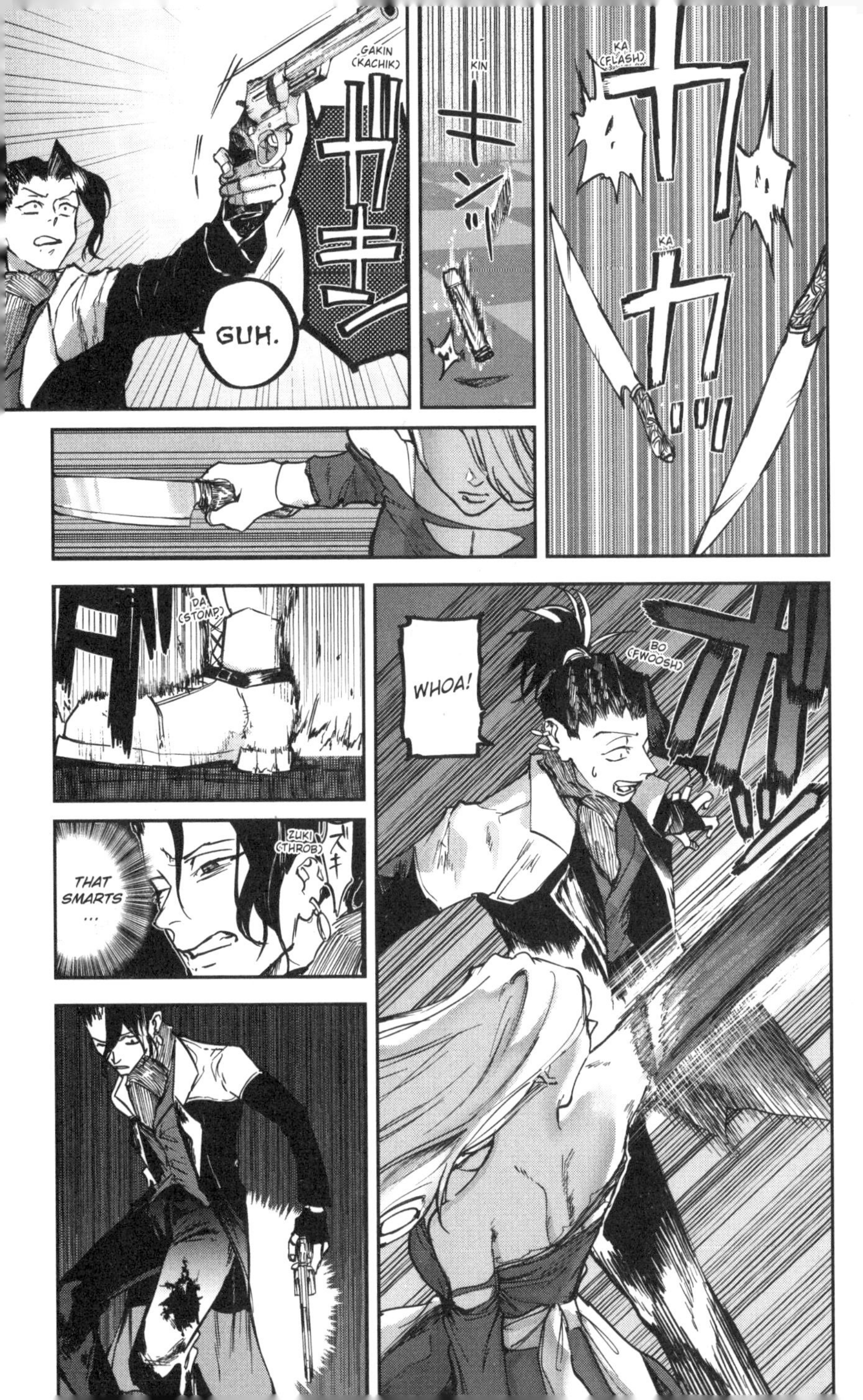
KA (FLASH)
KA
KIN
GAKIN (KACHIK)
GUH.
BO (FWOOSH)
WHOA!
DA (STOMP)
ZUKI (THROB)
THAT SMARTS ...

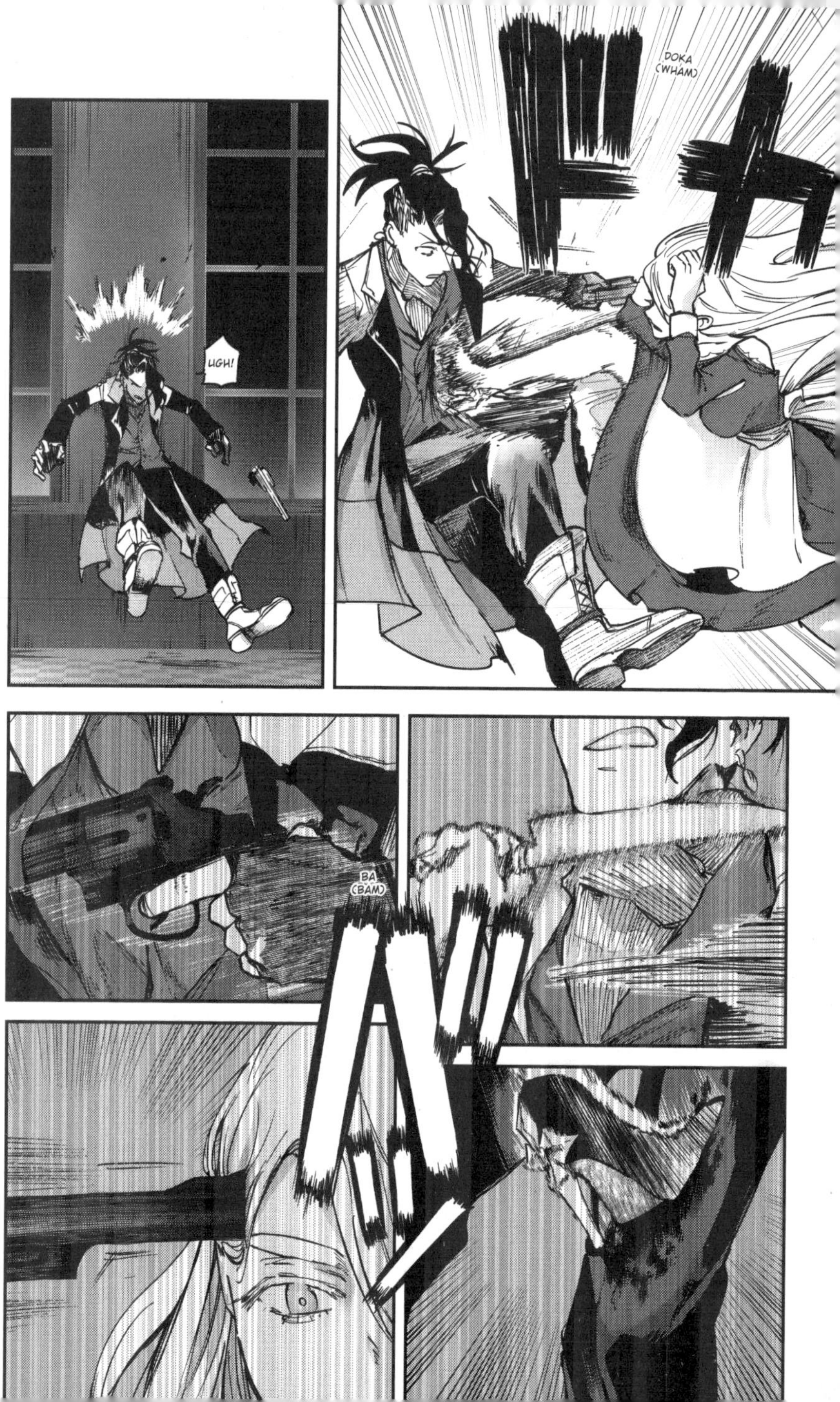
DOKA
(WHAM)
UGH!
BA
(BAM)

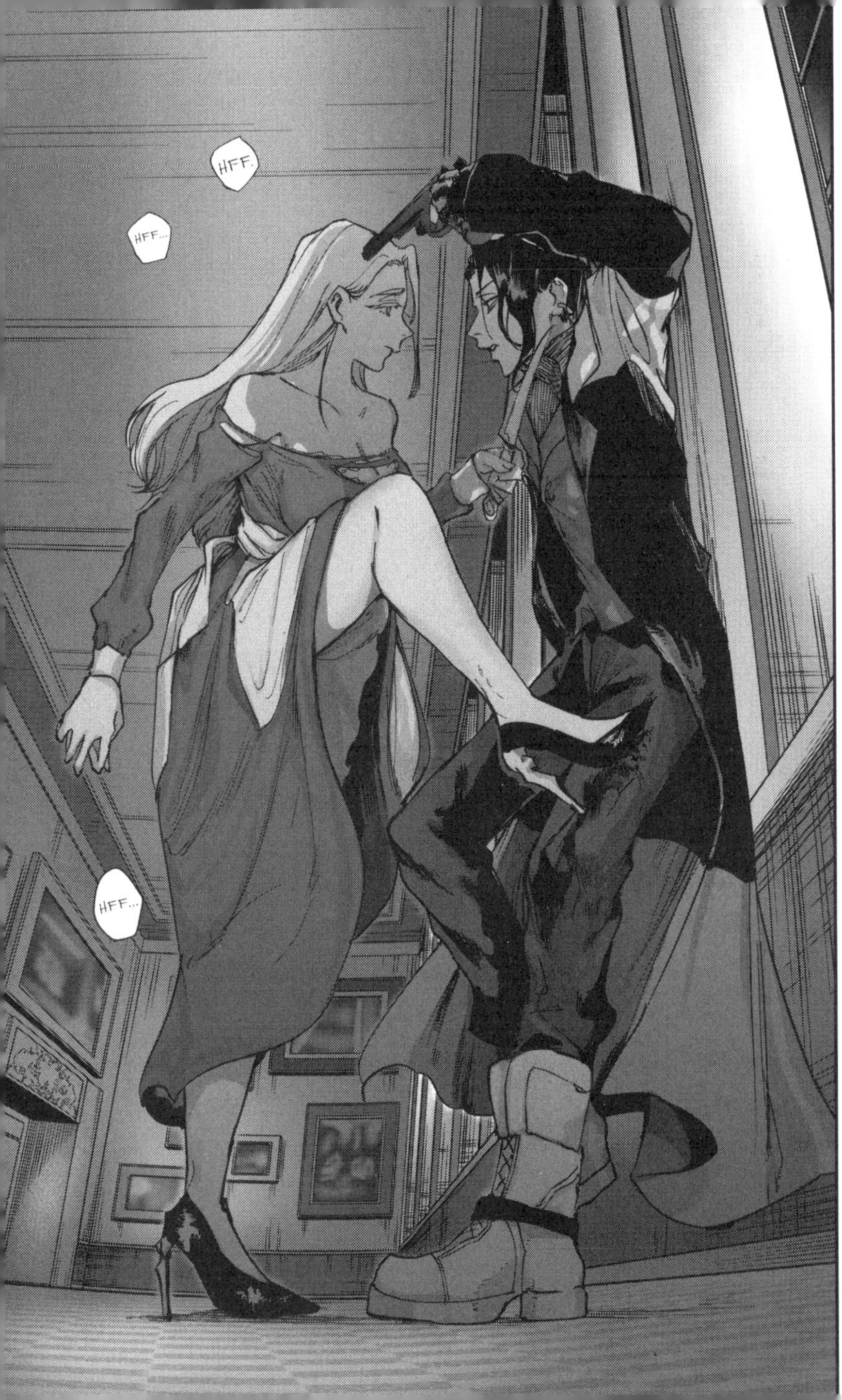
HFF.
HFF...
HFF...

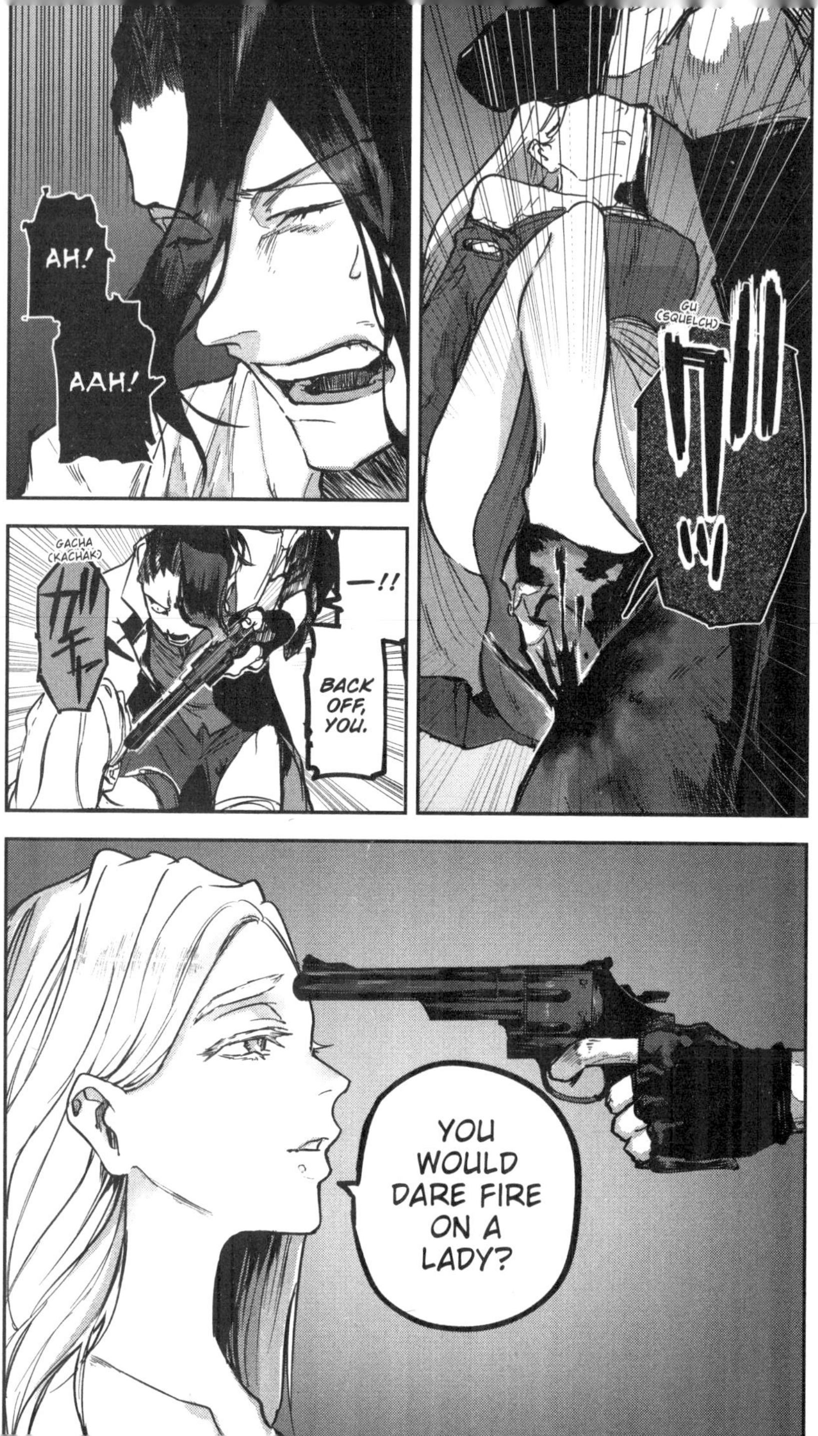
GU (SQUELCH)
AH!
AAH!
GACHA (KACHAK)
—!!
BACK OFF, YOU.
YOU WOULD DARE FIRE ON A LADY?

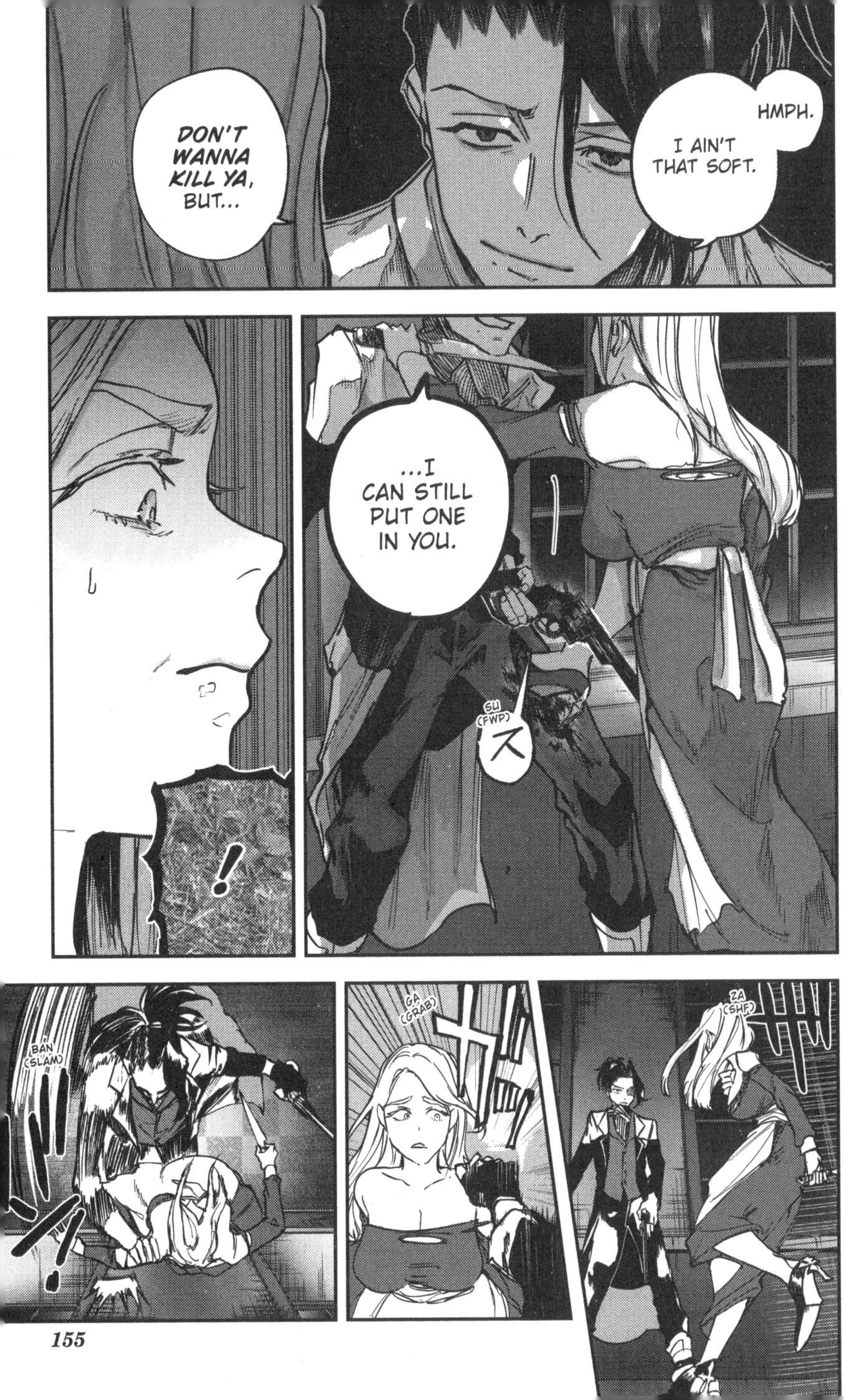
HMPH.
I AIN'T THAT SOFT.
DON'T WANNA KILL YA, BUT...
...I CAN STILL PUT ONE IN YOU.
SU (FWP) ス
!
ZA (SHF)
GA (GRAB)
BAN (SLAM)

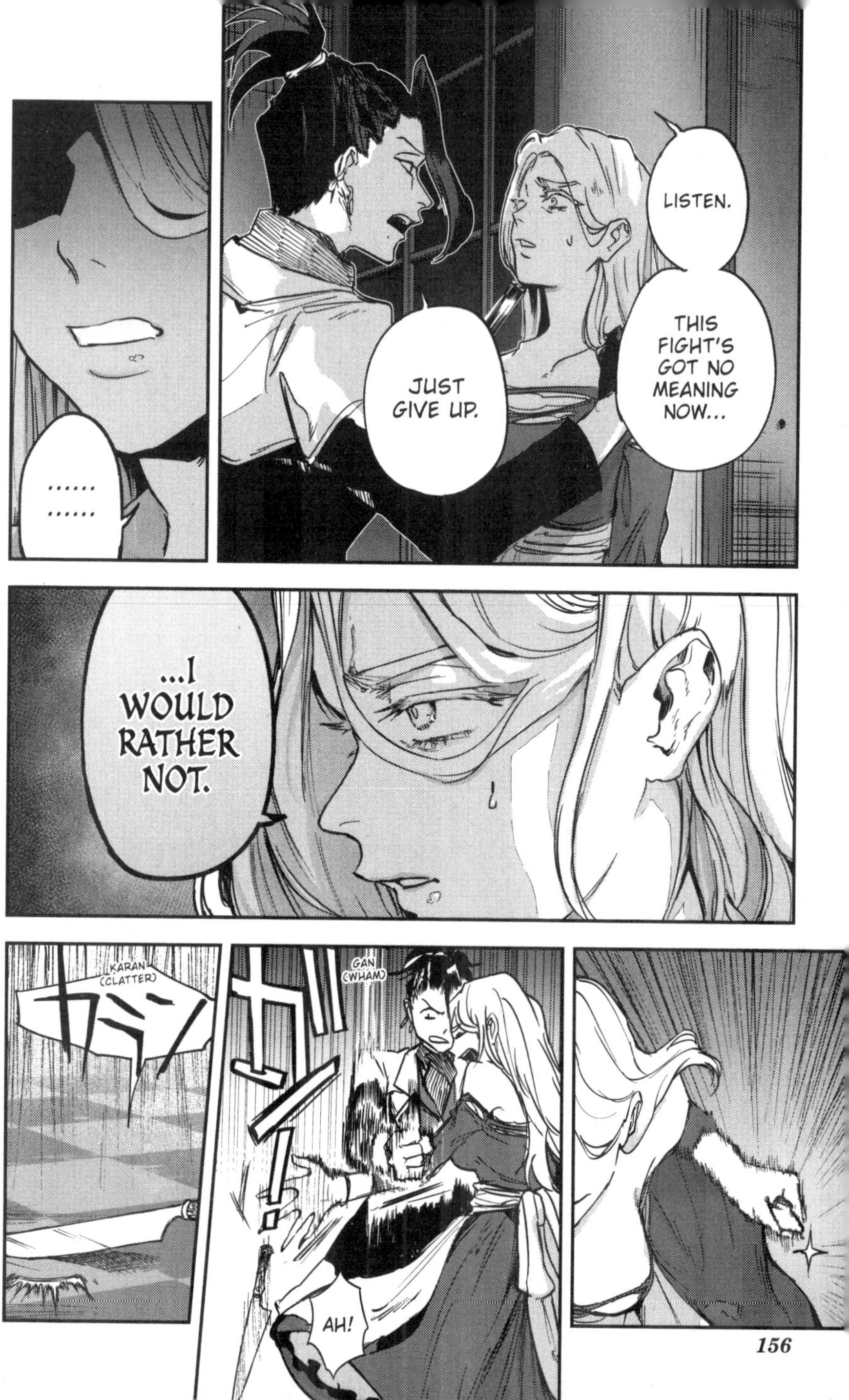
LISTEN.
THIS FIGHT'S GOT NO MEANING NOW...
JUST GIVE UP.
....
...I WOULD RATHER NOT.
GAN (WHAM)
!
AH!
KARAN (CLATTER)

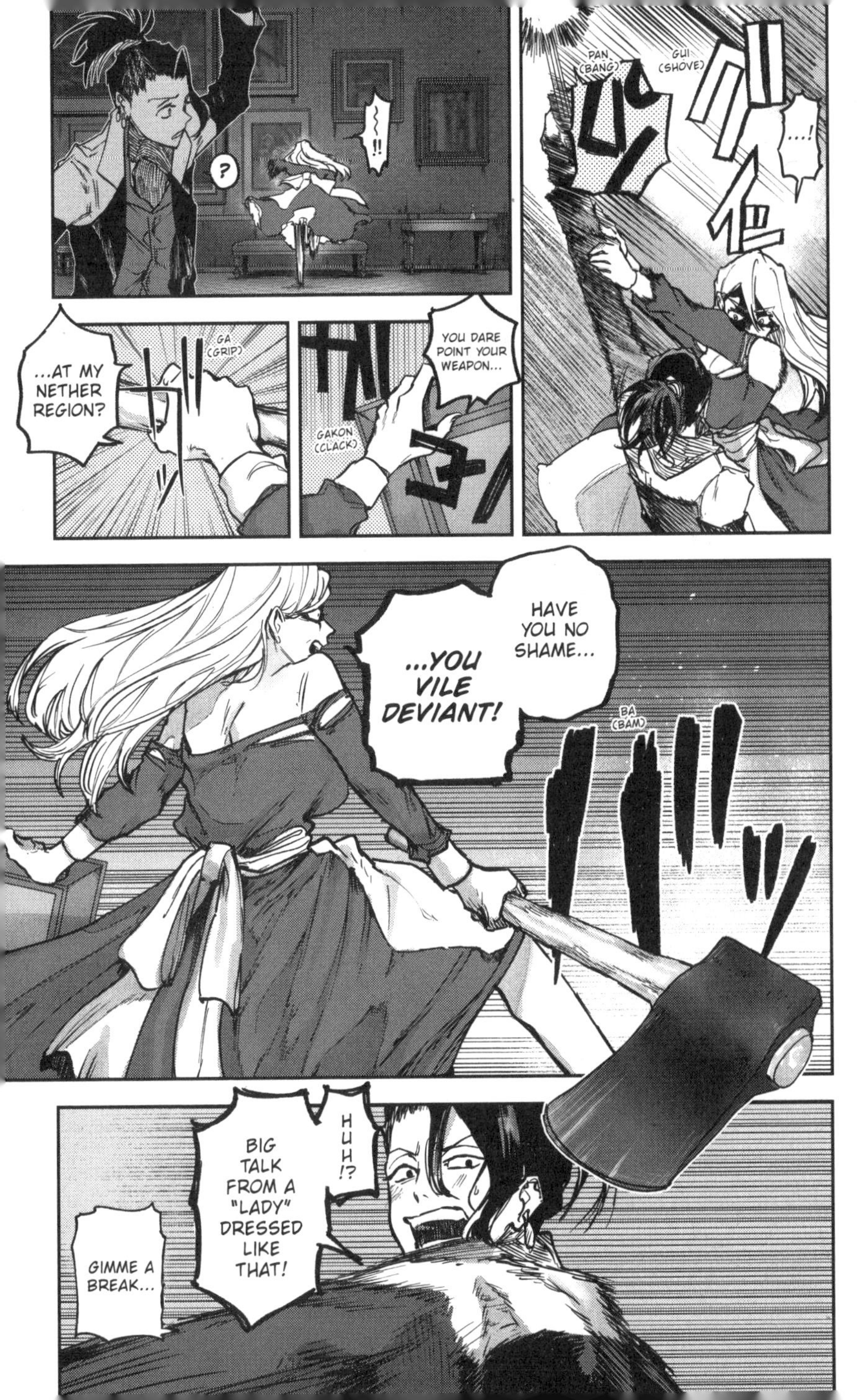
GUI (SHOVE)
PAN (BANG)
...!
~~~!!
?
YOU DARE POINT YOUR WEAPON...
GAKON (CLACK)
GA (GRIP)
...AT MY NETHER REGION?
HAVE YOU NO SHAME...
...YOU VILE DEVIANT!
BA (BAM)
HUH!?
BIG TALK FROM A "LADY" DRESSED LIKE THAT!
GIMME A BREAK...
~~~

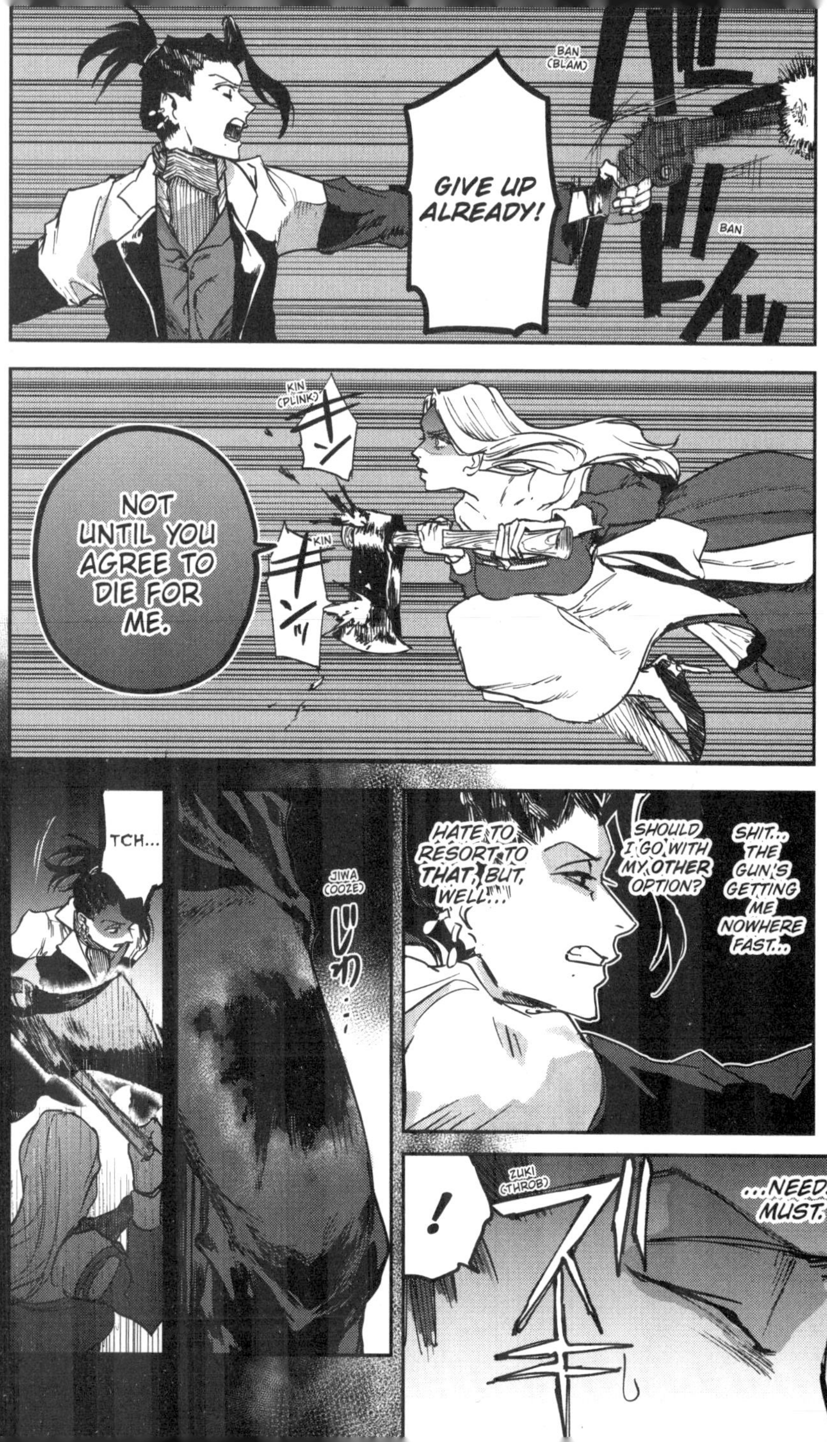
BAN (BLAM)
GIVE UP ALREADY!
BAN
KIN (PLINK)
KIN
NOT UNTIL YOU AGREE TO DIE FOR ME.
SHIT... THE GUN'S GETTING ME NOWHERE FAST...
SHOULD I GO WITH MY OTHER OPTION?
HATE TO RESORT TO THAT, BUT, WELL...
...NEEDS MUST.
ZUKI (THROB)
!
JIWA (OOZE)
TCH...

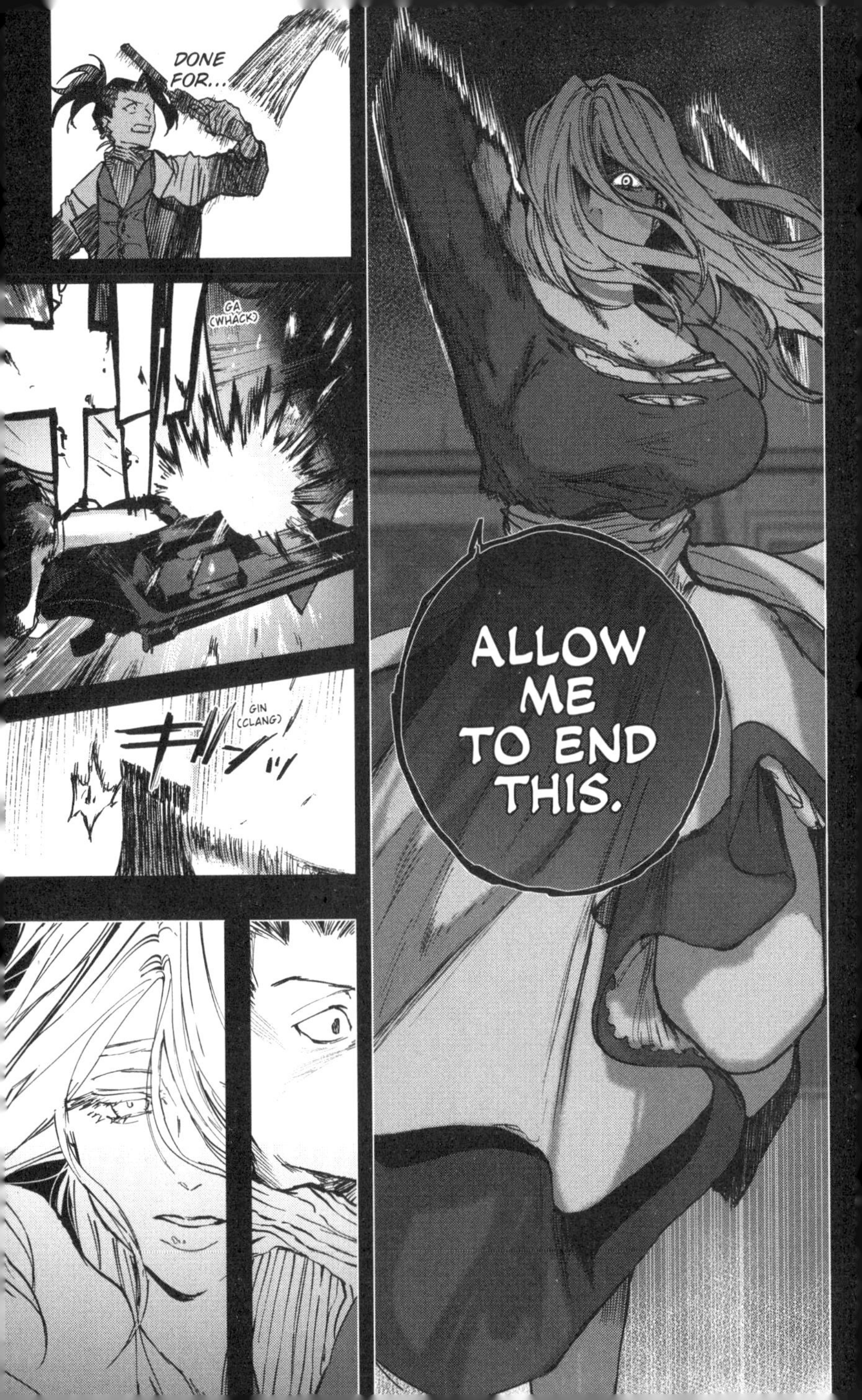
ALLOW ME TO END THIS.
DONE FOR...
GA (WHACK)
GIN (CLANG)

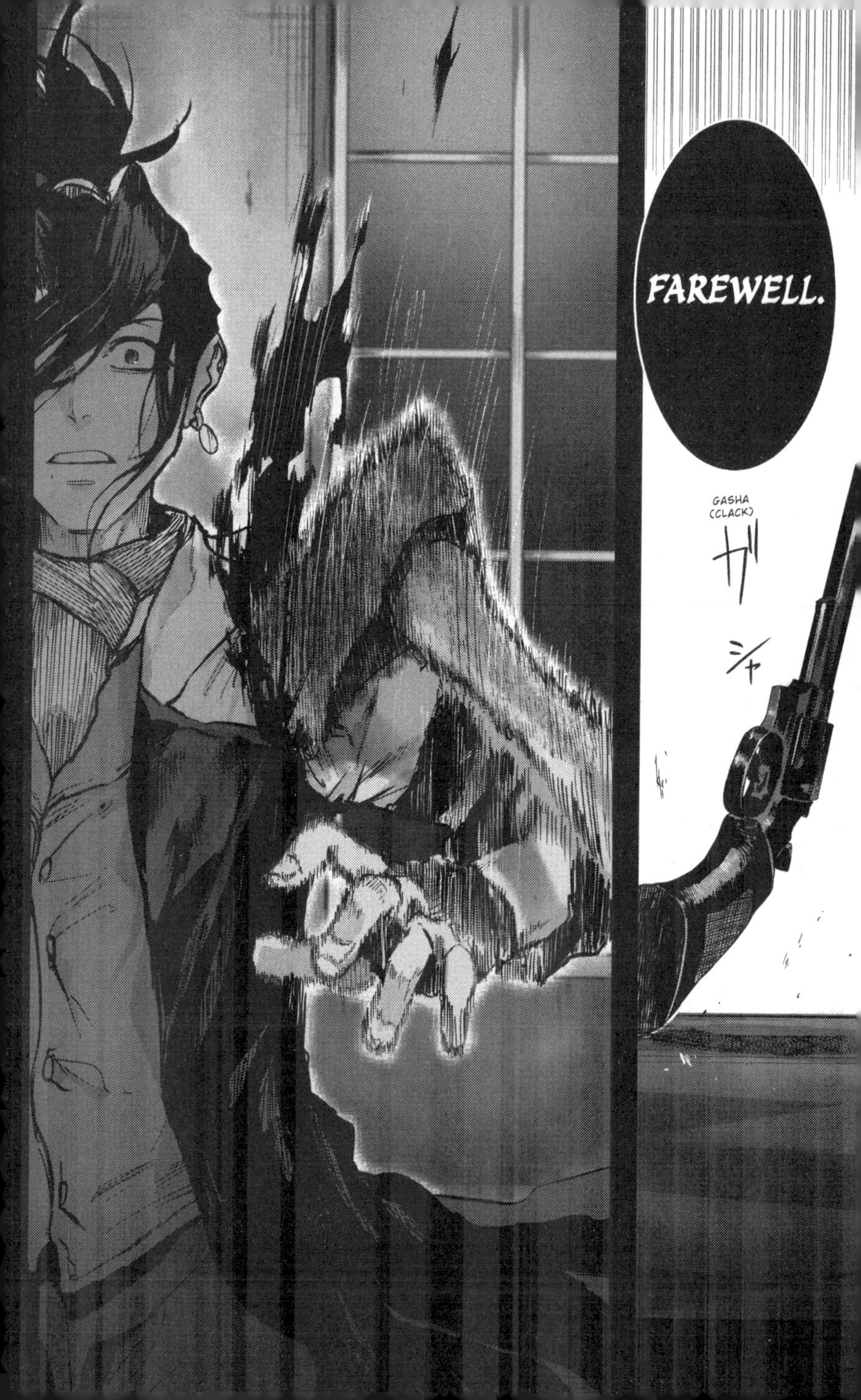
FAREWELL.
GASHA
(CLACK)
ガ
シャ

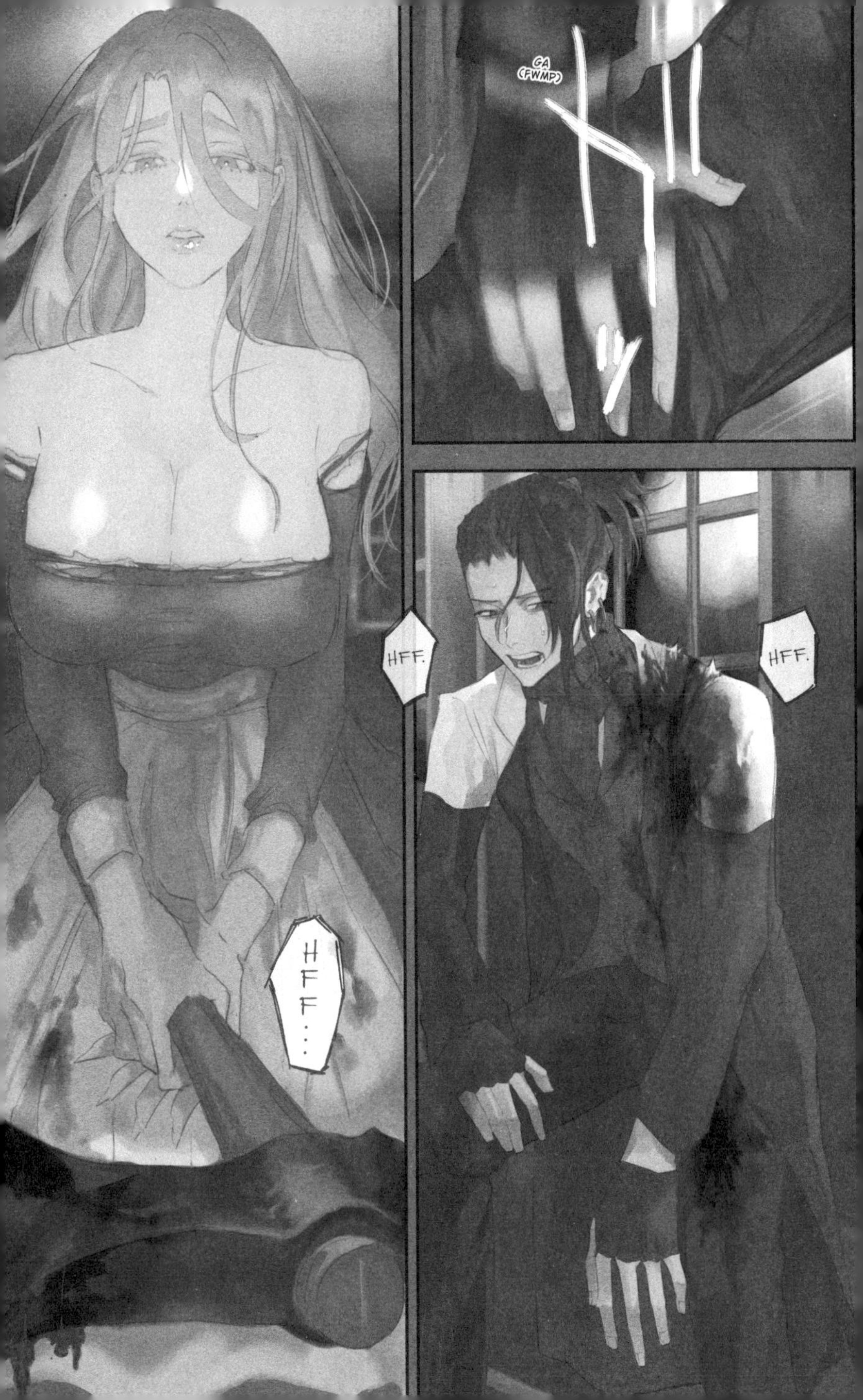
GA
(FWMP)
HFF.
HFF.
HFF...

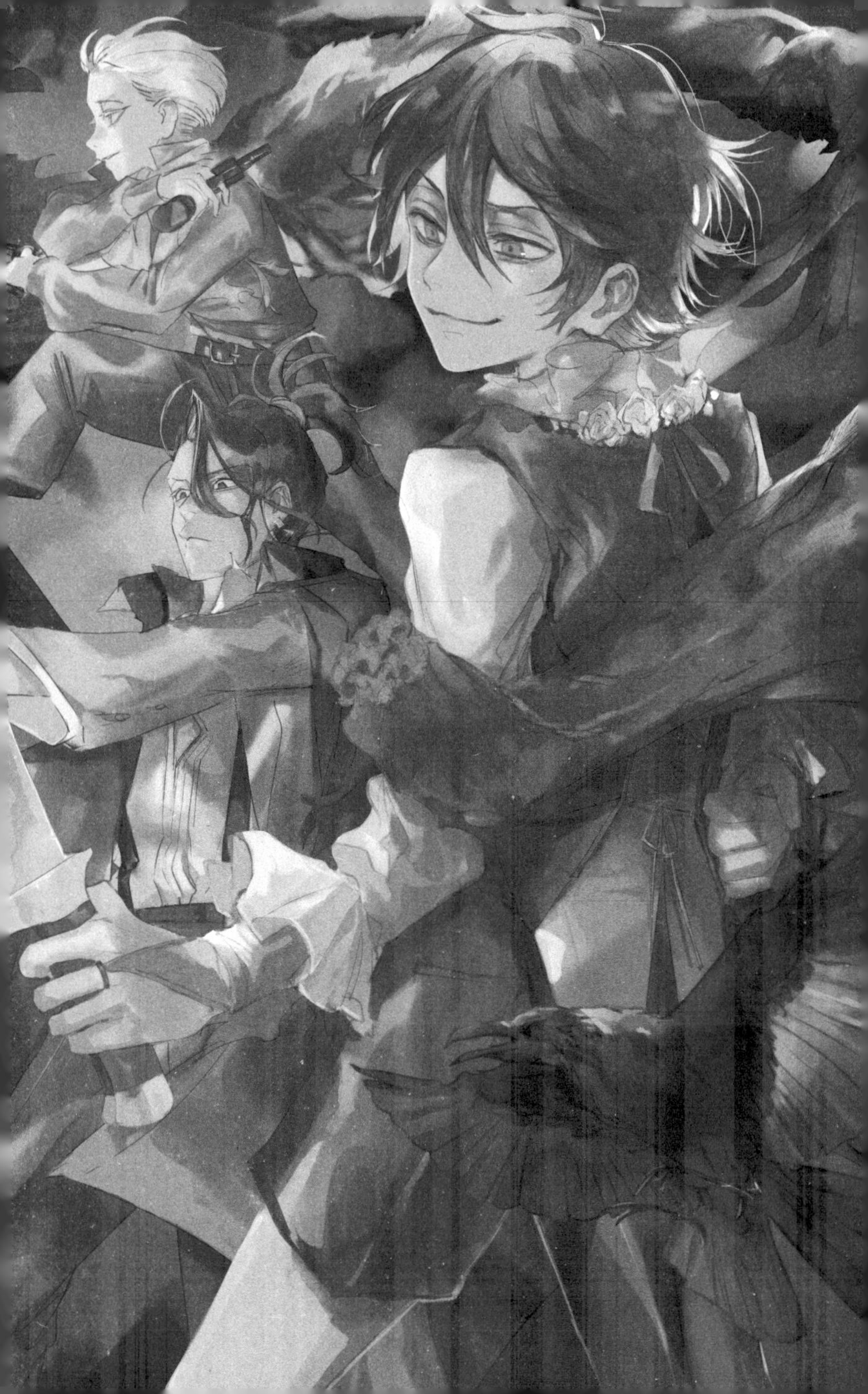

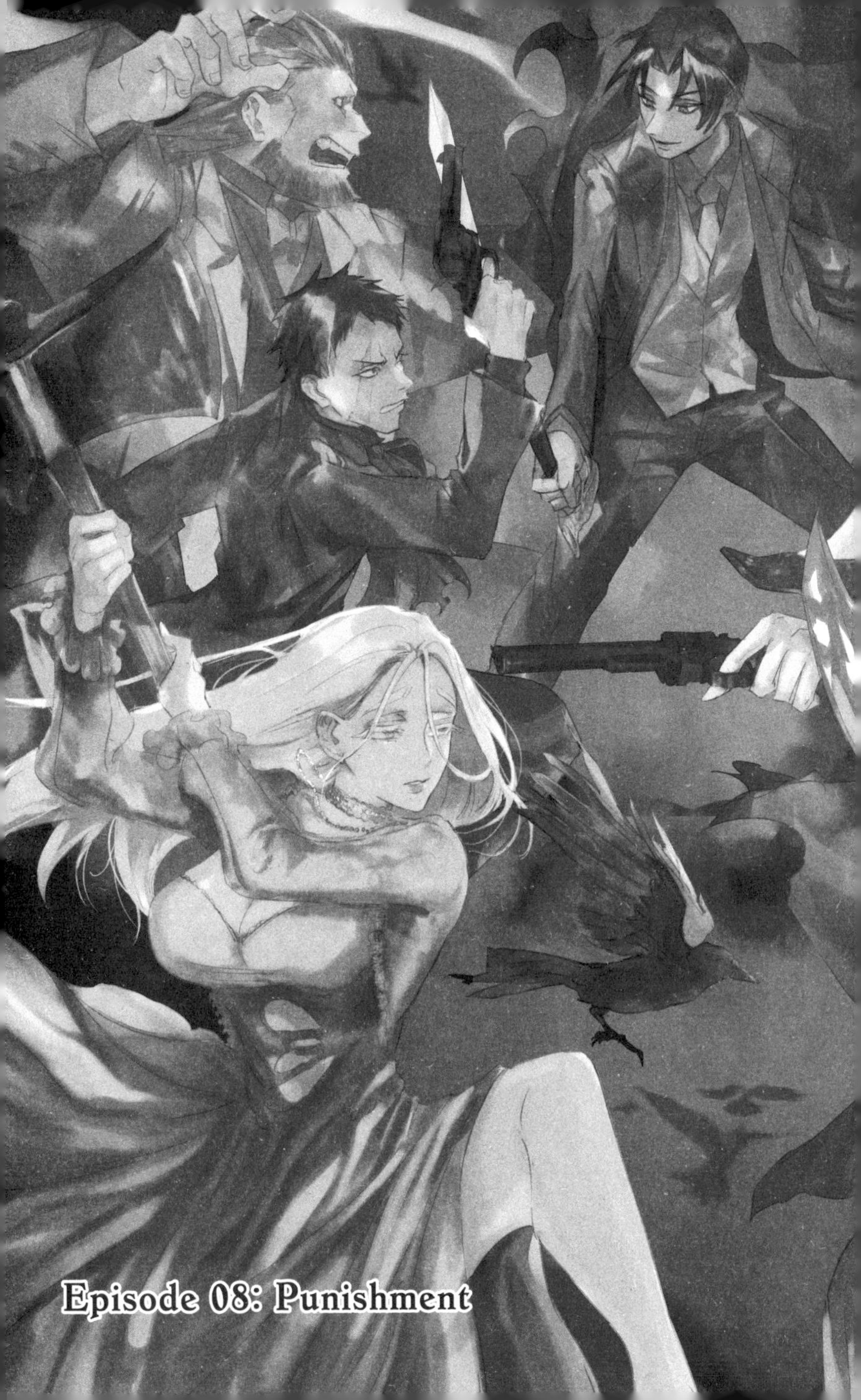
Episode 08: Punishment

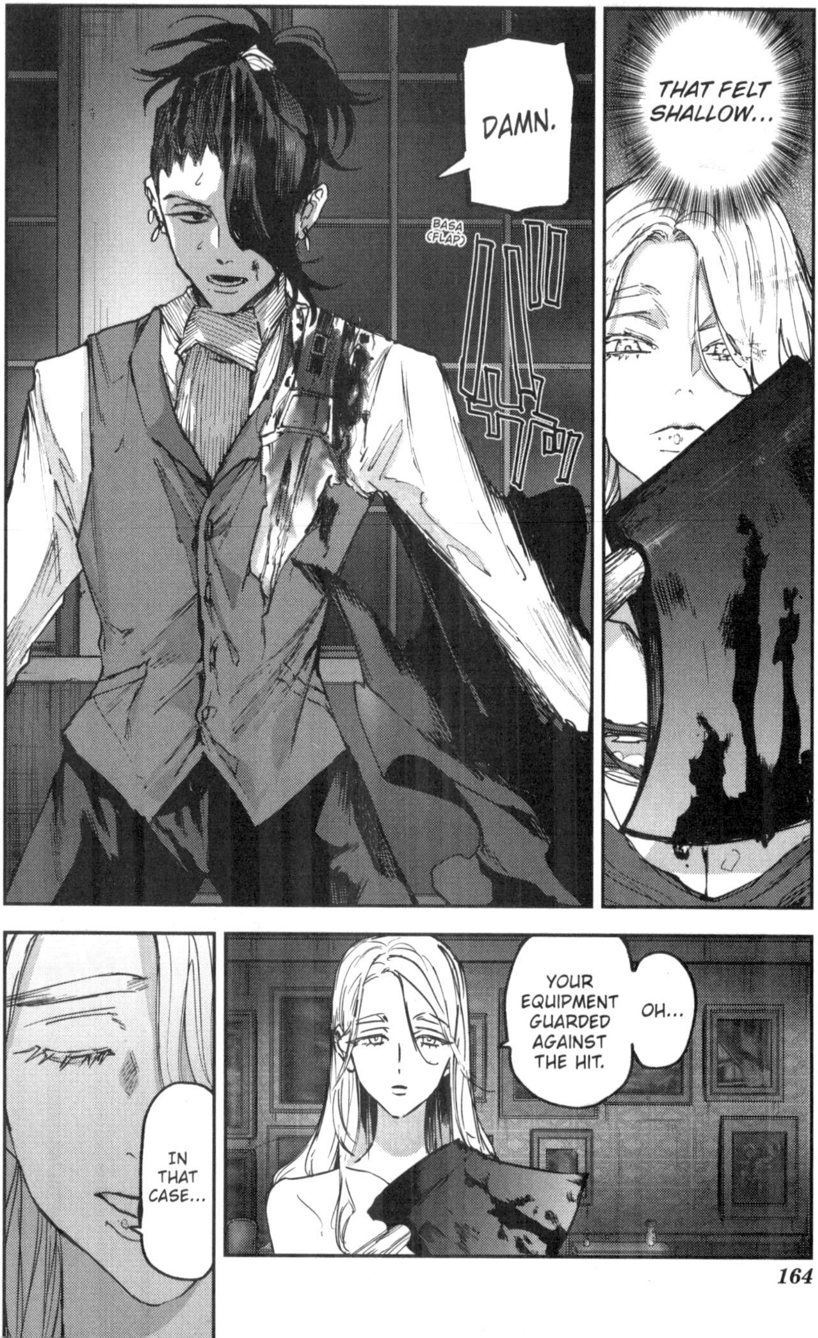
THAT FELT SHALLOW...
DAMN.
BASA (FLAP)
OH...
YOUR EQUIPMENT GUARDED AGAINST THE HIT.
IN THAT CASE...

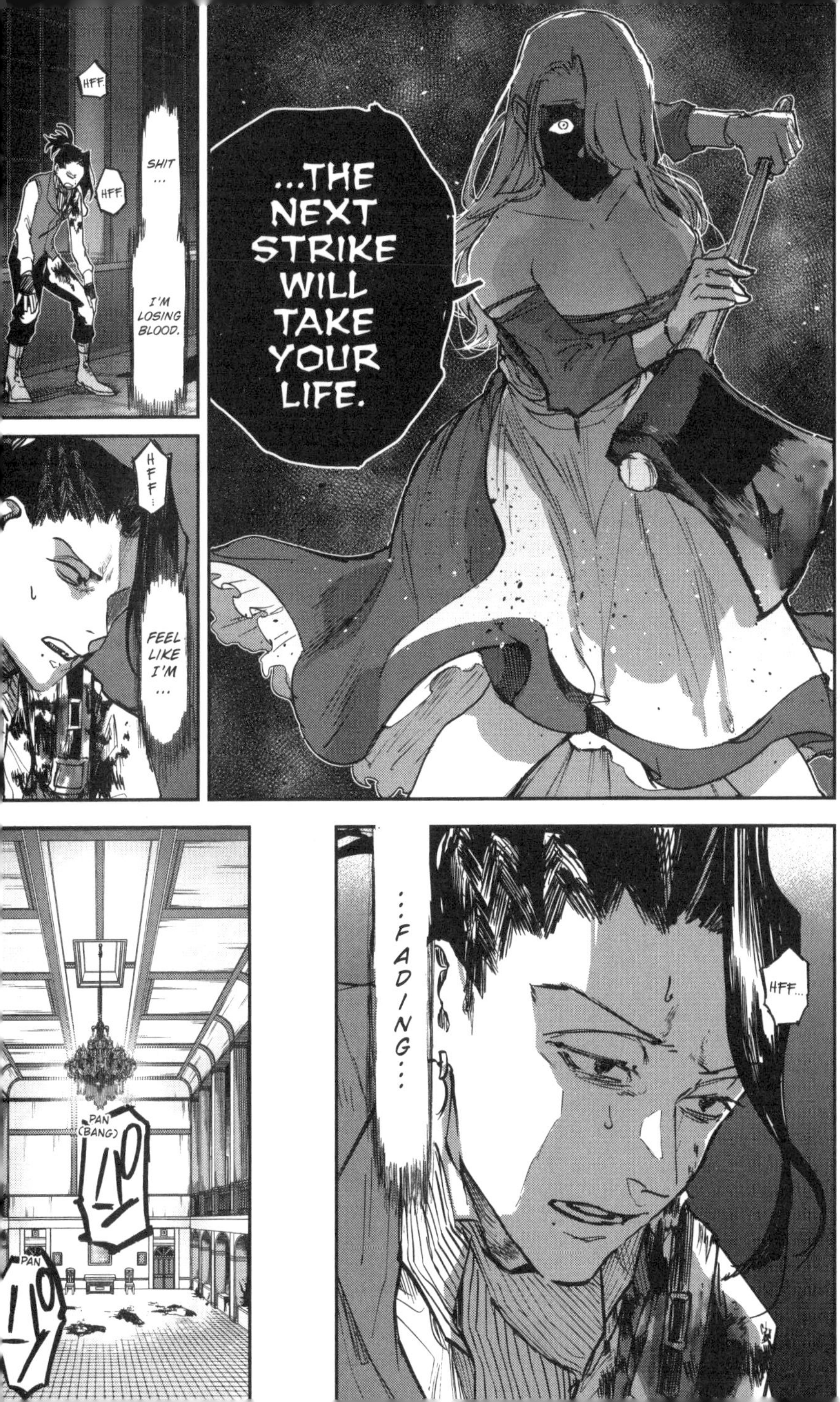
...THE NEXT STRIKE WILL TAKE YOUR LIFE.
HFF.
SHIT...
HFF.
I'M LOSING BLOOD.
HFF...
FEEL LIKE I'M...
...FADING...
HFF...
PAN (BANG)
PAN

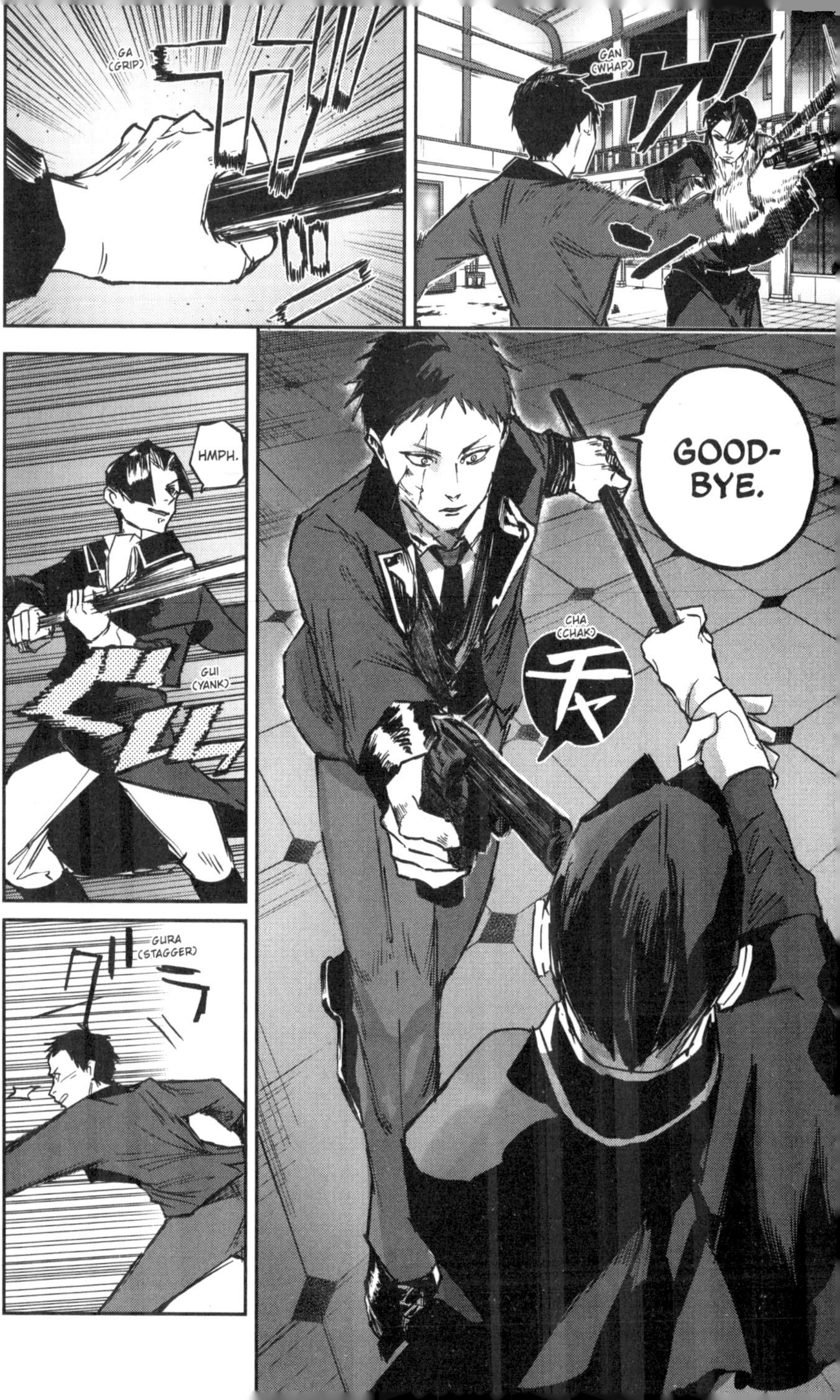
GAN (WHAP)
GA (GRIP)
GOOD-BYE.
CHA (CHAK)
HMPH.
GUI (YANK)
GURA (STAGGER)

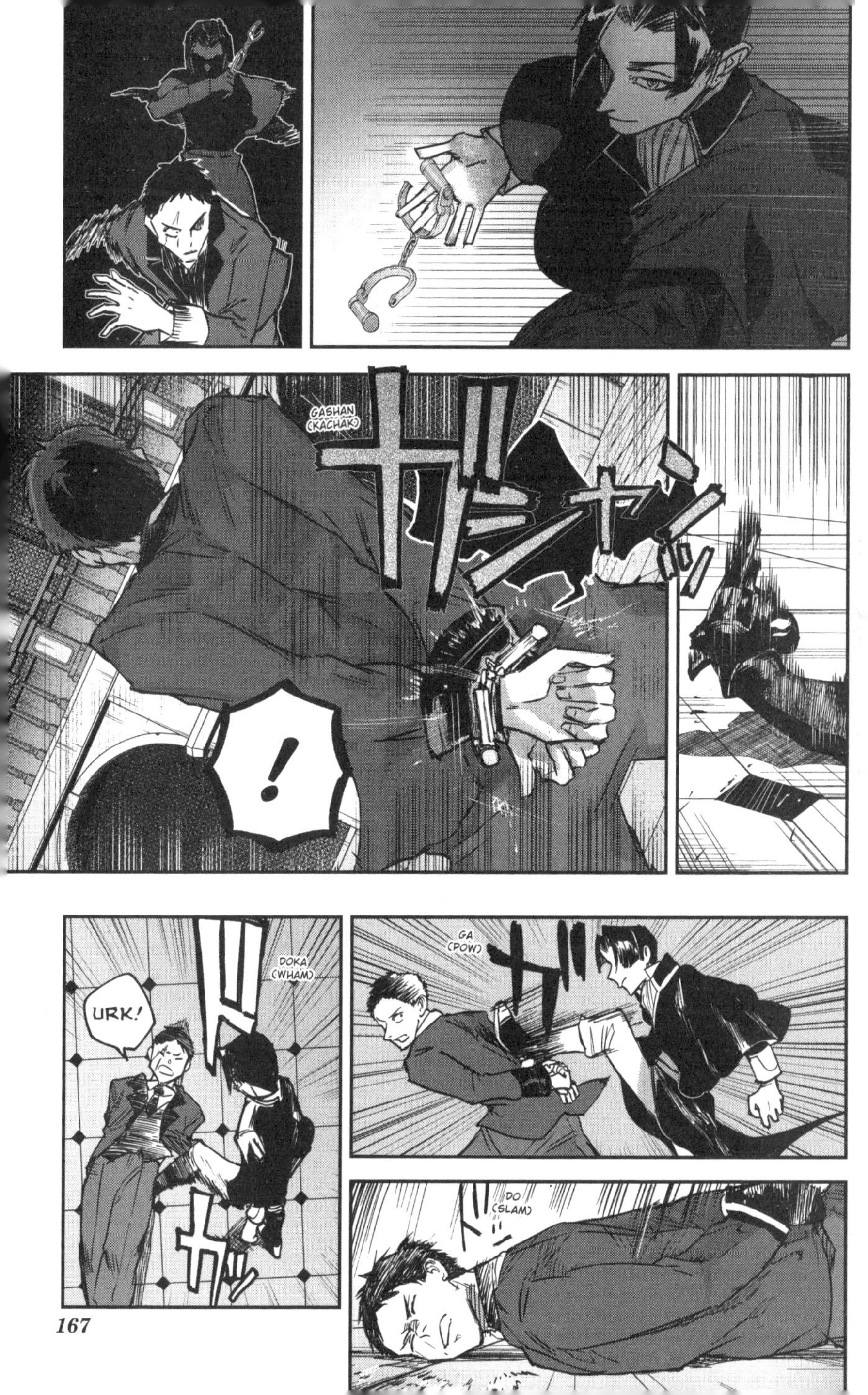

GASHAN (KACHAK)
!
GA (POW)
DO (SLAM)
DOKA (WHAM)
URK!

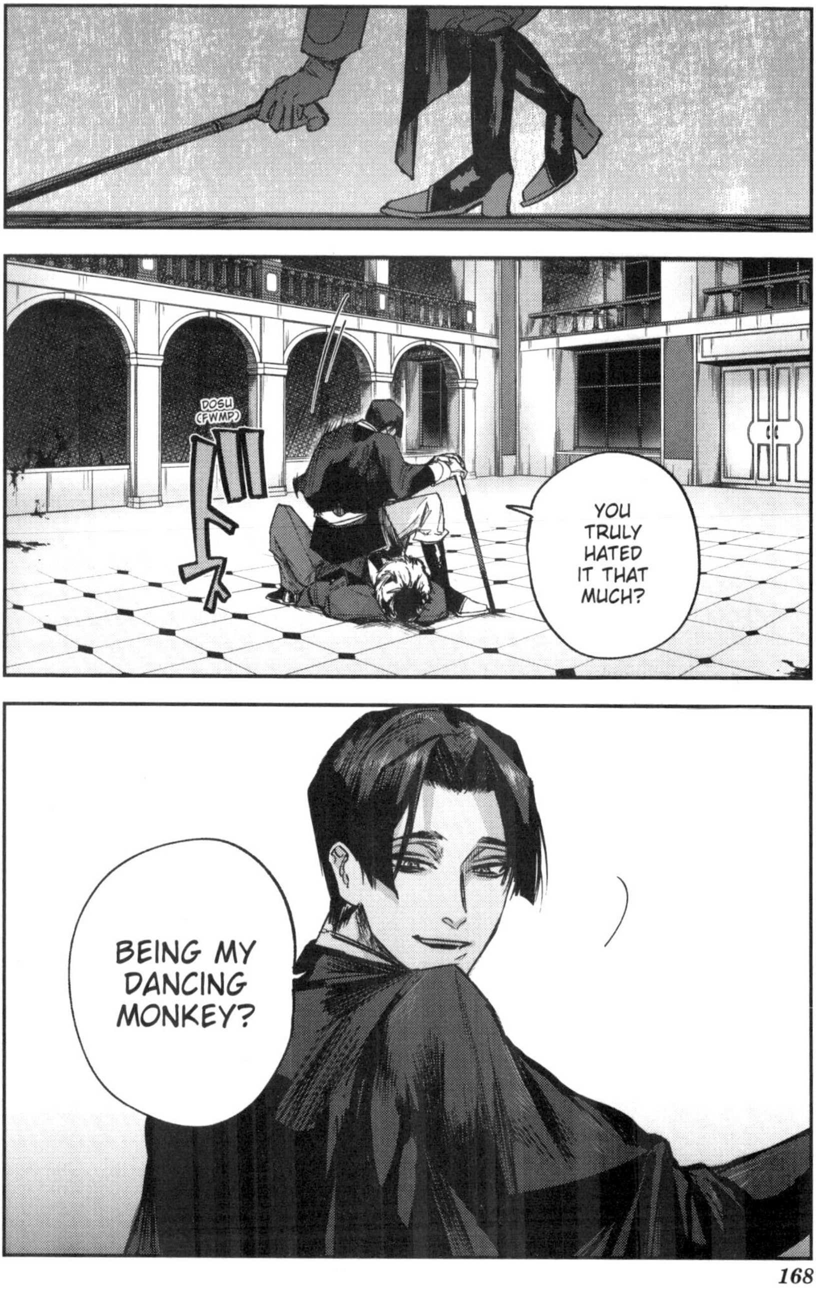
DOSU (FWMP)
YOU TRULY HATED IT THAT MUCH?
BEING MY DANCING MONKEY?

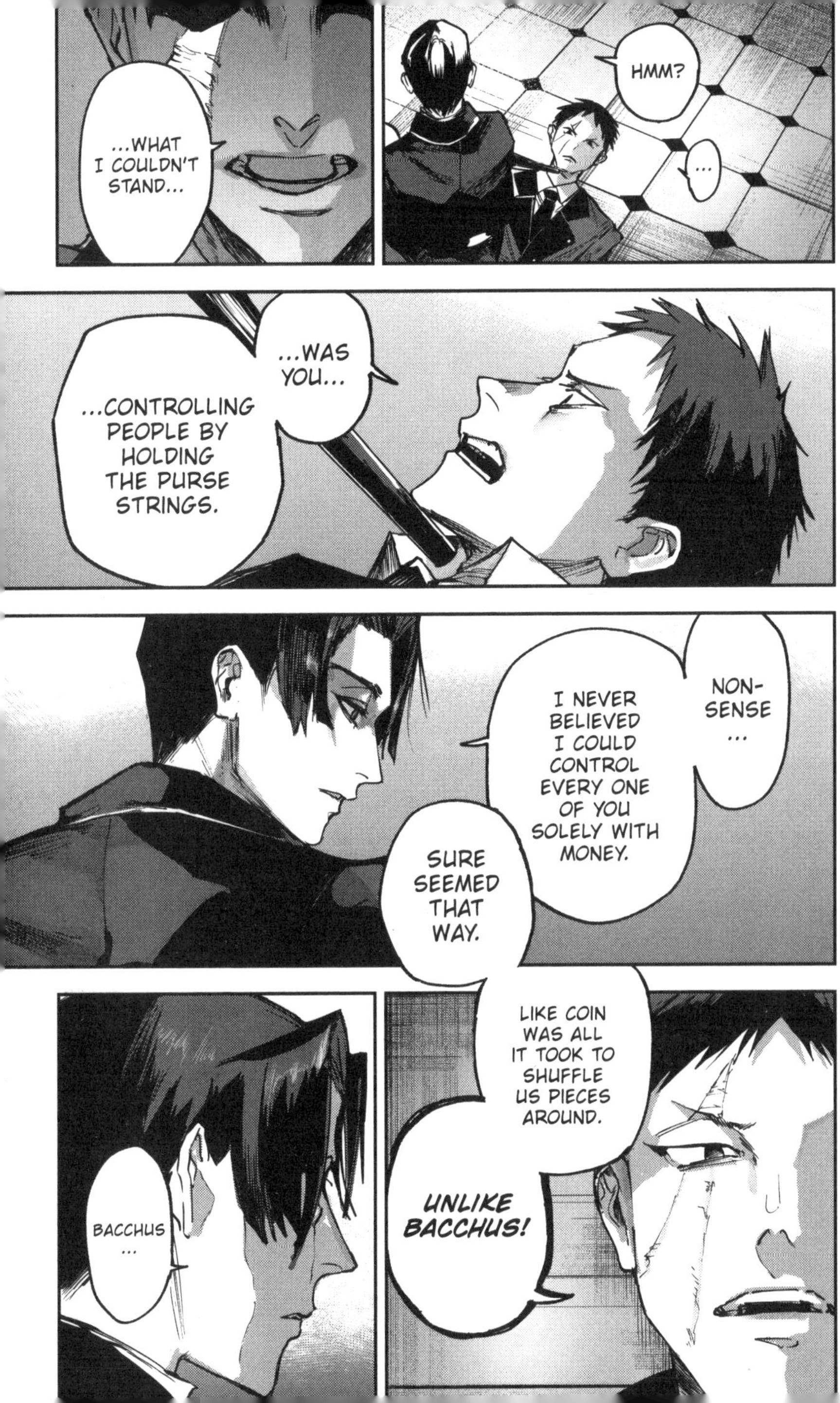
HMM?
...
...WHAT I COULDN'T STAND...
...WAS YOU...
...CONTROLLING PEOPLE BY HOLDING THE PURSE STRINGS.
NON-SENSE...
I NEVER BELIEVED I COULD CONTROL EVERY ONE OF YOU SOLELY WITH MONEY.
SURE SEEMED THAT WAY.
LIKE COIN WAS ALL IT TOOK TO SHUFFLE US PIECES AROUND.
UNLIKE BACCHUS!
BACCHUS...

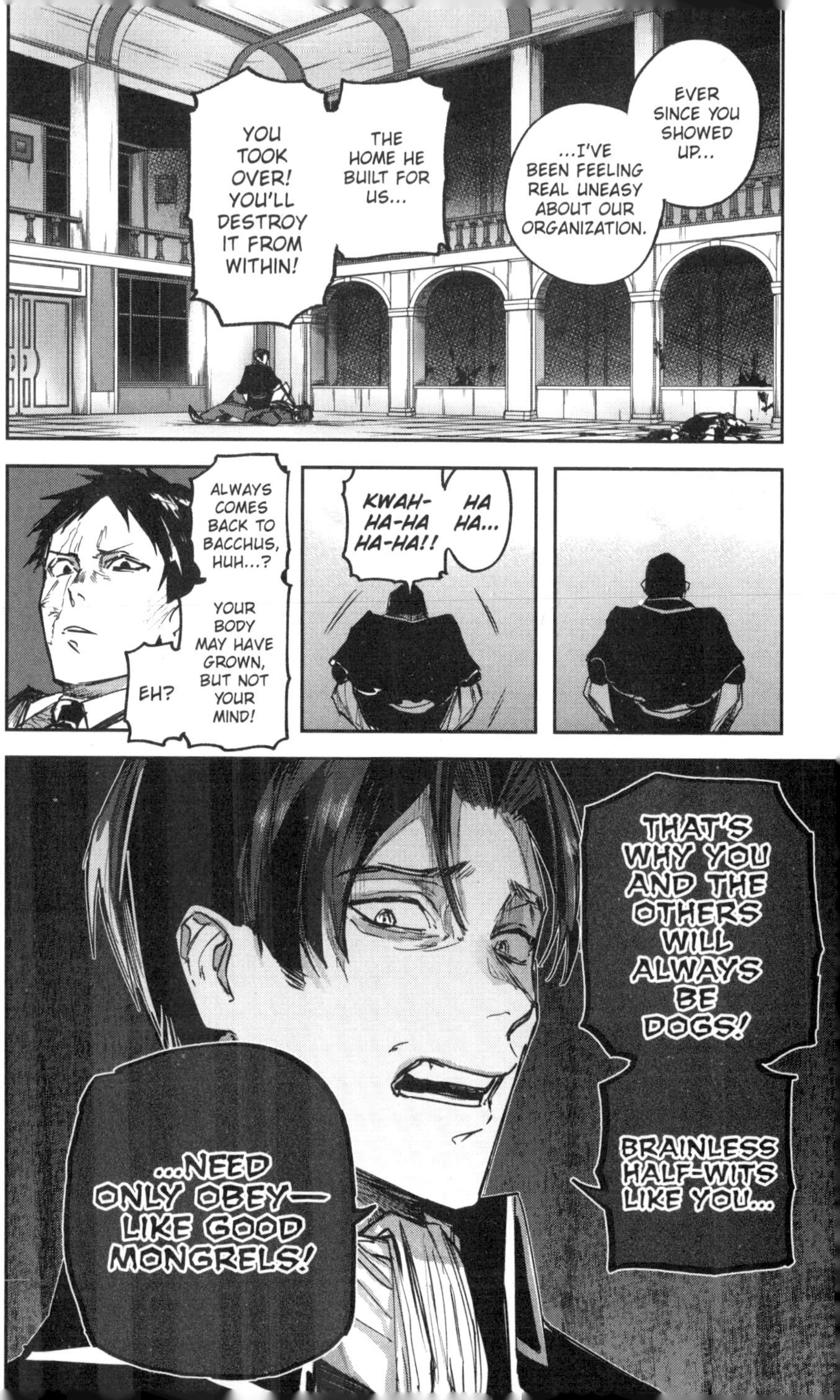
EVER SINCE YOU SHOWED UP...
...I'VE BEEN FEELING REAL UNEASY ABOUT OUR ORGANIZATION.
THE HOME HE BUILT FOR US...
YOU TOOK OVER! YOU'LL DESTROY IT FROM WITHIN!
HA HA...
KWAH-HA-HA HA-HA!!
ALWAYS COMES BACK TO BACCHUS, HUH...?
YOUR BODY MAY HAVE GROWN, BUT NOT YOUR MIND!
EH?
THAT'S WHY YOU AND THE OTHERS WILL ALWAYS BE DOGS!
BRAINLESS HALF-WITS LIKE YOU...
...NEED ONLY OBEY—LIKE GOOD MONGRELS!

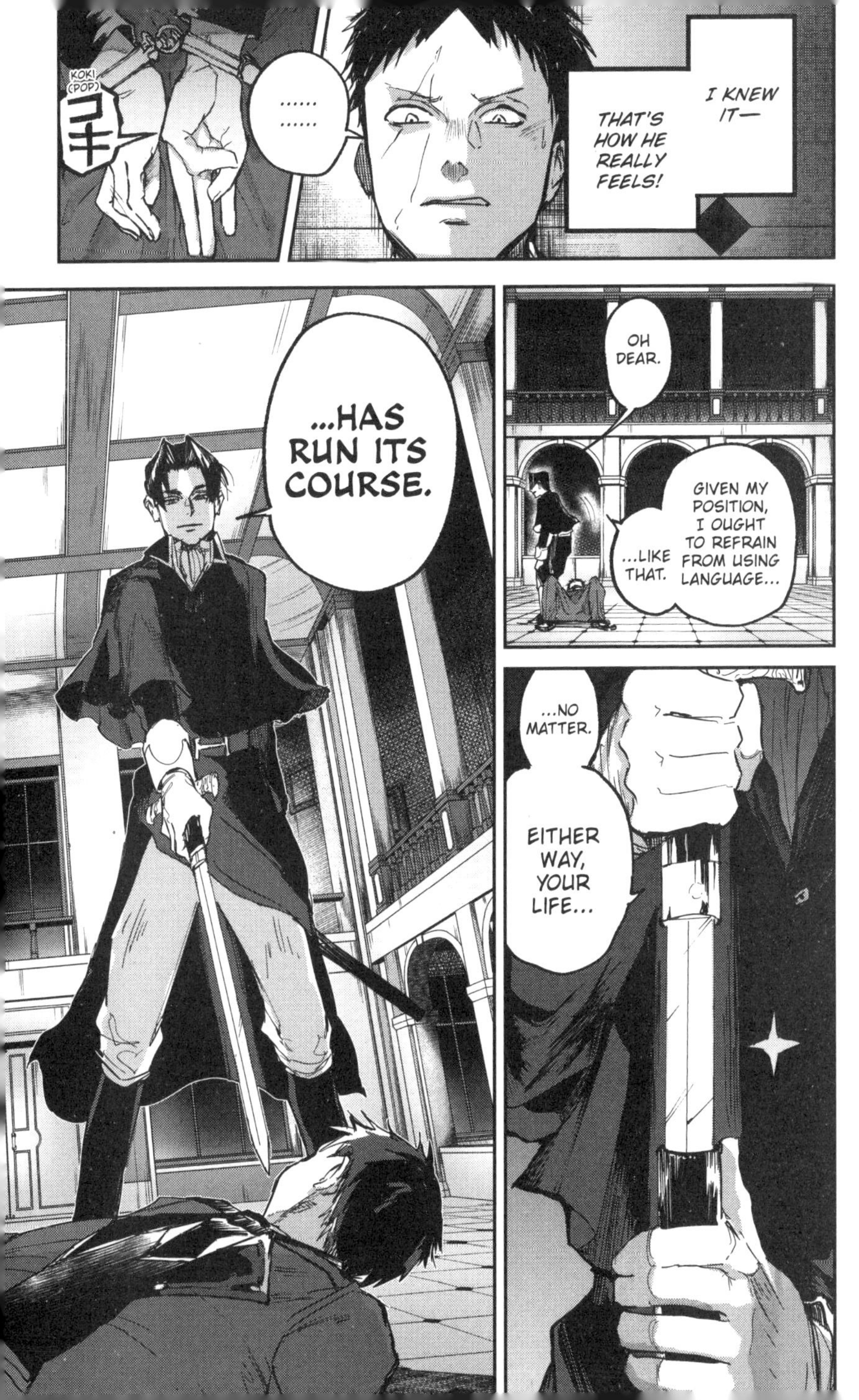
I KNEW IT—
THAT'S HOW HE REALLY FEELS!
....
KOKI (POP) コキ
OH DEAR.
GIVEN MY POSITION, I OUGHT TO REFRAIN FROM USING LANGUAGE...
...LIKE THAT.
...NO MATTER.
EITHER WAY, YOUR LIFE...
...HAS RUN ITS COURSE.

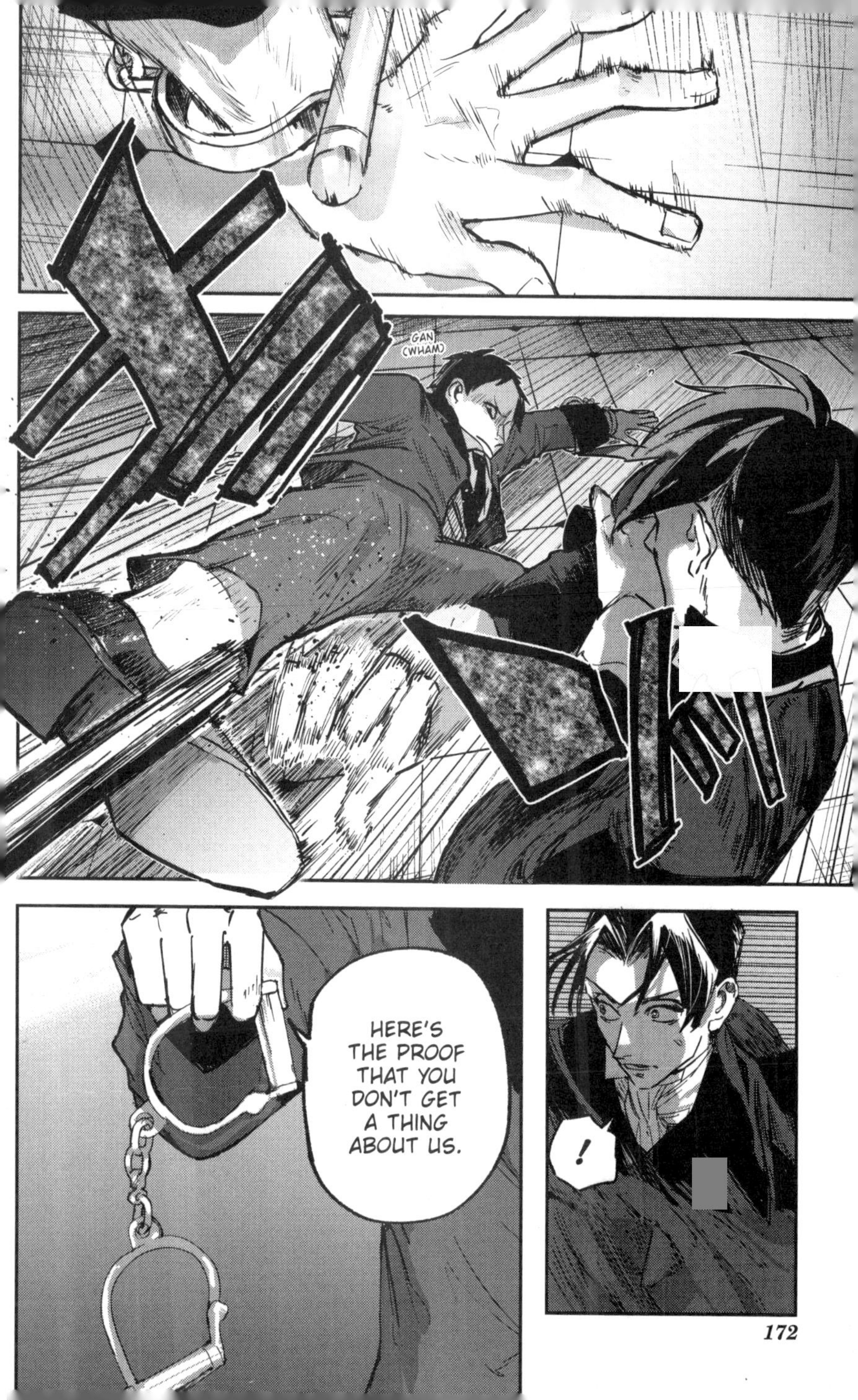
GAN
(WHAM)
!
HERE'S THE PROOF THAT YOU DON'T GET A THING ABOUT US.

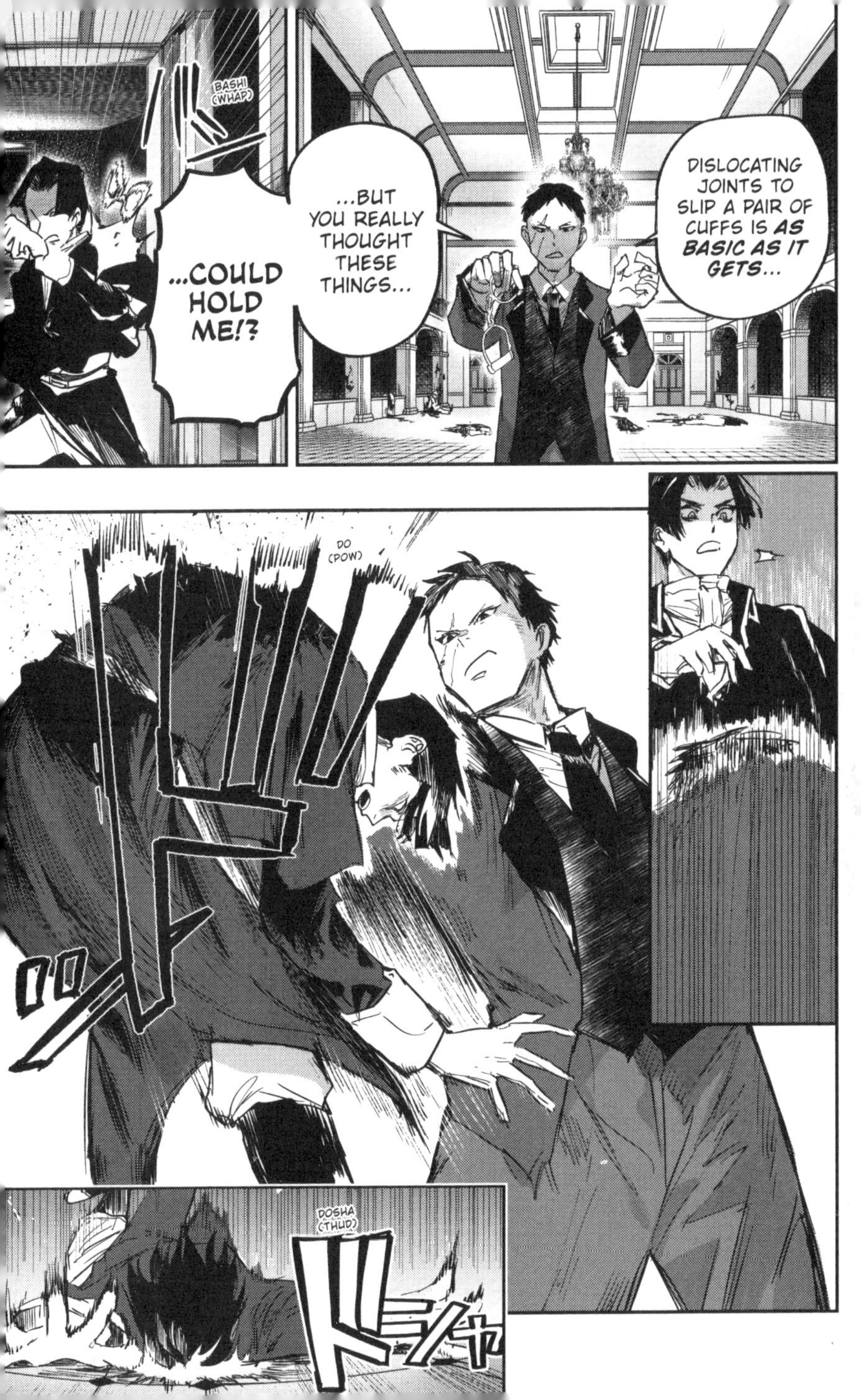
DISLOCATING JOINTS TO SLIP A PAIR OF CUFFS IS AS BASIC AS IT GETS...
...BUT YOU REALLY THOUGHT THESE THINGS...
BASHI (WHAP)
...COULD HOLD ME!?
DO (POW)
DOSHA (THUD)

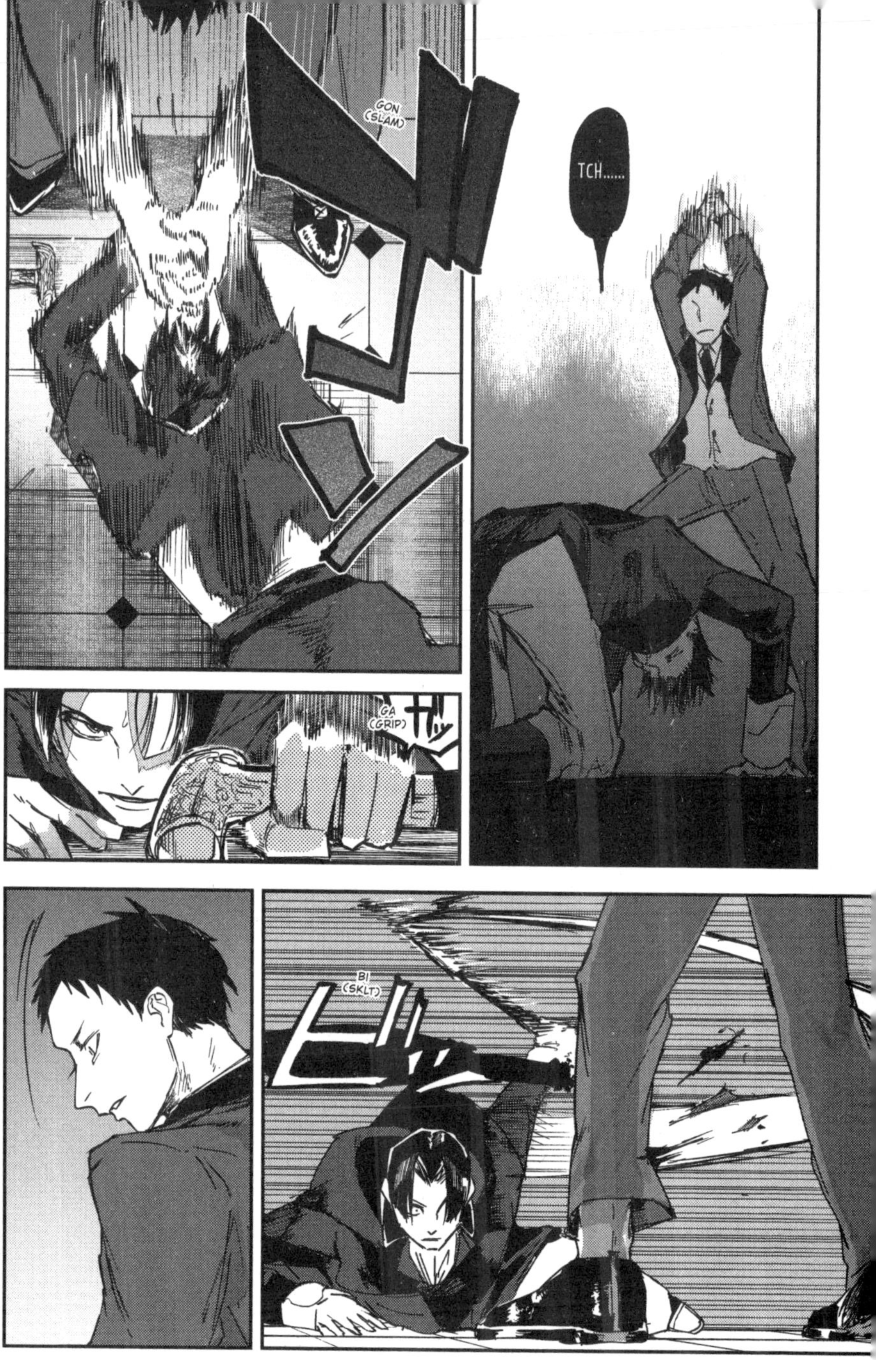
TCH......
GON
(SLAM)
GA
(GRIP)
BI
(SKLT)

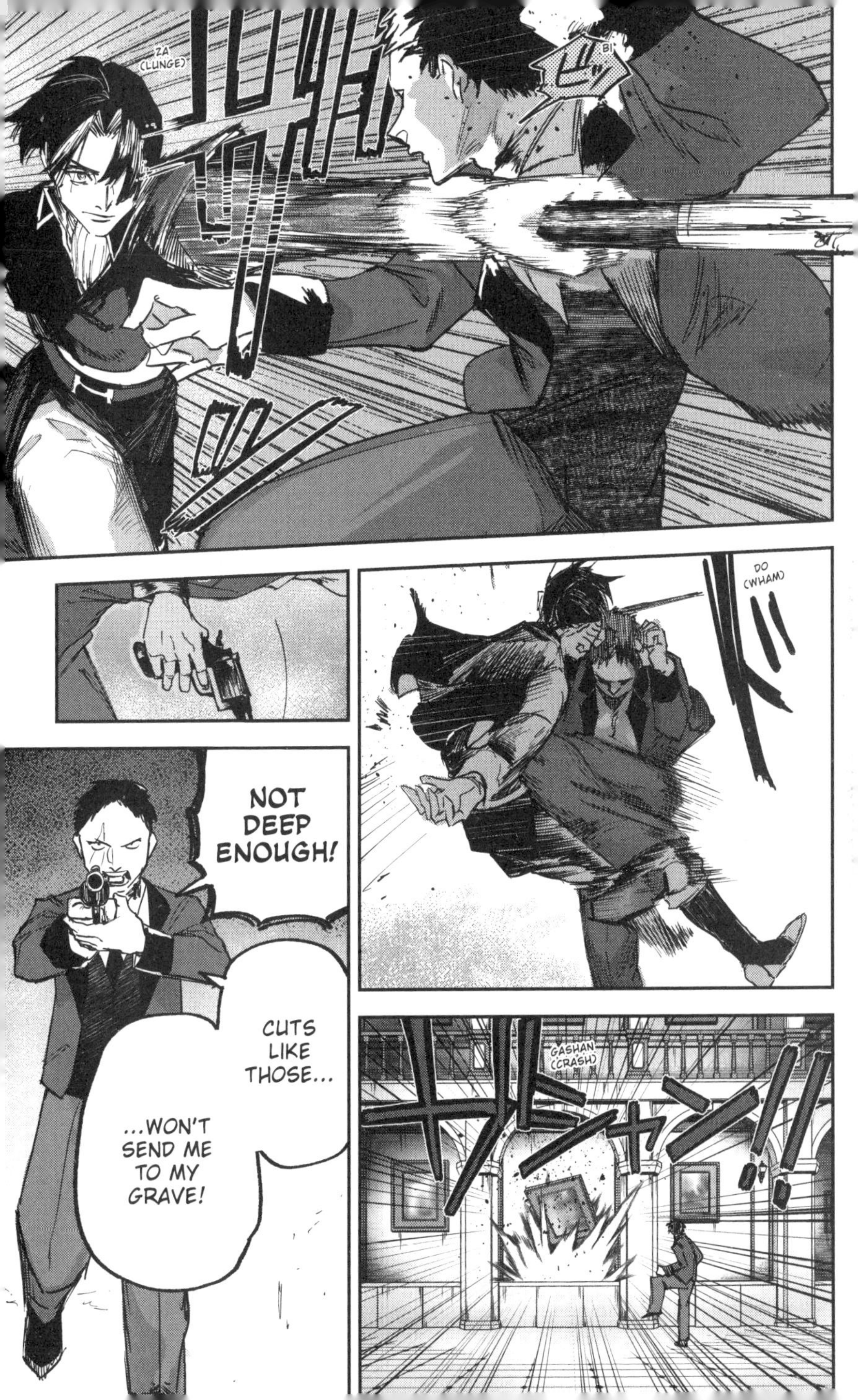
BI
ZA (LUNGE)
DO (WHAM)
NOT DEEP ENOUGH!
CUTS LIKE THOSE...
...WON'T SEND ME TO MY GRAVE!
GASHAN (CRASH)

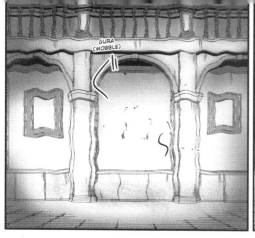

GURA
(WOBBLE)

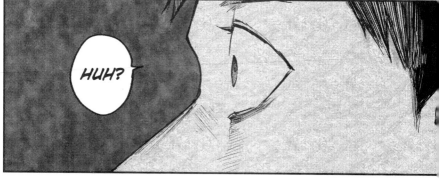

HUH?

KWAH
HA-HA-
HA!

MY
EYES
...?

176

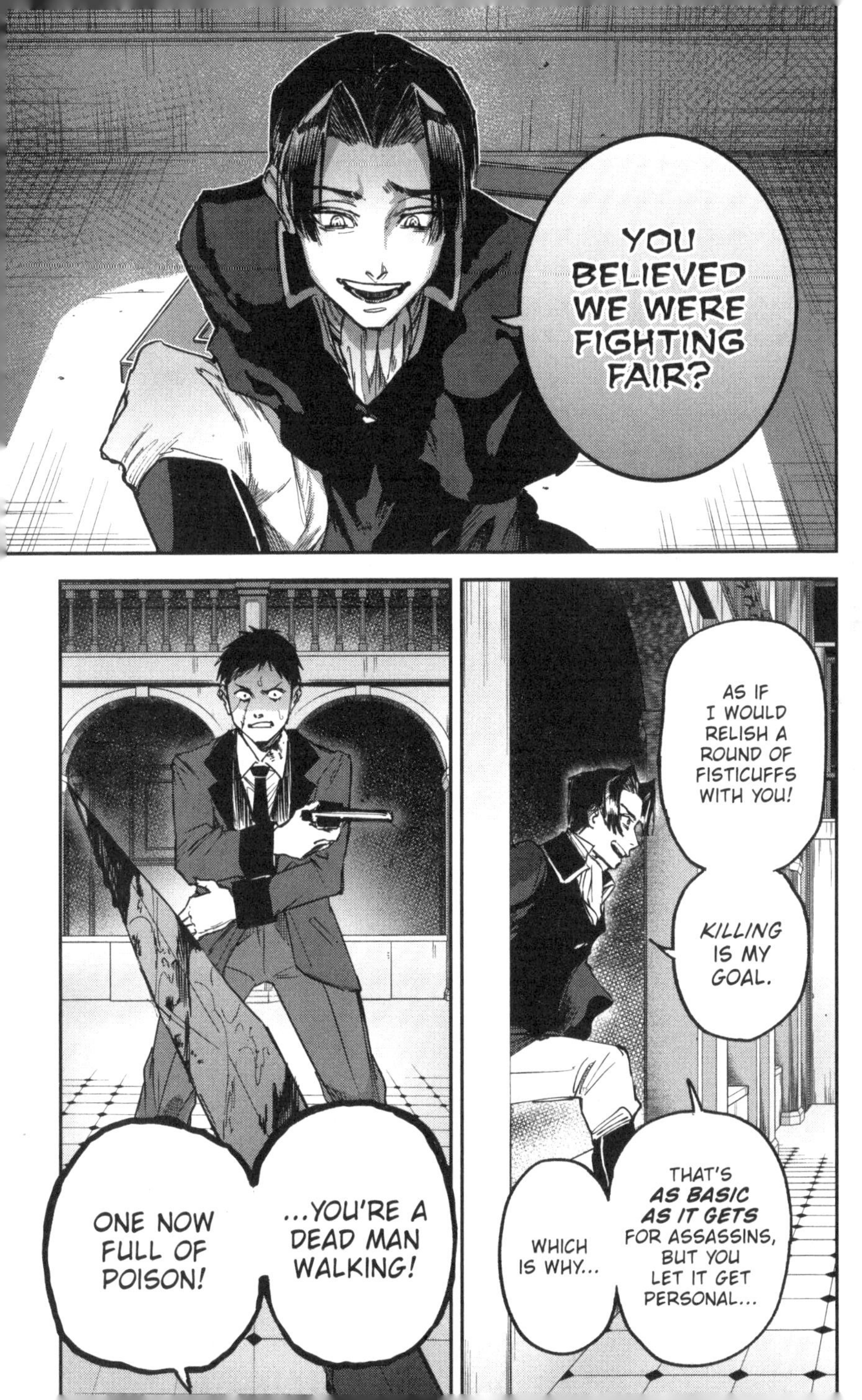
YOU BELIEVED WE WERE FIGHTING FAIR?
AS IF I WOULD RELISH A ROUND OF FISTICUFFS WITH YOU!
KILLING IS MY GOAL.
THAT'S ***AS BASIC AS IT GETS*** FOR ASSASSINS, BUT YOU LET IT GET PERSONAL...
WHICH IS WHY...
...YOU'RE A DEAD MAN WALKING!
ONE NOW FULL OF POISON!

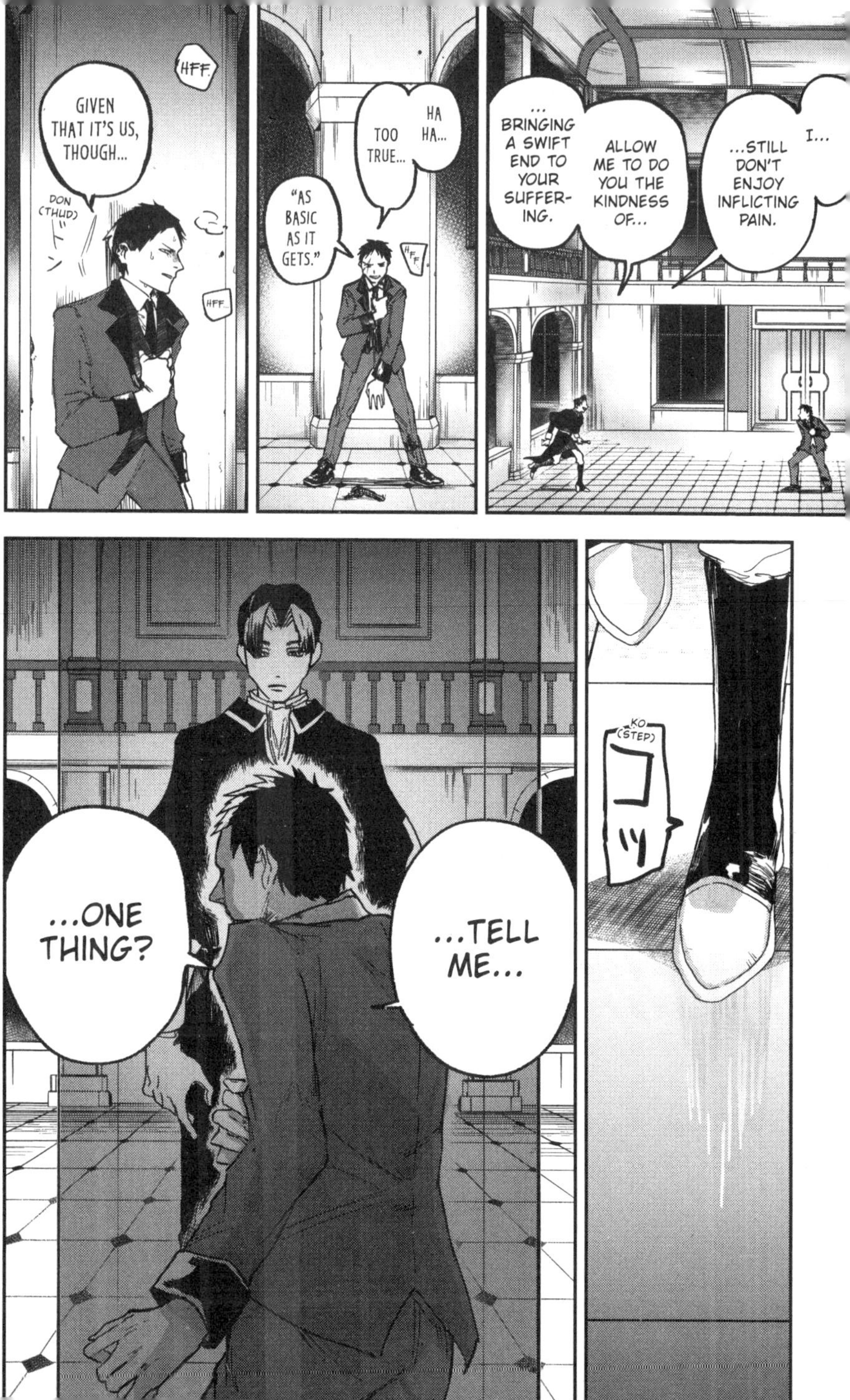
I...
...STILL DON'T ENJOY INFLICTING PAIN.
ALLOW ME TO DO YOU THE KINDNESS OF...
...BRINGING A SWIFT END TO YOUR SUFFER-ING.
HA HA...
TOO TRUE...
“AS BASIC AS IT GETS.”
HFF.
HFF.
GIVEN THAT IT'S US, THOUGH...
DON (THUD)
HFF...
KO (STEP)
...TELL ME...
...ONE THING?

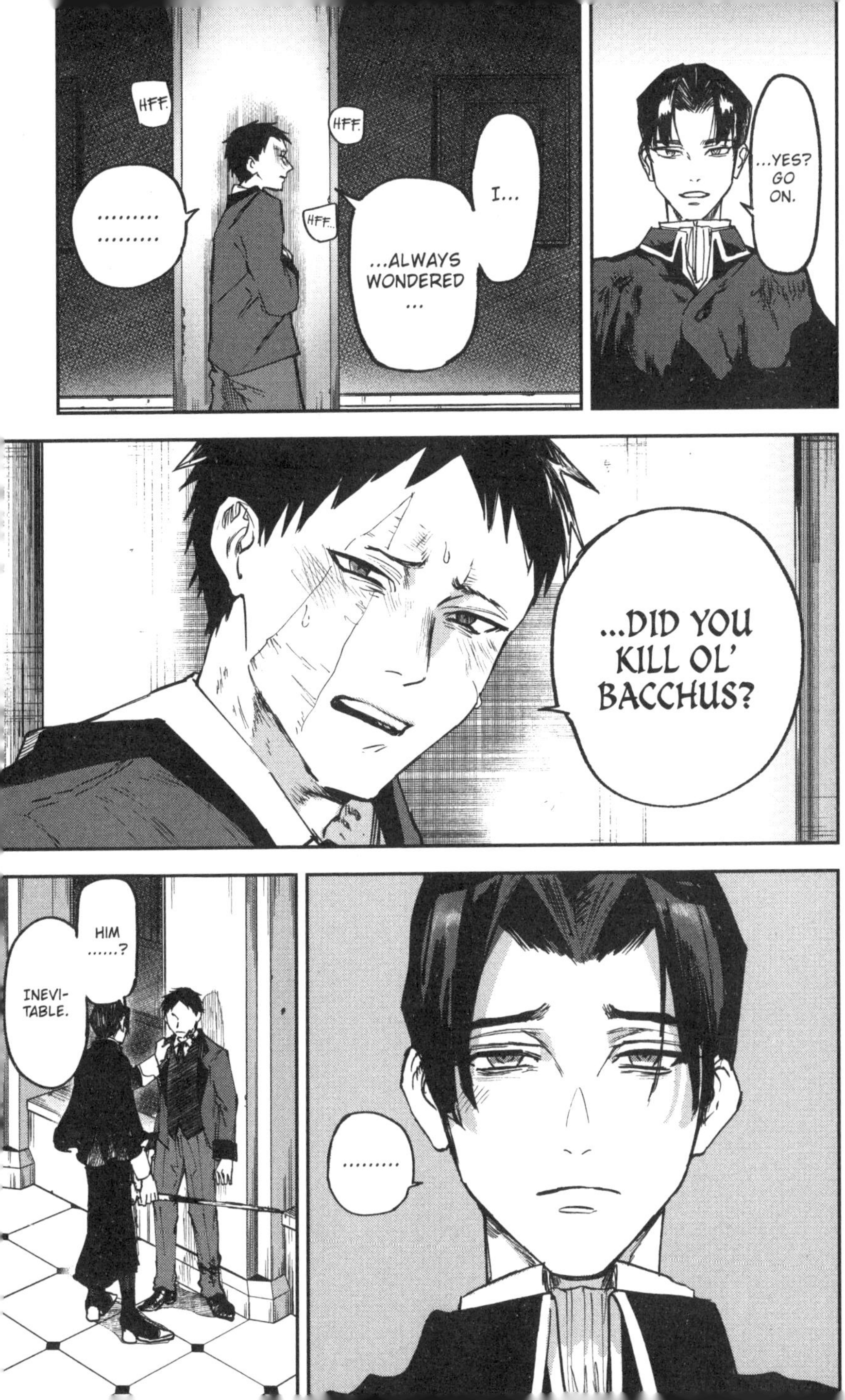
...YES? GO ON.
I...
...ALWAYS WONDERED ...
HFF.
HFF...
HFF.
....
....
...DID YOU KILL OL' BACCHUS?
....
HIM ......?
INEVI-TABLE.

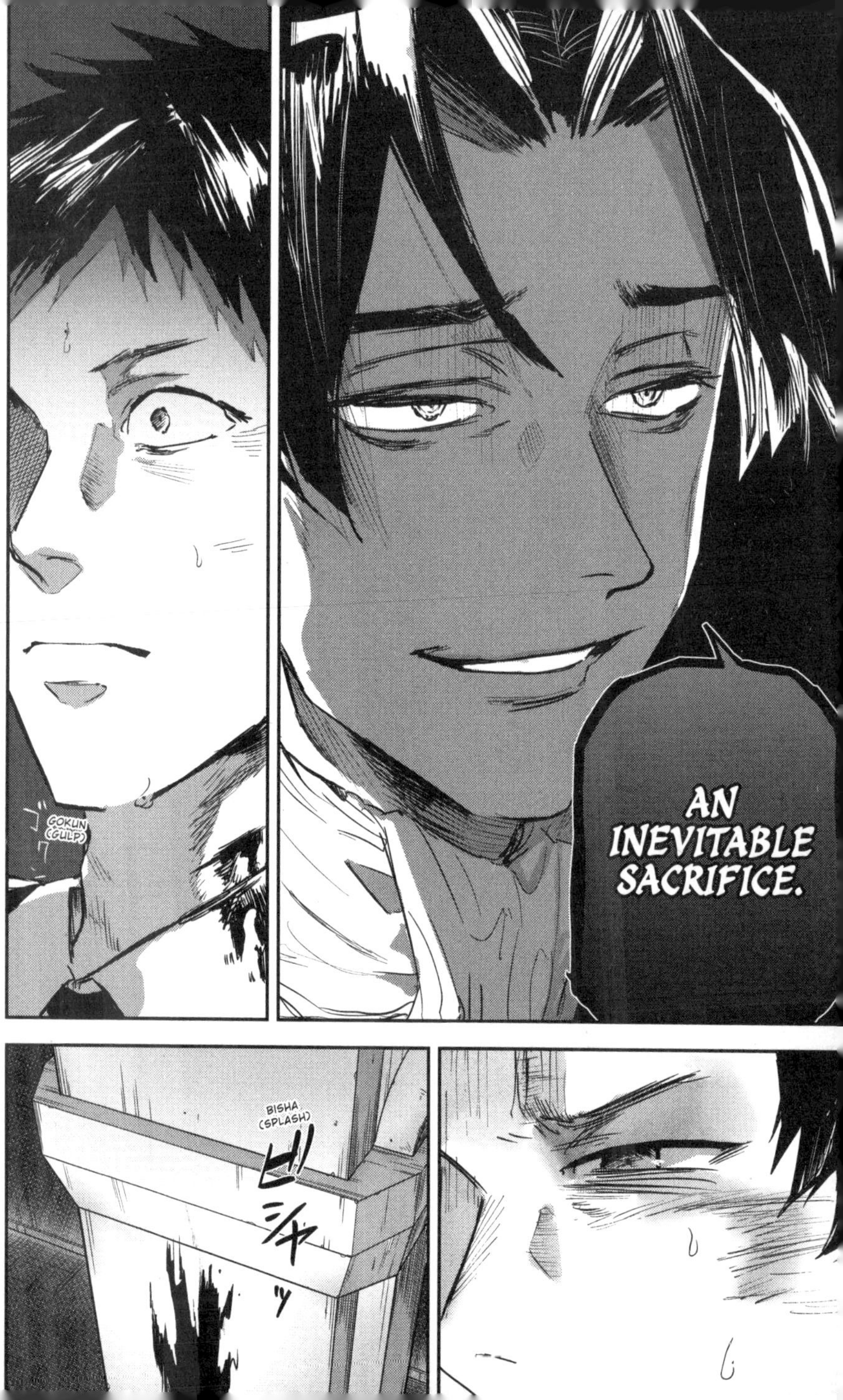
AN INEVITABLE SACRIFICE.
GOKUN (GULP)
BISHA (SPLASH)

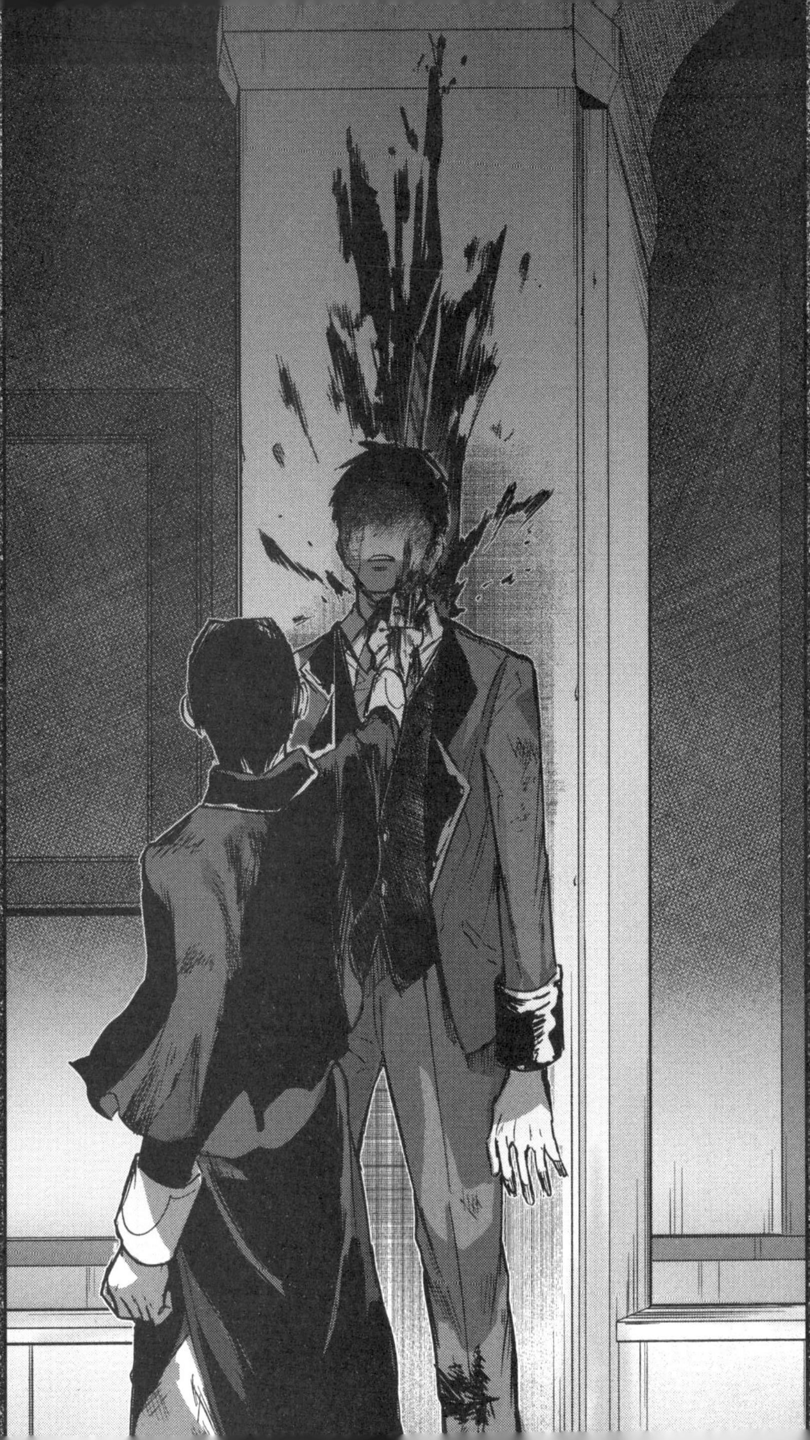

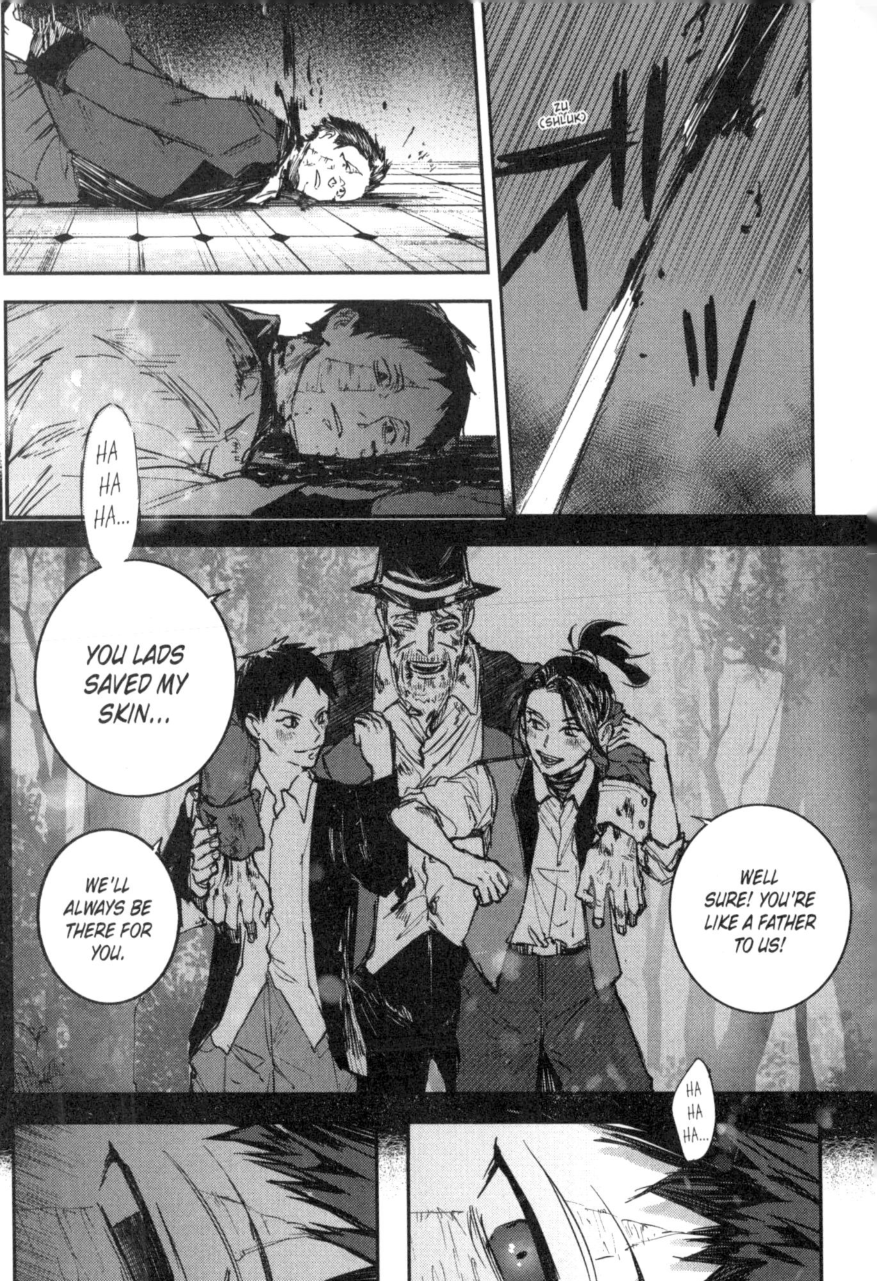
ZU
(SHLUK)
HA HA HA...
YOU LADS SAVED MY SKIN...
WELL SURE! YOU'RE LIKE A FATHER TO US!
WE'LL ALWAYS BE THERE FOR YOU.
HA HA HA...

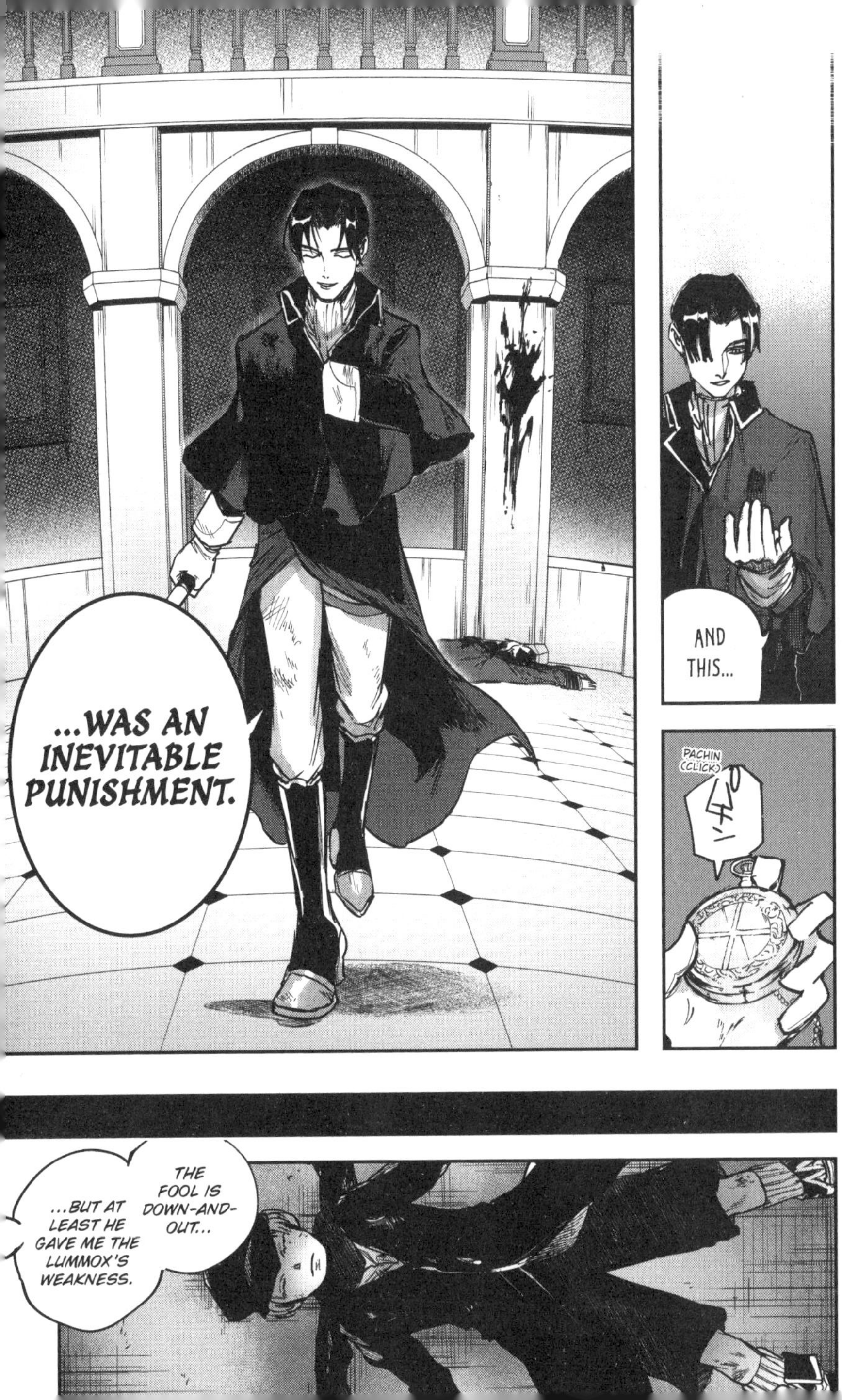
AND THIS...
PACHIN (CLICK)
...WAS AN INEVITABLE PUNISHMENT.
THE FOOL IS DOWN-AND-OUT...
...BUT AT LEAST HE GAVE ME THE LUMMOX'S WEAKNESS.

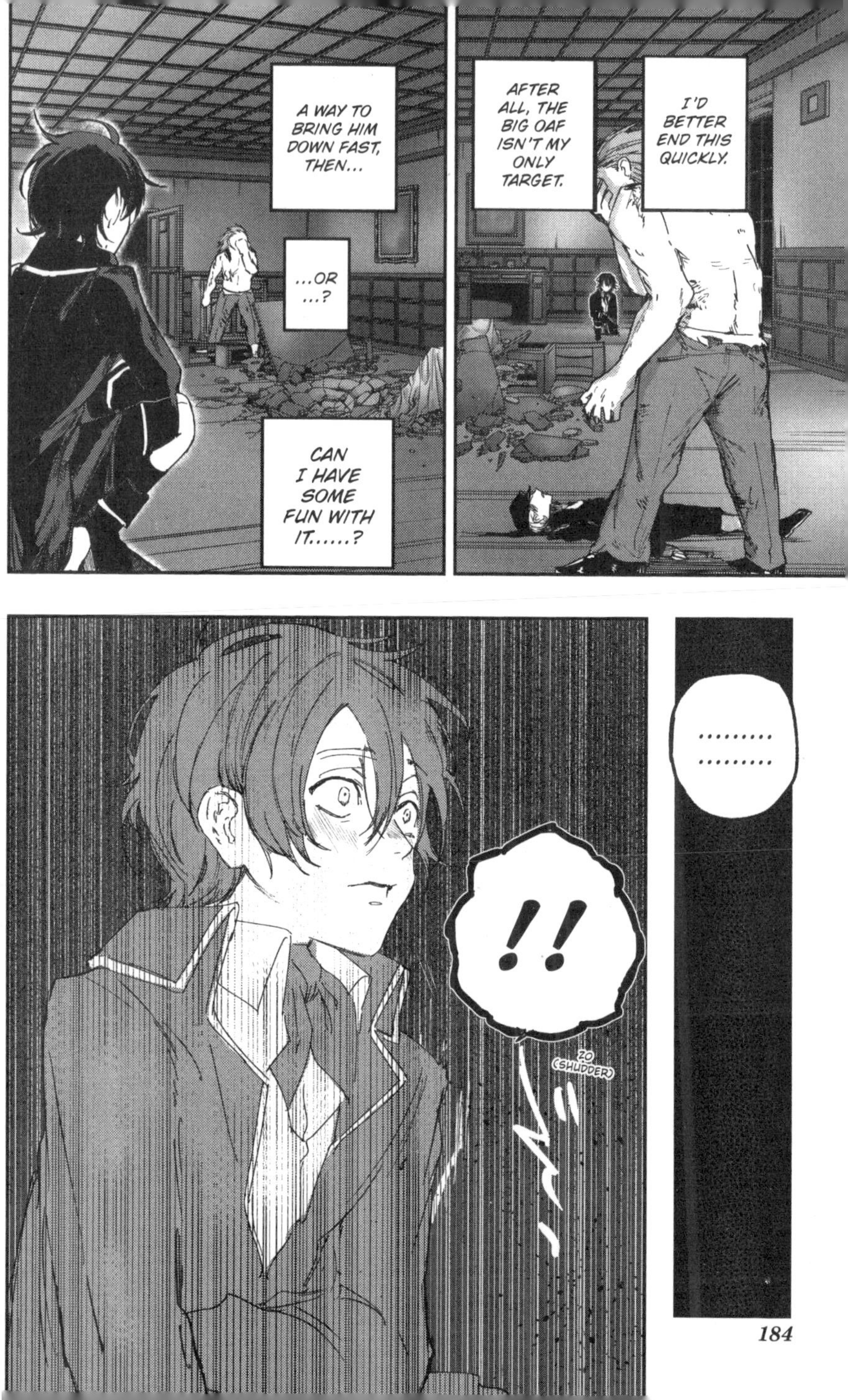
I'D BETTER END THIS QUICKLY.
AFTER ALL, THE BIG OAF ISN'T MY ONLY TARGET.
A WAY TO BRING HIM DOWN FAST, THEN...
...OR ...?
CAN I HAVE SOME FUN WITH IT......?
....
....
!!
ZO (SHUDDER)

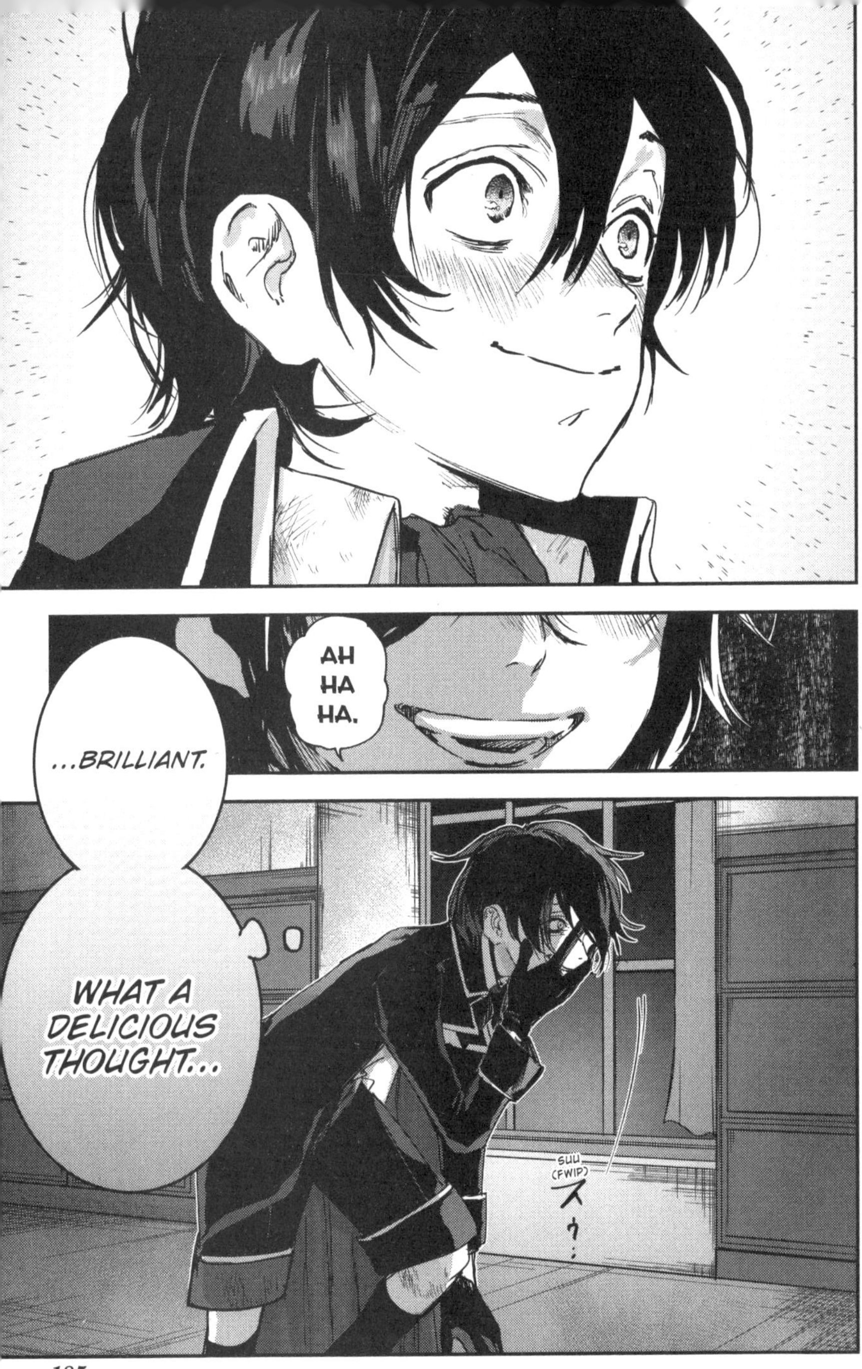
AH HA HA.
...BRILLIANT.
WHAT A DELICIOUS THOUGHT...
SUU (FWIP)
スゥ…

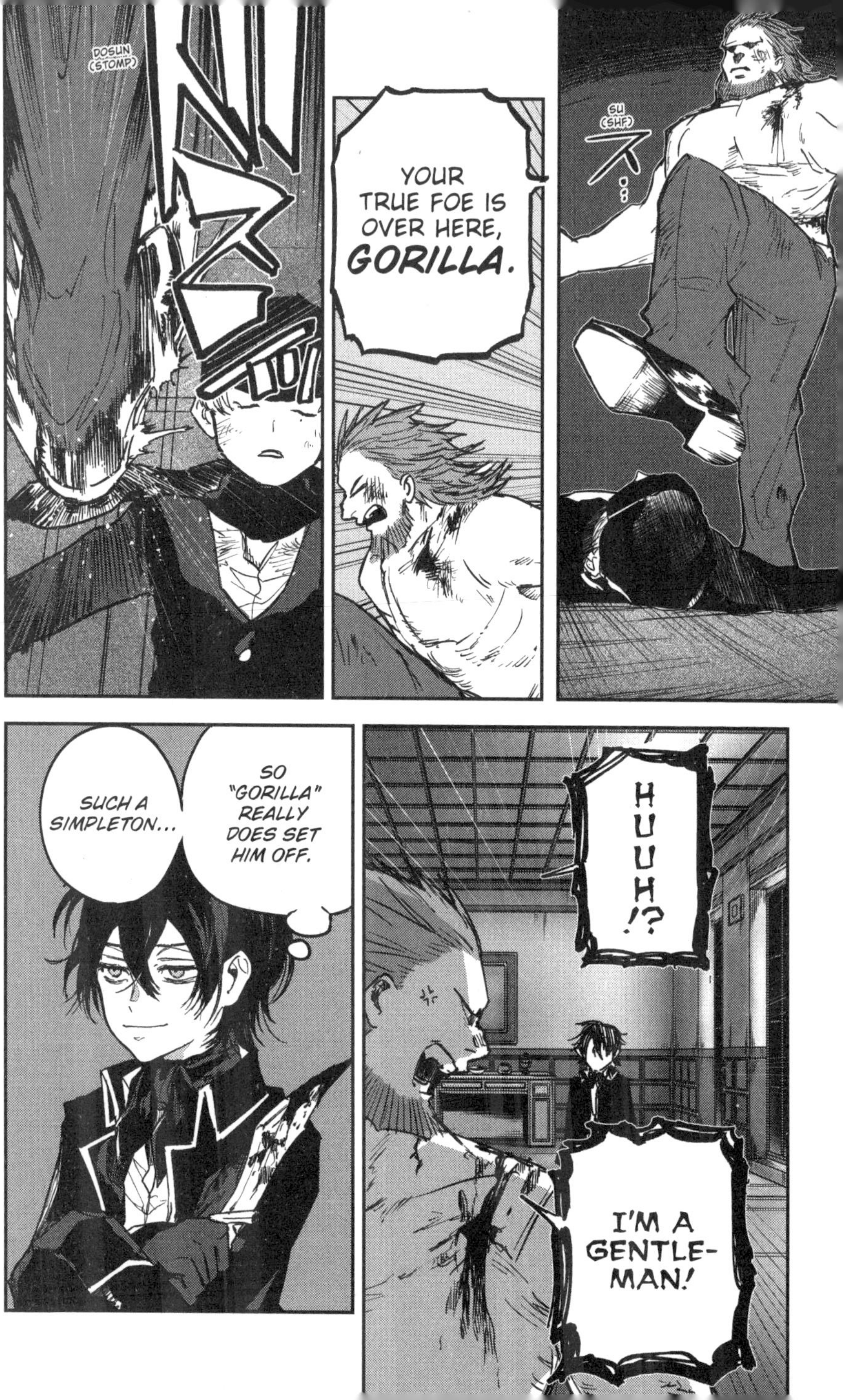
SU (SHF)
YOUR TRUE FOE IS OVER HERE, GORILLA.
DOSUN (STOMP)
HUUH!?
I'M A GENTLEMAN!
SO "GORILLA" REALLY DOES SET HIM OFF.
SUCH A SIMPLETON...

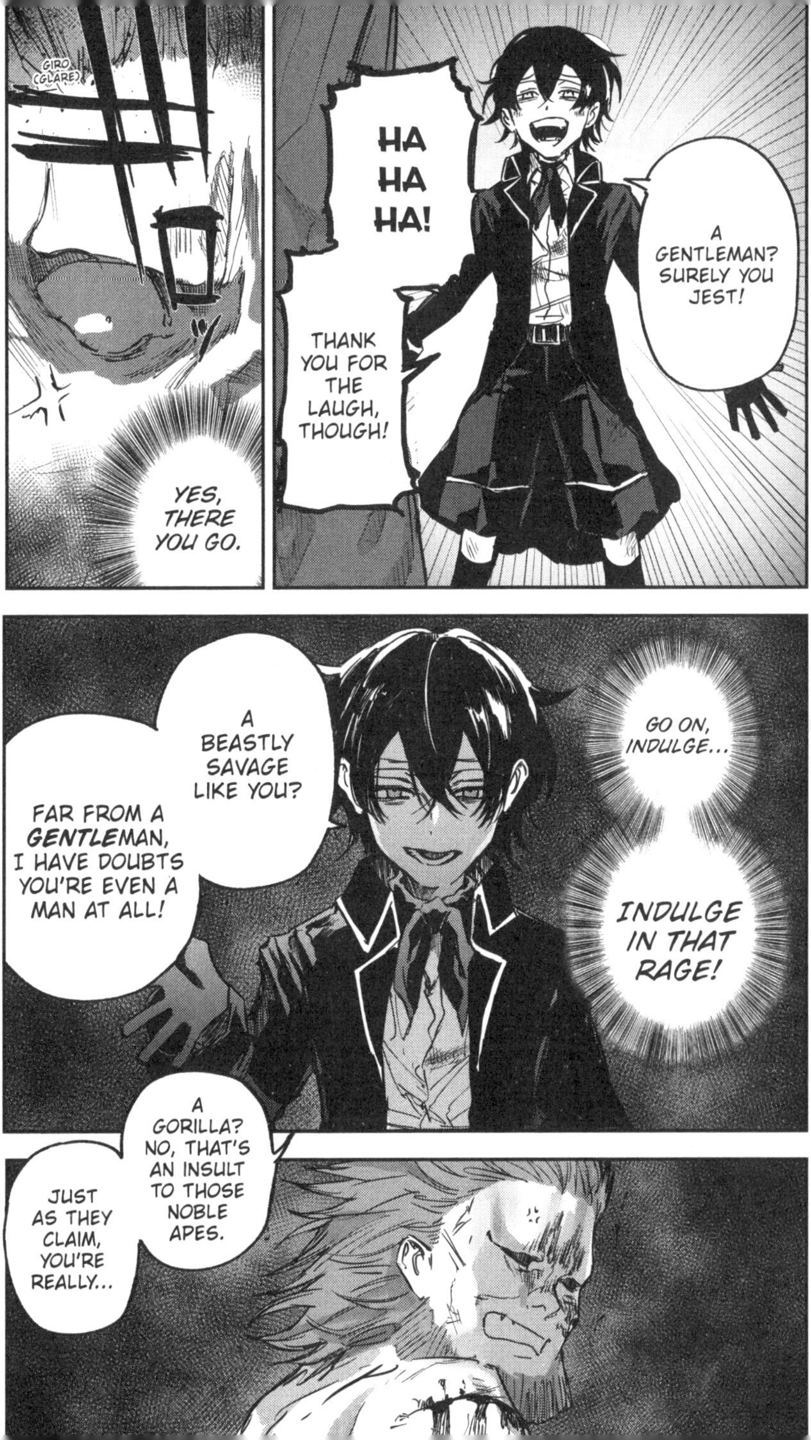
A GENTLEMAN? SURELY YOU JEST!
HA HA HA!
THANK YOU FOR THE LAUGH, THOUGH!
GIRO (GLARE)
YES, THERE YOU GO.
GO ON, INDULGE...
INDULGE IN THAT RAGE!
A BEASTLY SAVAGE LIKE YOU?
FAR FROM A GENTLEMAN, I HAVE DOUBTS YOU'RE EVEN A MAN AT ALL!
A GORILLA? NO, THAT'S AN INSULT TO THOSE NOBLE APES.
JUST AS THEY CLAIM, YOU'RE REALLY...

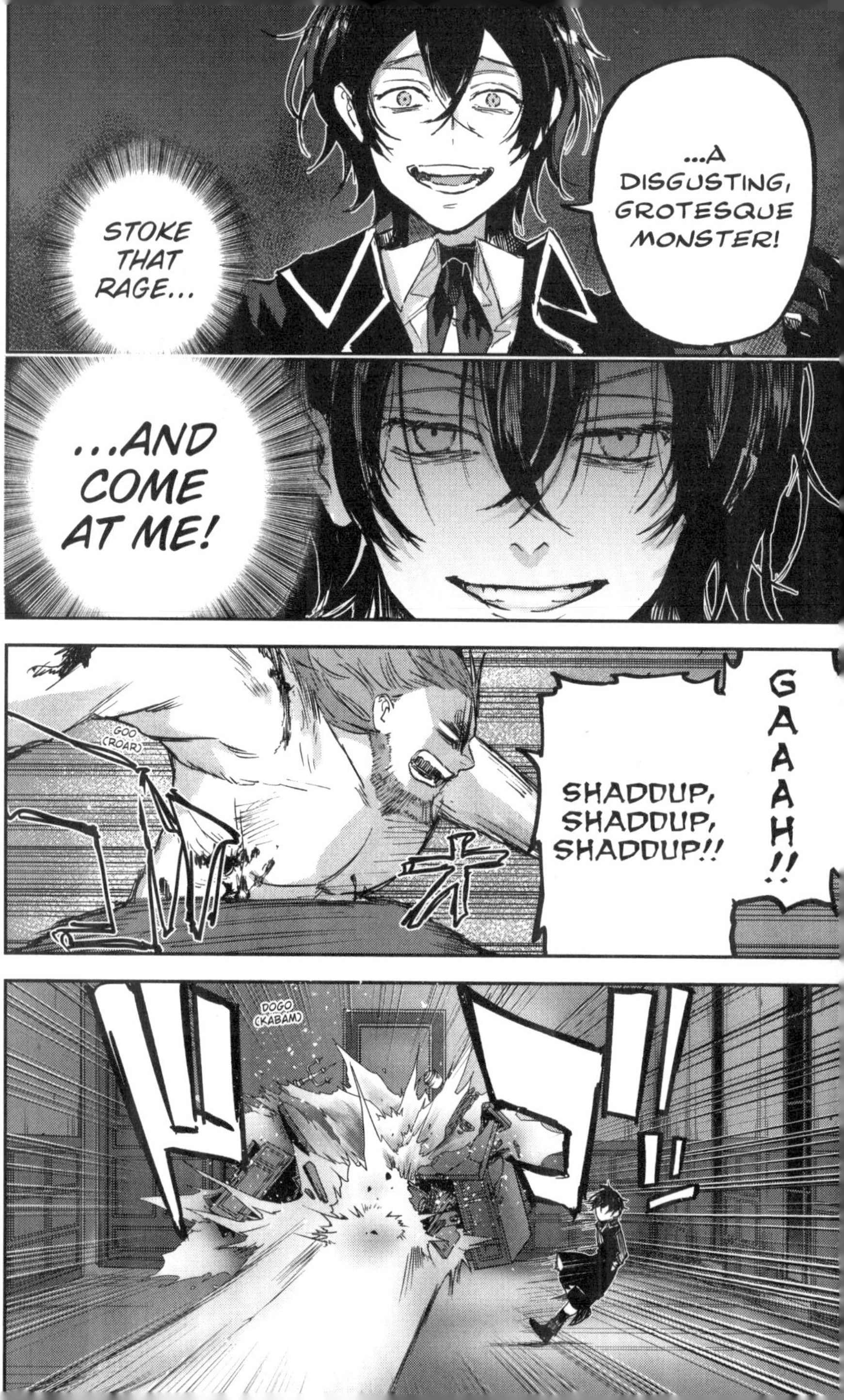
...A DISGUSTING, GROTESQUE MONSTER!
STOKE THAT RAGE...
...AND COME AT ME!
GAAAH!!
SHADDUP, SHADDUP, SHADDUP!!
GOO (ROAR)
DOGO (KABAM)

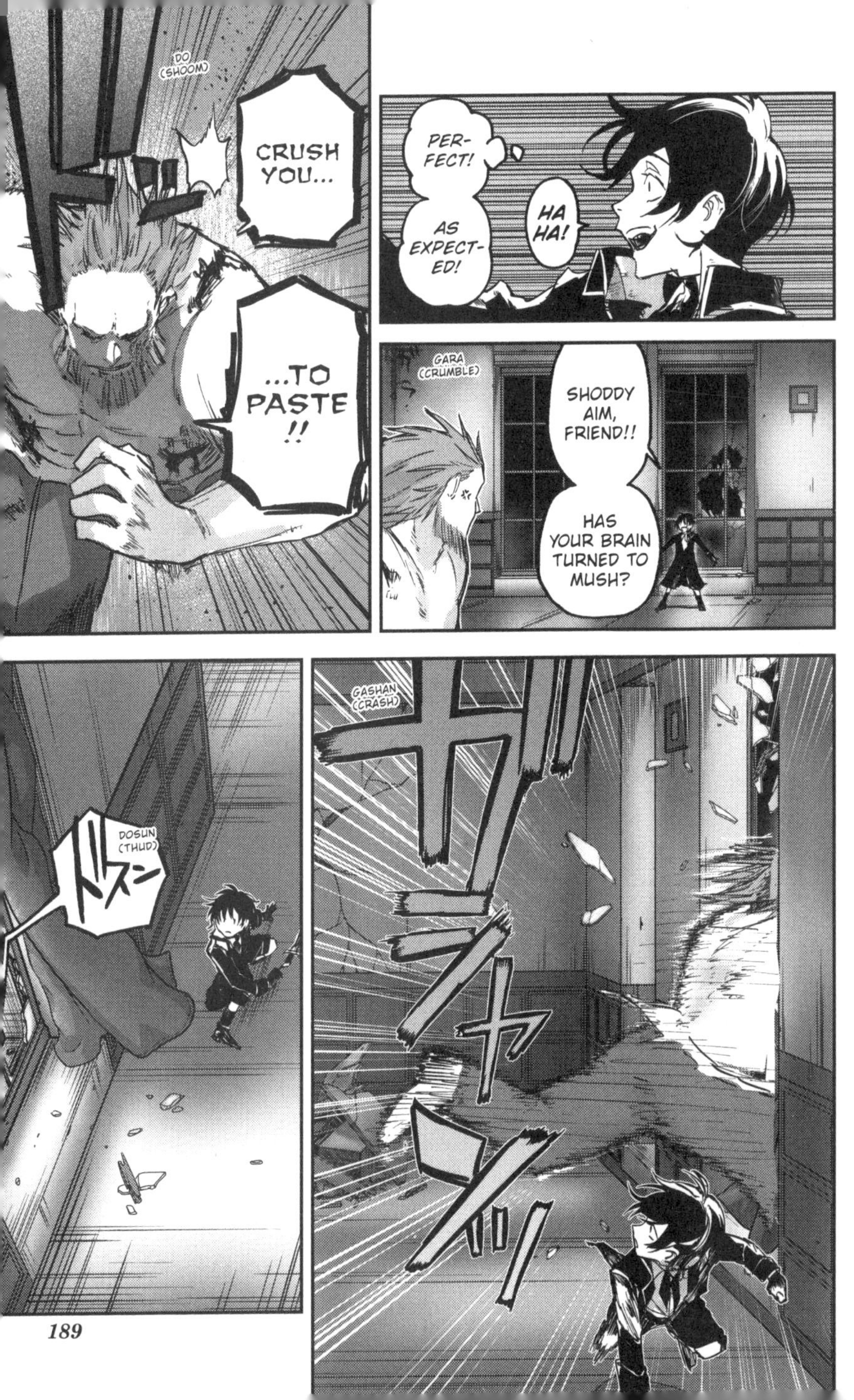
PER-FECT!
AS EXPECTED-ED!
HA HA!
GARA (CRUMBLE)
SHODDY AIM, FRIEND!!
HAS YOUR BRAIN TURNED TO MUSH?
DO (SHOOM)
CRUSH YOU...
...TO PASTE!!
GASHAN (CRASH)
DOSUN (THUD)
ドスン

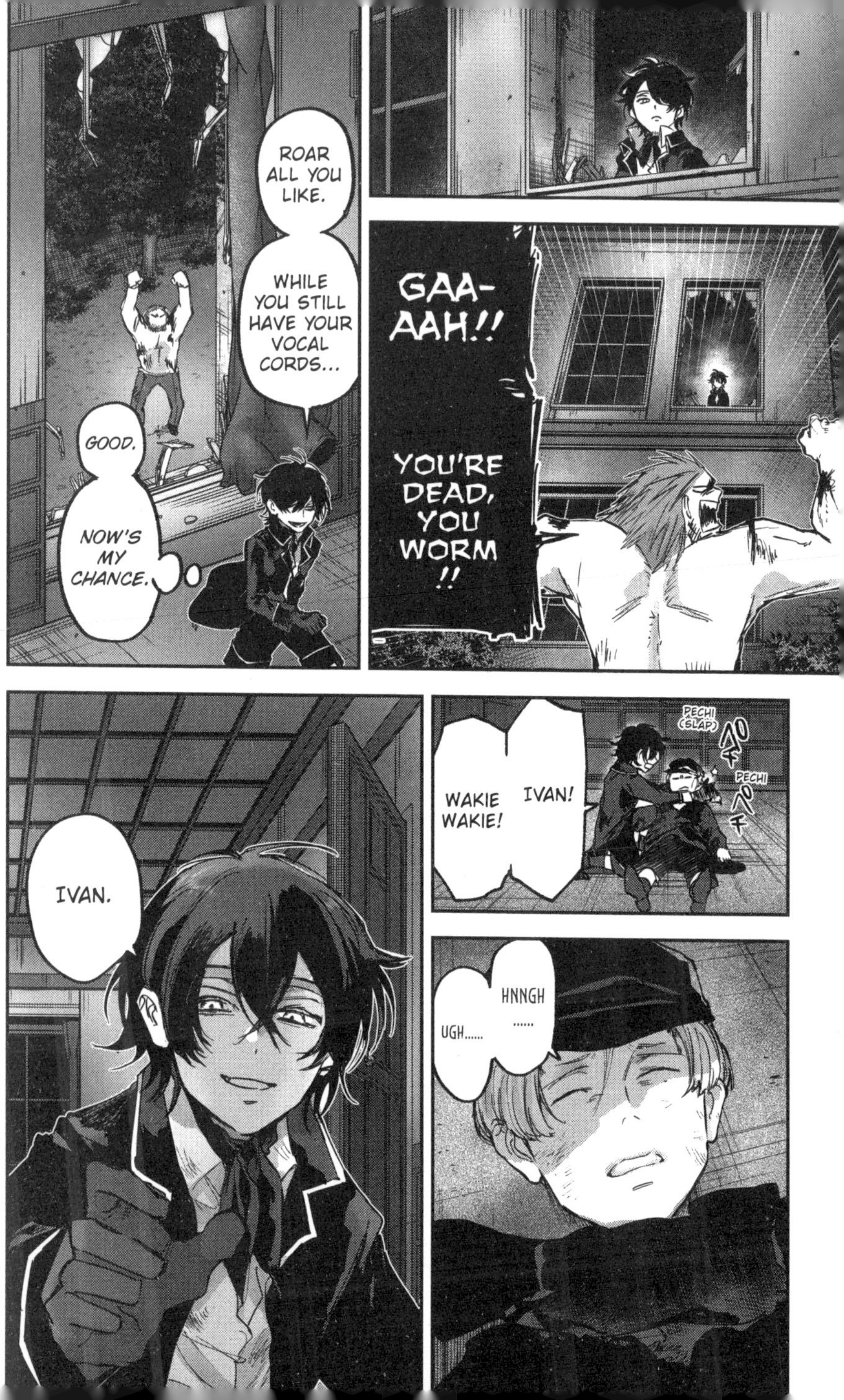
GAA-AAH!!
YOU'RE DEAD, YOU WORM!!
ROAR ALL YOU LIKE.
WHILE YOU STILL HAVE YOUR VOCAL CORDS...
GOOD.
NOW'S MY CHANCE.
PECHI (SLAP)
ペチ
PECHI
ペチ
IVAN!
WAKIE WAKIE!
HNNGH......
UGH......
IVAN.

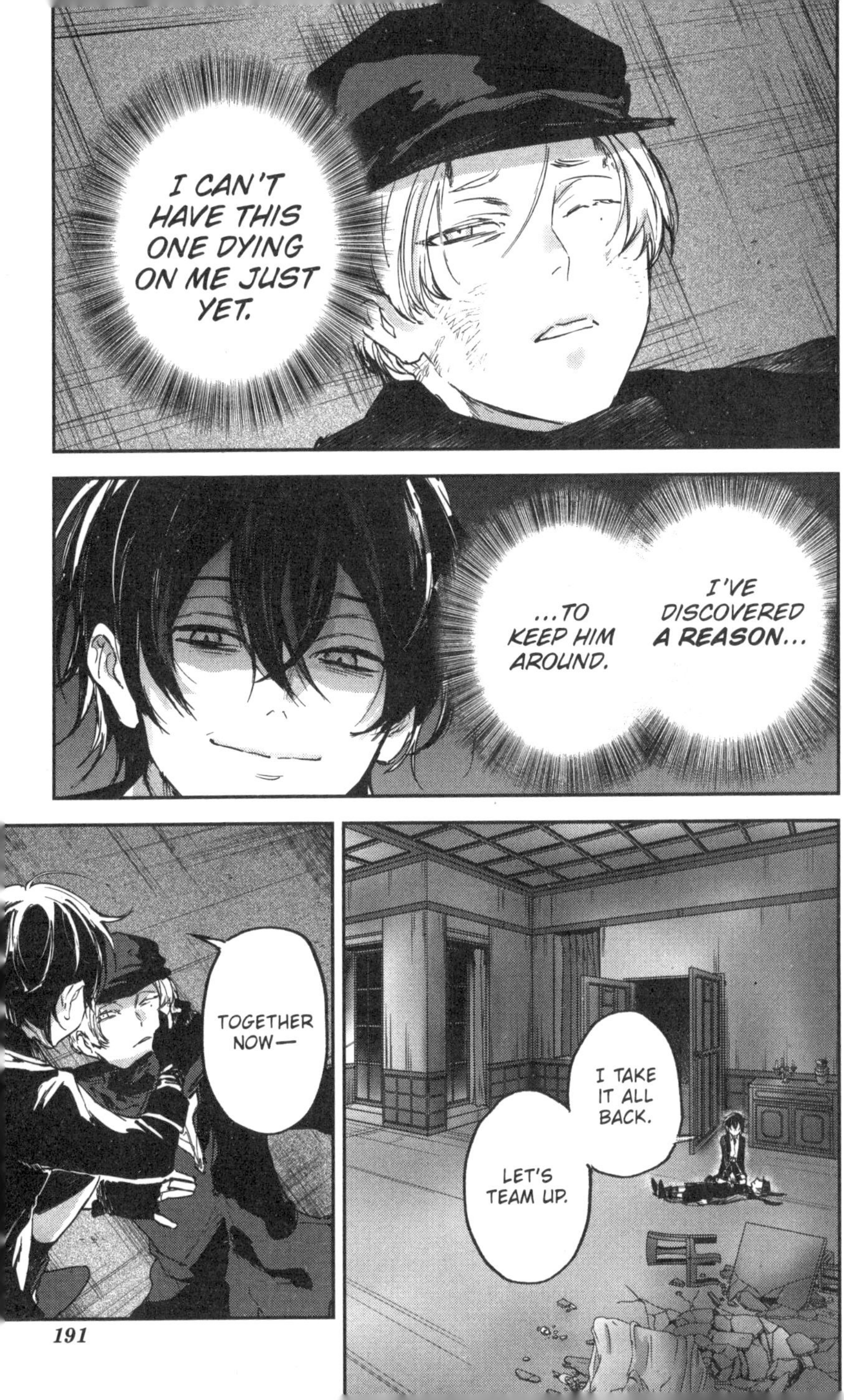
I CAN'T HAVE THIS ONE DYING ON ME JUST YET.
I'VE DISCOVERED A REASON...
...TO KEEP HIM AROUND.
I TAKE IT ALL BACK.
LET'S TEAM UP.
TOGETHER NOW—

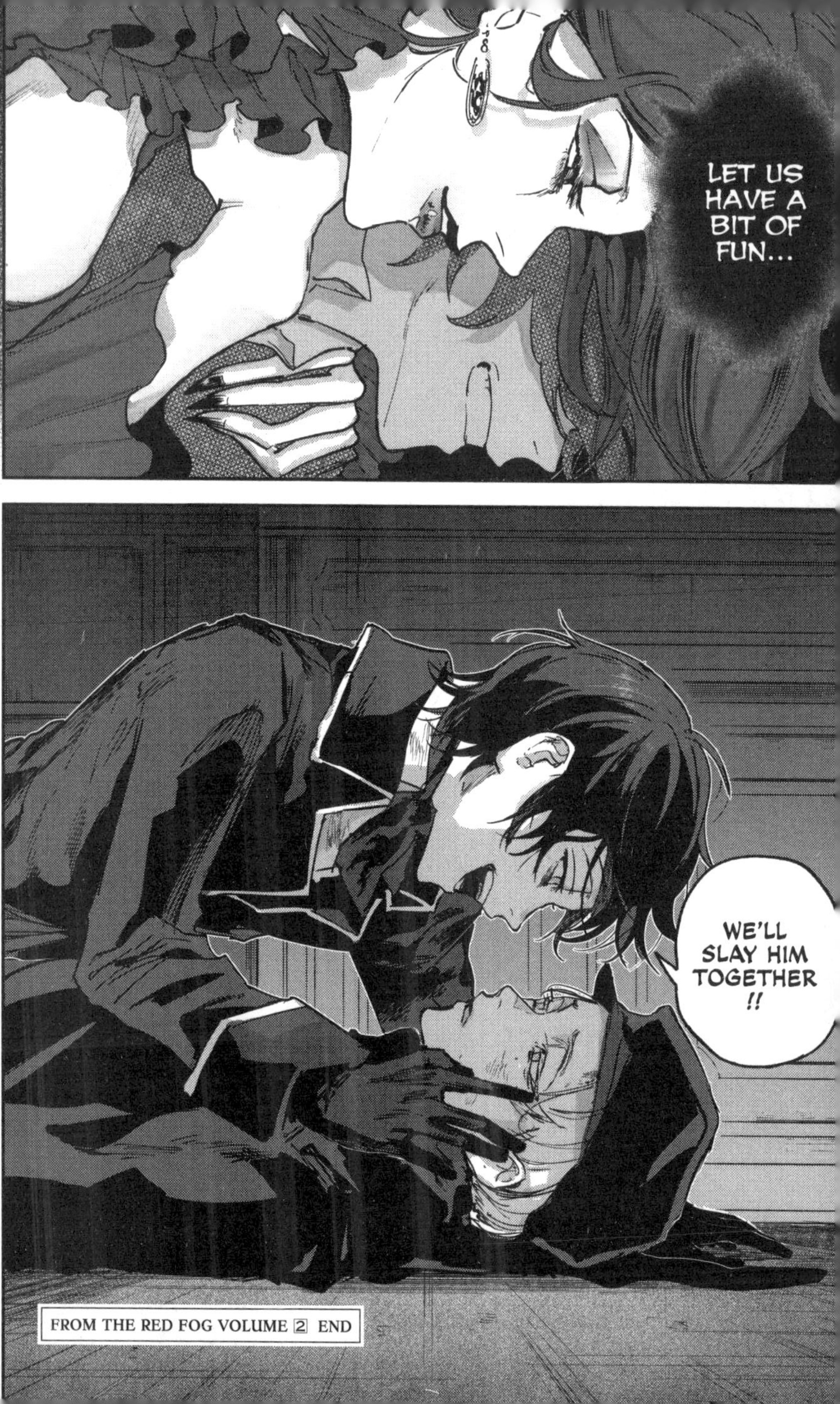
LET US HAVE A BIT OF FUN...
WE'LL SLAY HIM TOGETHER !!
FROM THE RED FOG VOLUME 2 END

AFTERWORD

HELLO, AND THANK YOU SO MUCH FOR
PICKING UP VOLUME 2 OF *FROM THE RED FOG*.

I'M SO GRATEFUL TO THE READERS WHO CHEER
ME ON, EVERYONE WHO CONTRIBUTES TO THIS WORK,
AND THOSE WHO SUPPORT ME IN OTHER WAYS.

VOLUME 2 FEATURES A LOT OF FIGHTING, BUT I DARESAY
THAT I'LL NEVER WRITE SUCH A LONG SEQUENCE OF
BATTLES EVER AGAIN...MAYBE. I'M PLANNING TO HAVE
A LOT MORE HUMAN DRAMA IN THE NEXT VOLUME.

TO BE BLUNT, I'M STILL LEARNING AND GROWING. I'M
INCOMPLETE. UNFINISHED. IMPERFECT. DESPITE MY BEST
EFFORTS, THERE ARE PLENTY OF MOMENTS WHERE I FAIL...
EVEN SO, I TELL MYSELF, "YOU'D BETTER NOT LOSE HEART,
ME!" (HA-HA). SO EVERY DAY, I ENGAGE IN TRIAL AND ERROR
AS I STRIVE TO DELIVER A BETTER STORY TO YOU READERS.
I JUST HOPE YOU'LL STICK AROUND AND—USING
MY WORK AS A LENS—WATCH ME IMPROVE.

AT THE RISK OF REPEATING MYSELF, I'D LIKE TO SAY
THAT THERE ARE MORE AND MORE MOMENTS WHERE
READER FEEDBACK MAKES ME THINK, "CREATING MANGA IS
WORTHWHILE WORK." IT'S ALL BECAUSE OF YOU GUYS THAT
I GET TO LIVE MY LIFE LIKE THIS. SO THANK YOU, TRULY!

I LOOK FORWARD TO CHATTING AGAIN IN THE NEXT VOLUME.

MOSAE NOHARA

Thanks! Assistant / Ken Sawada.
Editor / Noritaka Shimizu.

From The RED FOG 2

Mosae Nohara

Translation: Caleb D. Cook

Lettering: Chiho Christie

AKAI KIRI NO NAKA KARA Volume 2
©2021 Mosae Nohara/SQUARE ENIX CO., LTD.
First published in Japan in 2021 by SQUARE ENIX CO., LTD.
English translation rights arranged with SQUARE ENIX CO., LTD.
and Yen Press, LLC through Tuttle-Mori Agency, Inc.

English translation ©2022 by SQUARE ENIX CO., LTD.

Yen Press
150 West 30th Street, 19th Floor
New York, NY 10001

Visit us at yenpress.com · facebook.com/yenpress · twitter.com/yenpress · yenpress.tumblr.com · instagram.com/yenpress

First Yen Press Edition: July 2022
Edited by Yen Press Editorial: Danielle Niederkorn, Carl Li
Designed by Yen Press Design: Jane Sohn, Andy Swist

Yen Press is an imprint of Yen Press, LLC.
The Yen Press name and logo are trademarks of Yen Press, LLC.

Library of Congress Control Number: 2021949718

ISBNs: 978-1-9753-4368-2 (paperback)
978-1-9753-4369-9 (ebook)

1 3 5 7 9 10 8 6 4 2

WOR

Printed in the United States of America